Kaplan Publishing are constantly finding new ways to make a difference to your studies and our exciting online resources ~~ do offer something different to students l

This book comes with free MyKaplan o study anytime, anywhere. **This free or separately and is included in the pri**

C000171119

an

Having purchased this book, you have access to the following online study materials:

CONTENT	AAT	
	Text	Kit
Electronic version of the book	✓	✓
Progress tests with instant answers	✓	
Mock assessments online	✓	✓
Material updates	✓	✓

How to access your online resources

Kaplan Financial students will already have a MyKaplan account and these extra resources will be available to you online. You do not need to register again, as this process was completed when you enrolled. If you are having problems accessing online materials, please ask your course administrator.

If you are not studying with Kaplan and did not purchase your book via a Kaplan website, to unlock your extra online resources please go to www.mykaplan.co.uk/addabook (even if you have set up an account and registered books previously). You will then need to enter the ISBN number (on the title page and back cover) and the unique pass key number contained in the scratch panel below to gain access. You will also be required to enter additional information during this process to set up or confirm your account details.

If you purchased through the Kaplan Publishing website you will automatically receive an e-mail invitation to MyKaplan. Please register your details using this email to gain access to your content. If you do not receive the e-mail or book content, please contact Kaplan Publishing.

Your Code and Information

This code can only be used once for the registration of one book online. This registration and your online content will expire when the final sittings for the examinations covered by this book have taken place. Please allow one hour from the time you submit your book details for us to process your request.

Please scratch the film to access your unique code.

Please be aware that this code is case-sensitive and you will need to include the dashes within the passcode, but not when entering the ISBN.

KAPLAN

PUBLISHING

BUSINESS TAX

STUDY TEXT

Qualifications and Credit Framework

AQ2016

Finance Act 2020

For assessments from January 2021 until end January 2022

This Study Text supports study for the following AAT qualifications:

AAT Professional Diploma in Accounting – Level 4

AAT Level 4 Diploma in Business Skills

AAT Professional Diploma in Accounting at SCQF Level 8

British Library Cataloguing-in-Publication Data

A catalogue record for this book is available from the British Library.

Published by
Kaplan Publishing UK
Unit 2, The Business Centre
Molly Millars Lane
Wokingham
Berkshire
RG41 2QZ

ISBN 978-1-78740-791-6

We are grateful to HM Revenue and Customs for the provision of tax forms, which are Crown Copyright and are reproduced here with kind permission from the Office of Public Sector Information.

CONTENTS

STUDY TEXT

Chapter

Chapter

INTRODUCTION

HOW TO USE THESE MATERIALS

These Kaplan Publishing learning materials have been carefully designed to make your learning experience as easy as possible and to give you the best chance of success in your AAT assessments.

They contain a number of features to help you in the study process.

The sections on the Unit Guide, the Assessment and Study Skills should be read before you commence your studies.

They are designed to familiarise you with the nature and content of the assessment and to give you tips on how best to approach your studies.

STUDY TEXT

This study text has been specially prepared for the revised AAT qualification introduced in September 2016.

It is written in a practical and interactive style:

- key terms and concepts are clearly defined

- all topics are illustrated with practical examples with clearly worked solutions based on sample tasks provided by AAT in the new examining style

- frequent activities throughout the chapters ensure that what you have learnt is regularly reinforced

- 'pitfalls' and 'assessment tips' help you avoid commonly made mistakes and help you focus on what is required to perform well in your assessment

- 'Test your understanding' activities are included within each chapter to apply your learning and develop your understanding.

ICONS

The study chapters include the following icons throughout.

They are designed to assist you in your studies by identifying key definitions and the points at which you can test yourself on the knowledge gained, or to direct you towards other areas of your studies (past or future) where you will encounter similar issues or skills.

 Definition

These sections explain important areas of knowledge which must be understood and reproduced in an assessment.

 Example

The illustrative examples can be used to help develop an understanding of topics before attempting the activity exercises.

 Test your understanding

These are exercises which give the opportunity to assess your understanding of all the assessment areas.

 Links to other syllabus areas

These refer to areas of interaction with other parts of your syllabus, either in other AAT units which you have studied, or may go on to study, or even further professional qualifications that you may decide to pursue on completion of AAT.

Quality and accuracy are of the utmost importance to us so if you spot an error in any of our products, please send an email to mykaplanreporting@kaplan.com with full details, or follow the link to the feedback form in MyKaplan.

Our Quality Coordinator will work with our technical team to verify the error and take action to ensure it is corrected in future editions.

Progression

There are two elements of progression that we can measure: first how quickly students move through individual topics within a subject; and second how quickly they move from one course to the next. We know that there is an optimum for both, but it can vary from subject to subject and from student to student. However, using data and our experience of student performance over many years, we can make some generalisations.

A fixed period of study set out at the start of a course with key milestones is important. This can be within a subject, for example 'I will finish this topic by 30 June', or for overall achievement, such as 'I want to be qualified by the end of next year'.

Your qualification is cumulative, as earlier papers provide a foundation for your subsequent studies, so do not allow there to be too big a gap between one subject and another.

We know that exams encourage techniques that lead to some degree of short term retention, the result being that you will simply forget much of what you have already learned unless it is refreshed (look up Ebbinghaus Forgetting Curve for more details on this). This makes it more difficult as you move from one subject to another: not only will you have to learn the new subject, you will also have to relearn all the underpinning knowledge as well. This is very inefficient and slows down your overall progression which makes it more likely you may not succeed at all.

In addition, delaying your studies slows your path to qualification which can have negative impacts on your career, postponing the opportunity to apply for higher level positions and therefore higher pay.

You can use the following diagram showing the whole structure of your qualification to help you keep track of your progress.

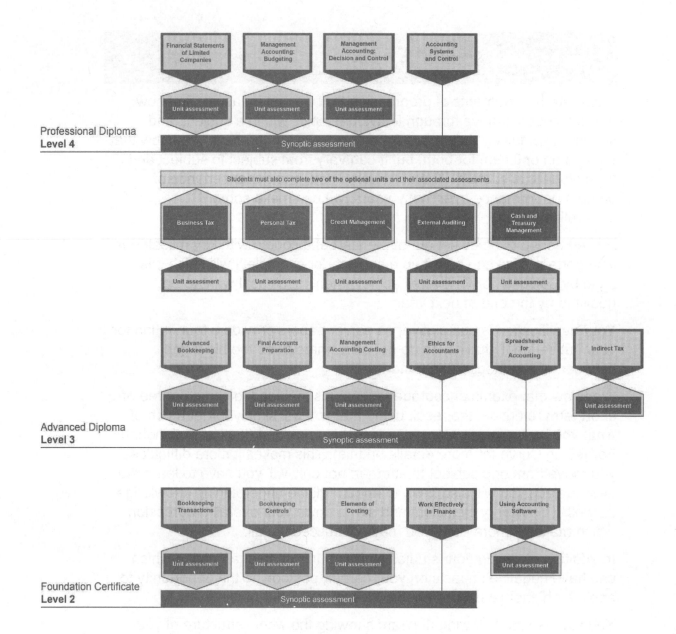

KAPLAN PUBLISHING

UNIT GUIDE

Purpose of the unit

This unit introduces the learners to UK taxation relevant to businesses. It is about the computing of business taxation, preparation of tax returns and how taxation has an impact on the running of a business for sole traders, partnerships and limited companies.

In learning how to prepare tax computations, learners will gain skills in the tax treatment of capital expenditure, and adjustment of accounting profits for tax purposes for sole traders, partnerships and limited companies. In addition, they will be able to allocate profits between partners in a partnership and be able to calculate National Insurance (NI) contributions for the self-employed.

The learner will become familiar with the completion of tax returns. They will know when these returns need to be filed with the UK's Revenue and Customs authority (HMRC), and the implications of errors in tax returns, the late filing of returns and the late payment of tax.

They will understand how to compute tax on the sale of capital assets and they will have an introduction to some of the tax reliefs available to businesses.

Tax advice is an important part of many accountancy roles. Learners will be able to discuss the ethical issues facing business owners and managers in reporting their business tax and the responsibilities that an agent has in giving advice on tax issues to business clients.

Learning outcomes

On completion of this unit the learner will be able to:

- Complete tax returns for sole traders and partnerships and prepare supporting tax computations.

- Complete tax returns for limited companies and prepare supporting tax computations.

- Provide advice on the UK tax regime and its impact on sole traders, partnerships and limited companies.

- Advise business clients on tax reliefs, and their responsibilities and their agent's responsibilities in reporting taxation to HM Revenue & Customs.

- Prepare tax computations for the sale of capital assets.

Scope of content

The unit consists of five learning outcomes, which are further broken down into assessment criteria. These are set out in the following table with reference to the relevant chapter within the text.

In any one assessment, students may not be assessed on all content, or on the full depth or breadth of a piece of content. The content assessed may change over time to ensure validity of assessment, but all assessment criteria will be tested over time.

Chapter

1 **Complete tax returns for sole traders and partnerships and prepare supporting tax computations**

1.1 **Analyse trading profits and losses for tax purposes**

Students need to be able to:

• apply rules relating to deductible and non-deductible expenditure	9
• classify expenditure as either revenue or capital expenditure	9
• adjust accounting profit and losses for tax purposes.	9

1.2 **Identify the correct basis period for each tax year**

Students need to be able to:

• identify the basis periods using the opening year and closing year rules	11
• determine overlap periods and overlap profits	11
• explain the effect on the basis period of a change in accounting date.	11

1.3 **Identify and calculate capital allowances**

Students need to be able to:

• identify the types of capital allowances	9
• calculate capital allowances including adjustments for private usage.	9

Chapter

1.4   Analyse taxable profits and losses of a partnership between the partners

Students need to be able to:

- apportion profits between a maximum of four partners   10

- determine the basis periods for continuing, new or departing partners   11

- allocate profits between the partners.   10

1.5   Calculate the NI contributions payable by self-employed taxpayers

Students need to be able to:

- determine who is liable to pay NI contributions   14

- calculate NI contributions.   14

1.6   Complete the individual and partnership tax returns relevant to sole traders and partnerships

Students need to be able to:

- accurately complete self-employed tax returns   9

- accurately complete partnership tax returns.   10

2   Complete tax returns for limited companies and prepare supporting tax computations

2.1   Analyse trading profits and losses for tax purposes

Students need to be able to:

- apply the rules relating to deductible and non-deductible expenditure   3

- classify expenditure as either revenue or capital expenditure   3

- adjust accounting profits and losses for tax purposes.   3

KAPLAN PUBLISHING

Chapter

2.2 Identify and calculate capital allowances

Students need to be able to:

• identify types of capital allowances	4
• calculate capital allowances.	4

2.3 Calculate total taxable profits and corporation tax payable

Students need to be able to:

• calculate the taxable total profits from trading income, property income, investment income and chargeable gains	2, 5
• calculate the total profits and corporation tax payable for accounting periods longer than, shorter than or equal to 12 months.	2, 5

3 Provide advice on the UK's tax regime and its impact on sole traders, partnerships and limited companies

3.1 Demonstrate an understanding of the tax return filing requirements and tax payments due

Students need to know:

• tax return filing deadlines	7, 13
• payment rules for sole traders and partnerships: amounts and dates	13
• payment rules for limited companies: amounts and dates.	7

3.2 Demonstrate an understanding of the penalties and finance costs for non-compliance

Students need to know:

• penalties for late filing of tax returns and failing to notify chargeability	7, 13
• late payment interest and surcharges	7, 13
• the enquiry window and penalties for incorrect returns.	7, 13

Chapter

4 **Advise business clients on tax reliefs, and their responsibilities and their agents responsibilities in reporting taxation to HMRC**

4.1 **Appraise the effective use of trading losses**

Students need to be able to:

• assess and calculate available loss relief	6, 12
• advise on the best use of a trading loss for sole traders, partnerships and limited companies.	6, 12

4.2 **Demonstrate an understanding of the current tax reliefs and other tax issues**

Students need to know:

• current tax reliefs available to businesses	6 and throughout
• current tax issues and their implications for businesses.	6 and throughout

4.3 **Discuss the responsibilities relating to tax for the business and its agent**

Students need to know:

• what the badges of trade are and how they evolved	9
• what records need to be maintained by a business, how long these records need to be maintained and the penalties for failing to keep these records	7, 13
• the distinction between tax planning, tax avoidance and tax evasion	21
• AAT's ethical standards relating to tax advice and professional conduct in relation to taxation.	21

Delivering this unit

This unit has the following links across the AAT Professional Diploma in Accounting.

Unit name	Content links	Suggested order of delivery
Personal Tax	This unit is an optional unit at Professional level, so it does not need to be taken after another unit has been studied. The Professional level unit, Personal Tax, is associated with this unit, although these units can be taken separately. Knowledge developed in either of these units will be useful in the later study of the other unit.	N/A

THE ASSESSMENT

Assessment type	Marking type	Duration of exam
Computer based unit assessment	Partially computer/ partially human marked	2 hours

The assessment for this unit consists of 11 compulsory, independent, tasks.

The competency level for AAT assessment is 70%.

Learning outcomes		Weighting
1	Complete tax returns for sole traders and partnerships and prepare supporting tax computations	29%
2	Complete tax returns for limited companies and prepare supporting tax computations	19%
3	Provide advice on the UK's tax regime and its impact on sole traders, partnerships and limited companies	15%
4	Advise business clients on tax reliefs, and their responsibilities and their agent's responsibilities in reporting taxation to HMRC	19%
5	Prepare tax computations for the sale of capital assets	18%
Total		100%

Sample assessments

The sample assessments have 11 tasks.

An analysis of the AAT sample assessments detailing the areas covered in each task and the marks available is set out below.

Task	Marks	Topic
1	10	Sole trader adjustment of profits and basis periods
2	10	Partnership allocation of profits National insurance contributions
3	13	Capital allowances (human marked)
4	6	Completion of tax return
5	9	Corporation tax computations (e.g. calculation of taxable total profits for long AP, calculation of tax, calculation of loss)
6	7	Administration: payment and filing dates (individuals and companies)
7	8	Administration: penalties for non-compliance (individuals and companies)
8	5	Relief for losses (individuals and companies)
9	14	Written task giving advice to clients regarding elements of tax legislation and ethics (human marked) (e.g. explaining legislation to client such as IR35, badges of trade)
10	8	Capital gains: individual gains, reliefs, tax
11	10	Capital gains: shares (human marked)

Reference material

Reference material is provided in this assessment. During your assessment you will be able to access reference material through a series of clickable links on the right of every task. These will produce pop-up windows which can be moved or closed.

The relevant section of the reference material has been included in the appropriate chapter of this study text. This is based on the version of the reference material that was available at the time of going to print.

The full version of the reference material is available for download from the AAT website.

STUDY SKILLS

Preparing to study

Devise a study plan

Determine which times of the week you will study.

Split these times into sessions of at least one hour for study of new material. Any shorter periods could be used for revision or practice.

Put the times you plan to study onto a study plan for the weeks from now until the assessment and set yourself targets for each period of study – in your sessions make sure you cover the whole course, activities and the associated test your understanding activities.

If you are studying more than one unit at a time, try to vary your subjects as this can help to keep you interested and see subjects as part of wider knowledge.

When working through your course, compare your progress with your plan and, if necessary, re-plan your work (perhaps including extra sessions) or, if you are ahead, do some extra revision/practice questions.

Effective studying

Active reading

You are not expected to learn the text by rote, rather, you must understand what you are reading and be able to use it to pass the assessment and develop good practice.

A good technique is to use SQ3Rs – Survey, Question, Read, Recall, Review:

1   **Survey the chapter**

    Look at the headings and read the introduction, knowledge, skills and content, so as to get an overview of what the chapter deals with.

2   **Question**

    Whilst undertaking the survey ask yourself the questions you hope the chapter will answer for you.

3   **Read**

Read through the chapter thoroughly working through the activities and, at the end, making sure that you can meet the learning objectives highlighted on the first page.

4   **Recall**

At the end of each section and at the end of the chapter, try to recall the main ideas of the section/chapter without referring to the text. This is best done after a short break of a couple of minutes after the reading stage.

5   **Review**

Check that your recall notes are correct.

You may also find it helpful to re-read the chapter to try and see the topic(s) it deals with as a whole.

Note taking

Taking notes is a useful way of learning, but do not simply copy out the text.

The notes must:

- be in your own words
- be concise
- cover the key points
- be well organised
- be modified as you study further chapters in this text or in related ones.

Trying to summarise a chapter without referring to the text can be a useful way of determining which areas you know and which you don't.

Three ways of taking notes

1   **Summarise the key points of a chapter**

2   **Make linear notes**

A list of headings, subdivided with sub-headings listing the key points.

If you use linear notes, you can use different colours to highlight key points and keep topic areas together.

Use plenty of space to make your notes easy to use.

3   Try a diagrammatic form

The most common of which is a mind map.

To make a mind map, put the main heading in the centre of the paper and put a circle around it.

Draw lines radiating from this to the main sub-headings which again have circles around them.

Continue the process from the sub-headings to sub-sub-headings.

Annotating the text

You may find it useful to underline or highlight key points in your study text – but do be selective.

You may also wish to make notes in the margins.

Revision phase

Kaplan has produced material specifically designed for your final assessment preparation for this unit.

These include pocket revision notes and an exam kit that includes a bank of revision questions specifically in the style of the new syllabus.

Further guidance on how to approach the final stage of your studies is given in these materials.

Further reading

In addition to this text, you should also read the 'Accounting Technician' magazine every month to keep abreast of any guidance from the assessors.

TAX RATES AND ALLOWANCES

These tables are provided in the reference material that you can access during your assessment. They will be available by clicking on the appropriate link to produce a pop-up window.

Taxation tables for business tax – 2020/21

Capital allowances

Annual investment allowance

Prior to 1 January 2019	£200,000
Between 1 January 2019 and 31 December 2020	£1,000,000
From 1 January 2021	£200,000

Plant and machinery writing down allowance

Assets other than motor cars	18%

Motor cars

CO_2 emissions up to 50 g/km	100%
CO_2 emissions between 51 and 110 g/km	18%
CO_2 emissions over 110 g/km –	
Prior to 1 April 2019/6 April 2019	8%
CO_2 emissions over 110 g/km –	
From 1 April 2019/6 April 2019	6%

Capital gains

Annual exempt amount	£12,300
Basic rate	10%
Higher rate	20%
Business asset disposal relief rate	10%
Investors' relief rate	10%
Business asset disposal relief lifetime allowance	£1,000,000
Investors' relief lifetime allowance	£10,000,000

National Insurance rates

Class 2 contributions:	£3.05 per week
Small profits threshold	£6,475 p.a.
Class 4 contributions:	
Main rate	9%
Additional rate	2%
Lower profits limit	£9,500
Upper profits limit	£50,000

Trading allowance

This allowance is available to individuals only.	£1,000

Corporation tax

Financial year	2020	2019
All profits and gains	19%	19%

Introduction to business tax

1

Introduction

This chapter presents an overview of business tax.

CONTENTS

1 Contents of the study text
2 Types of business entity
3 Introduction to the UK tax system
4 AAT code of professional ethics

1 Contents of the study text

1.1 Four categories

The study text can be split into four specific categories:

	Chapters
• Companies	2 – 7
• Unincorporated traders (sole traders and partnerships)	8 – 14
• Chargeable gains	15 – 20
• Duties and responsibilities of a tax adviser	21

The aim is to gradually consider each of the ways of taxing a business and then to consider the ethical implications for a tax adviser when giving advice.

Business taxation depends on whether an individual has decided to set up his business as a:

- company
- sole trader, or
- partnership.

2 Types of business entity

2.1 Company

A company is a legal entity, separate from its owners and managers.

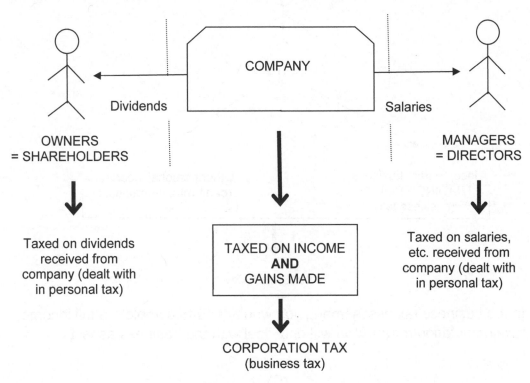

Note: In a lot of cases the shareholders and directors are the same people. However, this will have no effect on the business tax assessment.

2.2   Sole trader

An individual setting up an unincorporated business (i.e. not a company) on his/her own is known as a sole trader.

A sole trader is not a separate legal entity.

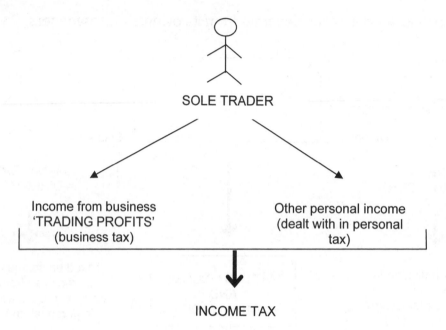

In the business tax assessment, you won't need to complete a full income tax computation/return. You will only deal with the business aspects.

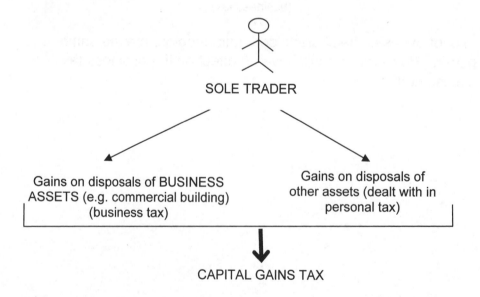

In the business tax assessment, you may be required to complete a capital gains tax computation. However, the sole trader will only have disposed of business assets.

2.3   Partnership

A partnership is another form of unincorporated business, but it is not a separate legal entity.

A partnership is formed when a number of individuals carry on a business together with a view to profit, i.e. a partnership is effectively a collection of sole traders working together.

Each partner pays his/her own income tax and capital gains tax on his/her share of the partnership's profits and gains.

3   Introduction to the UK tax system

3.1   Overall structure

Taxation is the raising of money by the State from the general public.

The UK Parliament passes tax legislation.

HMRC (Her Majesty's Revenue and Customs) is the body that controls and administers all areas of UK tax law.

3.2   Tax legislation

The basic rules of the UK tax system are contained in various statutes. These are amended and added to by annual Finance Acts.

Legislation can be given effect, or interpreted, in the following ways:

Statutory Instruments

Acts of Parliament confer powers on Ministers to make more detailed orders, rules or regulations by means of statutory instruments. An Act will often contain a broad framework and statutory instruments are used to provide the necessary detail that would be too complex to include in the Act itself.

Case law

Judges cannot make law relating to taxation, but they can be required to interpret the law which applies to the circumstances of the particular case. These rulings are binding and therefore provide guidance on the interpretation of tax legislation.

Extra-Statutory Concessions

In cases where there is doubt as to the meaning of the law, or where a strict application of the law produces an unacceptable result, HMRC does not always seek to apply the law strictly but instead makes an Extra-Statutory Concession.

HMRC Statements of Practice

These are public announcements of HMRC's interpretation of the legislation. They have no legal force and do not remove the taxpayer's right of appeal.

3.3 Tax planning, tax avoidance and tax evasion

Tax planning

This means arranging your tax affairs, using legal methods, so that you pay less tax.

For example, individuals and businesses can reduce their tax bills by claiming all the reliefs and allowances to which they are entitled. Sometimes a transaction can be timed to give maximum tax advantage.

Tax planning is legal.

Tax avoidance

Tax avoidance is legal but is not following the intent of the law.

For example, individuals and businesses may use unintended loopholes in the law, or artificially use foreign jurisdictions with low tax rates.

Tax evasion

Tax evasion is a criminal offence.

Tax evasion means using illegal methods to reduce tax due.

Typically this might be through concealing a source of income, deliberately understating income or over-claiming expenses and reliefs.

AAT reference material

These topics are covered in the reference material set out in section 6 below.

4 AAT code of professional ethics

4.1 Fundamental ethical principles

The AAT has set out a code of professional ethics which includes five fundamental principles which must be adhered to by all members.

Integrity

Members should be straightforward and honest in all professional and business relationships.

Objectivity

Members should not allow bias, conflicts of interest or the influence of others to override professional or business judgements.

Professional competence and due care

Members have an ongoing duty to maintain professional knowledge and skills at the required level to ensure that a client/employer receives a competent, professional service based on current developments.

Members should act diligently and in accordance with applicable technical and professional standards when providing professional services.

Confidentiality

Members should respect the confidentiality of information acquired as a result of professional and business relationships and should not disclose any such information to third parties unless they have proper and specific authority or there is a legal or professional right or duty to disclose.

Confidential information acquired as a result of professional and business relationships shall not be used for personal advantage of the member or third parties.

Professional behaviour

Members should comply with relevant laws and regulations and avoid any conduct that discredits the profession.

5 Summary

There are three types of business entity to consider:

- company
- sole trader
- partnership.

Each has its own special rules for calculating profits, gains and tax.

HMRC administers tax law which is passed by Parliament.

Tax planning is the legal use of reliefs and allowances for the purpose they were intended for, tax avoidance is legal but not using the law as it was intended, whilst tax evasion is illegal such as concealment of income or over-claiming of reliefs.

The AAT has set out a code of professional ethics including five fundamental ethical principles which members must abide by.

✳ Links to other syllabus areas

Within other Professional and prior level units, you gain an appreciation of the importance of tax within the financial statements of a company and the impact it can have on an entity's overall results and its overall business strategy.

In this unit we explore this particular cost heading in more detail and consider how a business calculates its tax liability for a specific period.

This is important to ensure that it is both recorded properly in the accounts (FSLC) and is factored in accurately when appraising past, or future, business decisions (MABU and MDCL).

6 AAT Reference material

Introduction to business tax

Administration

- Taxation administered by HM Revenue & Customs (HMRC).

- Rules covering tax are contained in statute (law) which is passed every year (Finance Act).

- Decisions reached by the courts interpreting the law are known as case law.

- HMRC also issue guidance – Extra Statutory Concessions and Statements of Practice.

Taxes

- Corporation Tax – paid by companies on both income and chargeable gains.

- Income Tax – paid by individuals on their income.

- Capital Gains Tax – paid by individuals on their capital gains.

Tax avoidance and tax evasion

- Tax evasion: any action taken to evade tax by illegal means; this carries a risk of criminal prosecution. Examples of tax evasion include failing to declare income and claiming false expenses.

- Tax avoidance: bending the rules of the tax system to gain a tax advantage that Parliament never intended. It involves operating within the letter of the law but not the spirit of the law.

- Tax planning: use of legitimate means to minimise taxpayer's tax liability, for example by investing in a tax-free ISA (Individual Savings Account).

Principles of corporation tax

2

Introduction

It is very likely that one of the tasks in the assessment will include the preparation of a corporation tax computation. This chapter sets the scene.

ASSESSMENT CRITERIA

Calculate the taxable total profits from trading income, property income, investment income and chargeable gains (2.3)

Calculate the total profits and corporation tax payable for accounting periods longer than, shorter than or equal to 12 months (2.3)

CONTENTS

1   Introduction to corporation tax
2   The principle of accounting periods
3   Pro forma corporation tax computation

1 Introduction to corporation tax

1.1 Corporation tax

Corporation tax is paid by companies. A company can be recognised in the assessment because its name will end with:

- Ltd (which means limited company), or
- plc (which means public limited company).

Sole traders and partnerships do not pay corporation tax.

 Example

Which of the following businesses pay corporation tax?

(a) Amy's Motor Dealers Ltd

(b) Bert & Sons

(c) Fozia Diamond plc

(d) Salman & Co

Solution

Corporation tax is paid by companies:

(a) Amy's Motor Dealers Ltd (name ends in Ltd), and

(c) Fozia Diamond plc (name ends in plc).

1.2 Corporation tax computation

Companies pay corporation tax on the total of their income and gains. Firstly, the period covered by the computation must be identified and then the income and gains to be included in the computation are calculated.

2 The principle of accounting periods

2.1 Accounting period

A 'period of account' is the period for which a company prepares a set of financial accounts.

However, a company must prepare a corporation tax computation for an 'accounting period' (AP).

In a normal situation, a company prepares a 12 month set of financial accounts and has a matching AP for corporation tax purposes.

 Example

Fast Ltd has prepared accounts for the year ended 31 December 2020. Smart plc has prepared accounts for the year ended 31 March 2021.

For what period will the companies prepare their corporation tax computations?

Solution

Fast Ltd – computation for year ended 31 December 2020.

Smart plc – computation for year ended 31 March 2021.

2.2 Accounts of less than 12 months

An AP can be any length up to 12 months.

Where a company prepares a set of financial accounts of less than 12 months, there is a short AP for corporation tax purposes.

 Example

Tardy Ltd has previously prepared accounts to 31 December, until 31 December 2019. The company has now changed to preparing accounts to 30 September.

What is its first accounting period using the new date?

Solution

Tardy Ltd has an AP of 9 months ended 30 September 2020.

2.3 Accounts of more than 12 months

An AP can never exceed 12 months.

Therefore, when a company prepares financial accounts for a period of more than 12 months, there must be two APs for corporation tax purposes.

The two APs are:

• AP for the first 12 months, and

• a separate AP for the balance of the period.

No other combination is acceptable.

A corporation tax computation is prepared for each AP.

```
              ┌──────────────────────────────┐
              │          Accounts            │
              │  18 months ended 31 March 2021│
              └──────────────────────────────┘
                   ↙                      ↘
┌──────────────────────────────┐   ┌──────────────────────────────┐
│          First AP            │   │         Second AP            │
│ 12 months ended 30 September │   │  6 months ended 31 March 2021│
│            2020              │   │                              │
└──────────────────────────────┘   └──────────────────────────────┘
```

The method of allocating profits from the accounts between the two periods is covered in Chapter 5.

Test your understanding 1

Ice Ltd has prepared accounts for the 15 months ended 31 July 2021.

What is/are the accounting period(s)?

A   15 months ended 31 July 2021

B   3 months ended 31 July 2020 and 12 months ended 31 July 2021

C   12 months ended 30 April 2021 and 3 months ended 31 July 2021

D   11 months ended 31 March 2021 and 4 months ended 31 July 2021

3 Pro forma corporation tax computation

In the assessment you may be expected to prepare a corporation tax computation using a similar layout to the pro forma set out below.

The pro forma will become more familiar as you work through the chapters.

The pro forma includes references to the chapters in the textbook where each entry is considered in detail.

Company name

Corporation tax computation for XX months ended.......(the AP)

	£	Chapter(s)
Trading profit	X	3, 4
Non-trade interest	X	5
Property income	X	5
Chargeable gains	X	5, 16
	—	
Total profits	X	
Less: Qualifying charitable donations	(X)	5
	—	
Taxable total profits (TTP)	X	
	—	
Corporation tax liability (at relevant rate)	X	5
	—	

4 Test your understanding

Test your understanding 2

Period of assessment

Read the following statements and state whether they are true or false.

1   Any business carrying on trading activities will pay corporation tax. *F*

2   Corporation tax computations are prepared for a period of account. *F*

3   The accounting period will always be the same as the period of account. *F*

4   When a period of account exceeds 12 months there will be two accounting periods; the first 12 months and then the balance of the period. *T*

Test your understanding 3

Harris Ltd

Harris Ltd started trading on 1 March 2020 and prepares its first set of accounts to 30 April 2021.

What is Harris Ltd's first accounting period?

A   2 months ended 30 April 2020

B   12 months ended 28 February 2021

C   13 months ended 31 March 2021

D   14 months ended 30 April 2021

5 Summary

A corporation tax computation must be prepared for each accounting period.

Identifying the correct accounting period(s) is an essential first step in correctly calculating corporation tax.

✳ Links to other syllabus areas

At Advanced level, within the IDRX unit, you gained an understanding of how VAT works. An appreciation of the way in which corporation tax is levied on business transactions is important to your understanding of the figures which are reported in the financial statements or which may inform key operating decisions going forward.

There are therefore direct links here with other Professional level papers such as FSLC, or MABU and MDCL.

The tax charge, and resulting liability, is also likely to represent a material number within any set of financial statements and therefore is generally going to form an item of key focus for any external auditor (ETAU).

Test your understanding answers

Test your understanding 1

The correct answer is C.

Explanation

The financial accounting period must be split into the first 12 months and then the remaining period.

Ice Ltd therefore has the following accounting periods:

　　12 months ended 30 April 2021, and

　　3 months ended 31 July 2021.

Two corporation tax computations must be prepared.

Test your understanding 2

1	False	Corporation tax is only paid by companies (Ltd or plc).
2	False	Corporation tax computations are prepared for an accounting period.
3	False	A period of account can exceed 12 months but an accounting period cannot.
4	True	

Test your understanding 3

The correct answer is B.

Explanation

B is the correct answer because the long period of account is divided into two accounting periods as follows:

1　　the first for the 12 months ended 28 February 2021

2　　the second for the remaining 2 months to 30 April 2021.

Adjusted trading profits

Introduction

It is likely that in the assessment there will be a task that involves the computation of adjusted profits for sole traders, partnerships and limited companies.

This chapter deals with adjustments for companies.

See Chapter 9 for further information on the taxation of trading profits for a sole trader or partnership.

ASSESSMENT CRITERIA	CONTENTS
Apply the rules relating to deductible and non-deductible expenditure (2.1)	1 Introduction to adjusted trading profits
Classify expenditure as either revenue or capital expenditure (2.1)	2 Adjustment of profits calculation
Adjust accounting profits and losses for tax purposes (2.1)	3 Disallowable expenditure
	4 Income included in the accounts but not taxable as trading profits
	5 Detailed pro forma adjustment of profits

1 Introduction to adjusted trading profits

The first entry shown on the pro forma corporation tax computation is the adjusted trading profits of the company.

The starting point in determining the amount of adjusted trading profits is the net profit (this is the profit before tax) as shown in the accounts (i.e. the statement of profit or loss, formerly known as the income statement). However, the accounts may, for example, contain expenditure items which are not allowable for tax purposes.

The net profit shown in the accounts of the company must be adjusted for tax purposes to give the adjusted trading profit.

The rules in this Chapter are also largely applicable to the calculation of the adjustment of profits for an unincorporated business. The differences in that calculation are set out in Chapter 9.

2 Adjustment of profits calculation

2.1 Pro forma adjustment of profits calculation

	£	Detail in:
Net profit as per accounts	X	
Add: Disallowable expenditure	X	Section 3
	X	
Less: Income included in the accounts but not taxable as trading profit	(X)	Section 4
Adjusted trading profit before capital allowances	X	
Less: Plant and machinery capital allowances	(X)	Chapter 4
Adjusted trading profit	X	

The three categories of adjustment are considered in turn, in the sections and chapter indicated above. In this chapter you will calculate the 'adjusted trading profit before capital allowances'.

An adjustment may be required in the assessment. It is essential that you understand the entries made.

Information about adjustment of profits is contained in the AAT reference material in section 8 below.

3 Disallowable expenditure

3.1 The principle of disallowable expenditure

Expenditure included in the accounts has the effect of reducing the profits of the company.

However, some items of expenditure are acceptable deductions for financial accounting purposes but are not acceptable for corporation tax purposes.

As a result, the reduction that was made in the accounts must be reversed for corporation tax purposes (i.e. the expenditure must be added back).

This is known as 'disallowable expenditure'.

The general principle to be applied in relation to any particular item of expenditure is that it will only be allowable in arriving at the taxable trading profits if it has been incurred 'wholly and exclusively' for the purposes of the trade.

If the expense is too remote from the trade it fails the remoteness test and will not be allowable. Expenditure is regarded as being too remote from the trade when it is incurred in some capacity other than that of trading.

Example

Jersey Ltd has the following statement of profit or loss for its year ended 31 March 2021:

	£
Sales	100,000
Less: Cost of sales	(40,000)
Gross profit	60,000
Less: Expenditure (Note)	(35,000)
Net profit per accounts	25,000

Note: The expenditure can be analysed as follows:

	£
Wholly and exclusively for the purposes of the trade	33,000
Not wholly and exclusively for the purposes of the trade (i.e. disallowable expenditure)	2,000
	35,000

Calculate the adjusted trading profits of Jersey Ltd for the year ended 31 March 2021.

Solution

Jersey Ltd – Adjusted trading profit – year ended 31 March 2021

	£
Net profit per accounts	25,000
Add: Disallowable expenditure	2,000
Adjusted trading profits	27,000

3.2 Examples of disallowable expenditure

The general principle of expenditure being incurred 'wholly and exclusively' for the purposes of the trade can be used in the assessment if you are in doubt.

However, there are many common examples of disallowable expenditure that tend to appear regularly in assessments. The common examples are set out in the remainder of section 3.

3.3 Fines

Fines on the business should be disallowed as the business is expected to operate within the law. Typical examples are penalties for late payment of VAT or for breaking health and safety regulations.

In practice, however, HM Revenue and Customs usually allow a deduction for parking fines incurred by employees while on company business. This does not, however, apply to directors' parking fines. Nor does it apply to any form of speeding or other motoring fines (irrespective of who they are incurred by).

> ### 💡 Example
>
> King plc is a chemical manufacturing company
>
> **King plc – Statement of profit or loss – year ended 31 March 2021**
>
> | | £ | £ |
> |---|---|---|
> | Sales | | 700,000 |
> | Less: Cost of sales | | (200,000) |
> | | | |
> | Gross profit | | 500,000 |
> | Less: Expenditure | | |
> | Fine for polluting rivers | 20,000 | |
> | Other allowable expenditure | 200,000 | |
> | | | (220,000) |
> | | | |
> | Net profit per accounts | | 280,000 |
>
> Calculate the adjusted trading profits for the year ended 31 March 2021.
>
> **Solution**
>
> **King plc – Adjustment of profits – year ended 31 March 2021**
>
> | | £ |
> |---|---|
> | Net profit per accounts | 280,000 |
> | Add: Disallowable expenditure | |
> | Fine for polluting rivers | 20,000 |
> | | |
> | Adjusted trading profit | 300,000 |

3.4 Fraud

Fraud undertaken by directors is disallowed. This is because the loss does not relate to the company's trading activities.

However, petty theft by non-senior employees which is not covered by insurance is generally allowable.

3.5 Donations

Donations to charity usually fail the wholly and exclusively test.

In practice, this means that there is no deduction for donations to national charities or political parties, unless there is some clear benefit to the trade.

However, small donations to local charities are allowable as they can effectively be classed as advertising.

Other charitable donations are always disallowed in the adjustment of profits computation.

These other charitable donations are however allowable for corporation tax purposes, but instead of being allowed in the adjustment of profits, they are deducted in arriving at the company's taxable total profits as qualifying charitable donations. This is considered in detail at Chapter 5.

Example

Larkspur Ltd has a net profit before tax of £123,000. In calculating this profit, a deduction has been made for charitable donations as follows:

	£
To NSPCC – national charity	7,000
To local children's hospital	300
	7,300

Calculate the adjusted trading profit assuming all other expenses are allowable.

Solution

Larkspur Ltd – Adjusted trading profit

	£
Net profit per accounts	123,000
Add: Donation to national charity	7,000
Adjusted trading profit	130,000

3.6 Capital expenditure

As a rule, capital expenditure charged to the statement of profit or loss (e.g. depreciation, purchase of small capital items) is not an allowable expense for tax purposes.

For this reason, 'repairs' expenditure requires careful review, as it often contains items of a capital nature.

In general, repairs and redecoration are considered to be revenue expenditure and are therefore allowable. Improvements, however, are disallowable.

In practice, the distinction between a repair and an improvement is not clear-cut. Repairs usually involve restoring an asset to its original condition or replacing part of an asset with a modern equivalent. Improvements usually involve enhancing the asset in some way.

For example, the replacement of a single glazed window with a double glazed window would be a repair, whilst installing a new window in a brick wall would be an improvement.

Second-hand non-current assets

If a non-current asset (i.e. fixed asset) is purchased in a dilapidated state, and the purchase price reflects this, then initial 'repairs' expenditure to bring the asset to a fit state for use in the business will not be allowable.

Two cases illustrate the difficulty of applying this rule in practice.

In *Law Shipping Co Ltd v CIR (1923)* the company purchased a ship which was not in a seaworthy condition. Expenditure on making the ship seaworthy was held to be capital and therefore disallowed.

In *Odeon Associated Theatres Ltd v Jones (1971)* the company purchased some cinemas which were in a run-down condition. Expenditure incurred in renovating the cinemas was held to be revenue and therefore allowable.

These two cases can be distinguished. In the *Law Shipping* case, the ship was not usable until the repairs were undertaken and the purchase price reflected the condition it was in. By contrast, in the Odeon case, the cinemas were capable of being used for the purpose of the trade prior to their renovation. In addition, the repairs were to remedy normal wear and tear.

You do not need to remember the names of the legal cases mentioned but the principle of the decision made is important.

Legal expenses of a capital nature

The general rule to determine whether legal expenses are allowable is to look at the nature of the expense.

If they relate to a capital item, such as the purchase of a building, then the expenses will be disallowed.

Note that for tax purposes, leases are always treated as capital in this context, therefore legal expenses relating to leases will normally be disallowed (but see exception below).

If they relate to a revenue item, such as the collection of trade receivables or employee issues such as drawing up contracts of employment, then they will be allowable.

There are some exceptions to the capital rule.

The following expenses are allowable:

- the legal costs of renewing a short lease (i.e. 50 years or less)
- the cost of registering a patent
- the legal costs of defending title to a non-current asset (e.g. disputes over land boundaries).

Depreciation

Depreciation, together with any loss on the sale of non-current assets, is disallowed and must be added back.

Relief for capital expenditure may be given through capital allowances instead of depreciation (see Chapter 4).

 Test your understanding 1

For each of the following items of expenditure, state if they would be treated as capital or revenue items for tax purposes.

1	Purchase of new office furniture	Revenue / Capital
2	Rates	Revenue / Capital
3	Repair to make asset usable after purchase	Revenue / Capital
4	Legal costs re purchase of new offices	Revenue / Capital
5	Legal costs re renewal of 20 year lease	Revenue / Capital

3.7 Irrecoverable debts (receivables)

The write off of a trade debt in the accounts as an irrecoverable debt is an allowable deduction from trading profits. Consequently, the recovery of a trade debt previously written off is taxable.

The write off of a non-trade debt (e.g. a loan to a former employee or a supplier), is not an allowable deduction from trading profits.

Note that 'irrecoverable debts' are also sometimes referred to as 'impaired debts' or 'bad debts'.

A provision for bad debts, which is calculated in accordance with IFRS® Standards is allowable when computing adjusted trading profits.

As a company's accounts are required to be drawn up using IFRS Standards and these standards require objective evidence of impairment in a debt, a bad debt provision in a company's accounts will be specific in nature and allowable for tax purposes. This may be different in an unincorporated business (see Chapter 9).

It is possible that a company's accounts could include a provision relating to matters other than receivables (e.g. inventory provision). Any movement in a provision described as general should be disallowed for tax purposes.

Example

The impaired debts account of Greenidge Ltd for the year ended 30 April 2021 appears as follows:

	£		£
		Provision for irrecoverable debts b/f	445
Written off:			
– Trade debts	274		
– Former employee	80	Recoveries – trade debts	23
Provision for irrecoverable debts c/f	419	Statement of profit or loss	305
	———		———
	773		773
	———		———

Show any adjustments required for tax purposes.

Solution

In this example, the information is presented in the form of a 'T' account.

The first stage is to establish a breakdown of the statement of profit or loss charge of £305.

Remember that this figure comprises amounts written off and recovered, and movements in provisions.

Statement of profit or loss charge:

	£	Allowable?
Decrease in provision for irrecoverable debts (£445 – £419)	(26)	✓
Amounts written off:		
Trade debt	274	✓
Former employee	80	✗
Recoveries – trade debts	(23)	✓
	———	
	305	
	———	

The write off of the debt owed by the former employee is disallowed.

The recovery of the trade debts is taxable.

The *decrease* in the provision for irrecoverable debts will be specific in nature and is therefore not adjusted for.

The adjustment to the trading profits for tax purposes is therefore:

Add: Former employee debt written off   £80
                                                    ─────

Write-offs of non-trading loans (such as here to the former employee) are not allowable deductions from trading profits, however they are allowed as a deduction from non-trade related interest income – take care, as it is easy to miss this point (see Chapter 5).

3.8 Interest payable

For the purpose of computing a company's adjusted trading profits you need to distinguish between trading and non-trading payments.

Interest payable on trading loans is an allowable expense in calculating trading profits. For example, interest payable on bank overdrafts or loan notes (also referred to as debentures) used for trading purposes.

Interest payable on non-trading loans is not an allowable expense in calculating trading profits. A loan to purchase an investment would be an example of a non-trading loan. Interest on such a loan should be added back in the adjustment to profits computation.

However, interest in respect of non-trading loans is allowable as a deduction from non-trade related interest income (see Chapter 5).

3.9 Other miscellaneous adjustments

Pre-trading expenditure

Expenditure incurred up to seven years before a trade commences is allowed as an expense of the first accounting period of trading, provided it would have been allowable had the trade existed at the time the expenditure was incurred.

Gifts

Gifts to employees are allowable (but may be taxed on employees).

Other gifts, for example gifts to customers, are only allowable if they fulfil the following three conditions.

- They incorporate a conspicuous advertisement for the business.
- The total cost per donee is not more than £50 per annum.
- The gift is not food, drink (alcoholic or otherwise) or tobacco or a voucher.

Note that if the cost exceeds the £50 limit, the whole amount is disallowed.

Therefore, desk diaries or pens embossed with the company name usually qualify, but a bottle of whisky carrying an advert for the company would not.

Entertaining

The cost of entertaining customers and suppliers is disallowed. However, the cost of entertaining staff is allowable.

Trade samples

Trade samples which are not for resale are allowable.

Hire or lease charges

The rules for disallowing part of the leasing charges for cars are based on the level of CO_2 emissions.

Leasing charges for cars with CO_2 emissions of 110g/km or less are allowed in full.

There is a standard disallowance of 15% of the leasing charges for a lease on a car with CO_2 emissions over 110g/km.

 Example

BSG Ltd started to lease two cars on 1 May 2020. The details of the leased cars are as follows:

(1)   The first car has a retail price of £21,000 and CO_2 emissions of 125g/km. The leasing charges up to 31 December 2020 are £6,400.

(2)   The other car has a retail price of £15,000 and CO_2 emissions of 105g/km. The leasing charges up to 31 December 2020 are £4,700.

Show the amount disallowed for the purposes of calculating the adjusted trading profits in the year ended 31 December 2020.

Solution

The only disallowance is for the first car as the CO_2 emissions exceed 110g/km.

The disallowed amount is (15% of £6,400) = £960.

Legal and professional fees

Legal and professional fees are allowable to the extent that they are related to the trade (e.g. debt collection fees).

Any professional costs relating to disputing a fine, tax penalty or connected with an enquiry into a return will usually be disallowable. HMRC guidance states that if the enquiry relates specifically to trading income and no additional profits are brought within the charge to tax, then the associated costs of dealing with the enquiry will be allowable.

3.10 Dividends

Dividends are paid out of profits after they have been subjected to tax. They are not expenses incurred in earning those profits. They are therefore not allowable expenditure.

However, there is normally no adjustment required as the computation starts with the 'net profit' which for a company is before the deduction of dividends paid. In a correctly drawn up statement of profit or loss dividends have not been deducted from net profit and so do not need to be added back.

An adjustment is only required if a question specifically tells you that the net profit given is **after** dividends have been deducted.

3.11 Summary

Common items of allowable and disallowable expenditure are summarised below.

Expenditure	Allowable	Disallowable
Fines	Employee parking fines	Other fines and penalties
Fraud	Petty theft by non-senior employees	By directors
Donations	Small donations to local charities	Other donations
In relation to non-current assets	Capital allowances on plant and machinery	Depreciation Profit or loss on sale
Repairs	Revenue expenditure Repairs and redecoration	Capital expenditure Improvements Work required on a newly-purchased asset to make it fit for use
Legal expenses	Relate to revenue matters – debt collection, employee contracts	Relate to capital matters – but note exceptions Relate to breaking the law
Irrecoverable debts	Trade debts	Non-trade debts
Interest payable	On trading loans	On non-trading loans
Entertaining	Staff	Customers and suppliers
Gifts	To employees Other gifts provided conditions satisfied	All other gifts
Car leasing	CO_2 emissions of 110g/km or less	Other cars – disallow 15% of leasing costs

Test your understanding 2

1   Jamaica Ltd operates a business selling high quality second-hand clothes.

Which of the following costs is NOT deductible in arriving at the tax adjusted trading profits?

A   Repairs to shop premises, carried out two weeks after the shop opened.

B   Advertising in the local paper.

C   Parking fine incurred by the Managing Director for parking outside the shop.

D   Cost of writing off stock that wouldn't sell.

2   Bakers R Us Ltd incurred the following expenses for the year ended 31 March 2021, but is unsure of their treatment for tax purposes.

Which of the following is NOT deductible in arriving at Bakers R Us Ltd's tax adjusted trading profit?

A   The cost of new plant and machinery that is used in the bread making process.

B   The write off of a trade debt owed by a customer.

C   Legal fees in chasing the debt owed by a customer.

D   A provision against the debt owed by a customer.

 4   **Income included in the accounts but not taxable as trading profits**

4.1   Types of income

The following are examples of income which may be included in the statement of profit or loss, but which is not taxable as trading profits.

*   Income taxed in another way, for example rental income (property income), interest receivable.

*   Dividends received.

*   Profits on sales of non-current (i.e. capital) assets.

4.2   Effect

As these types of income are not taxable as trading profits, they must be deducted to arrive at the correct adjusted trading profits.

5 Detailed pro forma adjustment of profits

5.1 Pro forma for a company

	+ £	– £
Net profit per accounts	X	
Add: Disallowable expenditure:		
Depreciation	X	
Loss on sale of non-current assets	X	
Capital expenditure	X	
Legal expenses of capital nature	X	
Fines and penalties	X	
Donations (unless small and to local charity)	X	
Entertaining (other than staff)	X	
Gifts to customers	X	
Proportion of car leasing costs	X	
Less: Income in accounts but not trading profits:		
Rental income		X
Profit on sale of non-current assets		X
Interest receivable		X
Dividend income		X
	X	X
	(X)	
Adjusted trading profit before capital allowances	X	

Example

The statement of profit or loss of SND Ltd for the year ended 31 March 2021 showed a net profit of £42,000 after accounting for the following items:

Expenditure:	£	Income:	£
Depreciation	9,500	Insurance recovery	
Loan note interest (Note 1)	8,000	re flood damage to	
Irrecoverable debts:		trading inventory	6,500
– Trade debts written off	4,000	Profit on sale of	
– Increase in provision	1,000	machine	3,200
Entertainment expenses			
(Note 2)	2,700		
Legal fees re new lease	3,200		
General expenses (Note 3)	1,800		

Notes:

(1) The loan note was issued to raise finance to purchase plant and machinery for the purpose of the trade.

(2) Entertainment consists of expenditure on:

	£
Entertaining customers	1,200
Staff dance (30 people)	900
Gifts to customers of food hampers	600

(3) General expenses comprise:

	£
Parking fines	
(relating to employees on company business)	300
Fees for employees attending training courses	1,500

Compute the adjusted trading profit for the above period.

Solution

Step 1: Start your solution with the company's net profit:

	+ £	− £
Net profit		42,000

Step 2: Add back any disallowable items of expenditure

Go through each expense in turn and decide whether or not it needs to be added back. If it does require adding back, add the figure to the plus column of your pro forma.

If you do not know how to treat a particular item, guess. You have a good chance of getting the right answer.

Step 3: Deduct income in the accounts which is not taxable as trading profits

Deal with any income in the order in which it appears in the accounts. For each item, ask yourself whether it relates to the company's trade.

If it does, no action is required. If it does not, include the figure in the minus column.

Step 4: Finish by totalling the pro forma

Note that it is not essential for you to put headings such as 'disallowable expenditure' on your pro forma. You could simply state 'add' and 'less'.

You do, however, need to list each adjusted item in words as well as figures.

Approach in computer based assessment (CBA)

You might be given a pro forma and will not have to type in expense headings and numbers. Instead you may have to select correct headings and numbers from drop down menus.

Alternatively, an assessment task may require you to drag and drop each item which needs adjustment into the appropriate part of the computation.

SND Ltd – Adjustment of profit for the year ended 31 March 2021

	+ £	– £
Net profit	42,000	
Depreciation	9,500	
Entertainment expenses	1,800	
Legal fees	3,200	
General expenses	–	
Profit on sale of machine		3,200
	56,500	(3,200)
	(3,200)	
Adjusted trading profit	53,300	

Explanation

1   Depreciation (capital expenditure) is not an allowable deduction.

2   Loan note interest is allowable (assuming the loan note proceeds were used for trading purposes).

3   Write-offs of trade debts and provisions in a company's accounts are allowable.

4   Expenditure on entertaining customers is not allowable. Expenditure on entertaining staff is allowable. The cost of the hampers is not allowable as they contain food.

5   The legal fees in respect of the new lease are a capital item, and are therefore not allowable.

6   Parking fines incurred by employees will generally be allowed. Training course fees are also allowable, assuming the course relates to the company's trade.

7   The insurance recovery is in respect of trading inventory. It is therefore taxable as trading profits, and no adjustment needs to be made.

8   Profits on the sale of non-current assets (such as plant and machinery) are effectively negative depreciation and are therefore not taxable.

In an assessment task you should try to work methodically through the statement of profit or loss and ensure you deal with all relevant items.

Example

The statement of profit or loss of DTS Ltd for the year ended 31 March 2021 showed a net profit of £53,000 after accounting for the following items:

Expenditure:	£	Income:	£
Depreciation	8,300	Rents received	8,400
Loss on sale of lorry	6,000	Profit on sale of	
Legal fees re employees'		machine	7,400
service contracts	600		
Penalty for late VAT return	2,200		
Repairs (Note)	6,400		

Note:

Included in the figure for repairs is an amount of £5,000 incurred in installing new windows in a recently acquired second-hand warehouse.

This building had suffered fire damage resulting in all of its windows being blown out shortly before being acquired by DTS Ltd. Other repairs were of a routine nature.

Compute the adjusted trading profit for the above period.

Solution

DTS Ltd – Adjustment of profit for the year ended 31 March 2021

	+ £	– £
Net profit	53,000	
Depreciation	8,300	
Loss on sale of lorry	6,000	
Legal fees re employees'		
service contracts	–	
Penalty for late VAT return	2,200	
Repairs	5,000	
Rents received		(8,400)
Profit on sale of machine		(7,400)
	74,500	(15,800)
	(15,800)	
Adjusted trading profit	58,700	

Explanation

1   Depreciation (capital expenditure) is not an allowable deduction.

2   Losses on the sale of non-current assets are treated in the same way as depreciation – they are added back. Conversely, profits on the sale of non-current assets are deducted.

3   Legal fees in connection with the service contracts are wholly and exclusively for the trade and are therefore allowable.

4   VAT penalties are not allowable.

5   The cost of new windows is not allowable. It is capital expenditure required to put a new asset into a usable state (*Law Shipping* case).

6   Rents received are taxable as property income and not trading profits, therefore deduct.

In an assessment you should try to work methodically through the information given and ensure you deal with all relevant items.

 Test your understanding 3

Brazil Ltd

The following is the statement of profit or loss of Brazil Ltd for the year ended 30 April 2021:

	£	£
Sales		240,458
Less: Cost of sales		(183,942)
Gross profit		56,516
Other income		5,000
Salaries and wages	24,174	
Rent and rates	8,560	
Legal and professional charges	3,436	
General expenses	1,211	
Depreciation	3,047	
		(40,428)
Net profit		21,088

The following further information is given:

(1) **Other income**

This comprises bank deposit interest for the year received on 30 April 2021.

(2) **Legal and professional charges**

This item includes the following:

	£
Legal fees in connection with new lease	325
Legal fees in connection with action by employee for unfair dismissal	830
Payment to employee for unfair dismissal	1,200
Accountancy charges	1,081

(3) **General expenses**

These include a payment of £200 to the Friends of the Local Hospital, and a donation of £25 to Save the Children.

Calculate the adjusted trading profit for the year for tax purposes.

✎ Test your understanding 4

Cashew Ltd

The following is the statement of profit or loss of Cashew Ltd for the year ended 31 March 2021:

	£	£
Gross profit		47,214
Other income		4,000
Salaries and wages	20,509	
Repairs to premises	3,263	
Travelling and entertaining expenses	1,964	
Irrecoverable debts	(630)	
Depreciation	2,120	
		(27,226)
Net profit		23,988

The following further information is given:

(1) **Other income**

This comprises bank deposit interest for the year which was received on 31 March 2021.

(2) **Repairs to premises**

Included in this item is £1,450 incurred in fitting a new shop-front to a former office and £250 for the initial repainting of a new shop.

(3) **Travelling and entertaining expenses**

These include expenses of entertaining UK customers of £326 and gifts to customers of Christmas hampers costing £528 (cost £48 each).

(4) **Irrecoverable debts**

The figure in the accounts is made up as follows:

	£
Trade debt recoveries	(232)
Decrease in provision for irrecoverable trade debts	(398)
	(630)

Calculate the adjusted trading profit for the year for tax purposes.

6 Test your understanding

Test your understanding 5

Karma Ltd

Karma Ltd incurred the following costs for the year ended 31 March 2021. For each item of expenditure state the tax treatment in arriving at Karma Ltd's trading profits.

Choice of treatment is 'Deductible' or 'Not deductible'.

1 Fees incurred in chasing a debt which was over 6 months old.

2 Legal fees incurred in acquiring a 5 year lease over new shop premises.

3 Qualifying charitable donation to a national charity.

4 Small donation to a local charity.

5 Costs of purchasing computer equipment.

Test your understanding 6

Adjustment of profits

What adjustment, if any, should you make for the following items included in a company's statement of profit or loss when calculating adjusted trading profits?

State 'Add back' or 'No adjustment required'.

1 Managing director's salary (he owns 99% of the shares)

2 Overdraft interest

3 Interest on a loan to purchase an investment property

4 Gifts of diaries to customers, costing £5 each and embossed with the company's name

5 Gifts of bottles of wine to customers, costing £5 each and embossed with the company's name

Test your understanding 7

Tricks Ltd

Tricks Ltd's statement of profit or loss for the year ended 31 March 2021 was as follows:

	£	£
Sales		370,150
Loan note interest receivable		4,100
UK dividends received		12,000
Profit on the sale of an investment		2,750
		———
		389,000
Allowable trading expenses	125,750	
Disallowable trading expenses	5,900	
Loan note interest payable (Note)	8,100	
	———	
		(139,750)
		———
Net profit		249,250
		———

Note: The funds raised by the issue of the loan note were used to purchase machinery for use in the business.

Calculate Tricks Ltd's adjusted trading profits for the year ended 31 March 2021.

Test your understanding 8

Cricket Limited

Cricket Limited has the following results for the year ended 31 December 2020:

	£		£
Salaries, wages	20,041	Gross trading profit	802,350
Legal charges (Note 1)	2,436		
Impaired debts (Note 2)	480		
Depreciation – Factory	20,000		
– Machine	10,000		
Repairs (Note 3)	7,800		
Sundry expenses (allowable)	3,492		
Net profit	738,101		
	802,350		802,350

Notes:

(1) **Legal charges**

	£
Debt collection	1,136
Staff service agreements	300
In connection with lease of new office premises	1,000
	2,436

(2) **Impaired debts**

	£
Loan to former employee written off	200
Increase in provision for impaired debts	280
	480

(3) **Repairs**

	£
Repainting	200
New office furniture	7,600
	7,800

Show Cricket Limited's adjusted trading profits for the year ended 31 December 2020.

Test your understanding 9

Uranus Ltd

The following items are charged against profit in the accounts of Uranus Ltd for the year ended 31 March 2021:

1   Running expenses of the managing director's BMW totalling £10,000 (including depreciation of £6,000). His total mileage in the year was 12,000 of which 6,000 was private. The car was owned by Uranus Ltd.

2   Entertainment expenditure totalling £25,000 of which £10,000 was incurred on overseas customers, £11,000 on UK customers and £4,000 on the annual company dinner for 200 employees.

3   Lease rental of £6,000 on sales director's car costing £20,000. The lease commenced on 1 April 2020. The car has CO_2 emissions of 145g/km.

State how you would deal with each of the above items when preparing the company's computation of adjusted trading profits for the year ended 31 March 2021.

 Test your understanding 10

Saturn Ltd

The following items are charged against profit in the accounts of Saturn Ltd for the year ended 31 March 2021:

1   A payment of £616 to the Royal National Lifeboat Institution (a registered national charity).

2   The write off of £8,000 against a trade debt of the company, being 80% of the debt. The liquidator of the debtor company had advised Saturn Ltd of this figure but in the event £5,000 of the debt was paid in May 2021.

3   Trade samples costing £7,000 in total which are put through the letter boxes of 2,000 homes in the East Midlands.

State how you would deal with each of the above items when preparing the company's computation of adjusted trading profits for the year ended 31 March 2021.

7 Summary

You should now be able to successfully attempt questions requiring you to calculate the adjusted trading profit for corporation tax purposes.

The starting point for computing adjusted trading profits is the net profit shown in the company's accounts. This must be adjusted in respect of the following items:

- Disallowable expenditure.

  The main types of disallowable expenditure are:

  - expenditure not wholly and exclusively for the purpose of the trade

  - expenditure disallowed under the detailed rules.

- Income included in the accounts but not taxable as trading profits. For example:

  - rents and interest

  - profits on the sale of capital assets.

When writing out answers on paper, it is advisable to use a '+' and '–' column and deal with each adjustment as you work methodically through the question. There is no need to arrange your answer into the two types of adjustment shown above. Either presentation may be seen in the assessment.

❋ Links to other syllabus areas

The accounting profits of a company (drawn up in accordance with generally accepted accounting policy) will either generally determine the tax treatment of certain key items of revenue and expenditure, or will form the starting point from which the tax treatment will then depart – your knowledge gained at Advanced level in AVBK and FAPR of how to account for business transactions is therefore of fundamental importance when it comes to establishing the basis on which the profits of the entity are to be taxed.

8 AAT Reference material

Adjustment of profits – sole traders, partnerships and companies

Pro forma for adjustment of profits

	£	£
Net profit as per accounts		X
Add: Expenses charged in the accounts that are not allowable as trading expenses	X	
	───	
	X	
		X
Less: Income included in the accounts which is not assessable as trading income	X	
	───	
		(X)
Adjusted profit/(loss)		X

Disallowed expenses

- Expenses that fail the remoteness test so not "wholly and exclusively" for trading purposes.

- Fines on the business or fraud by directors/owners.

- Donations to charity are generally disallowed in calculating trading profits (however qualifying charitable donations are deductible in the corporation tax computation).

- Political donations are never allowable.

- Capital expenditure, e.g. purchase of equipment included in profit and loss account.

- Depreciation. Capital allowances granted instead.

- Costs of bringing newly acquired second-hand assets to useable condition.

- Legal and professional expenses relating to capital items or breaking the law.

- Customer entertaining. Staff entertaining can be allowable.

- Customer gifts, unless gift incorporates business advertising, cost is less than £50 per annum per customer, and gift is not food, drink, tobacco or cash vouchers.

Non-assessable income

- Income taxed in any other way, e.g. interest or property income for individuals.

- Profits on sale of fixed assets.

Test your understanding answers

Test your understanding 1

1	Capital	The purchase of a new non-current asset is capital expenditure
2	Revenue	Rates are payable every year and are revenue expenditure
3	Capital	As the asset was purchased in a damaged condition and needed to be repaired before use, it is capital expenditure
4	Capital	Legal fees in relation to a capital purchase are treated as capital expenditure
5	Revenue	Legal fees in relation to the renewal of a short lease are specifically allowed as revenue expenditure

Test your understanding 2

Jamaica Ltd

1   The correct answer is C.

Bakers R Us Ltd

2   The correct answer is A.

Explanation

1   Fines incurred by directors are not deductible.

Parking fines incurred by employees whilst on business activity are generally deductible, but not those incurred by directors.

The other costs are deductible.

2   A is a capital cost, whereas the others are revenue costs, all of which are allowable as trading expenses, given the context.

The cost of plant and machinery will qualify for capital allowances (see Chapter 4).

Test your understanding 3

Brazil Ltd

Adjusted trading profits for the year ended 30 April 2021

	£	£
Net profit as per accounts	21,088	
Add: Legal fees re new lease	325	
National charity donation	25	
Depreciation	3,047	
Less: Bank deposit interest		(5,000)
	24,485	(5,000)
	(5,000)	
Adjusted trading profit	19,485	

Explanation

- Legal fees and payment in connection with unfair dismissal are allowable, as part of the cost of employing staff.

- The donation of £200 to the local charity is allowable as a business expense (small and local). Any donation to a national charity is not allowable.

Test your understanding 4

Cashew Ltd

Adjusted trading profits for the year ended 31 March 2021

	£	£
Net profit as per accounts	23,988	
Add: New shop-front	1,450	
Entertaining customers	326	
Gifts	528	
Depreciation	2,120	
Less: Bank deposit interest		(4,000)
	28,412	(4,000)
	(4,000)	
Adjusted trading profit	24,412	

Explanation

- The £250 initial repainting costs in respect of the new shop are considered to be allowable, following the decision in the *Odeon Theatres case*.

- Although the hampers cost less than £50 each, the cost is disallowed as the gift is of food.

- Recoveries of trade debts and movements in provisions for irrecoverable trade debts both relate to the trade and are therefore taxable and no adjustment is required.

Test your understanding 5

Karma Ltd

1	Deductible	
2	Not deductible	This is capital expenditure as it is a new lease.
3	Not deductible	Qualifying charitable donations are not deductible in calculating the taxable trading profits.
4	Deductible	
5	Not deductible	This is capital expenditure on which capital allowances may be claimed.

 Test your understanding 6

Adjustment of profits

1 No adjustment required – allowable expense.

2 No adjustment required – allowable expense.

3 Add back – not allowable deduction from trading profits but is deductible from non-trade related interest income.

4 No adjustment required – allowable expense.

5 Add back – gift of drink.

Note that the gift of any type of drink is not allowable (not just alcohol).

Test your understanding 7

Tricks Ltd

Adjusted trading profits for the year ended 31 March 2021

	£
Net profit	249,250
Add: Disallowable expenses	5,900
	255,150
Less: Loan note interest receivable	(4,100)
UK dividends	(12,000)
Profit on sale of investment	(2,750)
Adjusted trading profits	236,300

The funds raised by the issue of the loan note were used for the purposes of the trade and the interest paid is therefore an allowable deduction in computing the adjusted trading profits.

Note that this alternative presentation to the two columns shown previously is also acceptable.

 Test your understanding 8

Cricket Limited

Adjusted trading profits for the year ended 31 December 2020

	£
Net profit per accounts	738,101
Add: Legal charges re new office premises	1,000
Loan to former employee written off	200
New furniture	7,600
Depreciation	30,000
Adjusted trading profit	776,901

 Test your understanding 9

Uranus Ltd

1   Running expenses, except for depreciation, are an allowable deduction. The depreciation must be disallowed but relief for the cost of the car will be available through capital allowances.

The private use of the car by an employee of a company is irrelevant for profit adjustment purposes.

Therefore, add back £6,000.

2   Disallow all entertaining except staff entertaining.

Therefore, add back £21,000.

3   Part of this lease cost will be disallowed as the car has CO_2 emissions exceeding 110g/km.

The disallowable portion added back is as follows:
$(15\% \times £6,000) = £900$

 Test your understanding 10

Saturn Ltd

1   Donations to national charities are disallowed and treated as qualifying charitable donations. Therefore, add back £616.

2   No adjustment is required.

The write-off of a trade debt is allowable. There will be a credit in the following year's accounts, when the £5,000 is recovered, which will be taxable as part of the trading profit.

3   Trade samples, which are not for resale, are allowable. So no adjustment required.

Capital allowances – plant and machinery

Introduction

In the assessment it is likely that there will be tasks testing adjusting of profits (as per Chapter 3) and calculation of plant and machinery capital allowances.

Capital allowances are a very important topic.

ASSESSMENT CRITERIA	CONTENTS
Identify types of capital allowances (2.2) Calculate capital allowances (2.2)	1 Introduction to capital allowances 2 Qualifying expenditure 3 The allowances 4 Calculating the allowances 5 Capital allowances treatment of cars 6 Special rate pool 7 Short life assets 8 Pro forma computation for capital allowances on plant and machinery 9 Impact of the length of the accounting period 10 Business cessation

1 Introduction to capital allowances

1.1 Capital allowances

Capital allowances are a form of depreciation that is allowable for tax purposes. The allowances are only given on certain items of capital expenditure. This syllabus covers plant and machinery capital allowances only. A separate allowance is available for certain buildings (the structures and buildings allowance or SBA), however the AAT have confirmed this will not be tested in assessments under FA2020.

The rules in this Chapter are also largely applicable to the calculation of capital allowances for an unincorporated business. The differences in that calculation are set out in Chapter 9.

1.2 Capital allowances v depreciation

Each business can decide its own rate of depreciation for accounting purposes. In theory, identical businesses with the same assets could have different amounts of depreciation.

In order for everyone to be treated the same, HMRC use a standard calculation of capital allowances for tax purposes.

The capital allowances are deducted instead of depreciation, to arrive at the adjusted trading profit.

 Example

Opalite Ltd and Pyrite Ltd are two companies making the same products. In the year ended 31 December 2020, both companies made profits before depreciation/capital allowances of £200,000. Both have only one piece of machinery that they bought in the year for £150,000.

The companies have different methods of calculating depreciation, giving the following amounts:

Opalite Ltd	£25,000
Pyrite Ltd	£35,000

For tax purposes, both companies would have capital allowances of £150,000.

Compare the accounting profits and adjusted trading profits of both companies.

Solution

	Opalite Ltd £	Pyrite Ltd £
Profit before depreciation	200,000	200,000
Less: Depreciation	(25,000)	(35,000)
Accounting profits	175,000	165,000

Adjustment of profits computation

Accounting profits	175,000	165,000
Add: Depreciation	25,000	35,000
Adjusted profit before capital allowances	200,000	200,000
Less: Capital allowances	(150,000)	(150,000)
Adjusted trading profit	50,000	50,000

In reality there are likely to be many more adjustments that could give rise to different adjusted trading profits for tax purposes (as per Chapter 3).

However, this example illustrates that identical businesses could have different accounting profits, but have the same adjusted trading profits on which their tax is calculated.

2 Qualifying expenditure

2.1 What qualifies as plant and machinery?

There is no automatic right to tax relief for capital expenditure.

In order to qualify for capital allowances, expenditure must usually be in respect of plant or machinery.

There is no statutory definition of plant, however the courts have established a **function test**:

Does the asset perform:	This means that the asset is:	Plant and machinery?
An active function	Apparatus **with which** the business is carried on	Yes
A passive function	The setting **in which** the business is carried on	No

The dividing line between an asset that is functional and one that is merely setting is not always clear. Examples below show how the courts have reacted to claims for capital allowances in these circumstances.

- A canopy covering petrol filling pumps was held to be part of the setting and not plant and machinery. (It did not assist in serving petrol to customers.)

- False ceilings in a restaurant were not plant. (All they did was hide pipes.)

- Swimming pools at a caravan park were held to be plant and machinery – the caravan park as a whole was the setting.

The most common types of capital expenditure found in a set of financial accounts that are treated as 'plant and machinery' for tax purposes are:

- plant and machinery including moveable partitioning

- fixtures and fittings

- motor vehicles including cars, vans and lorries

- computer equipment and software.

In addition, the cost of alterations to buildings needed for the installation of plant qualifies as plant and machinery.

3 The allowances

3.1 Main types of capital allowances

The following are the main types of capital allowances that may be available to a company in respect of plant and machinery.

(a) Writing-down allowance (WDA)

- given at 18% on a reducing balance basis on most assets

- given at 6% (8% before 1 April 2019) on a reducing balance basis for items in the special rate pool (see section 6 below).

(b) Annual investment allowance (AIA)

- a 100% allowance for the first £1,000,000 (£200,000 before 1 January 2019 and from 1 January 2021) of expenditure incurred by a company on plant and machinery in a 12-month period

- where a company has an accounting period straddling 1 January 2019 or 1 January 2021, the maximum AIA is found via time apportionment

  for example, the maximum AIA for the year ended 31 March 2021 is £800,000

  (£1,000,000 × 9/12) + (£200,000 × 3/12)

- where a company spends more than the maximum AIA, the excess expenditure may qualify for a WDA.

(c) First year allowance (FYA)

- a 100% allowance is available on new (not second-hand) low emission cars with CO_2 emissions of 50g/km or less (see section 5 below)

- additions qualifying for the FYA are added into the capital allowances computation after the deduction of WDAs.

Example

Howlite Ltd purchased a machine costing £1,210,000 on 1 May 2020 in its year ended 31 December 2020. This is its only capital item.

Calculate the capital allowances for the first three years of ownership.

Assume the rates of allowances for the year ended 31 March 2021 continue into the future.

Solution

Howlite Ltd – Capital allowances

	£	Allowances £
Year ended 31 December 2020		
Cost	1,210,000	
AIA (max)	(1,000,000)	1,000,000
	210,000	
WDA (18% × £210,000)	(37,800)	37,800
	172,200	1,037,800
Year ended 31 December 2021		
WDA (18% × £172,200)	(30,996)	30,996
	141,204	
Year ended 31 December 2022		
WDA (18% × £141,204)	(25,417)	25,417
	115,787	

Example

Deacon Ltd prepares its accounts to the end of February each year. The company purchased a machine costing £875,000. This was the company's only acquisition.

Calculate the capital allowances for the accounting period of purchase if:

(a) the machine was purchased on 3 February 2019, or

(b) the machine was purchased on 3 December 2020.

Solution

(a) **Deacon Ltd – Capital allowances:**
     Purchase on 3 February 2019

	£	Allowances £
Year ended 28 February 2019		
Cost	875,000	
AIA (W)	(333,334)	333,334
	541,666	
WDA (18% × £541,666)	(97,500)	97,500
	444,166	430,834

Working: AIA

The accounting period straddles 1 January 2019. Ten months of the accounting period falls before 1 January 2019 and two months falls after.

The maximum AIA for the period is:

(£200,000 × 10/12) + (£1,000,000 × 2/12) = £166,667 + £166,667

= £333,334

(b) **Deacon Ltd – Capital allowances:**
Purchase on 3 December 2020

	£	Allowances £
Year ended 28 February 2021		
Cost	875,000	
AIA (W)	(866,666)	866,666
	8,334	
WDA (18% × £8,334)	(1,500)	1,500
	6,834	868,166

Working: AIA

The accounting period straddles 1 January 2021.

The maximum AIA for the period is:

(£1,000,000 × 10/12) + (£200,000 × 2/12) = £833,333 + £33,333
= £866,666

4 Calculating the allowances

4.1 Expenditure not pooled

As companies may have many assets, it would be extremely time-consuming to calculate allowances separately for each asset. Therefore, all qualifying expenditure is added to the main pool, apart from:

- cars with CO_2 emissions exceeding 110g/km, and

- assets for which a short life asset election has been made.

4.2   General pool (or main pool)

Most items of plant and machinery go into the general pool (also known as the main pool). Once an asset enters the pool, it loses its identity. This means that the writing down allowance (WDA) is calculated on the balance of the whole pool of assets, rather than on the individual assets.

When a new asset is acquired, the purchase price increases the value of the pool. When an asset is disposed of, the pool value is reduced by the lower of the sale proceeds or the original cost of the asset (see section 4.6 below).

Allowances are given for accounting periods. Allowances commence in the year in which the expenditure is incurred. A full WDA is given in the year of purchase irrespective of the date of purchase within that year.

4.3   Annual investment allowance (AIA)

The AIA is a 100% allowance for expenditure incurred by a company on plant and machinery. The precise amount of AIA depends, as we have seen, on the date to which a company is making up its accounts.

The AIA:

- is not available for expenditure on cars

- is available for expenditure on other vehicles

- applies for a 12-month accounting period. The allowance is time apportioned for short accounting periods.

Where expenditure on plant and machinery in an accounting period exceeds the maximum AIA, the excess is added to the pool balance on which a WDA can be claimed. If the expenditure incurred in the period is less than the available AIA, the remaining balance of any AIA is wasted.

 Example

Marble Ltd commenced trading on 1 April 2020. In its first year of trading the company made the following purchases:

- plant and machinery (purchased 1 September 2020)   £1,137,500

- a car for the office manager (CO_2 emissions 100g/km)   £11,000

(a)   Calculate how much of Marble Ltd's capital expenditure is eligible for writing down allowances after deduction of the AIA.

(b)   What would your answer to part (a) be if the plant and machinery had cost £780,000?

Solution

(a)   Marble Ltd – Capital allowances – year ended 31 March 2021

	£	General pool £
Additions:		
Not qualifying for AIA		
Car		11,000
Qualifying for AIA		
Plant and machinery	1,137,500	
AIA (W)	(800,000)	
Balance eligible for 18% WDA	337,500	337,500
Eligible for WDA		348,500

Working: AIA

The maximum AIA for the period is:
(£1,000,000 × 9/12) + (£200,000 × 3/12) = £750,000 + £50,000
= £800,000.

(b)   If the plant and machinery had cost £780,000

	£	General pool £
Additions:		
Not qualifying for AIA		
Car		11,000
Qualifying for AIA		
Plant and machinery	780,000	
AIA (Note)	(780,000)	
		Nil
Eligible for WDA		11,000

Note

The unused AIA of £20,000 (£800,000 – £780,000) is lost.

4.4 First year allowance (FYA)

A first year allowance is given in the year that a qualifying asset is purchased.

A 100% FYA is given for expenditure on new low emission cars (see section 5).

First year allowances are given in full in the period of purchase, **regardless** of the length of the accounting period (i.e. the FYA is never time apportioned).

The additions qualifying for FYA are usually included in the capital allowances computation after the deduction of the WDAs.

4.5 Writing down allowances (WDA)

A WDA of 18% is given on a reducing balance basis for a 12-month period.

It is given on:

* the unrelieved expenditure in the pool brought forward at the beginning of the accounting period (known as the tax written down value (TWDV))

* plus any additions eligible for WDAs

* less disposals of plant and machinery.

The TWDV brought forward includes all prior period expenditure, less capital allowances already claimed.

 Example

Plaster Ltd commenced trading on 1 January 2020 preparing accounts to 31 December each year.

On 1 May 2020 the company purchased £1,115,000 of machinery and a car costing £22,000 with CO_2 emissions of 105g/km.

Calculate the capital allowances available to Plaster Ltd for the year ended 31 December 2020.

Solution

Plaster Ltd – Capital allowances – year ended 31 December 2020

	£	General pool £	Allowances £
Addition not qualifying for AIA			
Car		22,000	
Addition qualifying for AIA	1,115,000		
AIA	(1,000,000)		1,000,000
Balance expenditure	115,000	115,000	
		137,000	
WDA (18% × £137,000)		(24,660)	24,660
TWDV c/f		112,340	
Total allowances			1,024,660

4.6 Disposal in the general pool

When a pool item is sold, the sale proceeds are deducted from the pool. However, this deduction cannot exceed the asset's original cost.

The following example illustrates the working of the general pool, including disposals.

 Example

Apple Ltd prepares accounts to 31 March each year.

On 1 May 2020 Apple Ltd incurred expenditure of £10,000 on the purchase of shop fittings and machinery. On 1 June 2020 the company sold some machinery for £6,000 (cost £4,000).

On 5 May 2021 the company sold equipment for £2,395 which had cost £11,200 in May 2016.

The tax written down value of the pool at 1 April 2020 was £8,260.

Compute the capital allowances for the years ended 31 March 2021 and 31 March 2022.

Assume the rates of allowances for the year ended 31 March 2021 continue into the future.

Solution

Step 1: **Identify the balance brought forward at the beginning of the accounting period**

This is the *tax written down value* (Tax WDV or TWDV).

	Pool
	£
Year ended 31 March 2021	
TWDV brought forward	8,260

Step 2: **Identify the accounting periods in which the additions and disposals occur**

In the year ended 31 March 2021, Apple Ltd acquired plant costing £10,000 and sold plant for £6,000 (cost £4,000).

The second disposal occurs in the second accounting period.

Step 3: **Identify any additions on which the AIA can be claimed**

The plant acquired on 1 May 2020 qualifies for the AIA.

Deal with this addition *before* calculating the WDA for that year on the other items in the general pool.

Consider the maximum AIA that can be claimed. The year ended 31 March 2021 straddles 1 January 2021, so the maximum AIA for the period is:

(£1,000,000 × 9/12) + (£200,000 × 3/12) = £800,000.

As the expenditure is less than £800,000 it will be covered in full by this AIA.

Step 4: **Prepare the capital allowances computation**

Deal with one accounting period at a time.

	£	General pool £	Allowances £
Year ended 31 March 2021			
TWDV b/f		8,260	
Additions qualifying for AIA	10,000		
AIA	(10,000)		10,000
	———	Nil	
Disposals			
1 June 2020 (proceeds restricted to cost)		(4,000)	
		———	
		4,260	
WDA at 18%		(767)	767
		———	
TWDV c/f		3,493	
		———	
Total allowances			10,767
			———
Year ended 31 March 2022			
TWDV b/f		3,493	
Disposals			
5 May 2021		(2,395)	
		———	
		1,098	
WDA at 18%		(198)	198
		———	
TWDV c/f		900	
		———	
Total allowances			198

4.7 Balancing charges

If, on the disposal of an asset in the general pool, the disposal proceeds exceed the pool balance (after additions to the pool in the year have been added) a negative balance will be left on the pool.

This gives rise to a 'balancing charge'.

A balancing charge is added to the pool to bring the pool balance back to £Nil.

A balancing charge is treated as a negative capital allowance (i.e. added to the adjusted trading profit).

4.8   Small pools writing down allowance

The WDA is claimed each accounting period and if there are no additions in an accounting period to be added to the pool, the WDA will be claimed on an ever decreasing amount for many years. It will be quite common in many small businesses and companies for there to be no additions to the pool, since any purchases in the period are usually covered by the AIA.

To prevent the inconvenience of keeping records of small balances of expenditure, a 'small pool WDA' can be claimed.

The annual WDA available:

- applies to the general pool and special rate pool (see section 6 below)

- does not apply to short life assets (see section 7 below)

- is any amount up to £1,000, and

- applies for a 12-month accounting period. The WDA is time apportioned for short accounting periods.

Therefore, an allowance of up to £1,000 can be claimed on the general or special rate pool where the unrelieved expenditure on the pool (after dealing with additions qualifying for WDAs and disposals in the period) is £1,000 or less. This allows the balance on a 'small pool' to be written off at once.

The claim is optional. However, it is likely that the taxpayer will want to claim as much as possible and reduce the remaining balance on the pool to nil.

 Example

Eden Ltd prepares accounts to 31 March. During the year ending 31 March 2021 it incurred the following expenditure:

15 May 2020   Purchased new office furniture for £23,000.

In addition, on 1 July 2020 it sold office equipment for £10,000 (original cost £18,000).

As at 1 April 2020 the tax written down value on its general pool was £10,800.

Calculate Eden Ltd's capital allowances for the year ended 31 March 2021.

Solution

	£	General pool £	Allowances £
Year ended 31 March 2021			
TWDV b/f		10,800	
Additions qualifying for AIA	23,000		
AIA	(23,000)		23,000
	────	Nil	
Disposals			
1 July 2020		(10,000)	
		────	
		800	
Small pool WDA		(800)	800
		────	
TWDV c/f		Nil	
		────	────
Total allowances			23,800
			────

4.9 Not claiming allowances

It is not compulsory to claim capital allowances. If profits are low, it may be preferable not to claim writing down allowances in the current year and instead to carry forward a higher tax written down value. Larger writing down allowances will then be available in the future when profits may be higher.

5 Capital allowances treatment of cars

5.1 Capital allowances treatment of motor cars

The capital allowances available in respect of motor cars depend on the level of the car's CO_2 emissions.

- Motor cars with CO_2 emissions between 51 and 110g/km are added to the general pool and attract a WDA of 18%.

- If the car has emissions exceeding 110g/km then it must be added to the special rate pool where the WDA is only 6% (8% before 1 April 2019 – see section 6 below).

- New low emission motor cars are however eligible for a first year allowance (FYA) in the year of purchase.

  The rate of the FYA is 100% and it is only for new cars with low CO_2 emissions (50g/km or less).

  Second-hand low emission cars are treated as cars with CO_2 emissions between 51 – 110g/km, however, if the question does not specify, you should assume that the car is new.

You will be told the level of CO_2 emissions for each car in the assessment.

Remember also that motor cars **never** qualify for the 100% AIA.

5.2 Disposals of cars

(a) *General pool cars*

Deduct lower of disposal proceeds and original cost from general pool balance before WDA is calculated (i.e. like normal pool disposals).

(b) *Low emission cars*

As for (a).

(c) *Special rate pool cars*

Deduct lower of disposal proceeds and original cost from special rate pool balance.

If a positive balance remains – give WDA at 18% (main pool cars) or 6% (8% before 1 April 2019) (special rate pool cars).

If a negative balance remains – a balancing charge applies (see section 4.7 above).

Example

Thistle Ltd has a year ended 31 March 2021. Its general pool had a TWDV brought forward of £31,000 at 1 April 2020.

In the year ended 31 March 2021, it purchased two assets:

(a)   a new car (CO_2 emissions 109g/km) costing £9,000; and

(b)   a van costing £4,000 (on 1 February 2021).

There were no disposals in the year.

(a)   Calculate the capital allowances for the year.

(b)   What would your answer be to (a) if the car was low emission?

Solution

(a)   **Thistle Ltd – Capital allowances – year ended 31 March 2021**

	£	General pool £	Allowances £
TWDV b/f		31,000	
Addition not qualifying for AIA		9,000	
Addition qualifying for AIA			
Van	4,000		
AIA	(4,000)		4,000
	–––––	Nil	
Disposals		Nil	
		–––––	
		40,000	
WDA (£40,000 × 18%)		(7,200)	7,200
		–––––	
TWDV c/f		32,800	
		–––––	
Total capital allowances			11,200
			–––––

(b)   **Thistle Ltd – Capital allowances – year ended 31 March 2021**

	£	General pool £	Allowances £
TWDV b/f		31,000	
Addition qualifying for AIA			
Van	4,000		
AIA	(4,000)		4,000
	‾‾‾‾‾‾	Nil	
Disposals		Nil	
		‾‾‾‾‾‾	
		31,000	
WDA (£31,000 × 18%)		(5,580)	5,580
Addition qualifying for FYA			
Car	9,000		
FYA (100%)	(9,000)		9,000
	‾‾‾‾‾‾	Nil	
		‾‾‾‾‾‾	
TWDV c/f		25,420	
		‾‾‾‾‾‾	
Total capital allowances			18,580
			‾‾‾‾‾‾

Example

Joist Ltd prepares accounts to 31 March each year.

In the year ended 31 March 2021 it purchased the following cars:

(1)   Car costing £16,000 with CO_2 emissions of 108g/km

(2)   Car costing £20,000 with CO_2 emissions of 180g/km

The TWDV brought forward on the general pool was £21,480.

Calculate Joist Ltd's capital allowances for the year ended 31 March 2021.

Solution

Joist Ltd – Capital allowances – year ended 31 March 2021

	General pool £	Special rate pool £	Allowances £
TWDV b/f	21,480		
Additions not qualifying for AIA			
Car – CO$_2$ 51–110 g/km	16,000		
Car – CO$_2$ >110 g/km		20,000	
	————		
	37,480		
WDA at 18%	(6,746)		6,746
WDA at 6%		(1,200)	1,200
	————	————	
TWDV c/f	30,734	18,800	
	————	————	
Total capital allowances			7,946
			————

Note:

As the accounting period commences after 1 April 2019 a writing down allowance of 6% can be used for the high emission car (see section 6).

 Example

Grin Ltd prepares accounts to 31 March each year.

At 1 April 2020 the tax written down values brought forward were:

General pool   £15,400
Special rate pool £17,000

During the year ended 31 March 2021 the company purchased plant for £20,000 and two cars with CO$_2$ emissions of 170g/km costing £20,000 each.

There were no additions in the year ended 31 March 2022.

There were no disposals in the year ended 31 March 2021 but in the year ended 31 March 2022, one of the cars purchased in the previous year was sold for £13,500.

Calculate Grin Ltd's capital allowances for the years ended 31 March 2021 and 2022.

Assume the rates of allowances for the year ended 31 March 2021 continue into the future.

Solution

The first task is to decide how many columns are needed to answer this question. There are two balances brought forward which require their own columns and a column is required on the left to deduct the AIA.

A pro forma can then be set up as below

	£	General pool £	Special rate pool £	Allowances £
Year ended 31 March 2021				
TWDV b/f		15,400	17,000	

Now the additions can be put into the appropriate column and the allowances calculated.

Grin Ltd – Capital allowances

	£	General pool £	Special rate pool £	Allowances £
Year ended 31 March 2021				
TWDV b/f		15,400	17,000	
Additions:				
Not qualifying for AIA or FYA				
Cars over 110g/km			40,000	
			_____	
Qualifying for AIA			57,000	
Plant	20,000			
AIA	(20,000)			20,000
	_____			
WDA at 18%		(2,772)		2,772
WDA at 6%			(3,420)	3,420
		_____	_____	
TWDV c/f		12,628	53,580	_____
Total allowances				26,192
				_____
Year ended 31 March 2022				
Disposals			(13,500)	
			_____	
			40,080	
WDA at 18%		(2,273)		2,273
WDA at 6%			(2,405)	2,405
		_____	_____	
TWDV c/f		10,355	37,675	
		_____	_____	
Total allowances				4,678
				_____

The example below demonstrates the full capital allowances working.

 Example

Polar Ltd started trading on 1 January 2020, preparing accounts to 31 December each year.

The following assets have been purchased since the company began trading.

Date of purchase	Asset	Cost £
9 November 2020	Used car	1,472
10 December 2020	Used car	928
15 December 2020	Plant and machinery	1,002,800
8 June 2021	New car	19,500
20 October 2022	New car	18,071

The cars acquired on 9 November 2020 and 10 December 2020 have CO_2 emissions of between 51 – 110g/km.

The new car acquired on 8 June 2021 has CO_2 emissions of 180g/km and the one acquired on 20 October 2022 has CO_2 emissions of 40g/km.

All the cars are used by employees 60% for business and 40% privately.

Calculate the capital allowances due for the three years ending 31 December 2022.

Assume the rates of allowances for the year ended 31 March 2021 continue into the future.

Solution

The approach is as follows:

- Allocate additions and disposals to the relevant accounting periods. Any acquisitions made prior to the commencement of trading are treated as if made on the first day of trading.

- Identify which additions qualify for AIA and FYA.

- Ignore information about private use as this is not relevant to companies.

Polar Ltd – Capital allowances computation

		General pool	Special rate pool	Total allowances
	£	£	£	£
y/e 31 December 2020				
TWDV b/f				
Additions: No AIA				
Cars (£1,472 + £928)		2,400		
Qualifying for AIA				
Plant and machinery	1,002,800			
AIA (max)	(1,000,000)			1,000,000
	———	2,800		
		———		
		5,200		
WDA (18% × £5,200)		(936)		936
		———		
TWDV c/f		4,264		
				———
Total allowances				1,000,936
				———
y/e 31 December 2021				
Additions: No AIA				
Car – CO_2 > 110g/km			19,500	
WDA @ 18%/6%		(768)	(1,170)	1,938
		———	———	
TWDV c/f		3,496	18,330	
				———
Total allowances				1,938
				———
y/e 31 December 2022				
WDA @ 18%/6%		(629)	(1,100)	1,729
Additions qualifying for FYA				
Low emission car	18,071			
FYA @ 100%	(18,071)			18,071
	———	Nil		
		———	———	
TWDV c/f		2,867	17,230	
		———	———	———
Total allowances				19,800
				———

6 Special rate pool

6.1 Special rate pool treatment

The special rate pool is a pool of qualifying expenditure that operates in the same way as the general pool except that:

- the WDA is 6% for a 12 month period (8% before 1 April 2019).

This means that if an accounting period straddles 1 April 2019, the rate applicable to the special rate pool is found via time apportionment.

For example, the relevant rate to use for the special rate pool for the year ended 30 November 2019 is 6.67% (8% × 4/12) + (6% × 8/12). This calculation should be rounded to two decimal places.

6.2 Qualifying expenditure

The special rate pool groups together expenditure on high emission cars (with CO_2 emissions in excess of 110g/km) — see section 5.1 above.

Test your understanding 1

Entrance Ltd prepares accounts to 31 December annually.

On 1 January 2019 the tax written down value of plant and machinery brought forward on the general pool was £24,000.

The following transactions took place in the year to 31 December 2019.

15 April 2019	Purchased car for £12,600 (emissions 180g/km)
30 April 2019	Sold plant for £3,200 (original cost £4,800)
16 July 2019	Purchased car for £9,200 (emissions 100g/km) ✓
17 August 2019	Purchased car for £9,400 (emissions 105g/km) ✓
12 December 2019	Purchased new car for £26,150 (emissions ✓ 48g/km)

In the following year to 31 December 2020, Entrance Ltd sold for £7,900 the car originally purchased on 17 August 2019. The car originally purchased on 15 April 2019 was sold for £9,400 on 9 November 2020. There were no other transactions.

Compute the capital allowances for the years ended 31 December 2019 and 31 December 2020.

---

7 Short life assets

7.1 Short life asset treatment

Where an asset is expected to have a useful life of less than eight years from the end of the period of account in which it was acquired, it may be beneficial to remove it from the general pool and treat it as a short life asset.

Capital allowances are calculated separately for each short life asset. When the asset is sold there will be a balancing adjustment.

- Where it is sold for less than its TWDV there will be a tax deductible balancing allowance equal to the excess of the TWDV over the sales proceeds.

- Where it is sold for more than its TWDV there will be a taxable balancing charge equal to the excess of the sales proceeds over the TWDV.

A short life asset election will be advantageous if it is anticipated that the asset will be sold for less than its TWDV, such that a balancing allowance will arise, within the following eight accounting periods.

The following conditions apply:

- short life asset treatment is not available for cars

- if a short life asset is not sold within eight years of the end of the accounting period in which it was purchased, its TWDV will be transferred back into the general pool

- a short life asset election must be made within two years of the end of the accounting period in which the expenditure was incurred.

However, note that the AIA is available against short life assets and the business can choose the expenditure against which the AIA is matched.

If eligible for the AIA, there may be no expenditure left to 'de-pool' and the short life asset election will not be made.

If there is expenditure in excess of the maximum AIA on assets eligible for the AIA, it may be advantageous for the AIA to be allocated against the general pool expenditure rather than a short life asset and for the short life asset election to be made.

Example

View Ltd prepares accounts to 31 March each year.

On 1 May 2019 the company purchased a lathe for £20,000. The lathe was required for an 18-month contract and was sold on 30 November 2020 for £7,000. View Ltd claimed to treat the lathe as a short life asset.

View Ltd purchased other plant in the year ended 31 March 2020 so the AIA limit was exceeded. The AIA was not claimed in respect of the lathe.

Calculate the capital allowances available in respect of the lathe for the years ended 31 March 2020 and 2021.

Solution

Capital allowances are calculated separately for the lathe and it is not included in the general pool.

View Ltd – Capital allowances

	Short life asset £	Allowances £
Year ended 31 March 2020		
Additions:		
Not qualifying for AIA or FYA		
Lathe	20,000	
WDA at 18%	(3,600)	3,600
TWDV c/f	16,400	
Year ended 31 March 2021		
Disposals	(7,000)	
	9,400	
Balancing allowance	(9,400)	9,400
TWDV c/f	–	

View Ltd has accelerated the capital allowances in respect of the lathe by treating it as a short life asset. If no short life asset claim had been made, the tax written down value would have remained in the general pool and View Ltd would have continued to claim WDAs in respect of it.

Note that if the lathe had been sold for more than £16,400, the claim would not have been beneficial as it would result in a balancing charge.

8 Pro forma computation for capital allowances on plant and machinery

8.1 Plant and machinery allowances

Capital allowances are an important element of the syllabus. To answer capital allowances questions successfully, it is vital to use a methodical approach to work through the information in the question.

The following approach to computational questions together with the following pro forma will help you to deal with the information in the correct order.

Note that a pro forma is supplied in the AAT reference material set out in section 13 below. This uses two separate columns for the AIA and FYA instead of one. Either approach is fine.

The AAT computation also deals with FYAs at an earlier stage – this approach is acceptable, however, including them at the end minimises the chance of making a mistake.

8.2 Approach to computational questions

For plant and machinery capital allowances, adopt the following step-by-step approach:

1   Read the information in the question and decide how many columns you will require.

2   Draft the layout and insert the TWDV b/f (does not apply in a new trade).

3   Insert additions not eligible for the AIA or FYA into the appropriate column.

4   Insert additions eligible for the AIA in the first column, and then allocate the AIA to the additions. Be careful if the accounting period straddles 1 January 2019 or 1 January 2021 because you will need a working to establish the maximum amount of AIA available for the period. If additions exceed the maximum AIA available, then the remaining expenditure is added to the general pool and eligible for the WDA.

5   Deal with any disposal by deducting the lower of cost and sale proceeds.

6   Calculate the WDA at the appropriate rate on each of the pools. If the accounting period straddles 1 April 2019 remember to use a hybrid rate on the special rate pool.

7   Insert additions qualifying for 100% FYA in the first column and give the FYA.

8   Calculate the TWDV to carry forward to the next accounting period and add the 'total allowances' column.

9   Deduct the total allowances from the tax adjusted trading profits.

Pro forma capital allowances computation

		General pool	Special rate pool	Short life asset	Allowances
	£	£	£	£	£
TWDV b/f		X	X	X	
Additions:					
Not qualifying for AIA or FYA					
Cars (51 – 110g/km)		X			
Cars (over 110g/km)			X		
Qualifying for AIA					
Plant and machinery purchased	X				
AIA (do not exceed maximum)	(X)				X
Balance of AIA qualifying					
expenditure to general pool		X			
Disposals (lower of original cost					
and sale proceeds)		(X)	(X)	(X)	
		X	X	X	
Balancing allowance/(Balancing charge)				X/(X)	X/(X)
				Nil	
WDAs at appropriate rates		(X)	(X)		X
Qualifying for FYA					
Low emission cars (up to 50g/km)	X				
FYA at 100%	(X)				X
		Nil			
TWDV c/f		X	X		
Total allowances					X

8.3   Approach to assessment questions

In the CBA you will be given a blank grid to enter capital allowance figures.

It will not be necessary to enter lines dividing totals and subtotals, but otherwise you should be able to produce a computation that is the same as that which you would draw up on paper. It is recommended that you prepare the computation on the paper provided before entering it on screen.

This activity will be manually marked.

9   Impact of the length of the accounting period

9.1   Short accounting periods

Capital allowances are computed for accounting periods and deducted in calculating trading profits.

The allowances calculated so far have all been for 12-month accounting periods.

Where the accounting period is less than 12 months long, the AIA and WDA must be scaled down accordingly. You must perform this calculation to the nearest month.

If the period for which accounts are drawn up exceeds 12 months, the capital allowances are computed in two stages – the first 12 months, then the balance (see Chapter 2, section 2.3 and Chapter 5, section 2.8).

Note that first year allowances are never time apportioned.

Therefore, purchases of new low emission cars are always given the FYA in full, even if the length of the accounting period is less than 12 months.

 Example

Kyanite Ltd started to trade on 1 January 2020 and, on that day, purchased a machine costing £1,005,000.

Calculate the capital allowances due for the first period of account on the assumption that accounts are prepared to

(i)   31 December 2020

(ii)   31 October 2020

(iii)   31 May 2021

Solution

	(i) **31 Dec 2020** **(12 months)** £	(ii) **31 Oct 2020** **(10 months)** £	(iii) **31 May 2021** **(17 months)** £
First period of account:			
First AP (max 12 months)			
Addition:			
Qualifying for AIA			
Plant and machinery	1,005,000	1,005,000	1,005,000
AIA	(1,000,000)		(1,000,000)
(max £1,000,000 × 10/12)		(833,333)	
	5,000	171,667	5,000
WDA (18%)	(900)		(900)
WDA (18% × 10/12)		(25,750)	
TWDV c/f	4,100	145,917	4,100
Second AP			
(balance of period of account)			
WDA (18% × 5/12)	n/a	n/a	(308)
TWDV c/f	4,100	145,917	3,792

Note that in example (iii) corporation tax is charged separately on an accounting period of 12 months ending on 31 December 2020 and on an accounting period of 5 months ending on 31 May 2021 (see Chapter 2).

Test your understanding 2

Ammolite Ltd buys a car costing £16,000 in its accounting period of nine months to 31 December 2020. The car has CO_2 emissions of 105g/km.

What capital allowances are available?

A   £2,880

B   £960

C   £720

D   £2,160

[handwritten: 9-months]

[handwritten: 16,000 × 18% × 9/12 = 2160]

10 Business cessation

10.1 Final accounting period

In the accounting period of cessation no allowances are given other than balancing adjustments.

Any additions and disposals in the final period are allocated to the appropriate columns in the capital allowances working.

At the end of the period there will be no TWDV carried forward, so there must be a balancing adjustment on all columns in the capital allowances working.

- If there is a positive balance remaining, a balancing allowance is given.

- If there is a negative balance remaining, a balancing charge arises.

Please note that cessation is the only time a balancing allowance can occur on the general pool and the special rate pool.

 Example

Druzy Ltd, a company that had been trading for many years preparing accounts to 31 March, ceased trading on 30 September 2021.

The tax written down value of the pool at 1 April 2020 was £12,600. On 1 October 2020, Druzy Ltd purchased some plant for £4,600.

All items of plant were sold on 30 September 2021 for £8,000 (no item was sold for more than cost).

Calculate the capital allowances due for the year ended 31 March 2021 and the six months ended 30 September 2021.

Assume the rates of allowances for the year ended 31 March 2021 continue into the future.

Solution

Druzy Ltd – Capital allowances computation

	£	General pool £	Allowances £
Year ended 31 March 2020			
TWDV b/f		12,600	
Addition qualifying for AIA			
1 October 2020	4,600		
AIA	(4,600)		4,600
	———	Nil	
WDA (18%)		(2,268)	2,268
		———	
TWDV c/f		10,332	
			———
Total allowances			6,868
			———
6 months ended 30 September 2021			
Disposal		(8,000)	
		———	
		2,332	
Balancing allowance		(2,332)	2,332
		———	———

Note: If plant is not sold until after the date of cessation, the proceeds eventually realised are used as the market value on cessation.

In effect it is treated as if sold on cessation for market value.

Test your understanding 3

Jackal Ltd ceased trading on 31 March 2021 and sold all of its plant and machinery on that date. The tax written down value of the pool at 1 April 2020 was £2,000.

What capital allowances are due based on the disposal proceeds below?

Please tick whether it is a balancing allowance or balancing charge and complete the amount.

Disposal proceeds	Balancing allowance	Balancing charge	Amount £	
Scrapped for no proceeds	(2000)		200 0	c/f = 0
Sold for £500	2000 - 500 (1500)		1500	c/f = 0
Sold for £2,200	(220) -2000	200	(200)	c/f 0

11 Test your understanding

Test your understanding 4

Plant and machinery allowances

Which one of the following statements is false?

A   The cost of alterations to buildings needed for the installation of plant is specifically eligible for plant and machinery capital allowances.

B   The AIA is not available on a car, unless it is a low emission car.

C   If the period of account of a business is less than 12 months, the AIA and WDA are scaled down proportionately.

D   A short life asset election cannot be made in respect of a car.

Test your understanding 5

Annual Investment Allowance

Which of the following acquisitions will qualify for the annual investment allowance?

A   A warehouse

B   Display equipment in a shop

C   A car used partly for business purposes by an employee

D   A pool car used exclusively for business use

Test your understanding 6

Banks Ltd

Banks Ltd prepared accounts for the three month period ended
31 March 2021.

On 1 February 2021 a car with CO_2 emissions of 162g/km was
purchased for the sales director at a cost of £16,000. It is used by him
60% for business purposes.

What are the capital allowances available on this car for the three
months ended 31 March 2021?

$$16000 \times 6\% \times \frac{3}{12} = 240$$

240

Test your understanding 7

Faraday Ltd

Faraday Ltd has the following non-current asset information for the year
ended 30 June 2020.

	£
Balances brought forward at 1 July 2019:	
General pool	398,100
Special rate pool	28,060
Additions:	
Machinery (purchased on 1 March 2020)	620,000 AIA
Salesperson's car (CO_2 emissions 48g/km)	20,850
Office furniture (purchased on 5 June 2020)	33,610 AIA
Managing Director's car (CO_2 emissions 178g/km)	48,150
Disposals:	
Machinery (Cost £25,000)	16,875
Director's car (CO_2 emissions 198g/km, cost £31,000))	23,100

Calculate Faraday Ltd's total capital allowances and show the balances
to carry forward to the next accounting period.

Test your understanding 8

Deni Ltd

Deni Ltd is a manufacturing business preparing accounts to 31 January each year.

At 1 February 2020, the written-down value of plant and machinery in the general pool was £25,000 and £7,100 for a short life asset, which had been purchased in October 2016.

During the year ended 31 January 2021, the following transactions were undertaken:

Purchases		£
1 March 2020	Machinery	1,011,250
15 March 2020	Second-hand machinery	10,000
20 May 2020	MD's car with CO_2 emissions of	
	100g/km (used 80% for business)	19,600
Sales		
25 February 2020	Machinery (cost £6,000)	1,750
31 March 2020	Short life asset	500

Compute Deni Ltd's capital allowances for the accounting period ended 31 January 2021.

Test your understanding 9

Tense Ltd

Tense Ltd prepares accounts to 31 December annually. On 1 January 2020, the balance of plant and machinery brought forward was £16,000.

The following transactions took place in the year to 31 December 2020.

15 April 2020   Purchased car for £15,000 (CO_2 emissions 105g/km)

30 April 2020   Sold plant for £2,000 (original cost £1,600)

26 July 2020   Purchased two new cars for £9,300 each. Both of these cars qualify as low emission cars.

In the following year to 31 December 2021, Tense Ltd sold for £7,600 one of the cars originally purchased on 26 July 2020.

The car originally purchased on 15 April 2020 was sold for £8,000 on 9 May 2021. There were no other transactions.

Compute the capital allowances for the years ended 31 December 2020 and 31 December 2021.

Assume the rates of allowances for the year ended 31 March 2021 continue into the future.

 Test your understanding 10

Booker Ltd

Booker Ltd trades as a manufacturer in York and prepares accounts to 30 June each year. The directors decided to change the company's year-end and prepared accounts for the 9 month period to 31 March 2021.

The balance on the general pool was £18,150 at 1 July 2020. In August 2020, the company sold for £4,900 a car bought for £7,800 (the car had CO2 emissions of 107g/km). The company also purchased a new car with CO2 emissions of 45g/km for £25,750 in August 2020. There was 10% private use of both cars by employees.

In December 2020 Booker Ltd purchased plant for £753,750.

Calculate Booker Ltd's capital allowances for the 9 m/e 31 March 2021 and show the tax written down values carried forward.

12 Summary

Capital allowances are available, instead of depreciation, to give tax relief for the cost of plant and machinery over the life of the assets.

A tabular layout is essential for computing capital allowances on plant and machinery.

The table should have separate columns for each of the following:

- general pool
- special rate pool.

When an asset is expected to have a short life and to be sold for less than its tax written down value, it may be beneficial to exclude it from the general pool and treat it as a short life asset.

When an accounting period is less than 12 months long, the maximum annual investment allowance and writing down allowances must be scaled down accordingly.

First year allowances are never scaled down.

 Links to other syllabus areas

At Advanced level, in AVBK, you studied the ways for accounting for depreciation and its importance in ensuring that the cost of capital assets is spread over the periods expected to benefit from their use.

Capital allowances are the equivalent, for tax purposes, of accounts depreciation – many of the underlying principles with which you have already studied will be equally applicable here.

If you decide to pursue your studies beyond AAT, you will learn about deferred tax, which is an accounting adjustment that gives effect to timing differences between the profits for tax and for accounting purposes. Accounts depreciation compared to tax allowable capital allowance are one such difference. Ultimately, however, their overall objective is the same – to give relief for the cost of the asset concerned.

Therefore, your prior knowledge of how depreciation works will help with your understanding of the idea behind how capital allowances work, and what they set out to achieve.

13 AAT reference material

Capital allowances on plant and machinery

Layout of capital allowances on plant and machinery computation

(see taxation tables for rates)

	First Year Allowance (FYA)	Annual Investment Allowance(AIA)	General pool	Special rate pool	Short Life Asset	Total allowances
	£	£	£	£	£	£
WDV b/f			X	X	X	
Additions	X	X	X			
Disposals			(X)		(X)	
	X	X	X	X	X	
Balancing allowance/balancing charge(BA/BC)					X/(X)	X/(X)
					Nil	
AIA/FYA	(X)	(X)				X
Writing down allowance @ 18% pa			(X)			X
Writing down allowance @ X% pa				(X)		X
WDV c/f	Nil	Nil	X	X		
Total allowances						X

- Plant – defined by 'function/setting' distinction and case law.

- AIA – 100% allowance for expenditure (other than cars) in 12 month period (pro rata). Expenditure in excess of AIA qualifies for writing down allowance (WDA). If the accounting period straddles 1 January 2019 or 1 January 2021, the AIA must be pro-rated.

- Full WDA for the period is given regardless of date of purchase of item. WDA is scaled for periods other than 12 months.

- The WDA % on the special rate pool is calculated as: ((8 × number of months before 1 April 19) + (6 x number of months after 1 April 19)/number of months in the chargeable period. This % should be rounded to 2 decimal places.

- FYA – 100% allowance given on purchase of low CO_2 emission cars. FYA is not scaled for short accounting periods.

- If the written down value (WDV) on the general pool (= WDV b/f + additions – disposals) is £1,000 or less then an election can be made to write off the pool balance, known as a 'small pools allowance'.

- Short life assets (SLA) – de-pool asset if life expected to be less than 8 years. Not available for cars.

Test your understanding answers

Test your understanding 1

Entrance Ltd – Capital allowances computation

		General pool	Special rate pool	Allowances
	£	£	£	£
Y/e 31 Dec 2019				
TWDV b/f		24,000		
Additions – no AIA				
Cars:				
15 April 2019			12,600	
16 July 2019		9,200		
17 August 2019		9,400		
Disposals		(3,200)		
		39,400		
WDA @ 18%/6.5% (Note)		(7,092)	(819)	7,911
Car (low emissions)	26,150			
FYA (100%)	(26,150)			26,150
		Nil		
TWDV c/f		32,308	11,781	
Total allowances				34,061
Y/e 31 Dec 2020				
Disposals		(7,900)	(9,400)	
		24,408	2,381	
WDA @ 18%/6%		(4,393)	(143)	4,536
TWDV c/f		20,015	2,238	
Total allowances				4,536

Note: For the year ended 31 December 2019 the relevant rate for the special rate pool is (8% × 3/12) + (6% × 9/12) = 6.5%

Test your understanding 2

The correct answer is D.

Explanation

A WDA of (£16,000 × 18% × 9/12) = £2,160 is due.

 Test your understanding 3

Capital allowances computation

Disposal proceeds	Balancing allowance	Balancing charge	Amount £
Scrapped for no proceeds	✓		2,000
Sold for £500	✓		1,500
Sold for £2,200		✓	200

 Test your understanding 4

Plant and machinery allowances

The correct answer is B.

Explanation

The AIA is not available on any cars.

If the car is a low emission car it is entitled to a 100% first year allowance, but this is a FYA, not the AIA.

The other statements are all true.

Test your understanding 5

Annual Investment Allowance

The correct answer is B.

Explanation

The other acquisitions will not qualify for AIA because:

A   Buildings are not plant and machinery.

C/D Cars do not attract the AIA regardless of whether they are for business or private use.

 Test your understanding 6

Banks Ltd

The correct answer is £240.

Explanation

There is no adjustment to capital allowances as a result of private use of assets by employees. The WDA is time apportioned as the period is only three months. As the accounting period started after 1 April 2019 there is no need to calculate a hybrid WDA for special rate pool items.

3 months ended 31 March 2021		Allowances
	£	£
Additions – no AIA		
Car with emissions >110g/km	16,000	
WDA (6% × 3/12)	(240)	240
	———	———
TWDV c/f	15,760	
	———	

Test your understanding 7

Faraday Ltd – Capital allowances

	General pool £	Special rate pool £	Allowances £
Year ended 30 June 2020			
TWDV b/f	398,100	28,060	
Additions – no AIA			
Car		48,150	
Additions – AIA			
Machinery	620,000		
Office furniture	33,610		
	653,610		
AIA (Note)	(653,610)		653,610
	0		
Disposal	(16,875)	(23,100)	
	381,225	53,110	
WDA (18%)/(6%) (Note)	(68,621)	(3,187)	71,808
Additions – FYA			
Low emissions car	20,850		
FYA (100%)	(20,850)		20,850
	0		
TWDV c/f	312,605	49,923	
Total allowances			746,268

Note: The accounting period falls between 1 January 2019 and 31 December 2020 so the maximum AIA is £1,000,000. The qualifying expenditure is less than this so will be fully covered by this AIA with no balance to be transferred to the general pool.

Note: As the accounting period started after 1 April 2019, there is no need to calculate a hybrid WDA for the special rate pool.

Test your understanding 8

Deni Ltd

Capital allowances

	£	General pool £	Short life asset £	Allowances £
Year ended 31 January 2021				
TWDV b/f		25,000	7,100	
Addition not qualifying for AIA				
Car		19,600		
Additions qualifying for AIA				
Machinery				
(£1,011,250 + £10,000)	1,021,250			
AIA (W)	(933,333)			933,333
		87,917		
Disposal		(1,750)	(500)	
		130,767	6,600	
Balancing allowance (note)			(6,600)	6,600
WDA (18%)		(23,538)		23,538
TWDV c/f		107,229	0	
Total allowances				963,471

Working: AIA

The accounting period straddles 1 January 2021.

The maximum AIA for the period is:

(£1,000,000 × 11/12) + (£200,000 × 1/12) = £933,333

Note: The short life asset is sold which must give rise to a balancing charge or allowance. In this case it is an allowance as the asset is sold for less than the TWDV brought forward.

Test your understanding 9

Tense Ltd

Capital allowances

	General pool	Allowances
Year ending 31 December 2020	£	£
TWDV b/f	16,000	
Additions not qualifying for AIA		
Car	15,000	
Disposals		
Plant (restrict to cost)	(1,600)	
	–––––––	
	29,400	
WDA (18%)	(5,292)	5,292
Additions qualifying for FYA		
Cars (£9,300 × 2)	18,600	
FYA at 100%	(18,600)	18,600
	–––––––	
	Nil	
	–––––––	
TWDV c/f	24,108	
		–––––––
Total allowances		23,892
Year ending 31 December 2021		
Disposals (£7,600 + £8,000)	(15,600)	
	–––––––	
	8,508	
WDA (18%)	(1,531)	1,531
	–––––––	
TWDV c/f	6,977	
	–––––––	–––––––
Total allowances		1,531

Test your understanding 10

Booker Ltd

Capital allowances computation

	£	General pool £	Allowances £
9 months to 31 March 2021			
TWDV b/f		18,150	
Additions			
Qualifying for AIA			
Plant and machinery	753,750		
AIA (W)	(550,000)		550,000
		203,750	
Disposal		(4,900)	
		217,000	
WDA (18% × 9/12)		(29,295)	29,295
Additions qualifying for FYA			
Car	25,750		
FYA at 100% (Note)	(25,750)		25,750
		Nil	
TWDV c/f		187,705	
Total allowances			605,045

Working: AIA

The accounting period straddles 1 January 2021 and is only nine months long.

The maximum AIA for the period is:

(£1,000,000 × 6/12) + (£200,000 × 3/12) = £550,000

Note: The FYA is not time apportioned for short accounting periods.

Corporation tax computation

5

Introduction

In the previous chapters we have been working towards calculating the adjusted trading profit of a company, the major source of income found on most corporation tax computations.

In this chapter we add to that knowledge to enable a full computation of a company's corporation tax liability.

ASSESSMENT CRITERIA

Calculate the taxable total profits from trading income, property income, investment income and chargeable gains (2.3)

Calculate the total profits and corporation tax payable for accounting periods longer than, shorter than or equal to 12 months (2.3)

CONTENTS

1   Pro forma corporation tax computation
2   Taxable total profits
3   The corporation tax liability

1 Pro forma corporation tax computation

1.1 Pro forma

The first stage of a single company computation is to ascertain the company's taxable total profits. This comprises income and gains, less qualifying charitable donations.

The pro forma that was set out in Chapter 2 is set out again below. It will be referred to throughout this chapter.

Company name

Corporation tax computation for XX months ended…(the AP)

	£
Trading profit	X
Non-trade interest	X
Property income	X
Chargeable gains	X
Total profits	X
Less: Qualifying charitable donations	(X)
Taxable total profits	X
Corporation tax liability at relevant rate	X

The AAT reference material set out in section 6 below contains a pro forma corporation tax computation.

2 Taxable total profits

2.1 Adjusted trading profit

The adjusted trading profit and capital allowances have been covered in the previous chapters, so you can now compute the trading profit that is entered in the computation of taxable total profits.

	Chapter	£
Adjusted trading profit	3	X
Less: Capital allowances		
Plant and machinery	4	(X)
Trading profit		X

2.2 Interest income (the loan relationship rules)

We consider the loan relationship rules at this point because of their relevance to the computation of trading profit and non-trade interest.

The loan relationship rules apply when a company pays or receives interest, or incurs any cost relating to a loan.

The legislation distinguishes between trading purposes and non-trading purposes, in relation to the interest.

For assessment purposes:

If a company **receives** interest you can normally assume that it is for non-trading purposes.

For example:

- interest received on a building society account

- interest received on a bank deposit account.

If a company **pays** interest you can normally assume that it is for trading purposes.

For example:

- interest paid on a bank overdraft

- interest paid on a loan to purchase new machinery.

You will, however, need to read the question carefully to make sure that these assumptions are not contradicted.

Net or gross?

Most interest paid by or received by a company is paid or received gross (with the exception of interest paid to individuals).

All amounts shown on corporation tax computations must be shown gross.

If interest is paid to an individual by a company it is paid net of 20% tax. Hence, the interest must be grossed up.

The gross interest is calculated as follows:

Interest paid to individual × 100/80

> ### 💡 Example
>
> Rye Ltd pays and receives the following amounts of interest.
>
> | | | £ |
> |---|---|---:|
> | (a) | Interest received on deposit account with Bat East Bank plc | 5,000 |
> | (b) | Interest paid on overdrawn business bank account | (2,000) |
> | (c) | Interest paid on loan made to the company by Mr Smith | (2,000) |
>
> Compute the gross figures to be used in the corporation tax computation.
>
> ### Solution
>
> Gross amounts to be included in calculation of taxable total profits:
>
> | | | £ |
> |---|---|---:|
> | (a) | Interest received | 5,000 |
> | (b) | Interest paid on overdraft | (2,000) |
> | (c) | Interest paid on loan by Mr Smith (£2,000 × 100/80) | (2,500) |

Trading loans

Interest paid

All interest on trading loans deducted in the statement of profit or loss is an allowable deduction from trading profits.

This means you will not need to make any adjustments in converting the accounting profit into the adjusted trading profit.

Interest received

You are unlikely to see any interest received for trading purposes.

However, if you do, such interest is included in the trading profit and therefore needs no adjustment.

Non-trading loans

Interest paid

Interest deducted in the statement of profit or loss in relation to non-trading loans is disallowed in computing adjusted trading profits (i.e. add it back in the adjustment of profit computation).

Instead, the interest is an allowable deduction from non-trade interest income.

The main example of this type of interest will be interest paid on a loan to buy an investment property or shares.

Interest received

Interest income shown in the statement of profit or loss (e.g. interest on a deposit account) will be from a non-trade loan and therefore must be deducted from net profit in the adjustment of trading profit computation and instead treated as non-trade interest income.

Other costs incurred in respect of loan relationships

All other costs in relation to non-trading loan relationships are disallowed in computing adjusted trading profits, but are allowed as a deduction from non-trade interest income instead.

The main example of this will be loans to former employees, customers or suppliers which have been written off.

The AAT reference material included in section 6 below refers to the treatment of interest.

Accruals basis

All interest in corporation tax computations must be dealt with on an accruals basis (not received and paid basis).

The accruals basis means the amount due within the accounting period.

Example

Slam Limited has received the following interest on its bank deposit account that was opened on 1 April 2020:

Date received	£
30 June 2020	1,000
31 December 2020	3,000
30 June 2021	4,000

Assuming interest accrues evenly between each date, calculate the non-trade interest income to be shown in the corporation tax computation for the year ended 31 March 2021.

Solution

1 April 2020 account opened	30 June 2020 received £1,000	31 December 2020 received £3,000	30 June 2021 received £4,000

31 March 2021

Interest accrued

£1,000   £3,000   ⅜ × £4,000

Non-trade interest for year ended 31 March 2021
= (£1,000 + £3,000 + £2,000) = £6,000

The figure shown in the accounts will normally be the accrued amount. You are therefore unlikely to have to calculate this.

 Test your understanding 1

The statement of profit or loss of ABC Ltd includes interest received on an investment in Government securities.

How should this be dealt with in the computation of the taxable total profits?

A   Deducted from net profit only

B   Included as non-trading income only

C   Deducted from net profit and included as non-trading income

D   No adjustment

2.3   Patent royalties

Patent royalties paid or received by companies are dealt with for tax purposes on an accruals basis.

Royalties payable

Royalties are relieved as a trading expense against trading profits on a normal accruals basis. So if they have been correctly charged through the accounts no adjustment should be needed.

Royalties receivable

Royalties receivable on patents are taxed as trading profits. Again, if the income has been correctly shown on an accruals basis no adjustment should be needed.

Royalties subject to income tax deductions

Patent royalties are usually received gross, except that patent royalties received from individuals are received net of 20% tax.

Similarly, all patent royalties are usually paid gross, except that patent royalties paid to individuals are paid net of basic rate tax.

All amounts shown in corporation tax computations must be shown gross.

Therefore, patent royalties paid to/received from an individual must be grossed up. The gross patent royalties are calculated as follows:

Patent royalties (cash amount) × 100/80

💡 Example

Thorn Ltd receives the following patent royalties.

What are the gross figures to be used in the corporation tax computation?

(a)	Received from Rye Ltd	£3,000
(b)	Received from Eric	£3,900

Solution

Gross amounts to be used:

(a)	From Rye Ltd	£3,000
(b)	From Eric (£3,900 × 100/80)	£4,875

2.4 Dividend income

Dividend income received by companies is not chargeable to corporation tax. If dividend income is included in the net income, it must be deducted when computing the adjusted trading profits.

This is because dividend income is paid out of after-tax profits of another company (i.e. the profits generating the dividend have already been subject to UK corporation tax in that other company).

2.5 Property income

The calculation of property income is not in the business tax syllabus.

If a company has property income you will be given the figure to use in calculating the taxable total profits.

2.6 Chargeable gains

A company's taxable total profits include chargeable gains as well as income.

The calculation of the chargeable gain or loss on the disposal of capital assets is covered in a later chapter.

For the purpose of this chapter, all gains and losses on asset disposals are already computed. You will, however, need to be able to produce a summary of the position for the purpose of calculating taxable total profits.

This is shown as follows:

	£
Gain (transaction 1)	X
Gain (transaction 2)	X
Loss (transaction 3)	(X)
	X
Less: Capital losses brought forward	(X)
Net chargeable gains	X

Current period gains and losses are netted off automatically.

Excess capital losses are covered in Chapter 16.

Test your understanding 2

1   GHI Ltd made a chargeable gain on the disposal of shares during 2020 of £60,000. It had capital losses brought forward of £25,000.

How much should be included in taxable total profits? (35000)

2   How would your answer differ if capital losses brought forward had amounted to £75,000? (0)

2.7 Qualifying charitable donations

The final component in calculating taxable total profits is to deduct from the total profits (income and gains) any qualifying charitable donations. These are paid gross by companies.

The gross amount deductible for an AP is the amount *paid* in that AP. This may be a different figure from the amount accrued in the accounts.

A qualifying charitable donation is basically any donation made by a company to a charity unless it already qualifies as a trading expense. Only donations that are 'small' and 'local in effect' will normally be allowed as a trading expense. It is therefore usually donations made to national charities which are treated as qualifying charitable donations.

 Test your understanding 3

Laserjet Ltd (1)

Laserjet Ltd provided you with the following information for its year to 31 January 2021.

	£
Adjusted trading profit before capital allowances	500,600
Capital allowances	16,000
Rental income (net of expenses)	32,000
Bank loan interest payable on a loan to purchase rental property (accrued)	4,000
Building society interest receivable (accrued)	20,000
10% loan note interest receivable (accrued)	6,000
Donation paid to national charity	14,000

Calculate the taxable total profits for the year ended 31 January 2021.

Approach to the question

You need a methodical approach to calculate taxable total profits.

Step 1: Set up a skeleton CT computation pro forma (this may be given in the assessment).

	£
Trading profit (W1)	484,600
Non-trade interest (W2)	22,000
Property income	32,000
Total profits	538,600
Less: Qualifying charitable donations	(14,000)
Taxable total profits	524,600

Note that the labels in the computation are not required to be in any particular order, but it is accepted best practice to put the trading profit first.

Step 2: Prepare any necessary workings separately from the pro forma

Work through the information methodically. The figure for trading profit often (though not in this example) requires more than one working for the component parts of:

- adjusted trading profit

- capital allowances on plant and machinery.

As you complete each working, slot the result into the pro forma.

2.8 Long periods of account

As you know, although a company can draw up financial accounts for a period of more than 12 months, a company's 'accounting period' (AP) for corporation tax purposes can never exceed 12 months.

Therefore, if the financial accounts cover more than 12 months, two accounting periods are required; one for the first 12 months and one for the balance.

This section tackles the allocation of income, chargeable gains and qualifying charitable donations between the two periods in finding taxable total profits.

Item	Method of allocation
Trading profit before deducting capital allowances	Time apportioned
Capital allowances (see Chapter 4)	Separate computation for each AP
Property income	Period in which accrued (Note)
Non-trade interest	Period in which accrued (Note)
Chargeable gains	Period of disposal
Qualifying charitable donation	Period in which paid

Note: If information to apply the strict accruals basis is not available, then time apportion.

Be very careful when calculating the number of months in the second period – double check it – as it is crucial for time apportioning calculations and easy to get wrong.

Note that the rules for long periods of account are covered in the AAT reference material set out in section 6 below.

Example

Printer Ltd has prepared accounts for the 16 months to 31 August 2020, with the following information.

	£
Adjusted trading profit before capital allowances	381,000
Building society interest	
Received 30 June 2019 (of which £1,950 related to year ended 30 April 2019)	2,450
Received 30 June 2020	2,675
Accrued on 31 August 2020	200
Rents from property	26,010
Chargeable gains	
Disposal on 31 March 2020	25,700
Disposal on 1 May 2020	49,760
Qualifying charitable donations:	
Paid 31 July 2019	6,000
Paid 31 January 2020	6,000

Capital allowances for the two APs derived from the 16 month period of account are £20,000 and £6,250 respectively.

Show how the company's period of account will be divided into APs and compute the taxable total profits for each AP assuming, where relevant, that all income is deemed to accrue evenly.

Solution

The procedure to be followed is exactly the same as for a 12 month period, but incorporating the allocation rules.

	12 months to 30 April 2020 £	4 months to 31 August 2020 £
Trading profit (W1)	265,750	89,000
Non-trade interest (W2)	2,531	844
Property income (W3)	19,507	6,503
Chargeable gains	25,700	49,760
Total profits	313,488	146,107
Less: Qualifying charitable donations (W4)	(12,000)	Nil
Taxable total profits	301,488	146,107

Note: The chargeable gains are allocated according to the date of the transaction.

Workings

(W1) Trading profit

	Total £	12m £	4m £
Adjusted profit (see note)	381,000	285,750	95,250
Less: Capital allowances		(20,000)	(6,250)
Trading profit		265,750	89,000

Note: The adjusted trading profit before capital allowances is **time apportioned** (it is acceptable to apportion on a monthly basis in the assessment).

(W2) Non-trade interest – Building society interest

As the accrual at 30 April 2020 is not given, the total amount which would be included in the statement of profit or loss for the 16 month period on the accruals basis is calculated, then time apportioned:

		Total £	12m £	4m £
Received	30 June 2019	2,450		
	30 June 2020	2,675		
Add	Closing accrual	200		
Less	Opening accrual	(1,950)		
		3,375	2,531	844

(W3) Property income

Rental income is assessable as property income, which is assessed on an accruals basis for the 16 months and then time apportioned into the two APs:

	Total £	12m £	4m £
Property income	26,010	19,507	6,503

(W4) Qualifying charitable donations

	£	
31 July 2019	6,000	
31 January 2020	6,000	
	12,000	In y/e 30 April 2020

Nil in 4 months to 31 August 2020 as none paid.

Test your understanding 4

Chinny Ltd

Chinny Ltd has for many years prepared accounts to 30 September, but changed its accounting date to 31 December by preparing accounts for the 15 months ended 31 December 2020.

The accounts show a profit, as adjusted for tax purposes (but before deducting capital allowances), of £250,000.

Capital allowances for the two APs based on the 15 month period of account were £13,450 and £5,818 respectively.

The company also had income in the period as follows:

		£
Building society interest receivable	1 Oct 2019 – 30 Sept 2020	4,420
	1 Oct 2020 – 31 Dec 2020	780
Chargeable gains	Disposal 15 Dec 2020	55,000
Rents received	31 July 2020	8,000

The rents accrued at 30 September 2019 and 31 December 2020 were £3,000 and £5,000 respectively.

Calculate the amounts of taxable total profits for this 15 month period of account.

3 The corporation tax liability

3.1 Calculating the corporation tax liability

Once you have computed a company's taxable total profits, the next stage of the computation is to calculate the corporation tax liability.

Corporation tax is calculated using the rate (or rates) in force during the accounting period.

The rates of tax are fixed for a financial year (FY), which is the year that runs from 1 April to the following 31 March. For example, FY2020 is the period from 1 April 2020 to 31 March 2021 (note that it is labelled based on the year in which the period starts).

For FY2020 and FY2019 the rate of corporation tax for all companies is 19%. This is also known as the main rate.

Example

Tilly Ltd has taxable total profits of £350,000 in its year ended 31 March 2021.

Calculate Tilly Ltd's corporation tax liability.

Solution

The year ended 31 March 2021 is the FY2020, therefore the tax is calculated at 19%.

Corporation tax liability (£350,000 × 19%) = £66,500.

 Test your understanding 5

Osmond Ltd

Osmond Ltd had the following results for the year ended 31 March 2020:

	£
Trading profit	510,000
Loan note (debenture) interest receivable	8,000
UK dividends received	18,000
Chargeable gain on the sale of an investment	7,500

Calculate Osmond Ltd's corporation tax liability for the year ended 31 March 2020.

525,500
× 19%
99845

3.2 Non 31 March year ends

The AP of a company with a year end of 31 December 2020 falls into two financial years as follows:

- three months of the year (1 January 2020 to 31 March 2020) is the last three months of FY2019

- nine months of the year (1 April 2020 to 31 December 2020) is the first nine months of FY2020.

However, because the main rate of corporation tax is 19% in both of these financial years, the corporation tax liability is simply 19% of the taxable total profits.

If the two financial years had different main rates of corporation tax, the corporation tax liability would be calculated by:

- time apportioning the taxable total profits between the two financial years by reference to the number of months in each financial year

- then multiplying the taxable total profits for each financial year by the appropriate main rate of corporation tax.

For example:

		£
FY2019	Taxable total profits × 3/12 × x%	X
FY2020	Taxable total profits × 9/12 × y%	X
		X

 Example

Calculate the corporation tax liability for Printer Ltd in the example in section 2 for its two accounting periods.

Solution

The 12 months to 30 April 2020 falls partly into FY2019 (11 months) and partly into FY2020 (1 month). However, because the main rate of corporation tax is 19% for both financial years, the corporation tax liability is simply 19% of the taxable total profits.

12 months to 30 April 2020	£
(£301,488 × 19%)	57,282

4 months to 31 August 2020	£
(£146,107 × 19%)	27,760

Test your understanding 6

Uptown Ltd

Uptown Ltd is a UK resident company which makes fashionable ladies clothing. The company has previously prepared accounts to 31 March but has now changed its accounting date to 30 September.

In the 18 month period to 30 September 2020 the company had the following results:

	£
Adjusted trading profits (Note 1)	990,000
Donation to charity (Note 2)	(20,000)
Bank interest receivable (Note 3)	12,500
Dividend received on 28 February 2019	17,500

Note 1: Adjusted trading profits

No capital allowances are due.

Note 2: Donation

On 31 December 2019 the company made a payment of £20,000 to a national charity.

Note 3: Bank interest

	£
30 September 2019 received	5,000
31 March 2020 received	4,000
30 September 2020 received	3,500
	————
	12,500
	————

The interest is non-trading interest. The amounts received were the amounts accrued to date.

Calculate the corporation tax liability of Uptown Ltd for the period ended 30 September 2020.

4 Test your understanding

Test your understanding 7

DEF Ltd

DEF Ltd received dividends from another UK company. This amount has not been included in the profit figure on which the adjusted trading profits are based.

How should this be dealt with in the computation of the company's taxable total profits?

A   Add the amount received to taxable total profits

B   Gross up by 100/80 and include in taxable total profits

C   Deduct the amount received from taxable total profits

D   Make no adjustment

Test your understanding 8

Ballard Ltd

Ballard Ltd prepares accounts for the year ended 31 March 2021. The following information is available:

	£
Adjusted trading profits before capital allowances	56,000
Bank interest receivable	3,000
UK dividends received	9,000

The tax written down value of the general pool was £24,000 on 1 April 2020 and on 1 December 2020 the company purchased a lorry for £14,000.

What are Ballard Ltd's taxable total profits for the year ended 31 March 2021?

A   £40,680

B   £45,000

C   £49,680

D   £52,160

Test your understanding 9

Pitch Ltd (1)

Pitch Ltd has the following results for the year ended 31 December 2020:

	£
Adjusted trading profits (before capital allowances and patent royalties)	679,601
Capital allowances	24,688
Chargeable gains	136,400
Capital loss brought forward	63,200
Rents receivable	3,500
Patent royalties from an individual (£11,200 × 100/80)	14,000
Bank deposit interest receivable	2,400
Dividends received from UK companies	4,800
Qualifying charitable donation paid	(1,000)

Show Pitch Ltd's taxable total profits for the year ended 31 December 2020.

Test your understanding 10

Long period of account

When a company has a period of account that exceeds 12 months, how are the following apportioned:

	Time apportioned	Separate computation	Period in which arises
Adjusted trading profits	✓		
Capital allowances		✓	
Rental income	✓ ✗		✓
Interest income	✓ ✗		✓
Chargeable gains			✓
Qualifying charitable donation paid			✓

Tick the appropriate treatment.

 Test your understanding 11

G Ltd

The following details relate to the corporation tax computation of G Ltd for the 12 month accounting period ended 31 March 2021:

	£
Tax adjusted trading profit (after disallowing the write off of a loan to a customer of £600 and a national charity donation of £1,800)	677,500
Bank interest receivable	2,800
Loan interest received	22,000
UK dividends received	36,000

Calculate G Ltd's corporation tax liability for the year ended 31 March 2021.

5 Summary

Make sure you are very familiar with the pro forma corporation tax computation.

Setting out your computations as shown in the pro forma will help to ensure that your computations and submissions to HM Revenue and Customs (HMRC) are always made in accordance with the current law and take account of current HMRC practice.

If you are given a period of account of more than 12 months, the first step is to split it into the two APs and compile the two separate taxable total profit figures using the apportioning rules.

Each AP is then dealt with separately.

In FY2019 and FY2020 the rate of corporation tax is 19%.

✳ Links to other syllabus areas

Tax is a significant cost to any business – if cash flow forecasts and budgets are to be meaningful and relied upon, tax needs to be factored in to the overall analysis.

By the same token, if the financial statements are to represent a true and fair view of the past results of the business, tax liabilities must be accurately stated.

In these respects, understanding how to calculate a company's corporation tax liability links in with other Professional level papers such as MABU, MDCL and FSLC. And for those whose role it is to give a view on the truth and fairness of those results, there is a clear link in with another Professional level paper, namely that of ETAU.

6 AAT reference material

An outline of corporation tax

- Companies pay corporation tax on their profits for each accounting period.

- There is one rate of corporation tax set each financial year.

- Profits = Income + Gains – Qualifying charitable donations.

- Accounting periods are usually 12 months long but can be shorter.

- If a company's accounts are longer than 12 months, the first 12 months will be one accounting period and the remainder a second accounting period.

- All UK property income is pooled as a single source of income and taxed on an accruals basis.

- Borrowing or lending money by a company is a loan relationship.

- Trading loan relationships are part of trading income.

- Non-trading loan relationships (NTL-R) are pooled to give NTL-R credits or deficits.

- Donations to national charities are qualifying charitable donations.

- Company A is a related 51% group company of company B if:

  - A is a 51% subsidiary of B, or

  - B is a 51% subsidiary of A, or

  - A and B are both 51% subsidiaries of the same company.

  'A' is a 51% subsidiary of 'B' if more than 50% of its ordinary share capital is beneficially owned (directly or indirectly) by 'B'.

Note that related 51% group companies are covered in Chapter 7 of this study text.

The calculation of total profits and corporation tax payable

ABC Ltd

Corporation tax computation for the year/period ended DD/MM/20XX

	£
Trading income – accruals basis	X
Interest income (NTL-R) – accrual basis	X
Property income – accruals basis	X
Chargeable gains	X
	X
Less Qualifying charitable donations	(X)
Total taxable profits	X
Corporation tax payable – Total taxable profits × Corporation tax rate	X

Key points

- Trading income is adjusted from net profit per company accounts less capital allowances.

- Companies receive interest gross.

- Virtually all interest receivable is taxed as interest income (NTL-R).

- Dividends payable by a company are not an allowable expense.

- UK dividends receivable by a company are not taxable.

- Net-off current year capital losses against current year capital gains. If there is a net capital loss carry it forward.

- See taxation tables for corporation tax rates.

Long periods of account

- Will consist of two accounting periods = first 12 months and remainder of period.

- Split profits as follows:

  - Adjusted trading profit – time apportion.

  - Capital allowances – separate computations for each accounting period.

  - Interest income (NTL-R) and property income – accruals basis.

  - Chargeable gains – according to date of disposal.

  - Qualifying charitable donations – according to date paid.

Test your understanding answers

 ## Test your understanding 1

ABC Ltd

The correct answer is C.

Explanation

The interest received will be included in the net profit per the accounts. It therefore needs to be deducted in the adjusted trading profit computation. It is then included as non-trade interest income in the calculation of taxable total profits.

 ## Test your understanding 2

GHI Ltd

1   £35,000

2   £Nil

Explanation

1   GHI Ltd would include chargeable gains of (£60,000 – £25,000) = £35,000 in taxable total profits.

2   No chargeable gains would be included in taxable total profits as the losses exceed gains by (£75,000 – £60,000) = £15,000. The excess loss will be carried forward and deducted from the next gains.

📝 Test your understanding 3

Laserjet Ltd (1)

Corporation tax computation – year ended 31 January 2021

	£
Trading profit (W1)	484,600
Non-trade interest (W2)	22,000
Property income	32,000
Total profits	538,600
Less: Qualifying charitable donations	(14,000)
Taxable total profits	524,600

Workings

(W1) Trading profit

	£
Adjusted trading profit	500,600
Less: Capital allowances	(16,000)
Trading profit	484,600

Take care not to adjust a profit which has already been adjusted.

(W2) Non-trade interest

	£
Building society interest receivable	20,000
Loan note interest receivable	6,000
	26,000
Less: Loan interest payable – rental property (note)	(4,000)
Non-trade interest	22,000

Note: This interest is not an allowable deduction from property income but has to be dealt with as a 'non-trading' loan and is deductible from non-trade interest income.

Test your understanding 4

Chinny Ltd

Corporation tax computations

	Year ended 30 September 2020 £	3 months to 31 December 2020 £
Trading profit (W1)	186,550	44,182
Non-trade interest	4,420	780
Property income (W2)	8,000	2,000
Chargeable gains	–	55,000
Taxable total profits	198,970	101,962

Workings

(W1) Trading profit

	Year ended 30 September 2020 £	3 months to 31 December 2020 £
Adjusted trading profits (12/15:3/15)	200,000	50,000
Less: Capital allowances	(13,450)	(5,818)
Trading profit	186,550	44,182

(W2) Property income

Rent receivable for 15 months:

(£8,000 − £3,000 + £5,000) = £10,000

	Year ended 30 September 2020 £	3 months to 31 December 2020 £
Time apportioned	8,000	2,000

Test your understanding 5

Osmond Ltd

Corporation tax computation – year ended 31 March 2020

	£
Trading profit	510,000
Non-trade interest	8,000
Chargeable gains	7,500
Taxable total profits	525,500
Corporation tax liability (£525,500 × 19%)	99,845

Test your understanding 6

Uptown Ltd
Corporation tax payable – period 30 September 2020

	12 months to 31 Mar 2020 £	6 months to 30 Sept 2020 £
Trading profit (W)	660,000	330,000
Non-trade interest	9,000	3,500
Total profits	669,000	333,500
Less: Qualifying charitable donation	(20,000)	–
Taxable total profits	649,000	333,500
Corporation tax liability (£649,000/£333,500 × 19%)	123,310	63,365

Working: Trading profit

			£
Apportioned	12 months to 31 Mar 2020	12/18 × £990,000	660,000
	6 months to 30 Sep 2020	6/18 × £990,000	330,000
			990,000

Test your understanding 7

DEF Ltd

The correct answer is D.

Explanation

Dividends from another company are not subject to corporation tax and are therefore not included in taxable total profits.

 Test your understanding 8

Ballard Ltd

The correct answer is A.

Explanation

	£
Adjusted trading profits	56,000
Less: Capital allowances (W)	(18,320)
Tax adjusted trading profits	37,680
Bank interest receivable	3,000
Taxable total profits	40,680

Note: UK dividends are not chargeable to corporation tax

Working: Capital allowances

	£	General Pool £	Allowances £
TWDV b/f		24,000	
Addition with AIA	14,000		
AIA	(14,000)		14,000
		Nil	
WDA (18% × £24,000)		(4,320)	4,320
TWDV c/f		19,680	
Total allowances			18,320

Test your understanding 9

Pitch Ltd (1)

Taxable total profits – year ended 31 December 2020

	£
Trading profit (W)	668,913
Property income	3,500
Non-trade interest	2,400
Chargeable gains (£136,400 – £63,200)	73,200
	————
Total profits	748,013
Less: Qualifying charitable donations	(1,000)
	————
Taxable total profits	747,013

Working: Trading profit

	£
Adjusted trading profit	679,601
Add: Patent royalties	14,000
Less: Capital allowances	(24,688)
	————
Trading profit	668,913

Test your understanding 10

Long period of account

	Time apportioned	Separate computation	Period in which arises
Trading income	✓		
Capital allowances		✓	
Rental income			✓
Interest income			✓
Chargeable gains			✓
Qualifying charitable donation paid			✓

Test your understanding 11

G Ltd – Corporation tax computation – year ended 31 March 2021

	£
Trading profit	677,500
Interest income (W)	24,200
Total profits	701,700
Less: Qualifying charitable donation	(1,800)
Taxable total profits	699,900

	£
Corporation tax liability (£699,900 × 19%)	132,981

Working: Interest income

	£
Bank interest	2,800
Loan interest	22,000
Less: Customer loan written off	(600)
Interest income	24,200

Note: Loans written off are not allowable against trading income and are added back in the adjustment of profits computation. However, they are allowable against interest income as an allowable deduction relating to a non-trading loan relationship.

Corporation tax reliefs and other tax issues

Introduction

This chapter covers two forms of relief available to companies and one other tax issue.

The relief for trading and capital losses is dealt with first.

Secondly the research and development tax credit scheme that applies to small and medium sized enterprises is discussed.

Individuals may seek to minimise tax by the use of a personal service company. Anti-avoidance rules often referred to as IR35 seek to reduce any advantages.

ASSESSMENT CRITERIA	CONTENTS
Assess and calculate available loss relief (4.1)	1 Trading losses
	2 Capital losses
Advise on the best use of a trading loss for sole traders, partnerships and companies (4.1)	3 Research and development tax credits
Demonstrate an understanding of current tax reliefs available to businesses (4.2)	4 Personal service companies (IR35)
Demonstrate an understanding of current tax issues and their implications for business (4.2)	

Trading losses

1.1 Adjusted trading losses

In Chapter 3 we considered how to calculate an adjusted trading profit.

An adjusted trading loss is computed in the same way. However, when a company makes an adjusted trading loss, its trading profit assessment for the accounting period is nil.

💡 Example

Carlos Ltd had the following results for its year ended 31 March 2021:

	£	£
Gross profit		30,000
Less: Depreciation	5,000	
Allowable expenses	12,000	
		(17,000)
Net profit per accounts		13,000

The capital allowances for the year amount to £21,000.

Calculate the adjusted trading profit/(loss) for the year.

Solution

Step 1: Set up an adjustment of profits pro forma as in Chapter 3.

Step 2: Calculate the adjusted trading profit/(loss)

Work through the statement of profit or loss line by line as previously to calculate the adjusted trading profit/(loss).

Carlos Ltd

Adjustment of profit/(loss) – year ended 31 March 2021

	£
Net profit per accounts	13,000
Add: Disallowable expenses	
Depreciation	5,000
	18,000
Less: Capital allowances	(21,000)
Adjusted trading loss	(3,000)
Trading profit assessment	Nil

The trading profit figure to be entered onto the pro forma corporation tax computation is nil.

The accounts may show a net **loss** to be adjusted. If this is the case, adding disallowable expenses will **reduce** the loss.

Example

Assume Carlos Ltd in the previous example had a net loss per accounts of (£10,000). Calculate the adjusted trading loss.

Solution

	£
Net loss per accounts	(10,000)
Add: Depreciation	5,000
	(5,000)
Less: Capital allowances	(21,000)
Adjusted trading loss	(26,000)

1.2   Summary of trading loss reliefs

There are three forms of relief available to a company which makes a trading loss:

- current year relief
- carry back relief
- carry forward relief.

Details of these reliefs are set out below and a summary is provided in the AAT reference material, which is included in section 7 below.

1.3   Current year relief

A trading loss can be relieved against total profits of the loss making accounting period. The set off is against profits before the deduction of qualifying charitable donations.

A claim for current year (or carry back) relief must be made within two years of the end of the loss making accounting period.

Example

Sage Ltd had the following results for the year ended 31 March 2021.

	£
Adjusted trading loss	(40,000)
Property income	10,000
Chargeable gain	50,000
Qualifying charitable donation	10,000

Show how relief would be obtained for the loss in the current period.

Approach to the example

It is *essential* once a loss has been identified to set up a loss memorandum as a working and allocate the loss to it, so that the relief for the loss does not exceed the actual amount of loss available.

Even where there is a trading loss, this does not alter the basic approach to a question.

- Present the CT computation in the standard pro forma.
- Support it with workings where necessary (one of which will be the loss memorandum).

Solution

Sage Ltd – Corporation tax computation – y/e 31 March 2021

	£
Trading profit	Nil
Property income	10,000
Chargeable gain	50,000
Total profits	60,000
Less: Loss relief – Current year	(40,000)
	20,000
Less: Qualifying charitable donation	(10,000)
Taxable total profits	10,000

Working: Loss memorandum

	£
Year ended 31 March 2021	
Current period loss	(40,000)
Relieved in current period	40,000
Loss c/f	Nil

Setting off the loss before the deduction of qualifying charitable donations (QCDs) may result in the QCDs becoming unrelieved. Excess amounts of QCDs are lost.

Example

What if Sage Ltd in the previous example made a loss of £60,000?

Solution

	£
Total profits i.e. before QCDs (as before)	60,000
Less: Loss relief – Current year	(60,000)
	Nil
Less: QCDs	Wasted
Taxable total profits	Nil

The QCD is unrelieved. It has not been used as there are insufficient profits to set it against.

It is an important principle in the use of most loss reliefs that, where there is an available loss, no restriction in set off is permitted.

This means that it would *not* have been possible here to restrict the loss relief to (£50,000) so as to then relieve a QCD of (£10,000), and find an alternative use for the remaining (£10,000) loss.

Unused QCDs cannot be carried forward or back and are therefore wasted.

1.4 Carry back relief

A trading loss may be carried back for relief against total profits in the preceding 12 months, but only *after* the loss has first been relieved against any available current period total profits.

The loss is set off against total profits *before* deducting QCDs.

In other words, the order in which the loss is applied is as follows.

• First, against total profits of the current year *(before* QCDs).

• Second, against total profits of the previous 12 months (again, *before* the deduction of QCDs).

In questions this is often referred to as 'setting off the loss as soon as possible'.

When a company ceases to trade, it can carry back the loss for 36 months rather than 12.

Approach to losses questions

A longer style task in the assessment may involve utilising company losses over several years; a methodical approach is very important for these tasks.

• Lay out the years side by side in a table, leaving space to insert any loss reliefs.

• Keep a separate working for the trading loss – the memorandum.

• Firstly set the loss against the total profits (before QCDs) of the year of loss.

• Then carry the balance of the loss back against total profits (before QCDs) of the previous 12 months.

• State whether there is any unrelieved loss remaining.

• Keep a running tally in the loss memorandum working.

Here is a pro forma. The loss has been incurred in 2021.

Pro forma corporation tax loss computation

	2020	2021
	£	£
Trading profit	X	Nil
Non-trade interest	X	X
Property income	X	X
Chargeable gains	X	X
Total profits	X	X
Less: Loss relief		
– Current period		(X)
– Carry back	(X)	
	Nil	Nil
Less: QCDs	Wasted	Wasted
Taxable total profits	Nil	Nil

Loss memorandum:	
	£
Current year loss (2021)	X
Less: Current year relief	(X)
Carry back relief	(X)
Loss still available	X

Example

Marjoram Ltd has the following results for the three accounting periods to 31 December 2021.

Year ended 31 December	2019	2020	2021
	£	£	£
Trading profits/(loss)	11,000	9,000	(45,000)
Building society interest	500	500	500
Chargeable gains	–	–	4,000
Qualifying charitable donations	250	250	250

Show the taxable total profits for all periods affected, assuming that loss relief is taken as soon as possible.

Solution

Marjoram Ltd

Corporation tax computations

Year ended 31 December	2020 £	2021 £
Trading profit	9,000	Nil
Non-trade interest	500	500
Chargeable gains	Nil	4,000
	———	———
Total profits	9,500	4,500
Less: Loss relief		
– Current period		(4,500)
– Carry back	(9,500)	
	———	———
	Nil	Nil
Less: QCDs	Wasted	Wasted
	———	———
Taxable total profits	Nil	Nil
	———	———

Note: The year ended 31 December 2019 is not affected; the loss cannot be carried back that far.

Loss working

	£
Loss for the year ended 31 December 2021	45,000
Less: Current year relief	(4,500)
	———
	40,500
Less: Carry back 12 months	(9,500)
	———
Loss still available at 1 January 2022	31,000
	———

Test your understanding 1

Banks Ltd has the following results:

Year ended 31 March	2020	2021
	£	£
Adjusted trading profit/(loss)	50,000	(120,000)
Bank interest	2,000	3,000
Qualifying charitable donation	1,000	500

On the assumption that Banks Ltd uses its loss as early as possible, what is the trading loss carried forward to the year ended 31 March 2022?

A   £117,000

B   £68,000

C   £66,500

D   £65,000

Short previous accounting period

Losses can be carried back 12 months. This usually means the loss can be deducted from the profits of the previous accounting period. However, if the previous accounting period is less than 12 months long, it will be possible to carry the loss back to cover a proportion of the profits for the period preceding that.

 Example

Amla Ltd has the following results for the three accounting periods to 31 December 2020.

	12m to 30 April 2019	8m to 31 Dec 2019	12m to 31 Dec 2020
	£	£	£
Trading profits/(loss)	40,000	18,000	(100,000)
Bank interest	2,000	1,500	1,700
Qualifying charitable donations	1,000	1,000	1,000

Show the taxable total profits for all periods affected, assuming that loss relief is taken as soon as possible.

Solution

Amla Ltd

Corporation tax computations

	12m to 30 April 2019 £	8m to 31 Dec 2019 £	12m to 31 Dec 2020 £
Trading profits	40,000	18,000	Nil
Bank interest	2,000	1,500	1,700
Total profits	42,000	19,500	1,700
Less: Loss relief			
– Current period			(1,700)
– Carry back		(19,500)	
(max 4/12 × £42,000)	(14,000)		
	28,000	Nil	Nil
Less: QCDs	(1,000)	Wasted	Wasted
Taxable total profits	27,000	Nil	Nil

Note: The loss can be carried back 12 months. This covers the whole of the 8 months to 31 December 2019 and 4 months of the year ended 30 April 2019. The maximum loss that can be deducted for the year ended 30 April 2019 is equal to 4/12 of the total profits i.e. £14,000.

Loss working

	£
Loss for the year ended 31 December 2020	100,000
Less: Current year relief	(1,700)
	98,300
Less: Carry back 8m to 31 Dec 2019	(19,500)
	78,800
Carry back to year ended 30 April 2019	(14,000)
Loss still available at 1 January 2021	64,800

Test your understanding 2

Undergrowth Ltd

Undergrowth Ltd is a UK resident company that began trading on 1 July 2018. The company's results are summarised as follows:

	Year ended 30 Jun 2019	6 months to 31 Dec 2019	Year ended 31 Dec 2020
	£	£	£
Trading profit/(loss)	35,000	25,000	(350,000)
Non-trade loan interest receivable	–	15,000	22,000
Property income	25,000	–	–
Donation to national charity	1,000	1,000	1,000

Calculate the taxable total profits for all of the years in the question after giving maximum relief at the earliest time for the trading losses sustained and any other reliefs.

Also show any balance of losses carried forward.

1.5 Carry forward relief

Where any loss remains unrelieved after the current year and carry back claims have been made, the remaining loss can be carried forward indefinitely. This also applies where no current year and carry back claims are made, as there is no compulsory requirement to use such reliefs.

When trading losses are carried forward, provided the trade is still being carried on and has not become small or negligible, a claim can be made for them to be offset against **total profits** of the company.

Where this is the case losses do not have to be offset against the first available total profits – the company can choose how much, if any, to offset and how much to carry forward to future periods.

Example

Mint Ltd began trading on 1 April 2018 and has the following results:

Year ended 31 March	2019	2020	2021
	£	£	£
Adjusted trading profit/(loss)	15,000	(100,000)	40,000
Non-trade interest	5,000	10,000	10,000
Chargeable gain	–	40,000	–

Show how the loss relief would be claimed where relief is required as soon as possible.

Solution

Mint Ltd – Corporation tax computations

Year ended 31 March	2019	2020	2021
	£	£	£
Trading profit	15,000	Nil	40,000
Non-trade interest	5,000	10,000	10,000
Chargeable gain	–	40,000	–
	———	———	———
Total profits	20,000	50,000	50,000
Less: Loss relief			
– Current year		(50,000)	
– Carry back	(20,000)		
– Carry forward			(30,000)
	———	———	———
Taxable total profits	Nil	Nil	20,000
	———	———	———

Working: Loss memorandum

	£
Loss for the year ended 31 March 2020	100,000
Less: Current year relief	(50,000)
Carry back relief	
– Year ended 31 March 2019	(20,000)
	———
	30,000
Less: Used in year ended 31 March 2021	(30,000)
	———
Loss left to c/f	Nil
	———

Test your understanding 3

Potter Ltd

The following is the income of Potter Ltd which commenced to trade on 1 October 2019.

Year ended 30 September	2020	2021
	£	£
Adjusted trading profit (loss)	(35,000)	94,000
Bank interest receivable	11,400	8,400
Rents receivable (after deducting expenses)	21,300	21,400
Donation to national charity paid 30 Sept	500	500

(handwritten: (2300) = 91700)

(handwritten: (2300))

(handwritten: 121,000)

Calculate the taxable total profits for the years ending 30 September 2020 and 2021, indicating how you would obtain relief as soon as possible for the loss.

1.6 Factors to be considered when choosing loss relief

Companies have the following choices when considering loss relief:

- current year claim then carry back claim then carry forward the remaining loss or

- current year claim then carry forward the remaining loss or

- carry forward all the loss.

When deciding which choice to make there are two main considerations:

(1) **Cash flow**

Where the company wants earliest relief, a current and carry back claim would be preferred.

This enables the company to claim tax repayments for the previous year which is a useful cash flow for a company suffering losses.

(2) **Rate of relief**

Where the company wants to obtain the highest possible tax saving then the rate of tax saved is important.

A company would prefer to claim relief in the periods when it is paying tax at the highest rate of tax (however note that in the assessment tax is always paid at 19%). Remember current year relief must always be claimed before carry back relief.

It would also be preferable to avoid wasting QCDs. (Note that current year and carry back claims cannot be restricted to avoid wasting QCDs whereas the offset of brought forward losses is more flexible).

You may have to make a choice of relief in the assessment and/or may be asked to select what factors a company should take into account when choosing the best relief.

2 Capital losses

Both trading and capital losses may be examined in the assessment.

Capital losses may occur in questions in isolation, but where a mixture of losses appear it is essential to distinguish the reliefs available.

The treatment of capital losses will be covered in detail in Chapter 16. However, in summary:

- A capital loss incurred in the current period is automatically relieved against current period gains. Any excess is then carried forward for relief against gains in future accounting periods.

- There is no carry back facility and a capital loss cannot be used against any other profit.

 Test your understanding 4

Coriander Ltd

Coriander Ltd began trading on 1 April 2018 and has the following results:

	Trading profit or (loss) £	Non-trade interest £	Qualifying charitable donation £	Capital gains or (losses) £
Year ended 31 Mar:				
2019	37,450	1,300	3,000	(5,000)
2020	(81,550)	1,400	3,000	
2021	20,000	1,600	3,000	12,000

Calculate taxable total profits for all years, assuming all reliefs are claimed at the earliest opportunity. State the amounts of losses carried forward.

Approach to the question

- Set up CT pro formas for all years leaving space to enter any loss reliefs.

- Set up a loss memorandum for the trading loss for the year ended 31 March 2020.

- There is also a capital loss to deal with which has more restrictive use than a trading loss.

 Test your understanding 5

Read the following statements and state whether they are true or false.

1   Trading losses can be relieved by carry back before being offset in the year of loss. (F)

2   Trading losses are deducted from other income in the current period after deducting qualifying charitable donations. (F)

3   Trading losses carried forward can only be carried forward for 12 months. (F)

4   Capital losses can be offset against other income in the year of the loss, but only against chargeable gains in future years. (F)

---

3 Research and development tax credits

3.1   Introduction

In order to encourage more spending on research and development (R&D), additional tax reliefs are given for qualifying revenue expenditure incurred by companies.

There is a tax credit scheme for small or medium sized enterprises (SMEs).

An SME is a company with less than 500 employees with either:

- an annual turnover under 100 million euros, or

- a balance sheet under 86 million euros.

This definition is given in the AAT reference material, which is included in section 7 below, so you do not have to learn it.

3.2   Scheme details

The scheme works as follows.

- Enhanced relief is available if the company spends money on qualifying R&D.

- SMEs can deduct an additional 130% of qualifying expenditure for tax purposes, i.e. for every £100 spent on R&D the company can deduct the original £100 plus a further £130 as allowable expenses for tax purposes. This gives total tax relief of 230% of the £100.

- If the deduction creates a loss it may be surrendered in return for a cash payment from HMRC (see section 3.3 below).

Qualifying R&D expenditure must be revenue expenditure on a project that seeks to achieve an advance in science or technology that is relevant to the company's trade.

It can include expenditure on the following:

- staffing costs (of staff directly involved in the R&D activity)
- materials, water, fuel and power for R&D
- software directly used in R&D.

It cannot include:

- contributions to other bodies for independent research
- expenditure covered by a grant or subsidy.

 Example

Dax plc is a profitable company manufacturing audio visual equipment. It is a small enterprise for the purposes of R&D.

The company has recently decided to investigate the market for a new type of classroom projection equipment and has spent the following amounts in the year ended 31 December 2020 on the project:

	£
Market research	8,000
Staff directly involved in researching the project	20,000
Heat and light in the R&D department	9,000
Administrative support for staff in the R&D department	5,000
New software	4,000
	46,000

Advise the company of any tax relief available in respect of its expenditure.

Solution

The cost of market research and administrative support is not covered by the SME scheme so only the normal 100% deduction is available.

The cost of staff directly involved in the project, heat and light in the R&D department and new software qualifies for the enhanced deduction.

	£
Allowable expense for tax purposes:	
Market research	8,000
Administrative support for staff in the R&D department	5,000
	———
	13,000
	———
Staff directly involved in researching the project	20,000
Heat and light in the R&D department	9,000
New software	4,000
	———
	33,000
	———
Total amount allowed in the calculation of adjusted profits	
100% of £13,000	13,000
230% of £33,000	75,900
	———
	88,900
	———

3.3 Losses

If the deduction of the R&D relief creates a loss, then the company can choose:

* to use the loss in the normal way, or

* surrender the loss in return for a cash payment.

The cash payment will be 14.5% of the loss.

Note that the rate of the relief is not mentioned in the AAT reference material.

Example

Curzon plc is a small company. Its adjusted trading profit before any R&D expense is £40,000 for the year ended 31 March 2021. It has incurred £50,000 of qualifying R&D expenditure.

Advise the company of the amount of loss which arises in the year ended 31 March 2021 and the amount of tax credit which will be received if it is surrendered.

Solution

Loss:

	£
Adjusted trading profit before R&D expense	40,000
R&D (£50,000 × 230%)	(115,000)
Trading loss	(75,000)

The company can choose to use the loss as normal or claim a cash repayment of £10,875 (£75,000 × 14.5%).

 Test your understanding 6

Read the following statements and state whether they are true or false.

1   A small company incurs £42,000 of qualifying R&D. It can deduct a total expense of £54,600 from its business profits. (F)

2   An SME can have more than 500 employees provided its turnover is below 100 million euros and its balance sheet is under 43 million euros. (F)

3   Ezri plc is a small company which has an adjusted trading profit of £21,000 before R&D expense and has spent £35,000 on qualifying R&D. It has an adjusted trading loss of £59,500. (T)

4 Personal service companies (IR35)

4.1 Introduction

This section deals with tax avoidance by using personal service companies (PSCs). The legislation is often referred to as IR35, which was the name of the HMRC press release that first introduced the legislation.

4.2 What is a personal service company?

If an employee is employed and earning a salary then his/her employer has to deduct income tax and employee's national insurance contributions (NICs) from the salary paid to the employee, via the PAYE system. The employer also has to pay employer's NICs. These taxes are all covered in detail in the personal tax syllabus.

Alternatively, the employee could resign from the employment, set up a company and then use that company to offer his/her services to the former employer. In that case, the company would invoice the former employer, who would pay the invoice without having to deduct income tax or NICs before making the payment, and would avoid having to pay employers' NICs at all.

The PSC pays corporation tax at only 19% on profits, net of any expenses wholly and exclusively incurred for the trade.

The former employee, now the company owner, could pay himself/herself a small salary (which would avoid employee's NICs) and withdraw funds as dividends, which are not liable to NICs. This would result in a lower overall tax charge.

4.3 Relevant engagements

The PSC legislation is aimed at situations which are essentially disguised employments.

It is not limited to employees contracting with their former employer, but covers anything that is deemed to be a 'relevant engagement'.

A relevant engagement is a contract between the PSC and the client, which would have been a contract of employment if the client had contracted directly with the individual doing the work.

HMRC will look to see whether, without the intermediary company, the relationship between the worker and the client would constitute a 'contract of service' (employment) rather than a 'contract for services' (self-employment).

This will include a consideration of the following types of factors:

- An obligation on the worker to accept work offered, and on the client to offer work would indicate a relevant engagement.

- If the manner and method of the work is controlled by the client, this indicates a relevant engagement.

- When the hours of work are fixed by the client, this would suggest a relevant engagement. If the worker can determine his/her own hours of work, this is a factor arguing against this being a relevant engagement.

- In a relevant engagement, it is likely that the worker is being paid an agreed, regular remuneration. If the worker is bearing the financial risk, it is less likely to be a relevant engagement.

- If the worker is provided with tools and equipment by the client, this is an indication of a relevant engagement.

- Having rights under employment legislation, such as holiday or sick pay, would indicate a relevant engagement.

- If the worker works exclusively for the client. If the worker has various other clients this is not an indication of a relevant engagement.

- Having to perform the work themselves is a normal requirement for employees and an indication that this is a relevant engagement. If the worker can send a substitute to do the work, this would indicate it is not a relevant engagement.

4.4 Deemed employment income tax charge

The client company is not affected by the PSC legislation. It is only the PSC that is affected.

The PSC suffers a deemed employment income tax charge. It has to:

- Treat the income from relevant engagements arising in a tax year as if it were paid out as salary to the employee.

- Account for the income tax and NIC on the notional salary.

- Only expenses typically allowed to employees, plus a flat rate 5% deduction, can be deducted from the notional salary. The rules regarding which expenses can be deducted by an employee are more stringent than those applying to companies.

Note that the AAT reference material set out in section 7 below includes some information about the IR35 legislation.

5 Test your understanding

 Test your understanding 7

AB Ltd

The following details relate to AB Ltd.

Year ended	31 Dec 2019	31 Dec 2020
	£	£
Adjusted trading profit/(loss)	19,000	(67,000)
Bank interest received	2,000	1,000
Chargeable gains	4,000	4,000
Qualifying charitable donation	10,000	

Assuming AB Ltd uses its loss as early as possible, what is the amount of loss carried forward at 31 December 2020?

A   £62,000

B   £47,000

C   £42,000

D   £37,000

Test your understanding 8

Eldorado Ltd

Eldorado Ltd prepares accounts annually to 31 August in each year. The company commenced to trade on 1 September 2018.

The results for the first few years were as follows:

Year to 31 August	2019	2020	2021
	£	£	£
Trading profits/(loss)	18,000	(81,000)	(6,000)
Chargeable gain	3,000		
Property income	22,000	22,000	22,000

Show how relief is obtained for the trading losses, assuming that relief is claimed as soon as possible.

 Test your understanding 9

Read the following statements and state whether they are true or false.

1   Capital losses can only be offset against chargeable gains in the year of the loss, and then against chargeable gains in future years.

2   Trading losses carried forward must be offset against the first available future total profits.

3   Trading losses can be deducted from other income and chargeable gains of the current accounting period.

4   Where trading losses have been relieved against the total profits of the loss making period, any losses remaining must then be offset against the total profits of the previous 12 months.

6 Summary

Losses often appear in assessments.

The rules depend on the type of loss:

- trading losses – current year and carry back relief against total profits before qualifying charitable donations, carry forward against total profits

- capital losses – current year against chargeable gains only, carry forward against chargeable gains only.

Small and medium sized enterprises (SMEs) can claim extra tax relief on allowable R&D costs.

230% of the cost of qualifying R&D can be deducted as an allowable expense.

Qualifying R&D must be revenue expenditure that contributes to seeking an advance in science or technology.

If the deduction of the R&D tax relief creates a loss the loss can be surrendered for a cash sum = to 14.5% of the loss.

If a company is determined to be a PSC then any income from relevant engagements will be subject to a deemed employment charge.

 Links to other syllabus areas

Companies may not always be profitable – in both FAPR and FSLC you learn how to account for losses and then, in other management accounting style papers, the impact of an excess of costs over revenue in terms of the ongoing viability of the business venture in both the short and the medium term.

A loss can also arise for tax purposes – you need an appreciation of its overall consequences from a wider financial perspective and its impact in terms of accounts recognition (FSLC) and in terms of other budgetary and cash flow implications.

7 AAT reference material

Corporation tax – trade losses

- Can elect to set trading losses against current accounting period 'total profits'. Qualifying charitable donations will remain unrelieved.

- If the above election is made, can also carry back trading loss to set against 'total profits' within the previous 12 months.

- Losses not relieved in the current accounting period or previous 12 months are carried forward and an election can be made to set against total profits in future periods.

- If there is a choice of loss relief, firstly consider when the loss was incurred, the rate of loss relief and then the timing of relief.

- Set out the use of the losses in a loss memorandum.

Current tax reliefs and other tax issues

Research and development (R&D) tax credits for small and medium sized companies

A small or medium sized enterprise (SME) is a company with less than 500 employees with either:

- an annual turnover under €100 million, or

- a balance sheet under €86 million.

The SME tax relief scheme

The tax relief on allowable R&D costs is 230%.

R&D tax credits

If a company makes a loss, it can choose to receive R&D tax credits instead of carrying forward a loss.

Costs that qualify for R&D tax relief

To qualify as R&D, any activity must contribute directly to seeking an advance in science or technology or must be a qualifying indirect activity. The costs must relate to the company's trade – either an existing one, or one that they intend to start up based on the results of the R&D.

Intermediaries (IR35) legislation

IR35 legislation prevents personal service companies ("PSC") being used to disguise permanent employment.

The rules apply where the relationship between the worker and the client, would be considered to be an employment relationship if the existence of the PSC was ignored.

If the rules apply, a **deemed employment income tax charge** is charged on the PSC.

The **deemed employment income tax charge** is calculated based upon the actual payments made to the PSC by the client.

Test your understanding answers

Test your understanding 1

Banks Ltd

The correct answer is D.

Explanation

D is the correct answer. When you are asked to use the loss 'as early as possible' it means the loss is set off against total profits before qualifying charitable donations in the current year and then total profits before qualifying charitable donations in the preceding 12 months.

A current year claim must be made before a carry back claim, as follows:

		£
Trading loss		120,000
Less: Utilised	– Current year offset	(3,000)
	– Carry back claim	(52,000)
		————
Available to carry forward		65,000
		————

Test your understanding 2

Undergrowth Ltd

	Year ended 30 Jun 2019 £	6 months to 31 Dec 2019 £	Year ended 31 Dec 2020 £
Trading profit	35,000	25,000	Nil
Non-trade interest	–	15,000	22,000
Property income	25,000	–	–
Total profits	60,000	40,000	22,000
Less: Loss relief			
– Current year			(22,000)
– Carry back (W)	(30,000)	(40,000)	
	30,000	Nil	Nil
Less: QCDs	(1,000)	Wasted	Wasted
Taxable total profits	29,000	Nil	Nil

Balances carried forward

- There is a trading loss at 31 December 2020 to carry forward of £258,000 (W).

    Working: Trading losses

	£
Loss for 12 months to 31 December 2020	350,000
Current year relief	(22,000)
Carry back relief – 6 months to 31 December 2019	(40,000)
– 12 months to 30 June 2019 (£60,000 × 6/12)	(30,000)
Carry forward at 31 December 2020	258,000

Test your understanding 3

Potter Ltd

Year ended 30 September	2020 £	2021 £
Trading profit	Nil	94,000
Non-trade interest	11,400	8,400
Property income	21,300	21,400
Total profits	32,700	123,800
Less: Loss relief – Current year	(32,700)	
Less: Losses b/f (£35,000 – £32,700)	–	(2,300)
	Nil	121,500
Less: QCDs	(Wasted)	(500)
Taxable total profits	Nil	121,000

📝 **Test your understanding 4**

Coriander Ltd – Corporation tax computations

Year ended 31 March	2019	2020	2021
	£	£	£
Trading profit	37,450	Nil	20,000
Non-trade interest	1,300	1,400	1,600
Chargeable gains			
(£12,000 – £5,000 b/f)	Nil		7,000
	———	———	———
Total profits	38,750	1,400	28,600
Less: Loss relief			
– Current year		(1,400)[1]	
– Carry back	(38,750)[2]		
– Carry forward			(25,600)[3]
	———	———	———
	Nil	Nil	3,000
Less: QCDs	Wasted	Wasted	(3,000)
	———	———	———
Taxable total profits	Nil	Nil	Nil
	———	———	———
QCDs wasted	3,000	3,000	
	———	———	

Loss memorandum

	£
Trading loss in the year ended 31 March 2020	81,550
(1) Current period relief	(1,400)
(2) Carry back relief – year ended 31 March 2019	(38,750)
	———
	41,400
(3) Carry forward against total profits	
– year ended 31 March 2021	(25,600)
	———
Loss to carry forward at 31 March 2021	15,800
	———

Note that the use of losses in the year ended 31 March 2021 has been restricted to avoid wastage of QCDs.

Test your understanding 5

1	False	Trading losses can only be relieved by carry back after a claim for current year relief has been made.
2	False	Trading losses are deducted from other income before deducting qualifying charitable donations. Any excess QCDs remaining unrelieved are wasted.
3	False	Trading losses carried forward can be carried forward indefinitely.
4	False	Capital losses cannot be offset against other income. They can only be set against chargeable gains.

Test your understanding 6

1	False	If the company incurs £42,000 of qualifying R&D expenditure it can deduct a total of £96,600 (£42,000 × 230%).
2	False	An SME must have less than 500 employees.
3	True	The company has a trade profit of £21,000 before R&D. The R&D deduction is £80,500 (£35,000 × 230%). This gives a trading loss of £59,500 (£21,000 – £80,500).

Test your understanding 7

AB Ltd

The correct answer is D.

Explanation

Year ended 31 December	2019	2020
	£	£
Trading income	19,000	Nil
Interest income	2,000	1,000
Chargeable gains	4,000	4,000
	———	———
Total profits	25,000	5,000
Less: Loss relief – Current year		(5,000)
– 12 month carry back	(25,000)	
	———	———
Taxable total profits	Nil	Nil
	———	———

Note: Loss relief is given before qualifying charitable donations are deducted. As a result the qualifying charitable donation in 2019 is wasted.

Loss memorandum

	£
Year ended 31 December 2020	67,000
Less: Current year offset – y/e 31 Dec 2020	(5,000)
Carry back – 12 months to y/e 31 Dec 2019	(25,000)
	———
Loss carried forward at 31 December 2020	37,000
	———

Test your understanding 8

Eldorado Ltd

Corporation tax computations

Year to 31 August	2019 £	2020 £	2021 £
Trading profit	18,000	Nil	Nil
Property income	22,000	22,000	22,000
Chargeable gain	3,000	–	–
Total profits	43,000	22,000	22,000
Less: Loss relief			
– Current year		(22,000)	(6,000)
– Carry back	(43,000)		
– Carry forward			(16,000)
Taxable total profits	Nil	Nil	Nil

Loss memorandum

	£		£
Loss – y/e 31 Aug 2020	81,000	Loss – y/e 31 Aug 2021	6,000
Offset: Current year	(22,000)	Offset: Current year	(6,000)
Carry back	(43,000)		
Carry forward	(16,000)		
Losses carried forward	Nil		Nil

Test your understanding 9

1	True	Capital losses can only be offset against chargeable gains of the current and future periods.
2	False	Trading losses carried forward do not have to be offset against the first available future total profits; the company can choose when to offset such losses.
3	True	Trading losses can be offset against the total profits of the loss making accounting period; total profits include income and chargeable gains.
4	False	Where trading losses have been relieved against the total profits of the loss making period, a company can choose to offset any losses remaining against the total profits of the previous 12 months but it is not obliged to do so.

Payment and administration – companies

7

Introduction

This chapter looks at the payment and administration aspects of corporation tax (see Chapter 13 for sole traders and partnerships).

At the end of each section you will find a summary showing which information from that section is provided in the AAT reference material, and which information is not provided and therefore needs to be learnt.

ASSESSMENT CRITERIA	CONTENTS
Tax return filing deadlines (3.1)	1 Corporation tax self-assessment (CTSA)
Payment rules for limited companies: amounts and dates (3.1)	2 HM Revenue and Customs' (HMRC) compliance checks
Penalties for late filing of tax returns and failing to notify chargeability (3.2)	3 Record keeping requirements
Late payment interest and surcharges (3.2)	4 Payment of corporation tax
The enquiry window and penalties for incorrect returns (3.2)	5 Approach to preparing written answers
What records need to be maintained by a business, how long these records need to be maintained and the penalties for failing to keep these records (4.3)	

1 Corporation tax self-assessment (CTSA)

1.1 Scope

Corporation tax self-assessment (CTSA) requires companies to submit a tax return for each accounting period (AP) and a self-assessment of any tax payable.

1.2 Filing the return

A company is required to file a return (form CT600) when it receives a notice requiring it to do so.

All companies must file their returns online and submit their accounts and any tax computations using iXBRL (inline eXtensible Business Reporting Language).

A company which is chargeable to tax, but which does not receive a notice requesting a return, must notify HMRC within 12 months of the end of the accounting period.

Failure to notify may result in a penalty. The penalty is calculated in broadly the same way as penalties for incorrect returns (see below) and is a maximum of 100% of the tax outstanding.

The return must include a calculation (self-assessment) of the corporation tax payable for the accounting period covered by the return.

The return must be made within:

- 12 months of the end of the period of account or, if later

- three months from the date of the notice requiring the return.

Long periods of account

The return filing date is based on the period of account (which may be more than 12 months long).

For a set of accounts of more than 12 months long, there will be two APs, two corporation tax computations and therefore two returns to file.

However, both returns will have the same filing date; 12 months after the end of the period of account.

Example

Edgar Ltd has prepared a set of accounts for the 15 months ended 31 March 2021.

Identify the period(s) for which return(s) must be completed and the filing date(s).

Solution

The period of account is the period for which accounts are drawn up (i.e. 15 months to 31 March 2021).

	Periods for returns	Filing date
(i)	First 12 months	
	– 12 months ended 31 December 2020	31 March 2022
(ii)	Balance	
	– 3 months ended 31 March 2021	31 March 2022

Penalties for late filing

Failure to submit a return by the due date will result in a penalty.

The system operates as follows:

• Less than 3 months overdue	£100
• Delay of more than three months	£200
• Delay of more than six months	£200 plus 10% of tax due
• Delay of more than 12 months	£200 plus 20% of tax due

If the return is late three times in a row then the £100 penalty is increased to £500 and the £200 penalty to £1,000.

A penalty will not be charged if the taxpayer has a reasonable excuse for the late filing, for example a serious illness. A lack of knowledge of the tax system is not a reasonable excuse.

Note that many of the details about dates, time limits and penalties are contained in the AAT reference material set out below in section 8. You should refer to this throughout this chapter.

Example

Flat Ltd received a notice to file Form CT600 for the year ended 30 June 2019 on 31 August 2019. The company submitted the corporation tax return on 28 February 2021 and paid its corporation tax liability of £35,000 on the same date.

What are the maximum penalties that can be charged in respect of the late filing of the return?

Solution

The corporation tax return was due to be filed on 30 June 2020, 12 months after the end of the period of account. The return was filed more than six months but less than 12 months late.

A fixed penalty of £200 will be charged plus 10% of any tax still outstanding. In this case that will be an additional penalty of £3,500 (£35,000 × 10%) making a total due of £3,700.

1.3 Notification of chargeability

A company which is liable to tax for the first time must notify HMRC within three months of the start of its first accounting period for tax.

A company which is chargeable to tax, but does not receive a notice to file a return, must notify HMRC within 12 months of the end of its accounting period.

Failure to notify may result in a penalty. The penalty is calculated in broadly the same way as penalties for incorrect returns (see section 1.8 below) and is a maximum of 100% of the tax outstanding.

1.4 Amending the return

A company can amend a return within 12 months of the filing due date.

HMRC can amend a return to correct obvious errors and anything else which they believe to be incorrect by reference to the information they hold within:

- nine months of the date it was filed, or
- nine months of the filing of an amendment.

If the company disagrees with HMRC's amendment it may reject it.

This rejection should be made within:

- the normal time limit for amendments or
- if this time limit has expired, within three months of the date of correction.

 Test your understanding 1

Administration

Read the following statements and state whether they are true or false.

1 The filing date for a company which prepares accounts for the 11 months to 30 April 2021 is 30 April 2022. (T)

2 DEF Ltd filed its corporation tax return for the year ended 31 March 2021 on 19 May 2022. The latest date that it can amend the return is 19 May 2023. (F)

3 The maximum penalty for not filing a corporation tax return on time is £100. (F)

1.5 Recovery of overpaid tax

A company may claim a repayment of tax within four years of the end of an accounting period. An appeal against HMRC's decision on such a claim must be made within 30 days.

A company is not allowed to make such a claim if its return was made in accordance with a generally accepted accounting practice which prevailed at the time.

1.6 Interest on late payments of corporation tax

Interest is charged automatically on late paid corporation tax:

- from the due date
- to the date of payment.

Where there is an amendment to the self-assessment interest runs:

- from the date the tax would have been payable had it been correctly self-assessed in the first place.

Interest paid on late payments of corporation tax is allowable as a deduction from non-trade interest income.

1.7 Interest on overpaid corporation tax

If corporation tax is overpaid HMRC will pay interest:

- from the later of the normal due date (see below) and the date of overpayment

- to the date it is refunded.

Interest received on overpaid corporation tax is assessable as non-trade interest income.

Detailed computations of interest will not be required in the assessment (such as daily calculations), but the principles must be understood.

1.8 Penalties for incorrect returns

A penalty will be charged where:

- an inaccurate return is submitted to HMRC or

- the company fails to notify HMRC where an under assessment of tax is made by them.

The percentage depends on the reason for the error.

Taxpayer behaviour	Maximum penalty % of tax lost
Genuine mistake: despite taking reasonable care	No penalty
Careless error and inaccuracy due to failure to take reasonable care	30%
Deliberate error but not concealed	70%
Deliberate error and concealed	100%

The penalties may be reduced at HMRC discretion where the taxpayer discloses information to HMRC. The reduction depends on the circumstances of the penalty and whether the taxpayer discloses the information before HMRC discover the error (unprompted disclosure) or afterwards (prompted disclosure).

Taxpayer behaviour	Minimum penalties	
	Unprompted disclosure % of tax lost	Prompted disclosure % of tax lost
Careless error and inaccuracy due to failure to take reasonable care	Nil	15%
Deliberate error but not concealed	20%	35%
Deliberate error and concealed	30%	50%

Example

State the maximum and minimum penalties that may be levied on each of the following companies which have submitted incorrect tax returns.

L Ltd   Accidentally provided an incorrect figure even though the return was checked carefully. The company notified HMRC of the error three days after submitting the return. *(nil)*

S Ltd   Was unable to check the return due to staff being on holiday. The return included a number of errors. The return was checked thoroughly the following week and the company provided HMRC with the information necessary to identify the errors. *30% max* *0% min*

J Ltd   Deliberately understated its tax liability and attempted to conceal the incorrect information that had been provided. HMRC have identified the understatement and J Ltd is helping them with their enquiries. *100% / 50%*

Solution

Penalties for incorrect tax returns are a percentage of the under declared tax.

L Ltd   No penalty is charged where a taxpayer has been careful and has made a genuine mistake.

S Ltd   The maximum percentage for failing to take reasonable care is 30%. The minimum percentage for unprompted disclosure is nil.

J Ltd   The maximum percentage for a deliberate understatement with concealment is 100%. The minimum percentage for prompted disclosure of information (where the taxpayer provides information in response to HMRC identifying the error) in respect of deliberate understatement with concealment is 50%.

Summary of reference material

	Included in reference material	Not included in reference material
How to submit returns		✓
Deadline to notify HMRC if chargeable to tax but no return has been issued		✓
Filing deadline	✓	
Late filing penalties	✓	
Increases to late filing penalties where return is filed late three times in a row		✓
Deadline to notify chargeability	✓	
Penalties for failure to notify chargeability		✓
Deadline for company to amend return	✓	
Deadline for HMRC to amend return		✓
Rejections of amendments		✓
Recovery of overpaid tax		✓
Interest on late and overpaid tax	✓	
Dates between which interest is charged		✓
Penalties for incorrect returns	✓	

As penalties for incorrect returns are the same as for individuals these can be found in the payment and administration for sole traders and partners section of the reference material.

2 HM Revenue and Customs' (HMRC) compliance checks

2.1 Basic rules

HMRC have the right to enquire into a company's tax return under their compliance check powers. This may be a random check or because they have reason to believe that income or expenses have been misstated in the tax return.

Where a return is submitted on time, notice must normally be given within a year of the actual filing date.

Where a return is submitted late HMRC can give notice of a compliance check (also referred to as an enquiry) within a year of the 31 January, 30 April, 31 July or 31 October following the actual date of delivery of the return.

HMRC may also demand that the company produce documents for inspection. If the company fails to do so, a penalty of £300, plus up to £60 a day, may be imposed.

A compliance check (enquiry) ends when HMRC give notice that it has been completed and notify what amendments they believe to be necessary. The notice is referred to as a closure notice.

In more complex cases, if the compliance check covers several different aspects, then a partial closure notice (PCN) may be issued to bring one particular part of the compliance check to an end ahead of the final closure notice.

Example

CTS Ltd has produced accounts for the year ended 30 June 2020. The company filed its return on 1 April 2021.

What is the latest date by which HMRC must give notice of a compliance check (enquiry)?

How would your answer differ if CTS Ltd had filed its return on 1 September 2021?

Solution

HMRC must give notice within a year of the actual filing date. The actual filing date is 1 April 2021; therefore, notice must be given by 1 April 2022.

If the company had filed its return on 1 September 2021, (i.e. after the due filing date of 30 June 2021) HMRC would need to give notice by 31 October 2022 (i.e. 12 months after 31 October following the actual date of delivery of the return).

2.2 Discovery assessments

A discovery assessment may be issued if HMRC believe that insufficient tax has been collected.

The taxpayer can appeal to the Tribunal against a discovery assessment.

2.3 Appeals procedure

The taxpayer can request an informal review of a disputed decision.

Alternatively, a formal appeal may be made to the Tax Tribunal within 30 days of the closure notice or PCN being issued.

Appeals from the Tax Tribunal on a point of law (but not on a point of fact) may be made to the Court of Appeal and from there to the Supreme Court.

The Tax Tribunal is independent of HMRC.

2.4 Summary of reference material

Item	Included in reference material	Not included in reference material
Reasons why HMRC may open an enquiry		✓
Deadline for HMRC to open an enquiry where the return was filed on time	✓	
Deadline for HMRC to open an enquiry where the return was filed late		✓
Penalty for failure to produce enquiry documents	✓	
Details of closure notice/partial closure notice		✓
Discovery assessments		✓
Appeals		✓

3 Record keeping requirements

A company and its tax adviser must keep records to assist in dealings with and support evidence given to HMRC.

Companies must keep records until the latest of:

- six years from the end of the accounting period
- the date any enquiries are completed
- the date after which enquiries may not be commenced.

Failure to keep records can lead to a penalty of up to £3,000 for each accounting period affected.

Summary of reference material

Item	Included in reference material	Not included in reference material
Six year deadline for keeping records	✓	
Deadlines for keeping records where enquiries have taken place		✓
Penalty for failure to keep proper records	✓	

 Payment of corporation tax

4.1 Payment date

All payments of corporation tax must be made electronically.

Companies must normally pay corporation tax within nine months and one day of the end of the accounting period (AP).

A company with a year ended 31 January 2021 must pay corporation tax by 1 November 2021.

Note that Edgar Ltd (in an earlier example) which had a long period of account of the 15 months ended 31 March 2021 would have two payment dates.

Edgar Ltd would pay corporation tax for:

- AP 1 = 12 months ended 31 December 2020, by 1 October 2021

- AP 2 = 3 months ended 31 March 2021, by 1 January 2022.

From this we can see that a company with a long period of account can have:

- two separate payment dates

- but one common filing date.

Note that the payment dates are earlier than the filing date.

This normal payment date rule does not however apply to large companies (see below).

4.2 Payment by instalments

Large companies are required to make quarterly payments on account of their corporation tax liability.

A 'large' company is one with augmented profits of more than £1,500,000. This figure is time apportioned for short accounting periods and may have to be divided between 51% group companies.

Augmented profits are the company's taxable total profits plus its dividend income. Dividends received from 51% group companies are ignored when calculating augmented profits.

Two companies are 51% group companies if:

- one is a 51% subsidiary of the other, or
- both are 51% subsidiaries of the same company.

Broadly a 51% subsidiary is one where more than 50% of the shares are owned.

Therefore, a company with two other 51% group companies will be required to pay its corporation tax in instalments if its augmented profits exceed £500,000 (£1,500,000 ÷ 3).

Exceptions to the rule

A company is not required to make quarterly instalment payments in the first period in which it becomes large, unless its augmented profits exceed £10 million.

This £10 million limit is also shared between 51% group companies and time apportioned for short APs.

In addition, a company does not have to make quarterly instalment payments if its CT liability does not exceed £10,000.

Payment amounts and pay days

The quarterly payments should be based on the actual corporation tax liability for the current year.

The first payment is made on the 14th day of the seventh month of the accounting period.

The other quarterly payments are due on the 14th day of months 10, 13 and 16.

Note that the payments begin during the accounting period itself, not afterwards. So you must begin counting months from the start of the accounting period.

Example

State the instalment payment dates for a company with a 12 month accounting period ending on 28 February 2021.

Solution

The payments on account are due on:

- 14 September 2020
- 14 December 2020
- 14 March 2021
- 14 June 2021

Each payment due is a quarter of the corporation tax liability for the year.

Therefore, estimates of the corporation tax liability for the year need to be made at each payment date.

At least the first three (and probably all four instalments) usually have to be estimated in practice.

The first instalment payment would be a quarter of the best estimate at that date.

The second payment would require a revised estimate to which an amount is added or deducted for any under or over payment in respect of the first instalment and so on.

HMRC may expect to see some proof that the estimates were made with care.

A penalty may be imposed where a company deliberately makes insufficient quarterly payments.

Test your understanding 2

Russell plc prepares accounts to 31 December each year and its taxable total profits for the year ended 31 December 2020 are £1,600,000.

Russell plc has no subsidiaries, receives no dividend income and its taxable total profits for the year ended 31 December 2019 were £720,000.

Which one of the following statements is correct with respect to Russell plc's corporation tax liability for the year ended 31 December 2020?

A The liability is payable
  – in four equal instalments beginning on 14 July 2020

B The liability is payable
  – in four equal instalments beginning on 14 July 2021

C The liability is payable on 1 October 2021

D The liability is payable on 31 December 2021

4.3 Interest

Companies should revise the estimate of their corporation tax liability every quarter. It is a good idea to keep records showing how the estimate has been calculated. This will help to justify the size of a payment if HMRC should dispute the amount paid.

Interest runs from the due date on any underpayments or overpayments.

Interest paid by the company is a deductible expense. Interest received by the company is taxable income. Both are dealt with under the loan relationship rules as non-trade interest.

Penalties may be charged if a company deliberately fails to pay instalments of a sufficient size.

4.4 Summary of reference material

Item	Included in reference material	Not included in reference material
Due date for companies who are not large	✓	
Large company due dates	✓	
Definition of a large company	✓	
Exception to paying instalments if the company is large for the first time unless profits are greater than £10 million	✓	
Exception to paying instalments if the corporation tax liability is no more than £10,000		✓
Need to revise estimates	✓	
Penalties may be imposed where a company deliberately pays insufficient instalments	✓	

5 · Approach to preparing written answers

5.1 Written advice to clients

There will be a written task in the assessment that could cover a number of syllabus areas including those dealing with filing dates, payments of tax, penalties and interest for companies or individuals (see Chapter 13).

The chief assessor wrote a guidance document to assist learners with written answers in personal tax. However, much of the guidance is relevant for business tax.

Some of the key points from the advice are set out below.

Firstly, it's important you understand that the software in which you are answering the task is not Microsoft Word. So there's no:

- spell checker
- grammar checker
- automatic correcting of typos.

You **must** proofread what you've written and correct any obvious spelling and grammatical errors.

There's often a mark for presentation of the answer, and the assessor is looking for whether the way you've presented your work would be acceptable in the workplace. This mark is independent of the technical answer, and what we look for is whether a client would find the answer acceptable from a visual perspective.

Before you start to type:

You must read the question in detail. We've noticed that learners often scan read a question, decide what it's about in an instant and then write the answer without giving any thought or consideration to the details. You should:

- read through once to get the general feel of the question
- read through again, slower this time, concentrating on key words or phrases
- plan your answer, ensuring all key areas are covered
- decide the structure of your answer, considering where you'll use things like an email, a memo or bullet points
- type up your answer
- proof read your answer, correcting any errors.

Too many times it would seem that learners only follow the fifth of these points. If you do this it **will** affect your marks.

Consider exactly who you're writing to. Most likely it will be a client, so this needs to influence your approach.

Remember, if the client is writing to you for advice, they don't know the answer. We often see learners give half answers which the assessor will understand, but which a client would not. As a result, they lose marks.

Similarly, be sure to avoid:

*   abbreviations
*   technical jargon
*   SMS/text message speak.

 Test your understanding 3

Space plc, which has taxable total profits of £2 million annually, is preparing its budget for the year ending 31 March 2021. It does not have any dividend income.

(a)   Prepare a plan of projected corporation tax payments based on its results for the year, stating the amounts due and the due dates.

(b)   Advise of any other administrative requirements for corporation tax purposes.

Approach to the question

Step 1:   Calculate the corporation tax liability.

Step 2:   Consider the impact of the instalment system on this large company.

Step 3:   Consider the *returns* required, and the impact of late payments.

6 Test your understanding

Test your understanding 4

ABC Ltd

ABC Ltd has four 51% group companies. In the year to 31 March 2020 its profits were £200,000. In the year to 31 March 2021 it sold its factory and had profits of £3 million.

When is the corporation tax for the year to 31 March 2021 due?

A   The liability is payable in 4 equal instalments beginning on 14 October 2020

B   The liability is payable in 4 equal instalments beginning on 14 October 2021

C   The liability is payable on 1 January 2022

D   The liability is payable on 31 March 2022

Test your understanding 5

Wendell plc

Wendell plc has augmented profits above £1,500,000 every year and has taxable total profits in the year ended 31 January 2021 of £2,400,000.

Calculate the corporation tax liability of Wendell plc for the accounting period to 31 January 2021 and state when this liability is due for payment.

7 Summary

There are numerous deadlines and penalties under CTSA.

The key points are:

- A company must file a return within
    - 12 months of the end of its period of account or
    - if later, three months from the date of the notice from HMRC.

- Failure to submit a return on time results in an immediate penalty of £100.

- A company which is liable to tax for the first time must notify HMRC of its chargeability within three months of the start of its accounting period.

- The company can amend a return within 12 months of the due filing date.

- HMRC can conduct a compliance check (enquiry) into a return provided they give written notice within a year of the actual filing date.

- Companies must keep records for six years from the end of the accounting period. Failure to do so can result in a penalty of up to £3,000.

- The due date for corporation tax is nine months and one day after the end of the accounting period.

- Companies with augmented profits of more than £1,500,000 (adjusted for short accounting periods and 51% group companies) must pay their liability in quarterly instalments, commencing on the 14th day of the seventh month of the accounting period.

✳ Links to other syllabus areas

An accountant and business adviser needs an understanding of when liabilities are due and the potential consequences of failing to do things on a timely basis. This was an important aspect of your Advanced level IDRX syllabus and is equally important when it comes to direct tax in terms of ensuring that companies, sole traders and partnerships fulfil their legal obligations as and when they fall due and are aware of the penalty implications if they fail to do so.

8 AAT reference material

Corporation tax – payment and administration

Payment dates

- Small companies (annual profits less than £1.5 million): 9 months + 1 day after end of the accounting period (AP).

- Large companies (annual profits greater than £1.5 million) must estimate year's tax liability and pay 25% of the year's liability:
    - 6 months and 14 days after start of AP
    - 9 months and 14 days after start of AP
    - 14 days after end of AP
    - 3 months and 14 days after end of AP.

- Estimate must be revised for each quarter. Penalties may be charged if company deliberately fails to pay sufficient instalments.

- No instalments due for first year company is large unless profits are greater than £10 million.

- 51% group companies share the annual profit limit of £1.5 million equally.

Interest on late payments

- Interest charged daily on late payment. Overpayment of tax receives interest from HMRC. Interest is taxable/tax allowable as interest income.

Filing the return

- Filed on the later of 12 months after end of AP or 3 months after the notice to deliver a tax return has been issued.

- Late filing penalties are: less than 3 months late: £100; greater than 3 months late: £200; greater than 6 months late: 10% of tax due per return; greater than 12 months late: 20% of tax due per return.

- Company must notify HMRC it is within scope of corporation tax within 3 months of starting to trade.

- Company can amend return within 12 months of the filing date.

Enquiries and other penalties

- HMRC must notify company of enquiry within 12 months of submission of return.

- Basis of enquiry – random or HMRC believe income/expenses misstated.

- Penalty for failure to produce enquiry documents: £300 + £60 per day.

- Penalty for failure to keep proper records is up to £3,000. Records must be retained for six years after the end of the relevant accounting period.

- Penalties for incorrect returns are the same as for sole traders and partners – see sole traders and partners link.

The following table detailing penalties for incorrect returns can be found in the payment and administration for sole traders and partners section of the reference material:

Type of behaviour	Maximum	Unprompted (minimum)	Prompted (minimum)
Genuine mistake: despite taking reasonable care	0%	0%	0%
Careless error and inaccuracy are due to failure to take reasonable care	30%	0%	15%
Deliberate error but not concealed	70%	20%	35%
Deliberate error and concealed	100%	30%	50%

Test your understanding answers

 ### Test your understanding 1

Administration

1 True   The filing date is 12 months from the end of the period of account regardless of the length of the accounting period.

2 False The latest date that DEF Ltd can amend its return is 31 March 2023 (i.e. 12 months after the due filing date not the actual filing date).

3 False The immediate penalty for late filing of £100. There can then be additional penalties once the delay exceeds three months.

 ### Test your understanding 2

Russell plc

The correct answer is C.

Explanation

C is the correct answer because even though Russell plc has augmented profits of more than £1,500,000 for the year ended 31 December 2020, it is large for the first time and its profits are below £10 million.

Russell plc did not have augmented profits of more than £1,500,000 in the previous year and therefore (given its profits do not exceed £10 m) will not have to pay instalments for the year ended 31 December 2020.

Russell plc's corporation tax liability will be due within 9 months and 1 day of the end of the accounting period (i.e. by 1 October 2021).

Test your understanding 3

(a) **Space plc**

Projected corporation tax payments – y/e 31 March 2021

Taxable total profits and augmented profits	£2,000,000
Corporation tax liability (at 19%)	£380,000

The accounting period will be subject to quarterly instalments as the company is large and was large in the previous year.

The liability for the year ended 31 March 2021 should be settled by four equal instalments of £95,000 (£380,000 ÷ 4).

		£
Instalment 1	14 October 2020	95,000
Instalment 2	14 January 2021	95,000
Instalment 3	14 April 2021	95,000
Instalment 4	14 July 2021	95,000

(b) **Administrative requirements**

(1) A return, including statutory accounts and computations, must be submitted online by 31 March 2022 (i.e. within 12 months of the accounting period end otherwise penalties will be charged).

(2) Late payments of tax will give rise to interest charges, which will be deductible from non-trade interest income.

KAPLAN PUBLISHING

Test your understanding 4

ABC Ltd

The correct answer is A.

Explanation

ABC Ltd is a large company in the year to 31 March 2021.

It must pay its corporation tax in instalments even though it was not a large company in the year to 31 March 2020. This is because its profits in the year to 31 March 2021 exceed £2 million (i.e. £10 million × 1/5) (in addition to ABC Ltd, there are four 51% group companies so five in total).

The tax is due on:

14 October 2020, 14 January 2021, 14 April 2021 and 14 July 2021.

Test your understanding 5

Wendell plc

Corporation tax liability and payment dates

	£
Corporation tax due:	
Taxable total profits and augmented profits	2,400,000
Corporation tax liability (£2,400,000 × 19%)	456,000
Due date of instalments:	
14 August 2020 (£456,000 × 1/4)	114,000
14 November 2020	114,000
14 February 2021	114,000
14 May 2021	114,000
	456,000

Sole traders and partnerships – principles of taxation

Introduction

In Chapters 2 to 7 we have considered how we tax the profits and gains of one type of business entity – a company.

In the next few chapters we look at how we tax the profits of sole traders and partnerships (unincorporated businesses).

This chapter is an introduction to the main differences in the method of dealing with the tax affairs of these business entities.

CONTENTS

1   Sole trader
2   Partnerships

1 Sole trader

1.1 No separate legal entity

A sole trader is an individual who has set up his/her own business. The business is not a separate legal entity.

1.2 Types of tax payable

The individual who sets up as a sole trader pays:

- income tax, on income including adjusted trading profits, and
- capital gains tax, on chargeable gains.

Example

Which of the following business entities is a sole trader?

(a)   Fred Flint, haulage contractor.

(b)   Fred Flint Ltd, haulage contractor.

Solution

(a)   Fred Flint is a sole trader. Fred pays income tax on his adjusted trading profit and capital gains tax on his gains.

(b)   Fred Flint Ltd is a company (a separate legal entity). The company pays corporation tax on income and gains.

2 Partnerships

2.1 No separate legal entity

A partnership is a group of individuals carrying on in business together. The business is not a separate legal entity.

2.2 Types of tax payable

Each partner individually pays:

- income tax, on his share of the partnership's adjusted trading profit in addition to his other personal income.

A partnership is effectively a collection of sole traders working together, each responsible for his own tax liability.

The allocation of partnership profits is considered further in Chapter 10.

3 Summary

Sole traders and partnerships:

- DO NOT pay corporation tax
- DO pay income tax and capital gains tax
- ARE NOT separate legal entities.

✳ Links to other syllabus areas

Many of the principles you have considered in AVBK and FAPR, when accounting for unincorporated businesses (i.e. sole traders and partnerships), remain highly relevant. The figures used in the financial accounts form the starting point for calculating the base on which tax will be charged, in order to establish the tax adjusted profits of the business concerned.

Taxable trade profits for unincorporated businesses

Introduction

The assessment may include a task that looks at the taxable trading profits of a sole trader or partner (unincorporated businesses).

There are some differences in the computation of adjusted trading profits and capital allowances for unincorporated businesses compared to companies.

ASSESSMENT CRITERIA	CONTENTS
Apply rules relating to deductible and non-deductible expenditure (1.1)	1 Adjusted trading profits for individuals
Classify expenditure as either revenue or capital expenditure (1.1)	2 Adjustment of trading profits
Adjust accounting profit and losses for tax purposes (1.1)	3 Capital allowances for individuals
Identify the types of capital allowances (1.3)	4 Trading allowance
Calculate capital allowances including adjustment for private usage (1.3)	5 Income tax return – self-employment
Accurately complete self-employed tax returns (1.6)	
Know what the badges of trade are and how they evolved (4.3)	

1 Adjusted trading profits for individuals

1.1 Badges of trade

We are now concerned with taxing the profits of a trade of an individual.

Statute law defines a 'trade' as including any venture in the nature of trade. This is not particularly helpful in practice and it has been necessary for the courts to decide in a number of cases whether or not an activity is a trade.

In 1954 a Royal Commission summarised the existing case law relevant to 'trade' by identifying six attributes or 'badges' of trade. These have been further developed over the years by case law, and HMRC now refer to the following nine badges of trade.

- **Profit seeking motive**

  The presence of a profit motive is indicative of a trade.

- **Number of transactions**

  The more frequent a transaction the more likely a trade is being conducted.

- **Nature of asset**

  Assets are generally acquired either for personal use, or as an investment, or as inventory used in a trade (i.e. stock) or as a non-current asset (i.e. fixed asset) used in a trade.

  An investment may be income generating (e.g. shares) or for pleasure (e.g. a painting). If an asset is clearly neither acquired as an investment or for the use of the owner or his/her family or friends, the inference of trading arises.

- **Existence of similar trading transactions or interests**

  If the transaction is similar to an existing trade of the individual it is more likely that it will be held that a trade is being carried out than if the transaction is unrelated.

- **Changes to the asset**

  An asset bought and enhanced in some way before sale is more likely to be a trading asset than a similar asset simply bought and sold without improvement.

- **The way the sale was carried out**

  It can be argued that the forced sale of an asset to relieve a cash flow crisis is less likely to be a disposal in the course of a trade.

- **The source of finance**

  If the purchase of the asset was funded by a loan which is to be paid off on disposal this is an indication of trading.

- **Interval of time between purchase and sale**

  The shorter the period of ownership the more likely this is indicative of a trade.

- **Method of acquisition**

  If the asset was acquired through an inheritance or on a gift the existence of a trade is less likely to be assumed.

Note that these badges are listed in the AAT reference material included in section 8 below.

It is vital to appreciate that no one badge is conclusive. In any set of circumstances some badges may indicate trading whilst others may not.

All factors must be considered and an overall view taken.

 Example

Jameela renovates classic cars as a hobby in her spare time and exhibits them at classic car events. She has accepted the occasional offer to sell and usually makes a profit if the time she has spent is ignored.

Explain whether you think Jameela will be treated as trading in cars by HMRC.

Solution

- The situation has to be measured against the 'badges of trade'.

- A car could be a trading asset or an investment or for personal use so the 'nature of asset' badge is inconclusive.

- If Jameela owns the cars for only a brief period and is constantly buying, renovating and selling, perhaps even advertising, there comes a point where the hobby becomes a trade.

1.2 Professions and vocations

The profits made by a self-employed person from a profession or vocation, such as accountancy, are taxed in the same way as the profits of a trade.

2 Adjustment of trading profits

2.1 Comparison between individuals and companies

The starting point in determining the amount of taxable trading profits is the net profit as shown in the accounts, but this must be adjusted for tax purposes in a similar way to companies.

We have already seen in Chapter 3 in the context of a company how to adjust the accounting profits to find the adjusted trading profits for tax purposes. The first part of this chapter will concentrate on approaching the topic from an individual trader's perspective.

Taxable trading profits for an individual comprise adjusted trading profits (Chapter 3) less capital allowances (Chapter 4) for an accounting period in much the same way as for a company.

This chapter covers the minor adjustments needed to the rules seen earlier in the context of companies.

Outline pro forma for adjustment of profits computation			
	Section	£	£
Net profit per accounts			X
Add: Disallowable expenditure	2.2	X	
Income not included in the accounts but taxable as trading income	2.3	X	
			X
			X
Less: Income included in the accounts but not taxable as trading income	2.4	X	
Expenditure not in the accounts but allowable as a trading deduction	2.5	X	
			(X)
Adjusted trading profit (before deducting capital allowances)			X

The same profit adjustment rules for companies apply for individual (or 'sole') traders but with minor adjustments explained as follows.

Note that the AAT reference material set out in section 8 below lists some of the more common adjustments.

2.2 Disallowable expenditure differences

Adjustments for private expenditure

Any private expenditure of the owner of the business deducted in the accounts should be disallowed. This would include any payment of the trader's income tax or national insurance liabilities.

There will sometimes be an estimated proportion of business use, for example with motor expenses or telephone expenses. If this is the case, only the private element should be disallowed and therefore added back.

Under self-assessment the trader has to be prepared to justify his/her estimate of the private element if HMRC enquire into his/her self-assessment return.

Salary to proprietor

The salary or drawings paid to the owner is the equivalent of a dividend paid by a company. It is an appropriation of profit, not a business expense, and must therefore be added back to profit.

💡 Example

Gordon has his own business as a motor dealer. His accounts for the year ended 31 December 2020 show the following results:

	£	£
Gross profit		80,000
Less: Expenses		
Salaries	30,000	
Motor expenses	3,000	
Allowable expenses	22,000	
		(55,000)
Net profit per accounts		25,000

Included in motor expenses is £1,000 relating to the cost of running Gordon's car which is used 60% for business purposes and included in salaries is Gordon's 'salary' of £20,000.

Calculate Gordon's adjusted trading profit.

Solution

	£
Net profit per accounts	25,000
Add: Disallowable expenses	
Gordon's 'salary'/drawings	20,000
Private motor expenses (£1,000 × 40%)	400
Adjusted trading profit	45,400

Note: Do not add back salaries or private motor expenses of employees. These are allowable expenses for the business (just as they are in a company's computation).

Bad debts/Irrecoverable debts

We saw in Chapter 3 that as companies are required to produce their accounts in accordance with internationally accepted accounting practice, any provisions for irrecoverable debts (bad debts) included within the accounts are specific in nature and therefore allowable for tax purposes.

The accounts of an unincorporated business however are not bound by the Companies Act requirements and therefore may contain *general* provisions which are not allowable for tax purposes.

Movements in general provisions, for example the *general* bad debt provision, are not allowable. An increase in a general provision must be added back, and a decrease in a general provision must be deducted, to arrive at adjusted trading profits.

Movements in *specific* provisions are allowable and do not need adjusting for in calculating the adjusted trading profits.

Note that movements in any other general provisions charged to the statement of profit or loss should also be disallowed (e.g. inventory/stock provisions).

Example

The bad debts account of Gregor, an interior designer, for the year ended 30 June 2020 appears as follows:

	£		£
Written off:		Balance brought down:	
Trade	274	Specific provision	185
Former employee	80	General provision	260
Balance carried down:		Recoveries – trade	23
Specific provision	194	Profit and loss account	305
General provision	225		
	773		773

Show the adjustment required in computing the adjusted trading profit.

Solution

The first stage is to establish a breakdown of the statement of profit or loss charge of £305.

Remember that this figure comprises amounts written off and recovered, and movements in provisions.

Statement of profit or loss charge:

	£	Allowable?
Increase in specific provision (£194 – £185)	9	✓
Decrease in general provision (£225 – £260)	(35)	✗
Trade debt written off	274	✓
Former employee loan written off	80	✗
Recoveries – trade	(23)	✓
	305	

The movement in the general provision and the amount owed by the former employee are both disallowed. In this case, the movement in the general provision is a *decrease, so* the adjustment made is to *deduct* it from the profit per the accounts.

The adjustments required to compute the adjusted trading profit are therefore as follows:

		£
Add:	Former employee, debt written off	80
Less:	Decrease in general provision	(35)

Charitable donations

An unincorporated business may make charitable donations. These fall into three categories:

- Small and to a local charity – allowed as trade expenses.

- Donations via the gift aid scheme – these are not allowed as a trade expense but the trader will get relief for the payment via their personal income tax computation. This relief is not tested in the business tax assessment.

- Other charitable donations – not allowed as a trade expense and no other relief is available.

For a company all charitable donations that are not relieved as trade expenses are given relief as qualifying charitable donations and are deducted from total profits on the face of the corporation tax computation.

2.3 Income not included in the accounts but taxable as trading income

This category does not exist for the adjustment of profits for a company.

The most common example is goods taken by the owner for his/her own use. The proprietor must be taxed on the profit he or she would have made if the goods had been sold at market value (i.e. at retail or wholesale price as appropriate).

If the cost of sales in the statement of profit or loss has not been reduced for the goods taken for own use, then the amount to be added back to arrive at the adjusted profit will be the *selling price*.

If the cost of sales has been reduced by the cost of the goods taken for own use, then the amount added back will be the *profit.*

 Example

Samina operates a toy store and has taken goods for her own use costing £500 during the year ended 31 December 2020. An adjustment has already been made to reflect the cost of the goods taken.

What is the increase to net profit required if:

(a) Samina operates a mark-up basis of pricing of 40%, or alternatively

(b) Samina operates on a gross profit margin of 40%?

Read the requirement carefully in the assessment. These will give different results.

Solution

(a) Mark-up means that the cost of the goods represents 100% and that sales value is therefore 140%.

	%
Sales	140
Less: Cost	(100)
Profit	40

The profit is therefore (40% of £500) = £200.

(b) Where a gross profit margin is supplied, sales represent 100% of the value.

If the profit is 40% of sales then the cost of goods is 60%.

	%
Sales	100
Less: Cost	(60)
Profit	40

Therefore the profit element is (£500 × 40/60) = £333.

  Example

Ragna has taken £500 of goods from inventory. An adjustment has been made in the accounts for the cost of the goods taken.

An extract from the statement of profit or loss shows the following:

	£	£
Sales		450,000
Opening inventory	160,000	
Purchases	210,000	
Closing inventory	(120,000)	
Cost of sales		(250,000)
Gross profit		200,000

Explain the adjustments needed if the net profit shown in the accounts is £90,000.

Solution

The increase to net profit for the profit element of goods for own use must be calculated by reference to the correct relationship between cost and gross profit.

If cost of goods used is £500 and £250,000 of costs generates £200,000 of profit then:

Profit element = £500 × 200/250 = £400

Therefore, the net profit is adjusted as follows:

	£
Net profit	90,000
Add: Increase in profit for goods for own use	400
	_____
Adjusted profit	90,400
	_____

2.4 Income included in the accounts but not taxable as trading income

The following are examples of amounts which may be included in the statement of profit or loss, but which are not taxable as trading income. Hence they should be deducted when calculating taxable trading profits.

- Income taxed in another way (e.g. rent, interest receivable).

- Income exempt from income tax (e.g. interest received on delayed tax repayments).

- Profits on sales of non-current assets.

These adjustments are essentially the same as those for companies.

2.5 Expenditure not in the accounts but allowable

This category of adjustment does not arise for companies.

Any business expense not charged in the accounts but paid for or borne privately by the proprietor can be deducted as a business expense.

For example, where a home telephone is used for business calls the cost of the business calls can be deducted (although it is more common for the whole amount to be charged to the statement of profit or loss, in which case the private portion should be disallowed).

Test your understanding 1

Alphonse (1)

Alphonse is in business as a wine merchant and has prepared accounts to 30 June 2020. His statement of profit or loss was:

	£	£
Sales		183,658
Cost of sales		(119,379)
Gross profit		64,279
Dividend income		300
		64,579
Salaries	9,740	
Rent and business rates	9,860	
Repairs to premises	2,620	
Motor expenses	740	
Depreciation	4,150	
Bad and doubtful debts	6,030	
Sundry expenses	770	
Salary		
– Alphonse	14,000	
– Wife, as secretary	1,450	
		(49,360)
Net profit		15,219

The following information is given:

Repairs to premises	£
Alterations to flooring in order to install new bottling machine	1,460
Redecoration	1,160
	2,620

Bad and doubtful debts account

	£			£
Trade debts written off	1,300	Provision brought forward		
Loan to ex-employee		– General		1,850
written off	400	– Specific		580
Provisions carried forward		Statement of profit or loss		6,030
– General	5,200			
– Specific	1,560			
	8,460			8,460

Sundry expenses

	£
Fine re breach of Customs bonding regulations	250
Subscription to Wine Retail Trade Association	50
Miscellaneous allowable expenses	470
	770

During the year Alphonse had withdrawn goods from inventory for his own consumption. The cost of this inventory was £455. The business makes a uniform gross profit of 35% on selling price. No entry had been made in the books in respect of the goods taken.

Compute Alphonse's adjusted trading profit before capital allowances for the period ended 30 June 2020, giving reasons for the adjustments made.

Note: Reasons for the adjustments are unlikely to be required in the assessment. It is likely that an adjustment of profits question will involve dragging items of expenditure to the appropriate part of the adjustment of profits calculation or choosing the correct adjustment from a few options.

However, understanding why adjustments are made will help you to remember them better.

3 Capital allowances for individuals

3.1 The general rules

The capital allowance rules for plant and machinery have already been explained in detail for companies (Chapter 4). The modifications needed to apply these rules for sole traders are explained below.

3.2 Private use assets

Any item of plant or machinery used partly *by the proprietor/owner* for private purposes, such as a van, must be given a separate column in the capital allowances working. Such assets cannot be covered by a short life asset election.

The AIA, WDA or FYA on the asset is based on its full cost. However, the allowance actually *claimed* will be reduced for private use. Only the proportion relating to business use can be claimed.

Note that if applicable, the business can choose the expenditure against which the AIA is matched. It will be most beneficial for the AIA to be allocated against the general pool expenditure rather than any private use asset as only the business proportion of any AIA available can be claimed.

However, note that in the assessment the assets most commonly used for private purposes are cars, which are not eligible for the AIA.

On disposal, a balancing adjustment will be calculated. However, the balancing adjustment will be similarly reduced for private use. Only the business proportion can be claimed or is taxable.

The following example demonstrates this.

 Example

Gerard is a trader preparing accounts for calendar years.

In May 2020 he bought a motor car for £7,200 which has CO_2 emissions of 105g/km. He sold this car in February 2022 for £5,000 replacing it with a car costing £18,800 which has a CO_2 emission rate of 170g/km.

Gerard uses his cars for both business and private purposes and estimates an 80% business use proportion.

Show the capital allowances and balancing adjustments on the cars for the years ended 31 December 2020, 2021 and 2022.

Assume the rates of allowances for the tax year 2020/21 continue into the future.

Solution

This example involves two private use cars.

Each car will have a separate column, as a private use asset.

The first stage is to calculate the allowances in the normal way. Then multiply these allowances by 80%, the business use proportion, to find the allowances that can be claimed.

On disposal, the balancing allowance or charge will be calculated as usual, and again multiplied by 80% to find the actual amount to be deducted or added back to adjusted trading profits.

The answer is therefore as follows:

Gerard – Capital allowances

	Private use Car 1 £	Private use Car 2 £	Allowances £
Year ended 31 December 2020			
Additions	7,200		
WDA at 18%	(1,296) × 80%		1,037
	———		———
TWDV carried forward	5,904		
Year ended 31 December 2021			
WDA at 18%	(1,063) × 80%		850
	———		———
TWDV carried forward	4,841		
Year ended 31 December 2022			
Additions		18,800	
Disposal proceeds	(5,000)		
	———		
	(159)		
Balancing charge	159 × 80%		(127)
	———		
WDA at 6% (note)		(1,128) × 80%	902
		———	
TWDV carried forward		17,672	
		———	———
Total allowances			775
			———

Note: Gerard's new car has emissions of more than 110g/km and was purchased in an accounting period commencing after 6 April 2019. The rate of WDA is 6%.

Test your understanding 2

Ernest

Ernest prepares accounts to 31 March annually. On 1 April 2020 he had a qualifying general pool balance of plant and machinery brought forward of £24,000.

The following transactions took place in the year to 31 March 2021.

15 April 2020	Purchased car for £16,000 (wholly business usage)
30 April 2020	Sold plant for £3,200 (original cost £4,800)
16 July 2020	Purchased car for £9,200 (wholly business usage)
17 August 2020	Purchased car for £9,400 (30% private usage by Ernest)

In the following year to 31 March 2022, Ernest sold for £8,100 the car originally purchased on 17 August 2020. The car originally purchased on 15 April 2020 was sold for £9,400 on 9 March 2022. There were no other transactions.

All cars purchased had CO_2 emissions between 51 and 110g/km.

Compute the capital allowances and balancing adjustments for the years ended 31 March 2021 and 31 March 2022.

Assume the rates of allowances for the tax year 2020/21 continue into the future.

3.3 The impact of the length of the accounting period (sole traders)

As we have seen, capital allowances are computed for accounting periods and deducted in calculating taxable trading profits.

The writing down allowances calculated so far have all been for 12 month accounting periods.

Where the accounting period is more or less than 12 months long, the AIA WDA and small pools WDA must be scaled up or down accordingly. You must perform this calculation to the nearest month.

Note the important difference between companies and sole traders. A company cannot have an accounting period greater than 12 months, but a sole trader can. Therefore, the allowances are scaled up where there is a long period of account for a sole trader.

Remember however, that first year allowances are given in full regardless of the length of the accounting period. They are never scaled up or down according to the length of the accounting period.

Capital allowances for periods which are not twelve months long are very popular in the assessment and you should always watch out for them.

 Example

Kedarnath started to trade on 1 January 2020, and on that day he purchased three cars for the use of his employees at a total cost of £21,900 and plant which cost £22,000. All the cars had CO_2 emissions of 100g/km.

Calculate the allowances due for his first two accounting periods on the assumption that he prepares his first accounts to:

(i)   31 December 2020

(ii)   31 October 2020

(iii) 31 March 2021

and annually on those dates thereafter.

Assume the rates of allowances for the tax year 2020/21 continue into the future.

Solution

(i)   **First accounts – 12 months to 31 December 2020**

	£	General pool £	Allowances £
12 months to 31 December 2020			
Additions:			
No AIA: Cars		21,900	
Qualifying for AIA:			
Plant	22,000		
AIA	(22,000)		22,000
	———	Nil	
		———	
		21,900	
WDA (18%)		(3,942)	3,942
		———	
TWDV c/f		17,958	
			———
Total allowances			25,942
			———

12 months to 31 December 2021

		General pool £	Allowances £
WDA (18%)		(3,232)	3,232
TWDV c/f		14,726	

(ii) **First accounts – 10 months to 31 October 2020**

	£	General pool £	Allowances £
10 months to 31 October 2020			
Additions:			
No AIA: Cars		21,900	
Qualifying for AIA:			
Plant	22,000		
AIA (Note)	(22,000)		22,000
		Nil	
		21,900	
WDA (18% × 10/12)		(3,285)	3,285
TWDV c/f		18,615	
Total allowances			25,285
12 months to 31 October 2021			
WDA (18%)		(3,351)	3,351
TWDV c/f		15,264	

Note: Maximum AIA = (£1,000,000 × 10/12) = £833,333.

(iii) **First accounts – 15 months to 31 March 2021**

	£	General pool £	Allowances £
15 months to 31 March 2021			
Additions:			
No AIA: Cars		21,900	
Qualifying for AIA:			
Plant	22,000		
AIA (Note)	(22,000)		22,000
	———	Nil	
		———	
		21,900	
WDA (18% × 15/12)		(4,928)	4,928
		———	
TWDV c/f		16,972	
			———
Total allowances			26,928
			———
12 months to 31 March 2022			
WDA (18%)		(3,055)	3,055
		———	———
TWDV c/f		13,917	
		———	

Note: Maximum AIA = (£1,000,000 + (£200,000 × 3/12)) = £1,050,000.

 Test your understanding 3

Anjula commenced trading on 1 May 2020 and prepares her first set of accounts to 31 August 2021.

On 2 June 2020 she purchased equipment costing £2,500 and a car costing £6,200 with carbon dioxide emissions of 105g/km and 100% business use.

What are the capital allowances available for the period ended 31 August 2021?

A   £8,700

B   £3,988

C   £2,088

D   £3,616

4 Trading allowance

4.1 The trading allowance

A trading allowance of £1,000 is available to sole traders (not partnerships).

If a sole trader's trading income (not profit) is no more than £1,000 it is exempt and does not need to be declared.

If a sole trader's trading income is less than £1,000 but trading expenses exceed receipts, the trader can choose not to claim the trading allowance in order to get relief for the trading loss that would arise without the allowance (see Chapter 12 for details).

If a sole trader's trading income is in excess of £1,000 then he/she can choose to deduct the trading allowance from trading income rather than the actual expenses incurred.

 Example

Anahera designs T-shirts in her spare time and sells them online.

Calculate Anahera's assessable trading profit assuming her income and expenses are as follows:

	Income £	Expenses £
(i)	800	350
(ii)	1,100	480
(iii)	500	700

(i) **Income £800 and expenses £350**

As Anahera's income (not profit) is less than £1,000 it is exempt and she will not need to declare it to HMRC.

(ii) **Income £1,100 and expenses £480**

Anahera's income is in excess of £1,000 so she can choose whether to deduct her actual expenses incurred or the trading allowance of £1,000.

	Actual expenses £	Trading allowance £
Income	1,100	1,100
Less: Expenses/trading allowance	(480)	(1,000)
Trading profit	620	100

Deducting the trading allowance gives a lower assessable profit and so this is the method that should be chosen.

(iii) **Income £500 and expenses £700**

Anahera's expenses exceed her income and create a trading loss. If she were to claim the trading allowance she would not receive the benefit of this trading loss.

Anahera should not claim the trading allowance and should deduct her expenses incurred instead to recognise a trading loss of £200.

	£
Income	500
Less: Expenses	(700)
Trading loss	(200)

5 Income tax return – self-employment

5.1 Self-employment supplementary pages

An individual may be required to complete a tax return.

There is a main return (SA100) and several supplementary pages to be completed as appropriate. One of the sets of supplementary pages consists of four pages on self-employment (SA103).

5.2 Page SEF 2

This page records the expenses of the business. The detailed section on expenses need only be completed if the annual turnover of the business is at least £85,000. Otherwise it is only necessary to enter a total expenses figure in Box 31.

- The left hand column includes all expenses shown in the accounts (analysed as appropriate).

- The right hand column shows the disallowable expenditure included within the expenses figures.

It is possible that boxes in both columns could include the same figure; for example, if depreciation in the accounts is £3,000 then:

- Box 29 will show £3,000, and

- Box 44 will show £3,000.

Usually the boxes will show different figures; for example, if wages and salaries of £50,000 included the owner's drawings of £20,000 then:

- Box 19 will show £50,000, and

- Box 34 will show £20,000.

Note that this page **only** records expenses and does not include adjustments for:

- goods for own use

- income included in the accounts but not taxable as trading income

- capital allowances.

The following is important in connection with the completion of forms in the assessment.

- When completing the form in the assessment, figures must be entered in the correct boxes.

- You will be asked to complete just one page of any form.

- Commas need not be entered for numbers of four digits or more.

- You do not need to fill in every box, only relevant ones.

Business expenses

Please read the 'Self-employment (full) notes' before filling in this section.

Total expenses	Disallowable expenses
If your annual turnover was below £85,000, you may just put your total expenses in box 31	Use this column if the figures in boxes 17 to 30 include disallowable amounts

17 Cost of goods bought for resale or goods used

£ · 0 0

32

£ · 0 0

18 Construction industry – payments to subcontractors

£ · 0 0

33

£ · 0 0

19 Wages, salaries and other staff costs

£ · 0 0

34

£ · 0 0

20 Car, van and travel expenses

£ · 0 0

35

£ · 0 0

21 Rent, rates, power and insurance costs

£ · 0 0

36

£ · 0 0

22 Repairs and maintenance of property and equipment

£ · 0 0

37

£ · 0 0

23 Phone, fax, stationery and other office costs

£ · 0 0

38

£ · 0 0

24 Advertising and business entertainment costs

£ · 0 0

39

£ · 0 0

25 Interest on bank and other loans

£ · 0 0

40

£ · 0 0

26 Bank, credit card and other financial charges

£ · 0 0

41

£ · 0 0

27 Irrecoverable debts written off

£ · 0 0

42

£ · 0 0

28 Accountancy, legal and other professional fees

£ · 0 0

43

£ · 0 0

29 Depreciation and loss/profit on sale of assets

£ · 0 0

44

£ · 0 0

30 Other business expenses

£ · 0 0

45

£ · 0 0

31 Total expenses (total of boxes 17 to 30)

£ · 0 0

46 Total disallowable expenses (total of boxes 32 to 45)

£ · 0 0

SA103F 2020, page 2, HMRC

Test your understanding 4

Alphonse (2)

Complete page 2 of the self-employment supplementary pages (below) for the relevant expenses for Alphonse in test your understanding 1.

Business expenses
Please read the 'Self-employment (full) notes' before filling in this section.

Total expenses	Disallowable expenses
If your annual turnover was below £85,000, you may just put your total expenses in box 31	Use this column if the figures in boxes 17 to 30 include disallowable amounts
17 Cost of goods bought for resale or goods used	32
£ · 0 0	£ · 0 0
18 Construction industry – payments to subcontractors	33
£ · 0 0	£ · 0 0
19 Wages, salaries and other staff costs	34
£ · 0 0	£ · 0 0
20 Car, van and travel expenses	35
£ · 0 0	£ · 0 0
21 Rent, rates, power and insurance costs	36
£ · 0 0	£ · 0 0
22 Repairs and maintenance of property and equipment	37
£ · 0 0	£ · 0 0
23 Phone, fax, stationery and other office costs	38
£ · 0 0	£ · 0 0
24 Advertising and business entertainment costs	39
£ · 0 0	£ · 0 0
25 Interest on bank and other loans	40
£ · 0 0	£ · 0 0
26 Bank, credit card and other financial charges	41
£ · 0 0	£ · 0 0
27 Irrecoverable debts written off	42
£ · 0 0	£ · 0 0
28 Accountancy, legal and other professional fees	43
£ · 0 0	£ · 0 0
29 Depreciation and loss/profit on sale of assets	44
£ · 0 0	£ · 0 0
30 Other business expenses	45
£ · 0 0	£ · 0 0
31 Total expenses (total of boxes 17 to 30)	46 Total disallowable expenses (total of boxes 32 to 45)
£ · 0 0	£ · 0 0

SA103F 2020, page 2, HMRC

6 Test your understanding

 Test your understanding 5

Patrick

Patrick is a self-employed businessman. The following expenses are charged in Patrick's statement of profit or loss for the year to 31 December 2020:

	£	✓ or ✗
Patrick's business travelling expenses	5,175	
Christmas presents for staff	250	
Entertaining overseas suppliers	2,750	
Entertaining UK customers	2,300	
Gifts to customers that carry the business name:		
– Boxes of chocolates costing £5.00 each	125	
– Calendars costing £1.50 each	150	
Donation to national charity	50	
Donation to local political party	100	
Subscription to chamber of commerce	25	
A gift to a member of staff upon marriage	45	
Patrick's squash club subscription	250	
Advertising in trade press	280	

Patrick often uses his squash club as a place to take customers since several of them are keen squash players.

Mark each expense with either a ✓ (if the expense is allowable and requires no adjustment) or ✗ (if the expense is disallowable and must be added back).

Test your understanding 6

Georgina

Georgina runs a business which she started on 1 September 2020 and prepares her first set of accounts to 31 May 2021.

On 1 October 2020, she purchased a car with CO_2 emissions of 107g/km for £10,500 which she uses 30% for business purposes.

What are the capital allowances available to her for the period ended 31 May 2021?

A   £567

B   £1,418

C   £1,890

D   £425

 Test your understanding 7

Adam

Adam's business accounts for the year to 31 March 2021 include the following items.

For each item state what adjustments, if any, are required?

1   Motor expenses for a car used by an employee, private use estimated at 30%.

2   Motor expenses for a car used by Adam, private use estimated at 30%.

3   Overdraft interest on the business bank account.

4   Bank interest received on the business deposit account.

5   Goods taken by Adam which he paid for at cost.

The choices available are:

A   None

B   Add back full amount

C   Deduct full amount

D   Add back 30%

E   Add back selling price

F   Add back profit

Test your understanding 8

Manuel (1)

Manuel is a self-employed wholesale clothing distributor. His summarised accounts for the year ended 30 June 2020 are as follows:

	£	£
Sales		400,000
Opening inventory	40,000	
Purchases	224,000	
	264,000	
Closing inventory	(32,000)	
Cost of sales		(232,000)
Gross profit		168,000
Wages and National Insurance (Note 1)	84,655	
Motor car running expenses (Manuel's car) (Note 2)	2,000	
Lighting and heating	4,250	
Rent and business rates	31,060	
Repairs and renewals (all allowable)	3,490	
Legal expenses (Note 3)	1,060	
Depreciation	3,510	
Sundry expenses (all allowable)	5,770	
		(135,795)
Net profit		32,205

Notes to the accounts

(1) Wages

Included in wages are Manuel's drawings of £300 per week, his National Insurance contributions of £159 for the year and wages and National Insurance contributions in respect of his wife totalling £11,750. His wife worked full-time in the business as a secretary.

(2) Motor car running expenses

Manuel estimates that one-third of his mileage is private. Included in the charge is £65 for a speeding fine incurred by Manuel whilst delivering goods to a customer.

(3) Legal expenses

	£
Defending action in respect of alleged faulty goods	330
Defending Manuel in connection with speeding offence	640
Debt collection	90
	1,060

(4) Capital allowances on plant and machinery for the year to 30 June 2020 are £2,480.

Calculate the taxable trade profits for the accounting period to 30 June 2020.

Test your understanding 9

Manuel (2)

Following on from test your understanding 8, you are required to complete page SEF 2 (disallowable expenses) for Manuel's tax return for the tax year 2020/21.

Business expenses

Please read the 'Self-employment (full) notes' before filling in this section.

Total expenses

If your annual turnover was below £85,000, you may just put your total expenses in box 31

Disallowable expenses

Use this column if the figures in boxes 17 to 30 include disallowable amounts

17 Cost of goods bought for resale or goods used £ · 0 0
32 £ · 0 0

18 Construction industry – payments to subcontractors £ · 0 0
33 £ · 0 0

19 Wages, salaries and other staff costs £ · 0 0
34 £ · 0 0

20 Car, van and travel expenses £ · 0 0
35 £ · 0 0

21 Rent, rates, power and insurance costs £ · 0 0
36 £ · 0 0

22 Repairs and maintenance of property and equipment £ · 0 0
37 £ · 0 0

23 Phone, fax, stationery and other office costs £ · 0 0
38 £ · 0 0

24 Advertising and business entertainment costs £ · 0 0
39 £ · 0 0

25 Interest on bank and other loans £ · 0 0
40 £ · 0 0

26 Bank, credit card and other financial charges £ · 0 0
41 £ · 0 0

27 Irrecoverable debts written off £ · 0 0
42 £ · 0 0

28 Accountancy, legal and other professional fees £ · 0 0
43 £ · 0 0

29 Depreciation and loss/profit on sale of assets £ · 0 0
44 £ · 0 0

30 Other business expenses £ · 0 0
45 £ · 0 0

31 Total expenses (total of boxes 17 to 30) £ · 0 0
46 Total disallowable expenses (total of boxes 32 to 45) £ · 0 0

SA103F 2020, page 2, HMRC

KAPLAN PUBLISHING

Test your understanding 10

Freda

Freda supplies furniture and furnishings. Her summarised accounts for the year ended 31 December 2020 are as follows:

	£	£
Sales of furniture and furnishings (Note 1)		300,000
Cost of sales		(200,000)
		100,000
Design fees		85,000
Gross profit		185,000
Wages and National Insurance (Note 2)	75,000	
Rent and business rates	18,250	
Miscellaneous expenses (all allowable)	12,710	
Taxation (Freda's income tax)	15,590	
Depreciation	2,540	
Lease rental on car (Freda's car) (Notes 3 and 4)	8,400	
Motor car running expenses (Freda's car) (Note 4)	2,500	
Lighting and heating	1,750	
		(136,740)
Net profit		48,260

Notes to the accounts

(1) Cost of sales has been reduced by £1,000 reimbursed by Freda for furnishings taken from inventory. This reimbursement represented cost price.

(2) Wages include Freda's drawings of £1,000 per month and her National Insurance contributions of £159 for the year.

(3) A lease for a BMW for Freda (list price £50,000, CO_2 emissions 150g/km) was entered into on 1 July 2020.

(4) Freda estimates that one-half of her mileage is private.

(5) Capital allowances for the year to 31 December 2020 are £1,200.

Calculate the taxable trade profits for the year ended 31 December 2020.

Test your understanding 11

Hudson

Hudson has been carrying on a manufacturing business in a South London suburb since 1 April 2015 preparing accounts to 31 March each year.

He decided to retire on 31 October 2021, and drew up his final set of accounts for the 7-month period to 31 October 2021.

The balance on the general capital allowances pool as at 1 April 2020 was £6,500.

The following plant was acquired for cash on the dates shown:

1 May 2020	New plant costing	£10,858
1 June 2020	Second-hand plant costing	£1,000

On 10 July 2020, Hudson bought a car costing £16,000 through his business. Three-quarters of his usage of the car was for business purposes and one-quarter for private purposes. The car has CO_2 emissions of 105g/km.

No sale of plant took place during these periods, but at 31 October 2021, when the business closed down, all the plant was sold for £2,450 (no one item realising more than its original cost), and the motor car was disposed of to a dealer, who gave Hudson £14,000 for it.

Calculate the capital allowances for Hudson for the final two accounting periods to 31 October 2021.

Assume the rates of allowances for the tax year 2020/21 continue into the future.

Test your understanding 12

Etta

Etta prepares accounts to 31 March annually. In the year to 31 March 2021, she bought three cars for use in her business as follows:

11 May 2020	Purchased car for £17,000 (wholly business usage)
21 June 2020	Purchased car for £8,800 (wholly business usage)
16 September 2020	Purchased car for £11,600 (30% private usage by Etta)

All the cars have CO_2 emissions between 51 and 110g/km.

She had never previously acquired any plant and machinery for her business.

In the following year to 31 March 2022, Etta sold for £9,700 the car originally purchased on 16 September 2020. The car originally purchased on 11 May 2020 was sold for £10,000 on 12 June 2021. There were no other transactions.

Compute the capital allowances and balancing adjustments for the years ended 31 March 2021 and 31 March 2022.

Assume the rates of allowances for the tax year 2020/21 continue into the future.

Test your understanding 13

Raj

On 1 May 2020, Raj began a small manufacturing business in a rented factory.

He subsequently purchased the following machinery:

		£
2 November 2020	Machinery	20,000
1 February 2021	Car (20% private use by Raj with CO_2 emissions 180g/km)	16,000
1 February 2021	New tool grinder	6,000
2 October 2021	Car for salesman (with CO_2 emissions 102g/km)	11,600

Accounts are prepared to 31 March in each year.

Compute the capital allowances for each accounting period up to 31 March 2022.

Assume the rates of allowances for the tax year 2020/21 continue into the future.

 Test your understanding 14

Asha commenced trade on 1 November 2018 making her accounts up for the period to 30 April 2020. During this period she made the following acquisitions for her business:

		£
1 November 2018	Machinery	40,000
1 February 2019	Car (60% business use by Asha with CO_2 emissions 155g/km)	16,000
1 December 2019	Plant	280,000

Compute the capital allowances for the accounting period to 30 April 2020.

Test your understanding 15

Meg receives trading income of £1,555 in the tax year 2020/21. Her allowable expenses are £500 for the tax year.

Calculate Meg's taxable trading income for the tax year 2020/21 assuming all beneficial elections are made.

7 Summary

Sole traders must adjust their accounting profits in the same way as companies:

- add back disallowable expenditure
- deduct allowable expenditure which is not shown in the accounts
- deduct income shown in the accounts not taxable as trading income
- add income taxable as trading income which is not shown in the accounts.

The main adjustments applying to individuals but not companies are the disallowance of the proprietor's salary and private expenses, and the adjustment of goods taken for the proprietor's own use.

Capital allowances are then deducted from the adjusted trading profits to give the taxable trading profits. The capital allowances must be restricted for the proprietor's own use of business assets.

A trading allowance is available which means sole traders with trading income of no more than £1,000 do not have to declare income or pay tax on it.

 Links to other syllabus areas

In AVBK in particular you saw how to account for many transactions relevant to sole traders, for example the extraction of profits by way of drawings and taking goods out of the business for one's own use.

Since the accounts form the basis of the figure which is going to be used for tax purposes, your prior knowledge in terms of understanding how such transactions are accounted for is important when it comes to consideration of the tax treatment.

8   AAT reference material

The badges of trade

Badges of Trade

- Profit seeking motive
- Number of transactions
- Nature of asset
- Existence of similar trading transactions or interests
- Changes to the asset
- The way the sale was carried out
- The source of finance
- Interval of time between purchase and sale
- Method of acquisition

Adjustment of profits – sole traders, partnerships and companies

Pro forma for adjustment of profits

	£	£
Net profit as per accounts		X
Add: Expenses charged in the accounts that are not allowable as trading expenses	X	
		X
		X
Less: Income included in the accounts which is not assessable as trading income	X	
		(X)
Adjusted profit/(loss)		X

Disallowed expenses

- Expenses that fail the remoteness test so not "wholly and exclusively" for trading purposes.

- Fines on the business or fraud by directors/owners.

- Donations to charity are generally disallowed in calculating trading profits (however qualifying charitable donations are deductible in the corporation tax computation).

- Political donations are never allowable.

- Capital expenditure, e.g. purchase of equipment included in profit and loss account.

- Depreciation. Capital allowances granted instead.

- Costs of bringing newly acquired second-hand assets to useable condition.

- Legal and professional expenses relating to capital items or breaking the law.

- Customer entertaining. Staff entertaining can be allowable.

- Customer gifts, unless gift incorporates business advertising, cost is less than £50 per annum per customer, and gift is not food, drink, tobacco or cash vouchers.

Non-assessable income

- Income taxed in any other way, e.g. interest or property income for individuals.

- Profits on sale of fixed assets.

Unincorporated businesses – trading income

Trading income calculated for each period of account:

		£
Adjusted accounting profit		X
Less:	Capital allowances	(X)
Less:	Balancing allowances	(X)
Plus:	Balancing charges	X
Trading income for the period of account		X

Expenses charged in the accounts which are not allowable as trading expenses

- See adjustment of profits – sole traders, partnerships and companies.
- Transactions with the owner of the business. For example:
  - Add back salary paid to owner. Salaries paid to family members do not need to be added back.
  - Private expenditure included in accounts.
  - Class 2 and Class 4 National Insurance contributions.
  - Goods taken for own use.

Unincorporated businesses – private use assets

- Private use assets have separate column in Capital Allowance computation.
- Disallow private use % of WDA/AIA/FYA.

Capital allowances – business cessation

- In the cessation period of account, no WDA/AIA/FYA.
- Include additions and disposals as normal. Any asset taken over by owner, treat as a disposal at market value. Balancing adjustment made (balancing charge or balancing allowance).

Test your understanding answers

 Test your understanding 1

Alphonse (1)

Adjusted trading profit for 12 months ended 30 June 2020

Expenditure charged but not allowable

Most of the required adjustments will be under this heading.

Start at the top of the statement of profit or loss and work down considering the admissibility of each item in turn and reading any relevant notes.

Do not flit from item to item at random since this is a sure way to overlook something.

If you do not know for certain whether any particular item is allowable or not, do not waste time thinking too much about it – take an informed guess; more often than not you will guess right.

Remember the main rule of allowability – the expenditure must be 'incurred wholly and exclusively for the purposes of the trade', in this case the trade of a wine merchant.

The adjustments under this heading are as follows:

	£	Reason
Net profit per accounts	15,219	
Repairs to premises – floor alterations	1,460	Capital cost
Depreciation	4,150	Capital cost
Bad and doubtful debts		
General provision increase	3,350	An appropriation
Loan to ex-employee written off	400	Not wholly and exclusively
Sundry expenses		
Fine	250	Not wholly and exclusively
Salary – Alphonse	14,000	Appropriation

Notes:

(1)   A company could treat the ex-employee loan write-off as a non-trade interest expense under the loan relationship rules. No such relief is available for a sole trader incurring a similar loss.

(2)   It is assumed that Alphonse's wife's salary can be justified as a business expense.

Income credited but not taxable as trading income

It is fairly likely that all credit items will either be assessed as a type of non-trading income or will be capital items or will not be taxable.

The adjustment under this heading is as follows:

	£	**Reason**
Dividend income	300	Taxed as dividend income

Income not credited but assessable

An adjustment under this heading will normally arise because goods have been taken for the proprietor's own use. Legal precedent has established that this 'sale' is to be brought to account for tax purposes at full market price, i.e. (£455 × 100/65) = £700.

The £700 will be an addition to the profits per the accounts in calculating adjusted trading profits, i.e. an adjustment on the plus side of the computation.

Alphonse

Adjustment of profits for 12 months ended 30 June 2020

	+ £	− £
Net profit per accounts	15,219	
Repairs – alterations to flooring	1,460	
Depreciation	4,150	
Bad and doubtful debts		
General provision increase	3,350	
Loan to ex-employee written off	400	
Sundry expenses		
Fine	250	
Salary – Alphonse	14,000	
Dividends		300
Goods withdrawn by Alphonse (£455 × 100/65)	700	
	39,529	300
	(300)	——
Adjusted trading profit (before capital allowances)	39,229	

Test your understanding 2

Ernest

Capital allowances computation – plant and machinery

	General pool £	Private use asset £		Allowances £
Year ended 31 March 2021				
TWDV b/f at 1 April 2020	24,000			
Additions: No AIA				
Cars				
15 April 2020	16,000			
16 July 2020	9,200			
17 August 2020		9,400		
Disposals				
30 April 2020	(3,200)			
	46,000			
WDA (18%)	(8,280)	(1,692)	× 70%	9,464
TWDV c/f	37,720	7,708		
Total allowances				9,464
Year ended 31 March 2022				
Disposals				
Car proceeds	(9,400)	(8,100)		
		(392)		
Balancing charge		392	× 70%	(274)
	28,320			
WDA (18%)	(5,098)			5,098
TWDV at 31 March 2022	23,222			
Total allowances				4,824

Test your understanding 3

Anjula

The correct answer is B.

Explanation

B is the correct answer because:

- the equipment attracts 100% AIA. As this accounting period both straddles 1 January 2021 and is more than 12 months long the maximum AIA is £800,000 (£1,000,000 × 8/12 + £200,000 × 8/12). The expenditure is less than this so will be covered in full by the AIA.

- the car attracts a WDA of 18% multiplied by 16/12 as the first accounting period is 16 months long.

The calculation is therefore:

	£
AIA	2,500
WDA (£6,200 × 18% × 16/12)	1,488
	———
Total allowances	3,988
	———

Test your understanding 4

Alphonse (2)

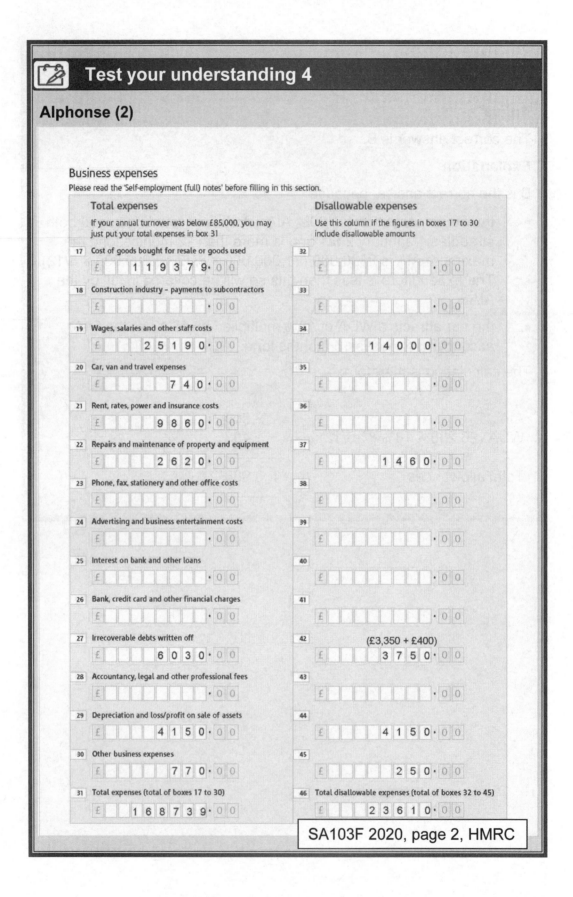

Business expenses

Please read the 'Self-employment (full) notes' before filling in this section.

Total expenses	Disallowable expenses
If your annual turnover was below £85,000, you may just put your total expenses in box 31	Use this column if the figures in boxes 17 to 30 include disallowable amounts
17 Cost of goods bought for resale or goods used £ 119379·00	**32** £ ·00
18 Construction industry – payments to subcontractors £ ·00	**33** £ ·00
19 Wages, salaries and other staff costs £ 25190·00	**34** £ 14000·00
20 Car, van and travel expenses £ 740·00	**35** £ ·00
21 Rent, rates, power and insurance costs £ 9860·00	**36** £ ·00
22 Repairs and maintenance of property and equipment £ 2620·00	**37** £ 1460·00
23 Phone, fax, stationery and other office costs £ ·00	**38** £ ·00
24 Advertising and business entertainment costs £ ·00	**39** £ ·00
25 Interest on bank and other loans £ ·00	**40** £ ·00
26 Bank, credit card and other financial charges £ ·00	**41** £ ·00
27 Irrecoverable debts written off £ 6030·00	**42** (£3,350 + £400) £ 3750·00
28 Accountancy, legal and other professional fees £ ·00	**43** £ ·00
29 Depreciation and loss/profit on sale of assets £ 4150·00	**44** £ 4150·00
30 Other business expenses £ 770·00	**45** £ 250·00
31 Total expenses (total of boxes 17 to 30) £ 168739·00	**46** Total disallowable expenses (total of boxes 32 to 45) £ 23610·00

SA103F 2020, page 2, HMRC

Test your understanding 5

Patrick

The correct answer is:

	£	✓ or ✗
Patrick's business travelling expenses	5,175	✓
Christmas presents for staff	250	✓
Entertaining overseas suppliers	2,750	✗
Entertaining UK customers	2,300	✗
Gifts to customers that carry the business name:		
– Boxes of chocolates costing £5.00 each	125	✗
– Calendars costing £1.50 each	150	✓
Donation to national charity	50	✗
Donation to local political party	100	✗
Subscription to chamber of commerce	25	✓
A gift to a member of staff upon marriage	45	✓
Patrick's squash club subscription	250	✗
Advertising in trade press	280	✓

✓ = allowable   ✗ = add back as disallowable expense

Test your understanding 6

Georgina

The correct answer is D.

Explanation

D is the correct answer because the car attracts a WDA at 18%, proportionately reduced for the short 9-month accounting period and adjusted for private use, as follows:

9 months ended 31 May 2021	Private use car		Allowances
	£		£
Addition – no AIA	10,500		
WDA (18% × 9/12)	(1,418)	× 30%	425
TWDV c/f	9,082		

Test your understanding 7

Adam

The correct answers are as follows:

1   A   These are fully allowable from the business point of view and, as they have already been deducted in the accounts, no adjustment is required. The employee may be assessed on the private use as a taxable benefit.

2   D   30% of the motor expenses should be added back as the private use is by the owner of the business.

3   A   This is an allowable trade expense and, as it has already been deducted in the accounts, no adjustment is required.

4   C   Bank interest is not taxed as trading profits, therefore deduct in full.

5   F   Add back the profit that would have been made had Adam paid the full selling price.

 Test your understanding 8

Manuel (1)

Adjustment of profits for 12 months ended 30 June 2020

	£
Net profit per accounts	32,205
Manuel's drawings (£300 × 52)	15,600
Manuel's NIC	159
Speeding fine	65
Motor expenses (1/3 of balance) (£2,000 – £65) × 1/3	645
Legal expenses in connection with speeding offence	640
Depreciation	3,510
	52,824
Less: Capital allowances	(2,480)
Taxable trade profits	50,344

Test your understanding 9

Manuel (2)

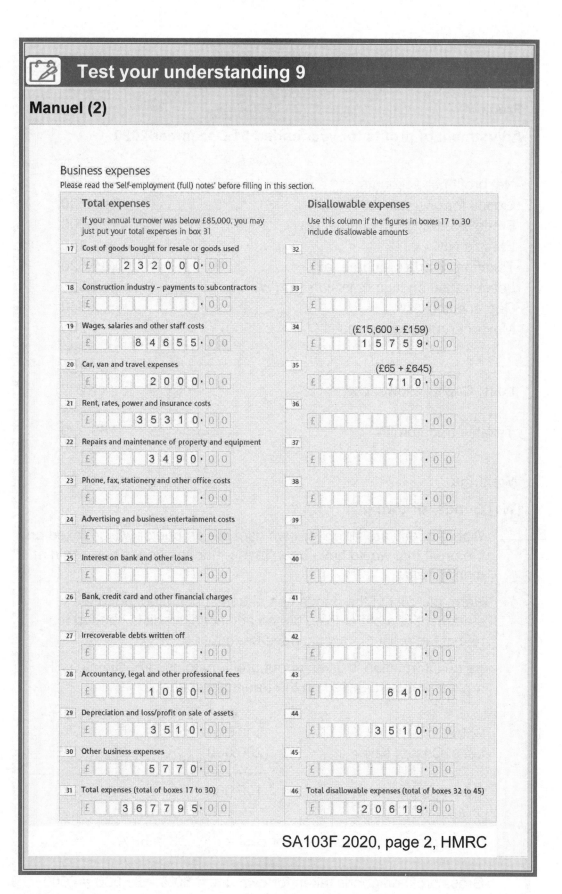

Business expenses

Please read the 'Self-employment (full) notes' before filling in this section.

Total expenses	Disallowable expenses
If your annual turnover was below £85,000, you may just put your total expenses in box 31	Use this column if the figures in boxes 17 to 30 include disallowable amounts

17 Cost of goods bought for resale or goods used

£ 2 3 2 0 0 0 · 0 0

32

£ · 0 0

18 Construction industry – payments to subcontractors

£ · 0 0

33

£ · 0 0

19 Wages, salaries and other staff costs

£ 8 4 6 5 5 · 0 0

34 (£15,600 + £159)

£ 1 5 7 5 9 · 0 0

20 Car, van and travel expenses

£ 2 0 0 0 · 0 0

35 (£65 + £645)

£ 7 1 0 · 0 0

21 Rent, rates, power and insurance costs

£ 3 5 3 1 0 · 0 0

36

£ · 0 0

22 Repairs and maintenance of property and equipment

£ 3 4 9 0 · 0 0

37

£ · 0 0

23 Phone, fax, stationery and other office costs

£ · 0 0

38

£ · 0 0

24 Advertising and business entertainment costs

£ · 0 0

39

£ · 0 0

25 Interest on bank and other loans

£ · 0 0

40

£ · 0 0

26 Bank, credit card and other financial charges

£ · 0 0

41

£ · 0 0

27 Irrecoverable debts written off

£ · 0 0

42

£ · 0 0

28 Accountancy, legal and other professional fees

£ 1 0 6 0 · 0 0

43

£ 6 4 0 · 0 0

29 Depreciation and loss/profit on sale of assets

£ 3 5 1 0 · 0 0

44

£ 3 5 1 0 · 0 0

30 Other business expenses

£ 5 7 7 0 · 0 0

45

£ · 0 0

31 Total expenses (total of boxes 17 to 30)

£ 3 6 7 7 9 5 · 0 0

46 Total disallowable expenses (total of boxes 32 to 45)

£ 2 0 6 1 9 · 0 0

SA103F 2020, page 2, HMRC

Test your understanding 10

Freda

Adjustment of profits for year ended 31 December 2020

	£
Net profit per accounts	48,260
Goods for own use (W1)	500
Freda's drawings (£1,000 × 12)	12,000
Freda's NIC	159
Taxation (Freda's income tax)	15,590
Lease rental on high emission car (W2)	4,830
Depreciation	2,540
Motor car running expenses (1/2 × £2,500)	1,250
	85,129
Less: Capital allowances	(1,200)
Taxable trade profits	83,929

Workings

(W1) Goods for own use

Where goods are taken for own use, the proprietor will be taxed on the profit that would have been made, had the goods been sold at market value.

Here, the cost of the goods has already been credited to the statement of profit or loss, but an additional credit is needed to reflect the profit that would have been made.

As no information is given about profit margins, an estimate will have to be used, based on the trading account.

	£
Sales	300,000
Less: Cost of sales	(200,000)
Gross profit	100,000

Gross profit as a percentage of cost = $\frac{100,000}{200,000}$ = 50%

Gross profit on goods taken for own use = 50% × £1,000 = £500

(W2) Lease rental on high emission car

Amount to be disallowed is 15% of hire charges:

Disallowed amount = 15% × £8,400 = £1,260

The car is also used privately so in addition to the disallowable amount calculated above, the private use element of the balance must also be disallowed.

Balance of expenditure £8,400 − £1,260 = £7,140

Private use element £7,140 × 1/2 = £3,570

Total amount disallowed:

	£
High emission element	1,260
Private use element	3,570
	4,830

Alternative calculation:

Amount allowed = (£8,400 × 85% × 50%) = £3,570

Amount to be added back = (£8,400 − £3,570) = £4,830

Test your understanding 11

Hudson

Capital allowances computation

	General pool £	Private use asset £	Allowances £
	£	£	£
Year ended 31 March 2021			
TWDV b/f	6,500		
Addition – No AIA		16,000	
Addition qualifying for AIA:			
– New plant	10,858		
– Second-hand plant	1,000		
	———		
	11,858		
AIA (Note 1)	(11,858)		11,858
	———		
	Nil		
WDA @ 18%	(1,170)	(2,880) × 75%	3,330
	———	———	
TWDV c/f	5,330	13,120	
			———
Total allowances			15,188
			———
7 months ended 31 Oct 2021			
Disposal proceeds	(2,450)	(14,000)	
	———		
Balancing allowance	2,880		2,880
	———	———	
Balancing charge		(880) × 75%	(660)
		———	———
Total allowances			2,220
			———

Notes:

(1) The year ended 31 March 2021 straddles 1 January 2021 so the maximum AIA available is £800,000 (£1,000,000 × 9/12) + (£200,000 × 3/12)

(2) No WDAs are given in the final accounting period.

Test your understanding 12

Etta

Capital allowances computation

	General pool	Private use asset	Allowances
	£	£	£
Year ended 31 March 2021			
Additions not qualifying for AIA			
11 May 2020	17,000		
21 June 2020	8,800		
16 September 2020		11,600	
	25,800		
WDA (18% × £25,800)	(4,644)		4,644
WDA (18% × 11,600) (Note 1)		(2,088)	1,462
TWDV c/f	21,156	9,512	
Total allowances			6,106
Year ended 31 March 2022			
Disposals	(10,000)	(9,700)	
	11,156	(188)	
Balancing charge (Note 2)		188	(132)
WDA (18% × £11,156)	(2,008)		2,008
TWDV c/f	9,148		
Total allowances			1,876

Notes:

(1) Business portion of WDA = (£2,088 × 70%) = £1,462

(2) Business portion of charge = (£188 × 70%) = £132

Test your understanding 13

Raj

Capital allowances computation

	£	General pool £	Private use asset £	Allowances £
11 m/e 31 March 2021				
Additions not qualifying for AIA				
Car			16,000	
Additions qualifying for AIA				
Machinery	20,000			
Tool grinder	6,000			
	26,000			
AIA (Note 1)	(26,000)			26,000
		Nil		
WDA (6% × 11/12 × £16,000)			(880) × 80%	704
TWDV c/f		Nil	15,120	
Total allowances				26,704
Year ended 31 March 2022				
Additions not qualifying for AIA				
Car		11,600		
		11,600		
WDA (18% × £11,600)		(2,088)		2,088
WDA (6% × £15,120)			(907) × 80%	726
TWDV c/f		9,512	14,213	
Total allowances				2,814

Notes:

(1) The period ended 31 March 2021 straddles 1 January 2021 so the maximum AIA available is £716,667 (£1,000,000 × 8/12 + £200,000 × 3/12)

(2) As all accounting periods start after 6 April 2019 the WDA for Raj's car is 6% p.a.

Test your understanding 14

Asha

Capital allowances computation

	£	General pool £	Private use asset £	Allowances £
18 m/e 30 April 2020				
Additions not qualifying for AIA				
Car			16,000	
Additions qualifying for AIA				
Machinery	40,000			
Plant	280,000			
	320,000			
AIA (Note 1)	(320,000)			320,000
		Nil		
WDA (9.83% × £16,000) (Note 2)			(1,573) × 60%	944
TWDV c/f		Nil	14,427	
Total allowances				320,944

Notes:

(1) The period ended 30 April 2020 straddles 1 January 2019 so the maximum AIA available is £1,366,667 (£200,000 × 2/12) + (£1,000,000 × 16/12)

(2) As the accounting period straddles 6 April 2019 a hybrid WDA must be used for Asha's car as this has emissions exceeding 110g/km. The appropriate WDA is calculated as (8% × 5/12) + (6% × 13/12) = 9.83%.

Test your understanding 15

Meg

Trading income computation

	£
Tax year 2020/21	
Income	1,555
Less: Trading allowance	(1,000)
Taxable trading income	555

Meg should elect to use the trading allowance as her income is over £1,000 and the allowance exceeds her actual expenses.

Partnership profit allocation

Introduction

Some of the tasks in the assessment will relate to either a sole trader or a partnership (i.e. an unincorporated business).

Both are given the same tax treatment with one extra step for partnerships, which is covered in this chapter.

ASSESSMENT CRITERIA	CONTENTS
Apportion profits between a maximum of four partners (1.4)	1 Allocation of profits
	2 Change in profit sharing arrangements
Allocate profits between the partners (1.4)	3 Partnership changes
	4 Partnership interest income
Accurately complete partnership tax returns (1.6)	5 Partnership tax return

1 Allocation of profits

1.1 Computation of taxable trade profits

There is no difference between a sole trader and a partnership when applying the rules for computing the adjustment of the profits of a partnership.

A partnership is merely treated for tax purposes as a collection of sole traders.

Each partner is assessed on his/her share of partnership profits as if he/she were a sole trader earning those profits.

1.2 Division of profits between partners

Profits are allocated according to the profit sharing arrangements during the *accounting period* in which profits are earned.

 Example

Andrew and Bernard have been in business for many years, drawing up their accounts to 31 December each year, and sharing profits in the ratio of 2:1.

The partnership's taxable trade profits for the year ended 31 December 2020 were £37,500.

Show how these profits are allocated to partners.

Solution

Year ended 31 December 2020	Total	Andrew	Bernard
Profits split (2:1)	£37,500	£25,000	£12,500

Test your understanding 1

John and Kyle

John and Kyle began in partnership on 6 April 2020 and have taxable trading profits for the year to 5 April 2021 of £24,047.

They have agreed to share profits and losses in the ratio of 3:2.

Calculate each partner's share of the taxable profits for the year ended 5 April 2021.

Some partnership agreements specify that one or more partners will receive a salary to reflect their work in the partnership or interest on the capital they have invested in the partnership. These are ways of apportioning profits and must be allocated to the respective partners before the balance of profits. The example below considers this further:

 Example

Fatma, Caroline, Nathan and Gita started in business on 1 January 2020. They shared profits as follows:

Interest on fixed capital	10%

Salaries

Fatma	£3,000 per annum
Caroline	£4,000 per annum
Nathan	£4,000 per annum
Gita	£3,000 per annum

Share of balance

Fatma	50%
Caroline	20%
Nathan	10%
Gita	20%

Capital account balances were as follows:

Fatma	£10,000
Caroline	£5,000
Nathan	£5,000
Gita	£5,000

The taxable trade profits of the partnership for the year ended 31 December 2020 were £100,000.

Show how these profits are allocated to the partners.

Solution

Profits are allocated as follows:

	Total £	F £	C £	N £	G £
Interest on capital (10% × capital)	2,500	1,000	500	500	500
Salaries	14,000	3,000	4,000	4,000	3,000
Balance (50:20:10:20)	83,500	41,750	16,700	8,350	16,700
Total taxable profits	100,000	45,750	21,200	12,850	20,200

It is important to realise that the whole profit of £100,000 is classed as taxable trade profits.

Even though there is reference to salaries and interest, this is merely a means of allocation. For example, Fatma is now treated as having taxable trade profits of £45,750; she is not regarded as having received interest income or employment income.

2 Change in profit sharing arrangements

2.1 Principle of allocating profits

Where there is a change in the profit sharing arrangements during the accounting period, the period must be split into two or more parts (depending on the number of changes), with a separate division among the partners for each part.

Example

Riya, Fran and Gilly have been in business for many years.

During the year ended 31 December 2020, their taxable trade profits were £94,000. Profits were shared as follows:

	Riya £	Fran £	Gilly £
To 30 June 2020			
Salary (per annum)	10,000	6,100	–
Balance	1	1	1
To 31 December 2020			
Salary (per annum)	Nil	Nil	Nil
Balance	2	1	1

Show how the profits would be allocated between the partners.

Solution

Beware, the salaries are quoted per annum; if a change occurs during an accounting period the salary must be time apportioned.

Year ended 31 December 2020

	Total £	Riya £	Fran £	Gilly £
Period 1 January 2020 – 30 June 2020 (6/12)				
Salary	8,050	5,000	3,050	
Balance (1:1:1)	38,950	12,983	12,983	12,984
(£94,000 × 6/12)	47,000			
Period 1 July 2020 – 31 December 2020 (6/12)				
Balance (2:1:1)	47,000	23,500	11,750	11,750
Total	94,000	41,483	27,783	24,734

The profits are deemed to accrue evenly over time.

Each partner now has her own taxable trade profits for the accounting period.

Test your understanding 2

Read the following statements and state whether they are true or false.

1 A partnership pays tax on the partnership profits.

2 Brian and Mary trade in partnership sharing profits equally and preparing accounts to 31 December. If they want to change their profit shares to 1/3:2/3 on 1 July 2020 they need to prepare accounts to 30 June 2020.

3 Partners' salaries and interest on capital are deductible in computing adjusted trading profit.

The AAT reference material set out in section 8 below includes brief details on partnership allocations. It also includes mention of basis periods which are dealt with in Chapter 11.

3 Partnership changes

3.1 Principle of allocating profits

Where there is a change in the partnership during the accounting period, the period must be split into two or more parts (depending on the number of changes), exactly as for a change in the profit share arrangement.

A change in the partnership may occur when a new partner is admitted.

 Example

Charbel and David began to trade in partnership with effect from 1 July 2017, preparing accounts to 30 June each year and sharing profits equally.

On 1 January 2019, Edward joined the partnership. Profits were then split in the ratio 2:2:1.

The tax adjusted trading profits of the partnership were as follows:

	£
Year ended 30 June 2018	70,000
Year ended 30 June 2019	73,200
Year ended 30 June 2020	74,000

Show the profit allocation for each partner for each accounting period.

Solution

Allocate accounting period profits to partners according to profit share, splitting the accounting period where appropriate.

	Total £	C £	D £	E £
Year ended 30 June 2018 (1:1)	70,000	35,000	35,000	–
Year ended 30 June 2019				
1 July 2018 – 31 Dec 2018 (1:1) 6/12	36,600	18,300	18,300	–
1 Jan 2019 – 30 June 2019 (2:2:1) 6/12	36,600	14,640	14,640	7,320
	73,200	32,940	32,940	7,320
Year ended 30 June 2020 (2:2:1)	74,000	29,600	29,600	14,800

A change in the partnership may also occur when a partner leaves the partnership or dies.

Example

Fahd, George and Hussain began to trade in partnership with effect from 1 July 2017, preparing accounts to 30 June each year and sharing profits equally.

On 31 October 2020 George died. Profits and losses were then split in the ratio 3:2.

The tax adjusted trading profits of the partnership were as follows:

	£
Year ended 30 June 2018	60,000
Year ended 30 June 2019	85,200
Year ended 30 June 2020	75,000
Year ended 30 June 2021	75,600

Show the profit allocation for each partner for each accounting period.

Solution

Allocate accounting period profits to partners according to profit share, splitting the accounting period where appropriate.

	Total £	F £	G £	H £
Year ended 30 June 2018 (1:1:1)	60,000	20,000	20,000	20,000
Year ended 30 June 2019 (1:1:1)	85,200	28,400	28,400	28,400
Year ended 30 June 2020 (1:1:1)	75,000	25,000	25,000	25,000
Year ended 30 June 2021				
1 July 2020 – 31 Oct 2020 (1:1:1) 4/12	25,200	8,400	8,400	8,400
1 Nov 2020 – 30 June 2021 (3:2) 8/12	50,400	30,240	–	20,160
	75,600	38,640	8,400	28,560

The assessor has confirmed that in the assessment there will be a maximum of four partners in any one scenario.

The assessment could test changes to a partnership agreement and/or changes to the members of a partnership.

Test your understanding 3

Michael, Nick and Liz (1)

Michael Peters and Nick Wyatt commenced business as printers on 1 October 2017, preparing accounts to 30 September each year and sharing profits equally.

On 1 January 2019, Liz Stretton was admitted to the partnership and profits continued to be shared equally.

On 30 June 2020, Nick retired. Profits continued to be shared equally.

On 31 December 2021 the partnership was dissolved.

The adjusted profits of the partnership, after deducting capital allowances, were as follows:

	£
Year ended 30 September 2018	30,000
Year ended 30 September 2019	36,000
Year ended 30 September 2020	42,500
Year ended 30 September 2021	40,000
Three months to 31 December 2021	17,500

Show the allocation of profits to each partner for all accounting periods.

 4 **Partnership interest income**

4.1 Allocation of partnership interest income

Interest received by a partnership must be deducted in the partnership adjustment of profits computation as it is not trading income.

The income must however be assessed on the partners.

The interest is therefore apportioned between the partners according to the profit sharing ratio applicable to the balance of trading income, on the date the interest is received.

Each partner then includes his/her share of the interest in his/her personal income tax return.

5 Partnership tax return

5.1 Partnership tax return

Although the partnership does not pay its own tax liability, there is still a requirement to file a tax return for the partnership. One partner will be nominated by the other members of the partnership to complete and submit the return.

The return covers details of the partnership income and related information. It also includes a partnership statement, which shows each partner's share of profits, losses and income. Each individual partner will then enter this information on his/her own personal tax return.

The partnership return consists of 8 pages, broken down as follows:

- Page 1 – There is no information to complete on the first page, which simply sets out the partners' responsibilities.

- The long form return (4 pages) – Pages 2 to 5.

- The short form return (2 pages) – Pages 6 and 7.

- Page 8 – Other information relevant to the partnership.

In an assessment you will only be required to complete the short form return.

5.2 Partnership tax return: Page 6

This page is the first page of the 'partnership statement (short)', which will be used by the individual partners to make entries on their personal tax returns.

Information is transferred from the remainder of the return and then allocated between the partners.

The tax adjusted trading profit of the partnership is put in Box 11, or the trading loss is inserted in Box 12.

It is possible that the partnership will also have received interest income. If so, this needs to be entered in Box 13.

The short statement caters for up to 3 partners when page 7 is used but in the assessment you will only have to complete one partner's information on page 6.

You should complete Boxes 6 – 10 for individual partner details with the information provided in the assessment, if applicable, regarding the name, address, unique taxpayer reference, NI number and date appointed or ceased as a partner.

The trading profit or loss should then be apportioned between the partners according to the profit sharing agreement, and entered in Boxes 11 or 12 on each partner's statement.

The partnership may have received payments under the Construction Industry Scheme (CIS). No knowledge of what these are is required. Any tax deducted from such payments should be entered in Box 24 for the partnership with the appropriate amounts entered in Box 24 for each of the individual partners.

You do not need to give any further information if the split is a simple profit sharing ratio, but if any partner is entitled to a salary or interest on capital, this should be explained in Box 3.116 – 'additional information' on page 5 of the long form return. This explanation on the long form return will not be required in the assessment.

Any interest received by the partnership will be apportioned between the partners according to the profit sharing ratio on the date of receipt of the interest, and entered in Box 13 on each partner's statement.

You should ignore the text which says 'Copy this figure to box ...' as this is only relevant when completing the partner's individual income tax returns.

5.3   Completing the tax return

The following is important in connection with the completion of forms in the assessment.

- When completing the form in the assessment, figures must be entered in the correct boxes.

- Commas need not be entered for numbers of four digits or more.

- You do not need to fill in every box, only relevant ones.

Page 6 is shown overleaf.

Partnership Statement (short) for the year ended 5 April 2021

Please read these instructions before completing the Statement

Use these pages to allocate partnership income if the only income for the relevant return period was trading and professional income or untaxed interest and alternative finance receipts from UK banks and building societies. Otherwise you must download the 'Partnership Statement (Full)' pages to record details of the allocation of all the partnership income. Go to www.gov.uk/taxreturnforms

Step 1   Fill in boxes 1 to 29 and boxes A and B as appropriate. Get the figures you need from the relevant boxes in the Partnership Tax Return. Complete a separate Statement for each accounting period covered by this Partnership Tax Return and for each trade or profession carried on by the partnership.

Step 2   Then allocate the amounts in boxes 11 to 29 attributable to each partner using the allocation columns on this page and page 7, read the Partnership Tax Return Guide, go to www.gov.uk/taxreturnforms
If the partnership has more than 3 partners, please photocopy page 7.

Step 3   Each partner will need a copy of their allocation of income to fill in their personal tax return.

PARTNERSHIP INFORMATION
If the partnership business includes a trade or profession, enter here the accounting period for which appropriate items in this statement are returned.

Start   **1**   /   /

End   **2**   /   /

Nature of trade   **3**

MIXED PARTNERSHIPS

Tick here if this Statement is drawn up using Corporation Tax rules   **4**   Tick here if this Statement is drawn up using tax rules for non-residents   **5**

Individual partner details

6   Name of partner

Address

Postcode

Date appointed as a partner
(if during 2019–20 or 2020–21) Partner's Unique Taxpayer Reference (UTR)

7   /   /   **8**

Date ceased to be a partner
(if during 2019–20 or 2020–21) Partner's National Insurance number

9   /   /   **10**

Partnership's profits, losses, income and tax credits

Tick this box if the items entered in the box had foreign tax taken off

Partner's share of profits, losses, income and tax credits
Copy figures in boxes 11 to 29 to boxes in the individual's Partnership (short) pages as shown below

- for an accounting period ended in 2020-21 ▼

from box 3.83	Profit from a trade or profession **A**	**11** £	Profit **11** £	Copy this figure to box 8
from box 3.82	Adjustment on change of basis	**11A** £	**11A** £	Copy this figure to box 10
from box 3.84	Loss from a trade or profession **B**	**12** £	Loss **12** £	Copy this figure to box 8
from box 3.94	Disguised remuneration	**12A**	**12A**	Copy to box 15

- for the period 6 April 2020 to 5 April 2021*

from box 7.9A	Income from untaxed UK savings	**13** £	**13** £	Copy this figure to box 28
from box 3.97	CIS deductions made by contractors on account of tax	**24** £	**24** £	Copy this figure to box 30
from box 3.98	Other tax taken off trading income	**24A** £	**24A** £	Copy this figure to box 31
from box 3.117	Partnership charges	**29** £	**29** £	Copy this figure to box 4, 'Other tax reliefs' section on page Ai 2 in your personal tax return

* If you're a 'CT Partnership' see the Partnership Tax Return Guide

Adapted from SA800 2020, HMRC

Test your understanding 4

Michael, Nick and Liz (2)

Following on from TYU 3, complete page 6 of the partnership return in respect of the year ended 30 September 2020 for Michael.

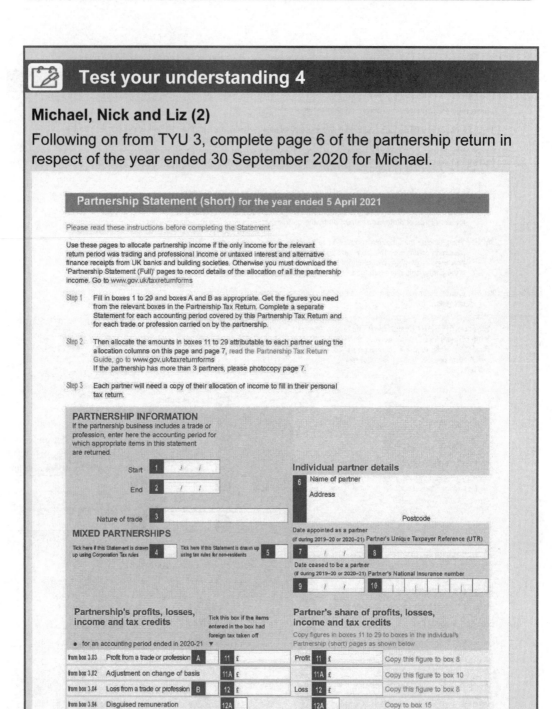

Adapted from SA800 2020, HMRC

6 Test your understanding

 Test your understanding 5

Lindsay, Tricia and Kate (1)

Lindsay and Tricia have been in partnership for many years, running a dry cleaning business. They prepare their accounts to 31 March each year. Their profit sharing ratio has always been 3:2.

On 1 August 2020, Kate joined the partnership and the profit sharing ratio was changed to 4:3:2 for Lindsay, Tricia and Kate.

For the year ended 31 March 2021, the trading profit was £150,000.

The division of profit would be calculated as:

	Total	Lindsay	Tricia	Kate
	£	£	£	£
Period to [ ]	1	2	3	
Period to [ ]	4	5	6	7

Options

1	A	£150,000
	B	£75,000
	C	£50,000
	D	£100,000
2	A	£30,000
	B	£20,000
	C	£45,000
	D	£90,000
3	A	£30,000
	B	£20,000
	C	£60,000
	D	£40,000

4	A	£150,000
	B	£75,000
	C	£50,000
	D	£100,000
5	A	£33,333
	B	£22,222
	C	£66,667
	D	£44,445
6	A	£22,222
	B	£25,000
	C	£33,333
	D	£44,445
7	A	£16,667
	B	£22,222
	C	£33,333
	D	£44,445

 Test your understanding 6

Ariana, Betty, Carlota and Diana

Ariana and Betty have been in partnership since 1 January 2008 sharing profits equally.

On 30 June 2019, Betty resigned as a partner and was replaced on 1 July 2019 by Carlota. Diana was admitted as a partner on 1 April 2020. Profits were shared equally throughout.

The partnership's taxable trade profits are as follows:

		£
Year ended	31 December 2019	60,000
Year ended	31 December 2020	72,000

Show the allocation of the taxable trade profits between the partners for each of the years to 31 December 2019 and 2020.

Test your understanding 7

Bishal and Harold

Bishal and Harold have traded in partnership for several years. Their accounts for the year ended 30 September 2020 show taxable trade profits of £16,500.

Bishal and Harold changed their profit-sharing ratio on 1 July 2020. The old profit-sharing ratio applies until 30 June 2020, and the new ratio applies from 1 July 2020.

	Bishal	**Harold**
Old ratio:		
Salaries p.a.	£3,000	£2,000
Share of balance	3/5	2/5
New ratio:		
Salaries p.a.	£6,000	£4,000
Share of balance	2/3	1/3

Show the allocation of the taxable trade profits between the partners for the year to 30 September 2020.

 Test your understanding 8

Peter and Nathan Flannery

Brothers Peter and Nathan Flannery have traded in partnership as Superhero Supplies for many years, trading in books and comics.

Their tax adjusted trading profits for the year ended 31 March 2021 are £130,400, and the partnership received interest of £16,210.

Peter and Nathan have always shared the profits of their business in the ratio 4:3.

Complete page 6 of the partnership tax return in respect of the year ended 31 March 2021 for the partnership as a whole and for Peter.

Partnership Statement (short) for the year ended 5 April 2021

Please read these instructions before completing the Statement

Use these pages to allocate partnership income if the only income for the relevant
return period was trading and professional income or untaxed interest and alternative
finance receipts from UK banks and building societies. Otherwise you must download the
'Partnership Statement (Full)' pages to record details of the allocation of all the partnership
income. Go to www.gov.uk/taxreturnforms

Step 1   Fill in boxes 1 to 29 and boxes A and B as appropriate. Get the figures you need
from the relevant boxes in the Partnership Tax Return. Complete a separate
Statement for each accounting period covered by this Partnership Tax Return and
for each trade or profession carried on by the partnership.

Step 2   Then allocate the amounts in boxes 11 to 29 attributable to each partner using the
allocation columns on this page and page 7, read the Partnership Tax Return
Guide, go to www.gov.uk/taxreturnforms
If the partnership has more than 3 partners, please photocopy page 7.

Step 3   Each partner will need a copy of their allocation of income to fill in their personal
tax return.

PARTNERSHIP INFORMATION

If the partnership business includes a trade or
profession, enter here the accounting period for
which appropriate items in this statement
are returned.

Start **1** [/   /   ]

End **2** [/   /   ]

Nature of trade **3** [   ]

Individual partner details

6 Name of partner

Address

Postcode

MIXED PARTNERSHIPS

Tick here if this Statement is drawn
up using Corporation Tax rules **4** [ ]

Tick here if this Statement is drawn up
using tax rules for non-residents **5** [ ]

Date appointed as a partner
(if during 2019–20 or 2020–21) Partner's Unique Taxpayer Reference (UTR)

7 [/   /   ]   **8** [   ]

Date ceased to be a partner
(if during 2019–20 or 2020–21) Partner's National Insurance number

9 [/   /   ]   **10** [   ]

Partnership's profits, losses, income and tax credits	Tick this box if the items entered in the box had foreign tax taken off ▼	Partner's share of profits, losses, income and tax credits	Copy figures in boxes 11 to 29 to boxes in the individual's Partnership (short) pages as shown below

● for an accounting period ended in 2020-21

from box 3.83	Profit from a trade or profession **A**	**11** £	Profit **11** £	Copy this figure to box 8
from box 3.82	Adjustment on change of basis	**11A** £	**11A** £	Copy this figure to box 10
from box 3.84	Loss from a trade or profession **B**	**12** £	Loss **12** £	Copy this figure to box 8
from box 3.94	Disguised remuneration	**12A**	**12A**	Copy to box 15

● for the period 6 April 2020 to 5 April 2021*

from box 7.9A	Income from untaxed UK savings	**13** £	**13** £	Copy this figure to box 28
from box 3.97	CIS deductions made by contractors on account of tax	**24** £	**24** £	Copy this figure to box 30
from box 3.98	Other tax taken off trading income	**24A** £	**24A** £	Copy this figure to box 31
from box 3.117	Partnership charges	**29** £	**29** £	Copy this figure to box 4, 'Other tax reliefs' section on page Ai 2 in your personal tax return

* If you're a 'CT Partnership' see the Partnership Tax Return G[ ]

Adapted from SA800 2020, HMRC

Test your understanding 9

Lindsay, Tricia and Kate (2)

For Lindsay in Test your understanding 5, complete page 6 in the partnership return in respect of the year ended 31 March 2021.

Partnership Statement (short) for the year ended 5 April 2021

Please read these instructions before completing the Statement

Use these pages to allocate partnership income if the only income for the relevant return period was trading and professional income or untaxed interest and alternative finance receipts from UK banks and building societies. Otherwise you must download the 'Partnership Statement (Full)' pages to record details of the allocation of all the partnership income. Go to www.gov.uk/taxreturnforms

Step 1   Fill in boxes 1 to 29 and boxes A and B as appropriate. Get the figures you need from the relevant boxes in the Partnership Tax Return. Complete a separate Statement for each accounting period covered by this Partnership Tax Return and for each trade or profession carried on by the partnership.

Step 2   Then allocate the amounts in boxes 11 to 29 attributable to each partner using the allocation columns on this page and page 7, read the Partnership Tax Return Guide, go to www.gov.uk/taxreturnforms
If the partnership has more than 3 partners, please photocopy page 7.

Step 3   Each partner will need a copy of their allocation of income to fill in their personal tax return.

PARTNERSHIP INFORMATION
If the partnership business includes a trade or profession, enter here the accounting period for which appropriate items in this statement are returned.

Start **1** / /

End **2** / /

Nature of trade **3**

Individual partner details

6 Name of partner

Address

Postcode

MIXED PARTNERSHIPS

Tick here if this Statement is drawn up using Corporation Tax rules **4**

Tick here if this Statement is drawn up using tax rules for non-residents **5**

Date appointed as a partner
(if during 2019–20 or 2020–21) Partner's Unique Taxpayer Reference (UTR)
7 / / **8**

Date ceased to be a partner
(if during 2019–20 or 2020–21) Partner's National Insurance number
9 / / **10**

Partnership's profits, losses, income and tax credits	Tick this box if the items entered in the box had foreign tax taken off ▼	Partner's share of profits, losses, income and tax credits Copy figures in boxes 11 to 29 to boxes in the individual's Partnership (short) pages as shown below
• for an accounting period ended in 2020-21		
from box 3.83 Profit from a trade or profession **A**	**11** £	Profit **11** £ Copy this figure to box 8
from box 3.82 Adjustment on change of basis	**11A** £	**11A** £ Copy this figure to box 10
from box 3.84 Loss from a trade or profession **B**	**12** £	Loss **12** £ Copy this figure to box 8
from box 3.94 Disguised remuneration	**12A**	**12A** Copy to box 15
• for the period 6 April 2020 to 5 April 2021*		
from box 7.9A Income from untaxed UK savings	**13** £	**13** £ Copy this figure to box 28
from box 3.97 CIS deductions made by contractors on account of tax	**24** £	**24** £ Copy this figure to box 30
from box 3.98 Other tax taken off trading income	**24A** £	**24A** £ Copy this figure to box 31
from box 3.117 Partnership charges	**29** £	**29** £ Copy this figure to box 4, 'Other tax reliefs' section on page Ai 2 in your personal tax return

* If you're a 'CT Partnership' see the Partnership Tax Return G[...]

Adapted from SA800 2020, HMRC

7 Summary

The taxable trade profits of a partnership are apportioned between the partners in accordance with the profit sharing arrangements during the accounting period.

Where there are salaries and interest on capital these should be dealt with first, and then any balance shared out using the profit sharing ratio.

Interest income is apportioned according to the profit sharing ratio on the date the interest is received.

 Links to other syllabus areas

In FAPR (Advanced level) you learned how to account for partnerships. This chapter builds directly on that knowledge and focuses on the tax consequences of carrying on business in partnership with others. Many of the underlying principles in terms of the way profits are shared between the partners for accounts purposes also apply when it comes to thinking about tax.

8 AAT reference material

Partnerships

- Each partner is taxed like a sole trader on their share of the partnership profits.

- First step is to share accounting profits between partners:
    - Allocate the correct salaries and interest on capital for the period to each partner.
    - Divide the remaining profit for each set of accounts between the partners based upon the profit sharing arrangement.
    - You may need to split the period if there is a change such as a partner joining or leaving.

- Opening year and cessation rules apply to partners individually when they join or leave the partnership.

- Allocate the profit for each partner to the correct tax year using usual basis period rules.

- Basis periods for continuing partners are unaffected by joiners or leavers.

- Each partner enters their share of profits for a tax year in the partnership pages of their own tax return.

Test your understanding answers

Test your understanding 1

John and Kyle

Year ending 5 April 2021	Total £	John £	Kyle £
Profits split (3:2)	24,047	14,428	9,619

Test your understanding 2

1	False	The partnership is not a separate legal entity from the partners. It is the partners who pay tax on their share of the partnership profits.
2	False	The profits are time apportioned to the period before and after 30 June, and then allocated using the profit sharing ratio in each period.
3	False	Salaries and interest must be added back in calculating adjusted trading profit as they are not actually salaries and interest. They merely represent a method chosen by the partners of allocating profits between them.
		They are taken into account in apportioning the profit between the partners, but the partners are assessed to their total share of trading profits of the partnership as trading income.

Test your understanding 3

Michael, Nick and Liz (1)

	Total £	Michael £	Nick £	Liz £
Year ended 30 September 2018	30,000	15,000	15,000	
Year ended 30 September 2019				
1 October 2018 – 31 December 2018 (3/12)	9,000	4,500	4,500	
1 January 2019 – 30 September 2019 (9/12)	27,000	9,000	9,000	9,000
	36,000	13,500	13,500	9,000
Year ended 30 September 2020				
1 October 2019 – 30 June 2020 (9/12)	31,875	10,625	10,625	10,625
1 July 2020 – 30 September 2020 (3/12)	10,625	5,313	–	5,312
	42,500	15,938	10,625	15,937
Year ended 30 September 2021	40,000	20,000		20,000
Period ending 31 December 2021	17,500	8,750		8,750

Test your understanding 4

Michael, Nick and Liz (2)

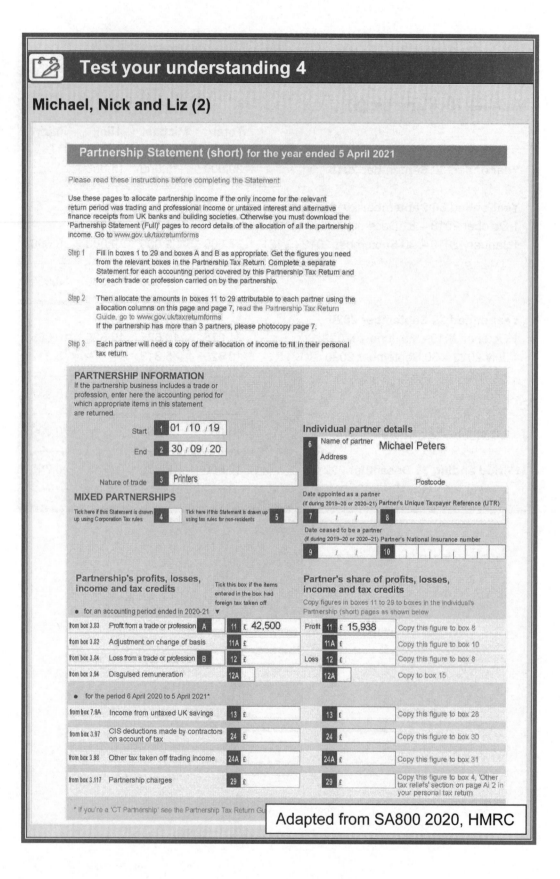

Partnership Statement (short) for the year ended 5 April 2021

Please read these instructions before completing the Statement

Use these pages to allocate partnership income if the only income for the relevant return period was trading and professional income or untaxed interest and alternative finance receipts from UK banks and building societies. Otherwise you must download the 'Partnership Statement (Full)' pages to record details of the allocation of all the partnership income. Go to www.gov.uk/taxreturnforms

Step 1   Fill in boxes 1 to 29 and boxes A and B as appropriate. Get the figures you need from the relevant boxes in the Partnership Tax Return. Complete a separate Statement for each accounting period covered by this Partnership Tax Return and for each trade or profession carried on by the partnership.

Step 2   Then allocate the amounts in boxes 11 to 29 attributable to each partner using the allocation columns on this page and page 7, read the Partnership Tax Return Guide, go to www.gov.uk/taxreturnforms
If the partnership has more than 3 partners, please photocopy page 7.

Step 3   Each partner will need a copy of their allocation of income to fill in their personal tax return.

PARTNERSHIP INFORMATION
If the partnership business includes a trade or profession, enter here the accounting period for which appropriate items in this statement are returned.

Start **1** `01 / 10 / 19`

End **2** `30 / 09 / 20`

Nature of trade **3** `Printers`

Individual partner details

6 Name of partner Michael Peters
Address

Postcode

MIXED PARTNERSHIPS

Tick here if this Statement is drawn up using Corporation Tax rules **4**

Tick here if this Statement is drawn up using tax rules for non-residents **5**

Date appointed as a partner
(if during 2019–20 or 2020–21) Partner's Unique Taxpayer Reference (UTR)
7 / /   **8**

Date ceased to be a partner
(if during 2019–20 or 2020–21) Partner's National Insurance number
9 / /   **10**

Partnership's profits, losses, income and tax credits	Tick this box if the items entered in the box had foreign tax taken off ▼	Partner's share of profits, losses, income and tax credits — Copy figures in boxes 11 to 29 to boxes in the individual's Partnership (short) pages as shown below

- for an accounting period ended in 2020-21

from box 3.83	Profit from a trade or profession	**A**	**11** £ 42,500	Profit **11** £ 15,938	Copy this figure to box 8
from box 3.82	Adjustment on change of basis		**11A** £	**11A** £	Copy this figure to box 10
from box 3.84	Loss from a trade or profession	**B**	**12** £	Loss **12** £	Copy this figure to box 8
from box 3.94	Disguised remuneration		**12A**	**12A**	Copy to box 15

- for the period 6 April 2020 to 5 April 2021*

from box 7.9A	Income from untaxed UK savings	**13** £	**13** £	Copy this figure to box 28
from box 3.97	CIS deductions made by contractors on account of tax	**24** £	**24** £	Copy this figure to box 30
from box 3.98	Other tax taken off trading income	**24A** £	**24A** £	Copy this figure to box 31
from box 3.117	Partnership charges	**29** £	**29** £	Copy this figure to box 4, 'Other tax reliefs' section on page Ai 2 in your personal tax return

* If you're a 'CT Partnership' see the Partnership Tax Return Gu...

Adapted from SA800 2020, HMRC

Test your understanding 5

Lindsay, Tricia and Kate (1)

The correct answers are as follows:

First period to: 31 July 2020

(1)   C

(2)   A

(3)   B

Second period to: 31 March 2021

(4)   D

(5)   D

(6)   C

(7)   B

Explanation:

The split of partnership profits will be as follows:

	Total £	Lindsay £	Tricia £	Kate £
Year ending 31 March 2021				
1 April 2020 – 31 July 2020 (4m)	50,000	30,000	20,000	
1 Aug 2020 – 31 March 2021 (8m)	100,000	44,445	33,333	22,222
	150,000	74,445	53,333	22,222

Test your understanding 6

Ariana, Betty, Carlota and Diana

	Total £	Ariana £	Betty £	Carlota £	Diana £
Year ended 31 Dec 2019					
1 Jan 2019 – 30 Jun 2019					
6/12 × £60,000	30,000	15,000	15,000		
1 Jul 2019 – 31 Dec 2019					
6/12 × £60,000	30,000	15,000		15,000	
	60,000	30,000	15,000	15,000	
Year ended 31 Dec 2020					
1 Jan 2020 – 31 Mar 2020					
3/12 × £72,000	18,000	9,000		9,000	
1 Apr 2020 – 31 Dec 2020					
9/12 × £72,000	54,000	18,000		18,000	18,000
	72,000	27,000		27,000	18,000

Test your understanding 7

Bishal and Harold

Allocation of taxable trade profits

The profit-sharing ratio was changed on 1 July 2020 which is 9 months into the accounting period. The profits will therefore be time-apportioned for allocation as follows:

Old ratio £16,500 × 9/12 = £12,375

New ratio £16,500 × 3/12 = £4,125

Allocation of taxable trade profits

	Total £	Bishal £	Harold £
1 Oct 2019 to 30 Jun 2020			
Salaries (9/12)	3,750	2,250	1,500
Balance (3:2)	8,625	5,175	3,450
	12,375	7,425	4,950
1 Jul 2020 to 30 Sep 2020			
Salaries (3/12)	2,500	1,500	1,000
Balance (2:1)	1,625	1,083	542
	4,125	2,583	1,542
Total allocation	16,500	10,008	6,492

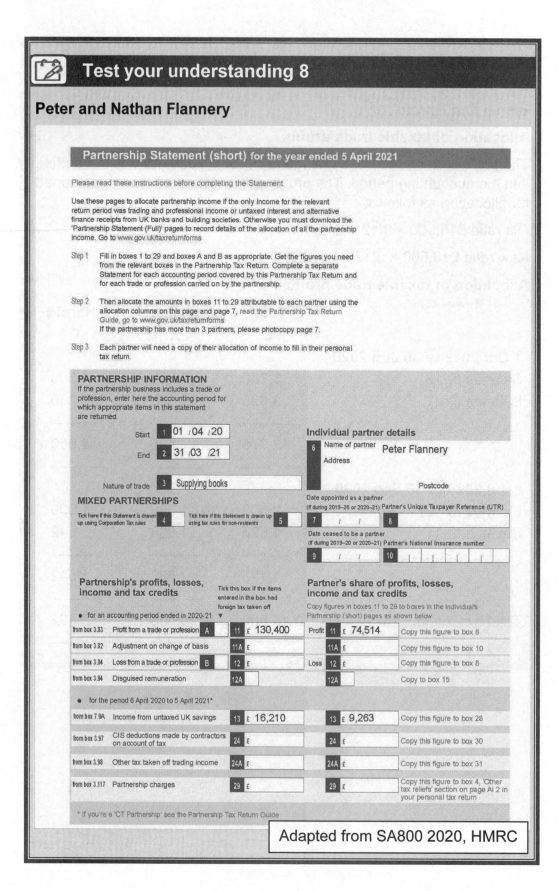

Test your understanding 8

Peter and Nathan Flannery

Partnership Statement (short) for the year ended 5 April 2021

Please read these instructions before completing the Statement

Use these pages to allocate partnership income if the only income for the relevant return period was trading and professional income or untaxed interest and alternative finance receipts from UK banks and building societies. Otherwise you must download the 'Partnership Statement (Full)' pages to record details of the allocation of all the partnership income. Go to www.gov.uk/taxreturnforms

Step 1   Fill in boxes 1 to 29 and boxes A and B as appropriate. Get the figures you need from the relevant boxes in the Partnership Tax Return. Complete a separate Statement for each accounting period covered by this Partnership Tax Return and for each trade or profession carried on by the partnership.

Step 2   Then allocate the amounts in boxes 11 to 29 attributable to each partner using the allocation columns on this page and page 7, read the Partnership Tax Return Guide, go to www.gov.uk/taxreturnforms
If the partnership has more than 3 partners, please photocopy page 7.

Step 3   Each partner will need a copy of their allocation of income to fill in their personal tax return.

PARTNERSHIP INFORMATION
If the partnership business includes a trade or profession, enter here the accounting period for which appropriate items in this statement are returned.

Start   **1** 01 / 04 / 20

End   **2** 31 / 03 / 21

Nature of trade   **3** Supplying books

MIXED PARTNERSHIPS

Tick here if this Statement is drawn up using Corporation Tax rules   **4**

Tick here if this Statement is drawn up using tax rules for non-residents   **5**

Individual partner details

6 Name of partner   Peter Flannery

Address

Postcode

Date appointed as a partner
(if during 2019–20 or 2020–21)   Partner's Unique Taxpayer Reference (UTR)
7 / /   **8**

Date ceased to be a partner
(if during 2019–20 or 2020–21)   Partner's National Insurance number
9 / /   **10**

Partnership's profits, losses, income and tax credits

Tick this box if the items entered in the box had foreign tax taken off ▼

Partner's share of profits, losses, income and tax credits

Copy figures in boxes 11 to 29 to boxes in the individual's Partnership (short) pages as shown below

- for an accounting period ended in 2020-21

from box 3.83	Profit from a trade or profession **A**	**11** £ 130,400	Profit **11** £ 74,514		Copy this figure to box 8
from box 3.82	Adjustment on change of basis	**11A** £	**11A** £		Copy this figure to box 10
from box 3.84	Loss from a trade or profession **B**	**12** £	Loss **12** £		Copy this figure to box 8
from box 3.94	Disguised remuneration	**12A**	**12A**		Copy to box 15

- for the period 6 April 2020 to 5 April 2021*

from box 7.9A	Income from untaxed UK savings	**13** £ 16,210	**13** £ 9,263		Copy this figure to box 28
from box 3.97	CIS deductions made by contractors on account of tax	**24** £	**24** £		Copy this figure to box 30
from box 3.98	Other tax taken off trading income	**24A** £	**24A** £		Copy this figure to box 31
from box 3.117	Partnership charges	**29** £	**29** £		Copy this figure to box 4, 'Other tax reliefs' section on page Ai 2 in your personal tax return

* If you're a 'CT Partnership' see the Partnership Tax Return Guide

Adapted from SA800 2020, HMRC

Test your understanding 9

Lindsay, Tricia and Kate (2)

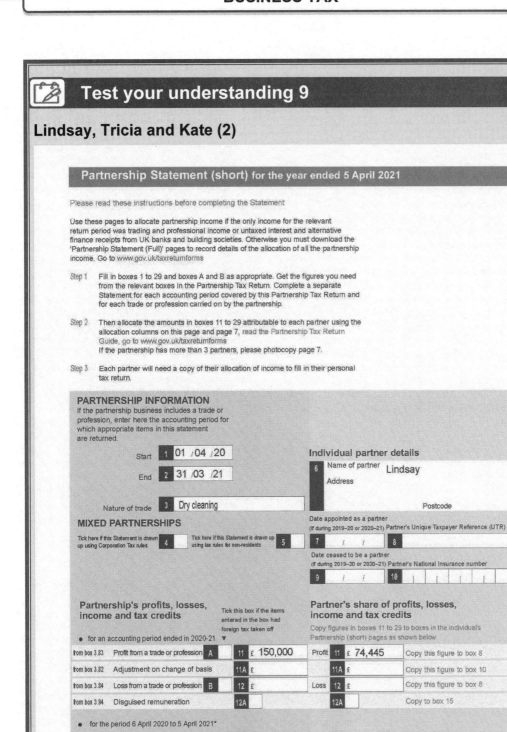

Partnership Statement (short) for the year ended 5 April 2021

Please read these instructions before completing the Statement

Use these pages to allocate partnership income if the only income for the relevant return period was trading and professional income or untaxed interest and alternative finance receipts from UK banks and building societies. Otherwise you must download the 'Partnership Statement (Full)' pages to record details of the allocation of all the partnership income. Go to www.gov.uk/taxreturnforms

Step 1   Fill in boxes 1 to 29 and boxes A and B as appropriate. Get the figures you need from the relevant boxes in the Partnership Tax Return. Complete a separate Statement for each accounting period covered by this Partnership Tax Return and for each trade or profession carried on by the partnership.

Step 2   Then allocate the amounts in boxes 11 to 29 attributable to each partner using the allocation columns on this page and page 7, read the Partnership Tax Return Guide, go to www.gov.uk/taxreturnforms
If the partnership has more than 3 partners, please photocopy page 7.

Step 3   Each partner will need a copy of their allocation of income to fill in their personal tax return.

PARTNERSHIP INFORMATION
If the partnership business includes a trade or profession, enter here the accounting period for which appropriate items in this statement are returned.

Start **1** 01 /04 /20

End **2** 31 /03 /21

Nature of trade **3** Dry cleaning

Individual partner details

6 Name of partner   Lindsay

Address

Postcode

MIXED PARTNERSHIPS

Tick here if this Statement is drawn up using Corporation Tax rules **4**   Tick here if this Statement is drawn up using tax rules for non-residents **5**

Date appointed as a partner
(if during 2019–20 or 2020–21) Partner's Unique Taxpayer Reference (UTR)

7 / /   **8**

Date ceased to be a partner
(if during 2019–20 or 2020–21) Partner's National Insurance number

9 / /   **10**

Partnership's profits, losses, income and tax credits	Tick this box if the items entered in the box had foreign tax taken off ▼	Partner's share of profits, losses, income and tax credits
• for an accounting period ended in 2020-21		Copy figures in boxes 11 to 29 to boxes in the individual's Partnership (short) pages as shown below
from box 3.83 Profit from a trade or profession **A** **11** £ 150,000		Profit **11** £ 74,445 Copy this figure to box 8
from box 3.82 Adjustment on change of basis **11A** £		**11A** £ Copy this figure to box 10
from box 3.84 Loss from a trade or profession **B** **12** £		Loss **12** £ Copy this figure to box 8
from box 3.94 Disguised remuneration **12A**		**12A** Copy to box 15
• for the period 6 April 2020 to 5 April 2021*		
from box 7.9A Income from untaxed UK savings **13** £		**13** £ Copy this figure to box 28
from box 3.97 CIS deductions made by contractors on account of tax **24** £		**24** £ Copy this figure to box 30
from box 3.98 Other tax taken off trading income **24A** £		**24A** £ Copy this figure to box 31
from box 3.117 Partnership charges **29** £		**29** £ Copy this figure to box 4, 'Other tax reliefs' section on page Ai 2 in your personal tax return

* If you're a 'CT Partnership' see the Partnership Tax Return G...

Adapted from SA800 2020, HMRC

Basis periods

Introduction

Sole traders and partners must complete a tax return each year.

There are rules to determine which profits go into each tax return, with special rules for the opening and closing years of a business.

There are also special rules when a business changes its accounting date after the opening years.

ASSESSMENT CRITERIA	CONTENTS
Identify the basis periods using the opening year and closing year rules (1.2)	1 Tax years 2 Current year basis 3 Opening year rules 4 Closing year rules 5 Change of accounting date 6 Partnerships
Determine overlap periods and overlap profits (1.2)	
Explain the effect on the basis period of a change in accounting date (1.2)	
Determine the basis periods for continuing, new or departing partners (1.4)	

1 Tax years

1.1 Tax year

An individual in business will need to complete a tax return for a tax year. A tax year runs from 6 April to the following 5 April.

> ### 💡 Example
>
> What time period is covered by the tax year 2020/21?
>
> **Solution**
>
> 2020/21 is the period:
>
>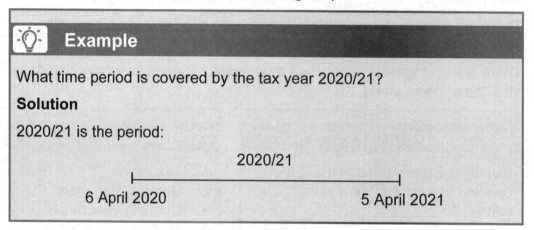
>
> 2020/21
>
> 6 April 2020   5 April 2021

We need to determine which taxable trade profits are to be assessed in each tax year.

2 Current year basis

2.1 Ongoing business

The basic rule is that the taxable trade profits assessed in any tax year will be based on the profit for the 12 month period of account ending in that tax year. This is known as the current year basis.

> ### 💡 Example
>
> Vivienne prepares accounts to 30 April each year.
>
> Her taxable trade profits after making all necessary adjustments, including capital allowances, were as follows:
>
> | | £ |
> |---|---|
> | Year ended 30 April 2019 | 20,000 |
> | Year ended 30 April 2020 | 25,000 |
>
> State in which tax years these profits will be taxed.

Solution

2019/20

6 April 2019   5 April 2020

30 April 2019

The year ended 30 April 2019 ends in 2019/20 and therefore all of the profits of that year will be taxed in the tax year 2019/20.

The year ended 30 April 2020 ends in 2020/21 and therefore all of the profits of that year will be taxed in the tax year 2020/21.

An individual can choose whichever accounting period end date he/she wants for his/her business, but care must be taken to tax the profits in the correct tax year.

Example

In which tax years will the following profits be taxed?

Profits for year ending: 30 April 2021
                               31 March 2021
                               30 June 2021
                               31 January 2021
                               31 December 2020

Solution

Profits for year ending:	Tax year of assessment
30 April 2021	2021/22
31 March 2021	2020/21
30 June 2021	2021/22
31 January 2021	2020/21
31 December 2020	2020/21

It often helps to draw a diagram showing the beginning and end of the tax year and mark on the accounting period end date to ensure you select the correct tax year.

3 Opening year rules

3.1 Special rules

Over the life of a business, it is important that:

- the total taxable trading profits of the business should be taxed, and

- there should be an assessment for each tax year of trading.

Suppose a business starts trading on 1 July 2020 and prepares accounts up to 30 June 2021.

Although the business starts in 2020/21 there is no accounting period ending in 2020/21, so if the normal 'current year basis' is applied, there would be no tax assessment in 2020/21.

To make sure that there is an assessment in every year the business trades, there are special opening year rules.

These are explained below.

(a) **First tax year**

The first tax year is the tax year in which the business started to trade.

The basis of assessment for the first tax year is *always* the period:

- from the date of commencement

- to the following 5 April.

This is known as the *actual basis of assessment*.

(b) **Second tax year**

In the second tax year, you need to ask the question:

Is there a set of accounts that ends in the second tax year?

If no accounts are prepared to a date ending in the second tax year, the basis of assessment is:

- the actual profits of the second tax year (6 April to 5 April).

If accounts are prepared to a date ending in the second tax year, you need to ask another question:

How long are the accounts that end in the second tax year?

If the accounts are:

- exactly 12 months long:

  - the basis of assessment is the profits of the 12 months (current year basis).

- more than 12 months long:

  - the basis of assessment is the profits of the 12 months to the end of that period.

- less than 12 months long:

  - the basis of assessment is the profits of the first 12 months trading.

(c) **Third year**

In the third tax year, the basis of assessment is:

- the profits of the 12 months to the accounting date ending in the third year.

This is usually the **current year basis**.

For the purposes of your assessment, any apportionments of profit are made on a monthly basis (not daily).

There are details of the opening year rules in the AAT reference material set out below in section 9.

The following examples will illustrate the three possibilities for the second tax year.

 Example

Lara started in business on 1 November 2018, preparing accounts to 31 October each year.

Her adjusted profits were as follows:

	£
Year ended 31 October 2019	18,000
Year ended 31 October 2020	37,500
Year ended 31 October 2021	44,000

State the taxable trade profits for the first four tax years of trading.

Solution

Her taxable trade profits are therefore as follows:

Year of Assessment	Basis period	Assessment £
2018/19	1 November 2018 – 5 April 2019 (£18,000 × 5/12)	7,500
2019/20	1 November 2018 – 31 October 2019	18,000
2020/21	1 November 2019 – 31 October 2020	37,500
2021/22	1 November 2020 – 31 October 2021	44,000

1 Nov 2018	31 Oct 2019	31 Oct 2020	31 Oct 2021

5 Apr 2019

2018/19

2019/20   2020/21   2021/22

3.2 Overlap profits

When an individual starts to trade, some profits may be taxed twice. Profits assessed in more than one tax year are called overlap profits.

In the previous example, the following profits are assessed in both 2018/19 and 2019/20:

1 November 2018 to 5 April 2019 = (£18,000 × 5/12) = £7,500

However, as stated before, it is very important that over the life of the business, the trader will be taxed on the total taxable profits of the business – and only once.

Therefore, relief for overlap profits is given by deducting them from the final assessment when an individual ceases to trade.

Note that there will be no overlap profits if the trader has a 5 April year end. Since we work to the nearest month for exams, this means that starting business and choosing a 31 March year end will also have no overlap profits.

 Example

Edrich started in business on 1 July 2018. He prepared his first set of accounts for the six months ended 31 December 2018 and then for calendar years thereafter.

His adjusted profits were as follows:

	£
Six months ended 31 December 2018	3,100
Year ended 31 December 2019	7,600
Year ended 31 December 2020	8,200
Year ended 31 December 2021	6,400

Show the taxable trade profits for the tax years 2018/19 to 2021/22 inclusive, and calculate the amount of any overlap profits.

Solution

His taxable trade profits are therefore as follows:

Year of assessment	Basis period	Assessment £
2018/19	1 July 2018 – 5 April 2019 £3,100 + (£7,600 × 3/12)	5,000
2019/20	1 January 2019 – 31 December 2019	7,600
2020/21	1 January 2020 – 31 December 2020	8,200
2021/22	1 January 2021 – 31 December 2021	6,400

There are overlap profits of £1,900 (£7,600 × 3/12) for the period from 1 January 2019 to 5 April 2019.

 Example

Hammond started in business on 1 January 2019. He prepared his first set of accounts for the seven months ended 31 July 2019 and annually to 31 July thereafter.

His adjusted profits were as follows:

	£
Seven months ended 31 July 2019	10,500
Year ended 31 July 2020	33,600
Year ended 31 July 2021	19,800

Show the taxable trade profits for the tax years 2018/19 to 2021/22 inclusive, and calculate the amount of any overlap profits.

Solution

The business commenced on 1 January 2019, which is in 2018/19.

The second tax year is 2019/20 and the accounts ending in that period are those for the seven months to 31 July 2019. This date is less than 12 months after the business started. Therefore, the second year assesses the first 12 months trading.

Remember we must tax 12 months of profits in the second year.

Hammond's taxable trade profits are therefore as follows:

Year of Assessment	Basis period	Assessment £
2018/19	1 January 2019 – 5 April 2019 £10,500 × 3/7	4,500
2019/20	1 January 2019 – 31 December 2019 £10,500 + (£33,600 × 5/12)	24,500
2020/21	1 August 2019 – 31 July 2020	33,600
2021/22	1 August 2020 – 31 July 2021	19,800

The overlap profits are:

	£
1 Jan 2019 – 5 April 2019 (£10,500 × 3/7)	4,500
1 Aug 2019 – 31 Dec 2019 (£33,600 × 5/12)	14,000
	18,500

1 Jan 2019	31 Jul 2019	31 Jul 2020	31 Jul 2021

5 Apr 2019

2018/19

31 Dec 2019

2019/20

2020/21

2021/22

Example

Farida started in business on 1 February 2019. She prepared her first set of accounts for the 18 months to 31 July 2020 and annually to 31 July thereafter.

Her adjusted profits were as follows:

	£
18 months ended 31 July 2020	9,000
Year ended 31 July 2021	2,680

Show the taxable trade profits for the tax years 2018/19 to 2021/22 inclusive, and calculate the amount of any overlap profits.

Solution

The taxable trade profits are as follows:

Year of Assessment	Basis period	Assessment £
2018/19	1 February 2019 – 5 April 2019	
	£9,000 × 2/18	1,000
2019/20	6 April 2019 – 5 April 2020	
	£9,000 × 12/18	6,000
2020/21	1 August 2019 – 31 July 2020	
	£9,000 × 12/18	6,000
2021/22	1 August 2020 – 31 July 2021	2,680

The overlap profits are:

1 Aug 2019 – 5 April 2020 (£9,000 × 8/18)   £4,000

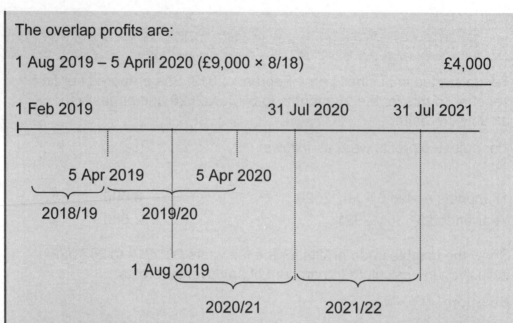

Note: In this example there is an 18 month period of account ending in the third tax year 2020/21.

In the second tax year where there are no accounts ending in that year, the actual profits from 6 April to 5 April are assessed.

In the third tax year, because we must only assess 12 months of profits, we take the last 12 months ending on the accounting date (i.e. 12 m/e 31 July 2020).

 Test your understanding 1

Navaro

Navaro started trading on 1 November 2017. He prepares his accounts to 30 April each year. The adjusted profits were as follows:

	£
Period ended 30 April 2018	12,000
Year ended 30 April 2019	27,000
Year ended 30 April 2020	30,000

1   In which tax year did Navaro start trading?

A   2016/17

B   2017/18

C   2018/19

D   2019/20

2   What are Navaro's taxable trading profits for the first tax year of trading?

A   £25,500

B   £12,000

C   £10,000

D   £9,600

3   What are Navaro's taxable trading profits for the second tax year of trading?

A   £12,000

B   £25,500

C   £26,750

D   £27,000

4   What are Navaro's taxable trading profits for the third tax year of trading?

A   £30,000

B   £29,750

C   £27,000

D   £26,750

5   What are Navaro's overlap profits?   £ [   ]

6   His overlap profits are relieved as follows:

A   There is no relief for overlap profits

B   From the taxable profits of his choice

C   From his taxable profits in the first tax year of trade

D   From his taxable profits in the final tax year of trade

Test your understanding 2

Ali and Sofia

(a) Ali started in business on 1 May 2018.

His first set of accounts was prepared to 30 September 2018 and he then retained 30 September as his year end.

Tax adjusted results in the early years were as follows:

	£
1 May 2018 – 30 September 2018	20,250
Year ended 30 September 2019	29,700
Year ended 30 September 2020	36,450
Year ended 30 September 2021	28,350

(b) Sofia started in business on 1 January 2018 and prepared her first set of accounts to 30 April 2019.

She then continued to prepare her accounts to 30 April. The tax adjusted results in the early years were as follows:

	£
1 January 2018 – 30 April 2019	37,800
Year ended 30 April 2020	26,325
Year ended 30 April 2021	29,350

Show the amounts assessable for all tax years affected by these results and compute any overlap profits.

 4 **Closing year rules**

4.1 Method of assessment

When an individual trader ceases to trade, any profits not yet assessed will be taxed in the tax year in which trading ceases.

The penultimate year (and the years prior to the penultimate year) is assessed on a current year basis. The final tax year assesses those profits that have not yet been assessed.

Note that this could result in the profits of more than one accounting period being assessed in the final tax year, as shown in the next example.

Example

Hutton has been in business for many years, preparing his accounts to 30 June each year. Owing to ill-health, he stopped trading on 31 January 2021.

His adjusted profits were as follows:

	£
Year ended 30 June 2019	12,000
Year ended 30 June 2020	10,000
Seven months ended 31 January 2021	3,640

Show the taxable trade profits for the last two tax years of assessment.

Solution

Step 1: Identify in which tax year the last few accounting periods end.

Accounting period	Ends in
Year ended 30 June 2019	2019/20
Year ended 30 June 2020	2020/21
Seven months ended 31 January 2021	2020/21

Step 2: Assess the profits in the tax years shown on the right hand side in step 1.

His taxable trade profits are therefore as follows:

Year of assessment	Basis period	Assessment
		£
2019/20	1 July 2018 – 30 June 2019	12,000
2020/21	1 July 2019 – 31 January 2021	
	(£10,000 + £3,640)	13,640

4.2 Overlap profits

As previously stated, over the life of the business, a trader will be taxed on his/her total taxable profits – and only once.

Therefore, relief for overlap profits in the opening years is given by deducting them from the assessment of the final tax year.

Example

Barrington started in business on 1 August 2017, preparing accounts to 31 July each year. He ceased to trade on 31 July 2021, on which date his business was acquired by another firm.

His adjusted profits were as follows:

	£
Year ended 31 July 2018	15,000
Year ended 31 July 2019	23,000
Year ended 31 July 2020	27,000
Year ended 31 July 2021	35,600
Total adjusted profits	100,600

Show the taxable trade profits for the tax years 2017/18 to 2021/22 inclusive and calculate the amount of any overlap profits.

Solution

Step 1: Identify the tax year in which trade commences

In this year profits from the date of commencement to 5 April will be assessed (1 August 2017 is in 2017/18).

Step 2: Deal with the second tax year

The second tax year has a 12 month period ending in it therefore those 12 months' profits are assessed.

After this you should be able to identify the amount of the overlap profits.

Step 3: Work out assessments for all years up to year of cessation

All other years will be taxed on the current year basis until the year of cessation.

Step 4: Work out the final year assessment

In the tax year of cessation (2021/22) all profits not yet assessed are taxed.

In this example it is straightforward as all periods are 12 months long.

Step 5: Deduct overlap profits

Finally, deduct from the final assessment the overlap profits.

The taxable trade profits are as follows.

Year of assessment	Basis period	Assessment £
2017/18	1 August 2017 – 5 April 2018 £15,000 × 8/12	10,000
2018/19	1 August 2017 – 31 July 2018	15,000
2019/20	1 August 2018 – 31 July 2019	23,000
2020/21	1 August 2019 – 31 July 2020	27,000
2021/22	1 August 2020 – 31 July 2021 (£35,600 – £10,000)	25,600
Total assessments		100,600

The overlap profits amount to £10,000. This sum is deducted from the assessment for the final tax year (2021/22).

Barrington's aggregate profits over his four years of trading total £100,600 and his aggregate taxable trade profits for the five tax years involved come to exactly the same figure.

5 Change of accounting date

5.1 Effect on basis period

An unincorporated trader or partnership may wish to change its accounting date for commercial or other reasons.

Where a trader who has previously prepared accounts to 30 June changes his/her accounting date to 30 September, the next set of accounts is going to be for either three months or 15 months.

However, in every tax year (other than the first and final tax years) the trader must be taxed on 12 months' worth of profits. Therefore, in the 'year of change' (the first tax year in which accounts are made up to the new date), there will either be new overlap profits created, or some overlap profits brought forward will be offset.

5.2 New date is earlier in the tax year

Where the new accounting date is earlier in the tax year than the old one, for example a change from 31 January to 30 November, the basis period for the tax year of change will be the **12-month period ending with the new accounting date**.

This will result in some profits being assessed more than once. Overlap profits will therefore arise, which are treated in exactly the same way as overlap profits arising on the commencement of trade.

It is possible to have either a long or short period of account ending on the new date.

 Example

(a) Andrea, a sole trader, has always prepared her accounts to 31 March. She decides to change her accounting date to 30 June by preparing accounts for the three month period to 30 June 2020.

Andrea's tax adjusted profits after capital allowances are as follows:

	£
Year ended 31 March 2020	60,000
Three months to 30 June 2020	20,000
Year ended 30 June 2021	85,000

Calculate Andrea's trading income assessments for 2019/20 to 2021/22.

Solution

(a) The accounting date has moved from March to June, i.e. to earlier in the tax year.

The tax year of change is the year in which accounts to the new accounting date are prepared (i.e. 2020/21).

The basis period for the tax year of change is the 12 months to the new accounting date.

Tax year	Basis period	Taxable income £
2019/20	Year to 31 March 2020	60,000
2020/21	12-month period to the new accounting date of 30 June 2020:	
	Year to 31 March 2020: (£60,000 × 9/12)	45,000
	Period to 30 June 2020	20,000
		65,000
2021/22	Year to 30 June 2021	85,000

Note: The change in accounting date has created further overlap profits of £45,000, as the 9 months to 31 March 2020 are assessed in both 2019/20 and 2020/21.

(b) Assume that instead of producing a three month set of accounts, Andrea had decided to change her accounting date to 30 June by preparing accounts for the fifteen month period to 30 June 2021 with tax adjusted profits of £105,000.

Calculate Andrea's trading income assessments for 2019/20 to 2021/22 and prove that the result would be virtually the same.

Solution

(b) The tax year of change is 2020/21 as Andrea does not adopt her normal 31 March year end here.

Andrea is allowed to adopt the new accounting date in this year, and the profits assessed are those for the 12 months to the new accounting date – 30 June.

Tax year	Basis period	Taxable income £
2019/20	Year to 31 March 2020	60,000
2020/21	12-month period to the new accounting date of 30 June 2020:	
	Year to 31 March 2020: (£60,000 × 9/12)	45,000
	Period to 30 June 2020:	
	(£105,000 × 3/15)	21,000
		66,000
2021/22	Year to 30 June 2021 (£105,000 × 12/15)	84,000

Note: Overlap profits still arise in respect of the 9 months to 31 March 2020 as before equal to £45,000.

5.3 New date is later in the tax year

Where the new accounting date is later in the tax year than the old one the basis period for the tax year of change will be **the period ending with the new accounting date**.

As the resulting basis period may be more than 12 months, a corresponding proportion of any overlap profits that arose upon the commencement of trading are offset against the taxable profits.

Again, it is possible to have either a short accounting period or a long accounting period creating the new date.

 Example

Peter, a sole trader, has always prepared his accounts to 30 June.

Peter has overlap profits of £13,500 from the period 1 July 2017 to 5 April 2018.

He has now decided to change his accounting date to 30 September by preparing accounts for the 15 month period to 30 September 2020.

Peter's tax adjusted trading profits after capital allowances are:

	£
Year ended 30 June 2019	24,000
Period ended 30 September 2020	30,000
Year ended 30 September 2021	36,000

Calculate Peter's trading income assessments for 2019/20 to 2021/22.

Solution

The tax year of change is the tax year in which accounts are prepared to the new accounting date (i.e. 2020/21).

As the new accounting date is later in the tax year, the basis period is the period ending with the new accounting date.

Tax year	Basis period	Taxable income £
2019/20	Year to 30 June 2019	24,000
2020/21	Period not yet assessed ending on the new accounting date	
	15-month period to 30 September 2020	30,000
	Less: Overlap profits (£13,500 × 3/9)	(4,500)
		25,500
2021/22	Year to 30 September 2021	36,000

Note: In 2020/21 the period of account not yet assessed and ending with the new accounting date is 15 months. As no assessment can exceed 12 months, Peter is allowed to offset 3 months of his overlap profits.

The remaining 6 months of overlap profits are carried forward as normal and are available for relief, either on a further change in accounting date or on the cessation of trade.

5.4 Conditions for a valid change

(1) The change of accounting date must be notified to HMRC on or before 31 January following the tax year in which the change is to be made.

E.g. if the year of change is 2020/21 then HMRC must be notified by 31 January 2022 (the latest filing date for the 2020/21 tax return).

(2) The first accounts to the new accounting date must not exceed 18 months in length.

The AAT reference material set out in section 9 below contains some details of the change of accounting date rules.

6 Partnerships

6.1 Separate traders

A partnership is treated as a collection of individual traders.

Therefore, if some individuals have been trading in partnership for many years, each will be assessed on his/her own share of the profits on a current year basis.

6.2 Partners joining

Where an individual joins the partnership, he/she alone will be assessed using the opening year rules on his/her share of the partnership profits.

The remaining partners will use the current year basis.

6.3 Partners leaving

Where an individual leaves the partnership, he/she alone will be assessed using the closing year rules on his/her share of the partnership profits.

The remaining partners will use the current year basis.

6.4 Procedure for partnerships

The correct procedure to follow for partnerships is:

Step 1: Adjust profits of the accounting period (including calculating capital allowances) for the partnership as a whole.

Step 2: Allocate the profits of the accounting period to the partners using the profit share arrangement.

Step 3: Consider each partner in turn, as if they were sole traders, to determine whether to apply current year basis, opening year rules or closing year rules.

Example

Using the results of the Fahd, George and Hussain example in Chapter 10 as set out below, calculate the taxable trade profits for each partner for the tax years 2017/18 to 2020/21.

	Total £	F £	G £	H £
Year ended 30 June 2018 (1:1:1)	60,000	20,000	20,000	20,000
Year ended 30 June 2019 (1:1:1)	85,200	28,400	28,400	28,400
Year ended 30 June 2020(1:1:1)	75,000	25,000	25,000	25,000
Year ended 30 June 2021				
1 July 2020 – 31 Oct 2020 (1:1:1)(4/12)	25,200	8,400	8,400	8,400
1 Nov 2020 – 30 June 2021 (3:2)(8/12)	50,400	30,240	–	20,160
	75,600	38,640	8,400	28,560

Solution

Steps 1 and 2 of the procedure have already been completed above.

Step 3: Determine the basis of assessment for each partner.

- Fahd and Hussain both commenced in partnership on 1 July 2017, hence apply the opening year rules. The following figures relate to Fahd.

Year of assessment	Basis period	Year of assessment
2017/18	1 July 2017 – 5 April 2018 (£20,000 × 9/12)	2017/18
2018/19	Year ended 30 June 2018	2018/19
2019/20	Year ended 30 June 2019	2019/20
2020/21	Year ended 30 June 2020	2020/21
2021/22	Year ended 30 June 2021	2021/22

Overlap profits = £15,000

- Hussain would be the same as Fahd until 2021/22 when his assessment would be £28,560.

- George commenced in partnership on 1 July 2017, and ceased on 31 October 2020, hence apply both opening and closing year rules:

Year of assessment	Basis period	Assessment £
2017/18	1 July 2017 – 5 April 2018 (£20,000 × 9/12)	15,000
2018/19	Year ended 30 June 2018	20,000
2019/20	Year ended 30 June 2019	28,400
2020/21	1 July 2019 – 31 October 2020 (£25,000 + £8,400 – £15,000)	18,400

Overlap profits = £15,000

In the assessment you will probably only need to perform Step 3 for one of the partners.

Test your understanding 3

Adam, Shanaya and Catrina

Adam, Shanaya and Catrina have been in partnership since 1 April 2015. The partnership prepares accounts to 31 December each year. On 1 November 2020, Adam retired from the partnership and the profit sharing arrangements were changed from that date onwards.

Which one of the following statements is correct?

A   The partnership is deemed to cease on Adam's retirement and the partners will apply the closing year rules to calculate their trading income assessments for the final years.

B   The final year of trading for Adam, Shanaya and Catrina will be 2020/21.

C   Shanaya and Catrina will have to apply the opening year rules to calculate their trading income assessments for 2020/21.

 D   Adam will apply the closing year rules in order to calculate his trading income assessment for 2020/21.

7 Test your understanding

Test your understanding 4

Xavier

Xavier commenced trading on 1 January 2020 and prepared his first set of accounts to 31 May 2021.

The period of profits which will be taxed in the second tax year is:

A   1 January 2020 to 5 April 2020

B   1 January 2020 to 31 December 2020

C   6 April 2020 to 5 April 2021

D   12 months ended 31 May 2021

Test your understanding 5

Mario

Mario commenced trading on 1 February 2020 and intends to prepare his accounts to 31 May each year. His first set of accounts is prepared to 31 May 2021.

For 2020/21, he will be assessed on trading profits for the 12 month period to 31 May 2021.

A   True

B   False

Handwritten notes (left/top margin):

1/7/19 — 5/4/20 = 13500
06/4/20 – 5/4/21 = 18000
01/5/20 – 30/4/21
18000
13,500
2019-20 = 13500
2020-21 = 18000
2021-22 = 18000

11 – months
01/5/20 – 5/4/21 ✓

Test your understanding 6

Amit

Amit commenced in business as a fashion designer on 1 July 2019, and prepared his first set of accounts to 30 April 2021.

His profit for the period, adjusted for taxation, was £33,000.

What is the amount of overlap profit that arises on the commencement of Amit's trade?

A   £18,000

B   £16,500

C   £4,500

D   £Nil

Handwritten notes (right):
2021/22 1/2 m
6/4/20 2020/21
5/4/20
1/7/19 9m
12 m
5/4/21 30/4/21
2019/20

Test your understanding 7

Katrina

Katrina ceased trading on 28 February 2021. Her tax adjusted trading profits for the final periods of trading are as follows:

	£
Year ended 30 June 2019	30,000
Year ended 30 June 2020	27,000
Period ended 28 February 2021	20,000

She has unrelieved overlap profits of £12,000.

What is Katrina's trading income assessment for 2020/21?

A   £8,000

B   £47,000

C   £35,000

D   £65,000

Handwritten notes (left margin):
6-4-19 = 5-4-20
2019/20 = 30000
6-4-20 – 5-4-21
2020/21 = 27000
20,000
OL   – 12000
35000 ✓

Test your understanding 8

James

James started in business on 1 January 2017 and prepared his first set of accounts to 30 April 2018.

He then continued to prepare his accounts to 30 April and his taxable trade profits in the early years were as follows:

	£
1 January 2017 – 30 April 2018	75,600
Year ended 30 April 2019	52,650
Year ended 30 April 2020	56,900

Show the amounts assessable for all tax years affected by these results and calculate the overlap profits arising.

 Test your understanding 9

Avril

Avril commenced trading on 1 January 2018. She prepared accounts to 30 June each year.

Her taxable trade profits for the first few years of trading were:

		£
Period ending	30 June 2018	80,000
Year ended	30 June 2019	100,000
Year ended	30 June 2020	110,000

Calculate the amounts assessable for 2017/18 to 2020/21, and show the overlap profit arising to be carried forward.

Test your understanding 10

Benny

Benny, a fashion designer, decided to commence his own business on 1 July 2018. He prepared accounts on a calendar year basis and his taxable trade profits for the first few periods of trading are as follows:

		£
Period ending	31 December 2018	14,000
Year ended	31 December 2019	36,000
Year ended	31 December 2020	28,000

Show the amounts assessable for 2018/19 to 2020/21, and state the overlap profit to be carried forward.

Test your understanding 11

Elle

Elle prepares accounts to 31 May annually.

Recent taxable trade profits have been as follows:

	£
Year ended 31 May 2019	22,000
Year ended 31 May 2020	26,000

Elle had overlap profits on commencement of the business totalling £5,000.

Show the assessments for all relevant tax years for the following alternative dates for cessation of trading.

(a) 31 May 2021 with taxable trade profits of £27,000.

(b) 31 January 2021 with taxable trade profits of £22,500.

Test your understanding 12

Bernadette

Bernadette opened a riding school on 1 October 2017.

Accounts were prepared regularly to 30 September and her taxable trade profits are as follows:

		£
Year ended	30 September 2018	21,280
Year ended	30 September 2019	24,688
Year ended	30 September 2020	28,816
Year ended	30 September 2021	30,304

She intends to cease trading on 28 February 2022. The forecast taxable trade profits for the period from 1 October 2021 to 28 February 2022 have been estimated at £16,792.

Show the assessable amounts for all tax years of the business.

Test your understanding 13

Bay

Bay, who has been carrying on a manufacturing business in a south London suburb since 1 January 2017, decided to retire on 31 October 2020, having reached 65 years of age.

His adjusted profits (before capital allowances) and capital allowances (CAs) over the life of the business are:

		Profits £	CAs £
Year ending	31 December 2017	19,487	4,343
Year ending	31 December 2018	17,840	3,879
Year ending	31 December 2019	16,928	3,310
Period ending	31 October 2020	18,040	1,326

Compute all the assessable amounts for Bay for the years 2016/17 to 2020/21 inclusive.

Note that you must proceed in the following order:

- deduct the CAs from the adjusted profits

- apply the basis period rules to the profits after deducting CAs.

Test your understanding 14

Ranjit

On 1 November 2018, Ranjit commenced a manufacturing business preparing accounts to 30 September in each year.

The adjusted profits for income tax purposes but before deducting capital allowances and the capital allowances are as follows:

		Profits £	CAs £
Period ended	30 September 2019	6,106	3,800
Year ended	30 September 2020	8,845	5,000
Year ended	30 September 2021	19,087	9,950

Compute the assessable amounts for each of the years affected by the results and calculate the amount of overlap profits.

 Test your understanding 15

Violet

Violet, a sole trader, has always prepared her accounts to 30 September.

Violet has six months of overlap profits of £7,200.

She has now decided to change her accounting date to 28 February by preparing accounts for the 17 month period to 28 February 2021.

Violet's tax adjusted trading profits after capital allowances are:

	£
Year ended 30 September 2019	15,600
Period ended 28 February 2021	42,500

Calculate Violet's trading income assessments for 2019/20 and 2020/21.

Test your understanding 16

Period of assessment

Read the following statements and state whether they are true or false.

1   The basis of assessment is always the 12 months to the accounting date ending in the tax year. (F)

2   If Paul started trading on 1 August 2019 and prepares account to 5 April each year, he will have no overlap profits. (T)

3   When a new partner joins a partnership, he/she is immediately taxed on his/her share of the profits of the accounting period ending in the tax year. (F)

 Test your understanding 17

Marty and Wendy

Marty and Wendy started trading on 1 April 2020 and made a tax adjusted trading profit for the year ended 31 March 2021 of £60,000. They agreed to split the profits equally.

Oz joined the partnership on 1 January 2021, at which point the profit sharing arrangement was changed and Marty, Wendy and Oz agreed to share profits in the ratio 3:2:1.

What is Oz's trading income assessment for 2020/21?

A   £2,500

B   £5,000

C   £10,000

D   £7,500

Test your understanding 18

Gita and Bader

Gita and Bader commenced in business on 1 October 2017 as hotel proprietors, sharing profits equally.

On 1 October 2019 their son Yousef joined the partnership and from that date each of the partners were entitled to one third of the profits.

Recent profits of the partnership adjusted for income tax are:

	£
Year ended 30 June 2020	50,000
Year ended 30 June 2021	60,000

What amount of profit is assessable on Yousef for 2020/21?

A   £12,500

B   £17,500

C   £8,333

D   £18,750

8 Summary

As the final step in assessing profits of an individual, we must consider whether to apply the:

- current year basis
- opening year rules (and calculate overlap profits)
- closing year rules (and deduct overlap profits).

There are additional rules to learn where there has been a change of accounting date. The rules ensure that 12 months of profits are subject to tax in all tax years other than the year in which the trade starts and the year in which it stops.

✳ Links to other syllabus areas

The ability to apply a set of rules to a practical situation is a key skill for any accountant and one which is therefore very relevant for the exams which you sit.

It's a technique which you will have used and will go on to use in many other areas of your syllabus – in FSLC, for example, you employ similar skills by applying a set of accounting rules when considering how to present the financial consequences of a particular business transaction.

9   AAT reference material

Sole traders – basis periods

Tax year – 2020/21 tax year runs from 6 April 2020 to 5 April 2021

Basis period rules

- First year – runs from start date of trading to the next 5 April.

- Second year and third year:

Later years – basis period is the period of account ending in the tax year = Current Year basis (CYB).

Final year – basis period is the period from the end of the basis period for the previous tax year to cessation date.

Overlap profits – opening year rules may lead to profits being taxed twice. Relief is given on cessation of the business.

Sole traders – change of accounting date

For an accounting date change to be recognised for tax purposes the following conditions must be satisfied:

- the first accounts ending on the new date must not exceed 18 months in length.

- the sole trader or partnership must give notice of the change in the tax return by the filing date of the tax return.

- the change will not be permitted if there has been a change of accounting date in the previous 5 years unless there are genuine commercial reasons for the change.

Steps:

Step 1: Identify the year of change. This is the first year when current year basis is not possible.

Step 2: For all years before the year of change, the basis period is the 12 months to the old year end date.

Step 3: For all years after the year of change, the basis period is the 12 months to the new year end date.

Step 4: In the year of change, identify the 'relevant period'. The relevant period is the time to the new accounting date from the end of the previous basis period (i.e. all profits which have not been assessed as a result of steps 2 and 3)

- If the relevant period > 12 months, tax the profits of the relevant period but deduct overlap profits from commencement such that 12 months in total are taxed. The basis period is the same as the relevant period.

- If the relevant period is < 12 months, tax the 12 month period to the end of the relevant period (this will mean taxing some profits from the previous period twice, creating additional overlap profits). The basis period is the 12 months to the end of the relevant period.

Example 1 – relevant period is less than 12 months

Jasmin changes her accounting date as follows:

Accounts	Year	Basis period
Year to 31 December 2019	2019/20	1/1/19 to 31/12/19
9 months to 30 September 2020	2020/21	1/10/19 to 30/9/20
Year to 30 September 2021	2021/22	1/10/20 to 30/9/21

Year of change – 2020/21

Relevant period – 9 months to 30 September 2020

Basis period for 2020/21 – 12 months to 30 September 2020

Example 2 – relevant period is greater than 12 months

Vaughan changes his accounting date as follows:

Accounts	Year	Basis period
Year to 31 December 2019	2019/20	1/1/19 to 31/12/19
15 months to 31 March 2021	2020/21	1/1/20 to 31/3/21
Year to 31 March 2022	2021/22	1/4/21 to 31/3/22

Year of change – 2020/21

Relevant period – 15 months to 31 March 2021

Basis period for 2020/21 – 15 months to 31 March 2021

Test your understanding answers

 Test your understanding 1

Navaro

1   The correct answer is B.

   Explanation

   1 November 2017 (the date of commencement of trade) falls in the 2017/18 tax year.

2   The correct answer is C.

   Explanation

   The taxable profits in the first tax year are always the actual profits arising in the tax year.

   Therefore, the taxable profits are:

5 months ended 5 April 2018 (5/6 × £12,000)	£10,000

3   The correct answer is B.

   Explanation

   As the accounting period ending in the second tax year (2018/19) is less than 12 months long, the taxable period will be the first 12 months of trade.

   Therefore, the taxable profits are:

	£
6 months ended 30 April 2018	12,000
6 months ended 31 October 2018 (6/12 × £27,000)	13,500
	25,500

4   The correct answer is C.

Explanation

In the third tax year of trade (2019/20) the taxable trading profits are the profits for the 12 months ending on the accounting date falling in the tax year.

Therefore, the taxable profits are the profits for the year ended 30 April 2019.

5   The correct answer is £23,500.

Explanation

There are two periods which are taxed twice.

Therefore, the overlap profits are:

	£
5 months ended 5 April 2018 (5/6 × £12,000)	10,000
6 months ended 31 October 2018 (6/12 × £27,000)	13,500
	———
	23,500
	———

6   The correct answer is D.

📝 Test your understanding 2

Ali and Sofia

(a) Ali

Year of assessment	Basis period	Assessment £
2018/19	1 May 2018 – 5 April 2019	
	£20,250 + (£29,700 × 6/12)	35,100
2019/20	Year ending 30 September 2019	29,700
2020/21	Year ending 30 September 2020	36,450
2021/22	Year ending 30 September 2021	28,350

Overlap profits are:
1 Oct 2018 – 5 April 2019 (£29,700 × 6/12)   £14,850
                                            ———

(b) Sofia

Year of assessment	Basis period	Assessment £
2017/18	1 January 2018 – 5 April 2018 (£37,800 × 3/16)	7,087
2018/19	Year ending 5 April 2019 (£37,800 × 12/16)	28,350
2019/20	Year ending 30 April 2019 (£37,800 × 12/16)	28,350
2020/21	Year ending 30 April 2020	26,325
2021/22	Year ending 30 April 2021	29,350

Overlap profits are:

1 May 2018 – 5 April 2019 (£37,800 × 11/16)   £25,987

 Test your understanding 3

Adam, Shanaya and Catrina

The correct answer is D.

Explanation

The partnership continues despite Adam's resignation. Only Adam has to consider the closing rules to calculate his trading income assessments for 2020/21 (i.e. his final year).

The remaining partners continue to be assessed on a current year basis.

Test your understanding 4

Xavier

The correct answer is C.

Explanation

C is the correct answer because Xavier commenced trading in 2019/20, the assessment for which is calculated as the profits between 1 January 2020 and 5 April 2020.

There is no set of accounts ending in the second tax year, 2020/21, and therefore Xavier will be taxed on the basis of profits arising between 6 April 2020 and 5 April 2021.

 Test your understanding 5

Mario

The correct answer is B.

Explanation

The statement is false because there are no accounts ending in 2020/21 and therefore Mario will be assessed on the basis of profits arising between 6 April 2020 and 5 April 2021.

Test your understanding 6

Amit

The correct answer is B.

Explanation

Assessable trading profits:

Year of assessment	Basis period	Assessment £
2019/20	Actual basis – 1 July 2019 to 5 April 2020 9/22 × £33,000	13,500
2020/21	Actual basis – 6 April 2020 to 5 April 2021 12/22 × £33,000	18,000
2021/22	12 months to 30 April 2021 12/22 × £33,000	18,000

There are overlap profits for the period 1 May 2020 to 5 April 2021 of £16,500 (£33,000 × 11/22).

 Test your understanding 7

Katrina

The correct answer is C.

Explanation

Assessable trading profits

Year of assessment	Basis period	Assessment £
2019/20	Year ended 30 June 2019	30,000
2020/21	1 July 2019 – 28 February 2021 (£27,000 + £20,000 – £12,000)	35,000

Test your understanding 8

James

Year of assessment	Basis period		Assessment £
2016/17	1 January 2017 to 5 April 2017	(£75,600 × 3/16)	14,175
2017/18	Actual basis (6 April 2017 to 5 April 2018)	(£75,600 × 12/16)	56,700
2018/19	12 months to 30 April 2018	(£75,600 × 12/16)	56,700
2019/20	Year ended 30 April 2019		52,650
2020/21	Year ended 30 April 2020		56,900
Overlap	1 May 2017 to 5 April 2018 (£75,600 × 11/16)		51,975

Test your understanding 9

Avril

Year of assessment	Basis period	Assessment £
2017/18	(1 Jan 2018 – 5 Apr 2018) (3 months) £80,000 × 3/6	40,000
2018/19	Accounting period is less than 12 months therefore use first 12 months Period ended 30 Jun 2018 (6 months)	80,000
	1 Jul 2018 – 31 Dec 2018 (6 months) £100,000 × 6/12	50,000
		130,000
2019/20	Current year basis to 30 Jun 2019	100,000
2020/21	Current year basis to 30 Jun 2020	110,000
Overlap	(1 Jan 2018 – 5 Apr 2018) £40,000 Plus (1 Jul 2018 – 31 Dec 2018) £50,000	90,000

Test your understanding 10

Benny

Year of assessment	Basis period	Assessment £
2018/19	(1 Jul 2018 – 5 Apr 2019) (9 months)	
	Period ended 31 Dec 2018 (6 months)	14,000
	1 Jan 2019 – 5 Apr 2019 (3 months)	
	(£36,000 × 3/12)	9,000
		23,000
2019/20	Current year basis to 31 Dec 2019	36,000
2020/21	Current year basis to 31 Dec 2020	28,000
Overlap	(1 Jan 2019 – 5 Apr 2019) (£36,000 × 3/12)	9,000

Test your understanding 11

Elle

(a) **Cessation on 31 May 2021**

Year of assessment	Basis period	Assessment £
2019/20	Current year basis to 31 May 2019	22,000
2020/21	Current year basis to 31 May 2020	26,000
2021/22	Current year basis to 31 May 2021	27,000
	Less: Overlap profits	(5,000)
		22,000

(b)   Cessation on 31 January 2021

Year of assessment	Basis period	Assessment £
2019/20	Current year basis to 31 May 2019	22,000
2020/21	Year to 31 May 2020	26,000
	Plus: Period to 31 Jan 2021 (cessation)	22,500
	Less: Overlap profits	(5,000)
		43,500

Test your understanding 12

Bernadette

Year of assessment	Basis period	Assessment £
2017/18	(1 October 2017 – 5 April 2018) (6/12 × £21,280)	10,640
2018/19	Year ended 30 September 2018	21,280
2019/20	Year ended 30 September 2019	24,688
2020/21	Year ended 30 September 2020	28,816
2021/22	Year ended 30 September 2021	30,304
	Plus period to cessation on 28 February 2022	16,792
	Less: Overlap profits (W)	(10,640)
		36,456

Working

Overlap profits (1 Oct 2017 to 5 April 2018) (£21,280 × 6/12) = £10,640

📝 Test your understanding 13

Bay

Year of assessment	Basis period	Assessment £
2016/17	1 January 2017 – 5 April 2017 (3/12 × £15,144) (W)	3,786
2017/18	Year ended 31 December 2017	15,144
2018/19	Year ended 31 December 2018	13,961
2019/20	Year ended 31 December 2019	13,618
2020/21	10 months to 31 October 2020 Less: Overlap relief (W)	16,714 (3,786)
		12,928

Workings

Overlap profits

(1 Jan 2017 to 5 April 2017) (3/12 × £15,144) = £3,786

Adjusted profits after capital allowances

	Trading profit £	Capital allowances £	£
Year to 31 December 2017	19,487	(4,343)	15,144
Year to 31 December 2018	17,840	(3,879)	13,961
Year to 31 December 2019	16,928	(3,310)	13,618
10 months to 31 October 2020	18,040	(1,326)	16,714

Test your understanding 14

Ranjit

Year of assessment	Basis period	Assessment £
2018/19	1 Nov 2018 – 5 Apr 2019 (5 months of the 11 month period to 30 Sep 2019) (£2,306 × 5/11)	1,048
2019/20	Accounting period less than 12 months so: First 12 months	
	11 months to 30 Sep 2019 plus	2,306
	1 month to 31 Oct 2019 (£3,845 × 1/12)	320
		2,626
2020/21	Year ended 30 Sep 2020	3,845
2021/22	Year ended 30 Sep 2021	9,137

Overlap profits = (£1,048 + £320) = £1,368

Workings: Adjusted trading profits after capital allowances

	Trading profit £	Capital allowances £	£
Period ending 30 Sep 2019	6,106	(3,800)	2,306
Year ended 30 Sep 2020	8,845	(5,000)	3,845
Year ended 30 Sep 2021	19,087	(9,950)	9,137

Test your understanding 15

Violet

The tax year of change is the tax year in which accounts are prepared to the new accounting date (i.e. 2020/21).

As the new accounting date is later in the tax year, the basis period is the period ending with the new accounting date.

Tax year	Basis period	Taxable income £
2019/20	Year to 30 September 2019	15,600
		———
2020/21	Period not yet assessed ending on the new accounting date	
	17-month period to 28 February 2021	42,500
	Less: Overlap profits (£7,200 × 5/6)	(6,000)
		———
		36,500
		———

Note: In 2020/21 the period of account not yet assessed and ending with the new accounting date is 17 months. As no assessment can exceed 12 months, Violet is allowed to offset 5 months of her overlap profits.

The remaining month of overlap profits is carried forward as normal and is available for relief, either on a further change in accounting date or on the cessation of trade.

 Test your understanding 16

Periods of assessment

1 False   This is not true in the opening and closing years

2 True   The taxable trade profits of 2019/20 will be those of the period to 5 April 2020, and for 2020/21 will be those of the year to 5 April 2021, and so on. There are no overlap periods.

3 False   The opening year rules apply to individuals joining a partnership as if they had commenced a new trade.

Test your understanding 17

Marty and Wendy

The correct answer is A.

Explanation

A is the correct answer because profits are allocated to Oz in his first year of assessment as follows:

	Marty £	Wendy £	Oz £
1 Apr 2020 – 31 Dec 2020 (£60,000 × 9/12) – split evenly	22,500	22,500	
1 Jan 2021 – 31 Mar 2021 (£60,000 × 3/12) – split 3:2:1	7,500	5,000	2,500
	30,000	27,500	2,500

 Test your understanding 18

Gita and Bader

The correct answer is B.

Explanation

This is the fourth year of trading for Gita and Bader, so they are assessed on the normal current year basis.

It is the second year for Yousef. The accounts ending in 2020/21 are for the 9 month period from the date he joined the partnership (1 October 2019 to 30 June 2020). As this period is less than 12 months his assessment is based on his first 12 months of trading.

The basis period for Yousef will be:

2020/21   1 Oct 2019 – 30 Sep 2020 (1st 12 months)

The profits assessable on Yousef will be:

$(9/12 × £50,000/3) + (3/12 × £60,000/3) = £17,500$

Trading losses for individuals

Introduction

Just like companies, individuals can also make trading losses. This chapter discusses how a loss is calculated and how it can be relieved.

ASSESSMENT CRITERIA
Assess and calculate available loss relief (4.1)
Advise on the best use of a trading loss for sole traders, partnerships and limited companies (4.2)

CONTENTS

1   Identification of a trading loss
2   Ongoing businesses
3   Trading losses set against chargeable gains
4   Partnership losses

1 Identification of a trading loss

A trading loss is calculated in exactly the same way as a trading profit.

In other words, the accounting profit (or loss) is adjusted for tax purposes, and capital allowances are taken into account.

The adjusted loss is then identified with the tax year in which it arose. This is shown in the examples below.

 Example

A trader has a net accounting profit of £9,000 for the year ended 31 December 2020 which includes £3,000 of disallowable expenses. Capital allowances of £14,000 are available.

Calculate the taxable trade profits assessed in 2020/21 and the trading loss available for relief.

Solution

Year ended 31 December 2020	£
Net profit	9,000
Add: Disallowable expenses	3,000
	12,000
Less: Capital allowances	(14,000)
Adjusted loss	(2,000)

In this situation when a loss has arisen, the 2020/21 trading profits assessment is determined as £Nil and there is a (£2,000) trading loss available for relief.

Example

A trader has a net accounting loss of £9,000 for the year ended 31 December 2020 which includes £3,000 of disallowable expenses. Capital allowances of £14,000 are available.

Calculate the taxable trade profits assessed in 2020/21 and the trading loss available for relief.

Solution

	£
Accounting loss	(9,000)
Add: Disallowable expenses	3,000
	(6,000)
Less: Capital allowances	(14,000)
Adjusted loss	(20,000)

The assessment for 2020/21 is £Nil.

The trading loss available is £20,000.

It is easy to identify the wrong amount of loss available by not paying sufficient attention to the arithmetic.

Capital allowances, which normally reduce a profit, will increase a loss.

2 Ongoing businesses

2.1 Options available

There are two main ways of relieving a trading loss in an ongoing business:

- relief against total income of the current and/or the preceding tax year

- relief against future trading profits only.

2.2   Set off of trading loss against total income

This relief allows the trading loss to be set **against total income** of:

(i)   the **tax year of the loss**, and/or

(ii)   the **preceding tax year**.

A claim can be made to obtain relief in either year in isolation, or in both years, in either order.

If the individual wants relief as early as possible then the losses should be carried back against the previous tax year. This will generate a repayment of tax which will benefit cash flow.

When applying the loss relief it cannot be restricted to preserve the personal allowance. The personal allowance is deducted from income after loss relief has been deducted.

The personal allowance for 2020/21 is £12,500. This means that if a trader has total income of £12,500 or less, it is not worth claiming loss relief against total income for that year as the income will be covered by the personal allowance.

Any excess loss over and above total income is available for relief by carrying forward.

The AAT reference material set out in section 7 below has the rules for this type of claim and factors to consider when considering which claim to make.

Example

Beryl has a trading loss in her accounting year ended 30 September 2020 of £18,000.

Her other income is as follows:

	2019/20	2020/21
	£	£
Taxable trade profits	14,000	Nil
Other income	2,000	6,000

State the alternative claims Beryl could make to obtain loss relief against her total income.

Solution

The loss for the year ended 30 September 2020 is identified with the tax year 2020/21 as the accounting period ends in the tax year 2020/21.

As a result the taxable trade profits for 2020/21 are £Nil.

The loss could be offset against her total income in that year (2020/21) and/or the previous tax year (2019/20) as follows:

- set off £6,000 in 2020/21 and relieve the balance of £12,000 in 2019/20, or

- set off £6,000 in 2020/21 and make no claim for 2019/20, or

- set off £16,000 in 2019/20 and relieve the balance of £2,000 in 2020/21, or

- set off £16,000 in 2019/20 and make no claim for 2020/21.

It is important to identify all of the available options before deciding the course of action you will take.

2.3 Future relief for trading losses

The individual taxpayer does not *have* to claim relief for the loss against total income as described in section 2.2. If no such claim is made, all of the loss will be carried forward for relief in the future.

Alternatively, a claim may have been made for loss relief against total income, but as it can only be used in the same tax year as the loss and/or the previous year, there may be an amount of trading loss still unrelieved after this relief. This remaining amount will be available to carry forward.

Whatever the reason, any trading loss *not* relieved in the same or previous tax year is automatically carried forward.

The trading loss carried forward must be relieved against the **first available** taxable **trading profits** from the **same trade**.

The set off cannot be restricted. If there are sufficient losses, future taxable trade profits will be reduced to £Nil.

Trading losses carried forward cannot be set against other sources of income.

 Test your understanding 1

Sole trader losses

Which one of the following statements is correct with regard to a sole trader's losses?

A   A loss can only be relieved against trading profits made in the same tax year

B   A loss can be relieved in the preceding tax year, but only after a claim for relief has been made in the current tax year

C   A carried forward loss must be relieved against profits from the same trade in future years

D   A loss can be relieved against total income arising in future years

 Example

Dong has been trading for some time preparing accounts to 31 July.

His recent adjusted trading results are as follows:

		£
Year ended 31 July 2018	Profit	18,000
Year ended 31 July 2019	Loss	43,200
Year ended 31 July 2020	Profit	13,000
Year ended 31 July 2021	Profit	15,000

Dong's other income in each year is £12,000.

Show Dong's net income after loss relief for all tax years affected by the above results assuming:

(a)   no claim is made against total income for the trading loss

(b)   full claims are made to obtain relief against total income as early as possible.

Solution

(a) If no claim is made against total income

The trading loss of 2019/20 is carried forward against future trading profits.

	2018/19 £	2019/20 £	2020/21 £	2021/22 £
Taxable trade profits	18,000	Nil	13,000	15,000
Less: Loss relief b/f			(13,000)	(15,000)
	18,000	Nil	Nil	Nil
Other income	12,000	12,000	12,000	12,000
Net income after reliefs	30,000	12,000	12,000	12,000

Loss memorandum

	£
Year ended 31 July 2019 – Loss	43,200
Less: Utilised – 2020/21	(13,000)
– 2021/22	(15,000)
Loss left to carry forward to 2022/23	15,200

(b) Full claims made against total income

Claims against total income can only be made for 2018/19 and/or 2019/20, and any balance is carried forward for relief against future trading profits.

	2018/19 £	2019/20 £	2020/21 £	2021/22 £
Taxable trade profits	18,000	Nil	13,000	15,000
Less: Loss relief b/f			(1,200)	–
			11,800	15,000
Other income	12,000	12,000	12,000	12,000
	30,000	12,000	23,800	27,000
Less: Loss relief				
– current year		(12,000)		
– preceding year	(30,000)			
Net income after reliefs	Nil	Nil	23,800	27,000

Loss memorandum

	£
Year ended 31 July 2019 – Loss	43,200
Less: Relief against total income – 2018/19	(30,000)
– 2019/20	(12,000)
	1,200
Less: Utilised in 2020/21	(1,200)
Loss left to carry forward	Nil

 Test your understanding 2

Caroline

Caroline has been in business as a gourmet caterer since 1 July 2017.

She prepares accounts for calendar years and her adjusted trading results were as follows:

	£
Six months ended 31 December 2017	4,900
Year ended 31 December 2018	10,500
Year ended 31 December 2019	(45,000)
Year ended 31 December 2020	350

Caroline also receives a salary of £12,000 per annum from part-time secretarial work.

She has also received interest as follows:

2018/19   £220
2019/20   £8,715
2020/21   £8,700

Required:

Calculate Caroline's net income after reliefs (but before the personal allowance) for the years 2018/19 to 2020/21 inclusive, assuming reliefs for losses are claimed as early as possible.

3 Trading losses set against chargeable gains

If a trader still has loss remaining after offset against the total income for the year, the loss can be treated like a capital loss and set off against chargeable gains of the same tax year. The claim can also be made for the previous tax year. Chargeable gains are dealt with in Chapter 18.

4 Partnership losses

4.1 Reliefs available to partners

Partners are allocated losses in the same way as profits. Each partner is then entitled to decide independently on how to use his/her individual share of the loss.

An ongoing partner could use the loss against total income in the current and/or preceding tax year or carry the loss forward against trading profits.

Test your understanding 3

Read the following statements and state whether they are true or false.

1 A sole trader can restrict the amount of loss relief claimed against total income in the current year so that the personal allowance is not lost.

2 Kate has been trading for many years. A trading loss for the year to 31 December 2020 can be relieved by set off against total income of 2019/20 and/or 2020/21 (in any order). Any balance unrelieved will be carried forward and set against future trading profits of the same trade.

3 If a partnership makes a loss, all partners must claim loss relief in the same way.

5 Test your understanding

Test your understanding 4

Belinda

Belinda has been trading for many years and incurred a tax adjusted trading loss for the period ended 31 December 2020.

Which one of the following statements is correct with regard to the use of the trading loss?

A   The trading loss may be carried forward and set against trading income for 2020/21 arising from the same trade

B   The trading loss can be set against total income for 2020/21, but only after the loss is set against total income for 2019/20

C   The trading loss can be set against total income for 2019/20, irrespective of whether the loss has been set against total income for 2020/21

D   The trading loss can be set against total income for 2019/20, but only after the loss is set against total income for 2020/21

Test your understanding 5

Bourbon

Bourbon has been trading as a self-employed biscuit maker for many years. His taxable trade profits or losses are given below.

		£
Year to 31 March 2020	Profit	12,200
Year to 31 March 2021	Loss	(24,050)
Year to 31 March 2022	Profit	12,750

Details of Bourbon's other income is as follows:

	2019/20 £	2020/21 £	2021/22 £
Building society interest received	7,250	17,100	5,250

Required:

(a) Set out the options to an established business continuing to trade for relief of the loss.

(b) Advise Bourbon, with calculations, as to the best method of obtaining loss relief.

6 Summary

The loss reliefs available to an ongoing business are summarised below.

- Relief against total income – current and/or preceding tax year.

- Carry forward against future profits of the same trade.

- Relief against gains – current and/or preceding tax year provided a claim is made against income of the same tax year first.

✳ Links to other syllabus areas

A trading loss will generally have cash flow implications for the business – either by giving rise to a tax repayment or in the form of a reduction in future tax liabilities.

An understanding of the impact on cash flow of tax losses is important and will need to be reflected in the budgets and forecasts of the business as well as considerations of its ongoing viability into the future. Therefore, there is a link in with other units such as MABU and MDCL.

7 AAT reference material

Trading losses for sole traders and partners

- A loss is computed in the same way as a profit, making the same adjustments to the net profit as per the accounts and deducting capital allowances.

Set off of trading loss against total income

- Set off loss against total income of the preceding tax year and/or the tax year of loss, e.g. loss in 2020/21 set off against total income in 2019/20 and/or 2020/21.

- Cannot restrict loss to preserve use of personal allowance so personal allowance may be wasted.

- For 2020/21 loss claim needed by 31 January 2023.

Carry forward of trading losses

- If any loss remains unrelieved after current year and carry back claim has been made, or no such claims are made, then carry forward the loss against first available profits of the same trade.

Choice of loss relief – consider the following:

- Utilise loss in the tax year in which income is taxed at a higher rate.

- Possible wastage of personal allowance.

- Review the projected future profits to ensure the loss can be utilised.

- If cash flow is important, a loss carry back claim may result in a tax refund being paid to the business.

Test your understanding answers

Test your understanding 1

Sole trader losses

The correct answer is C.

Explanation

Once a loss has been carried forward it must be set against future profits of the same trade. It cannot be set against total income in the future.

The taxpayer can choose whether to offset a trading loss against total income in the current tax year and/or the preceding year. It is not necessary to make these claims in any particular order.

Test your understanding 2

Caroline

Income tax computations

	2018/19 £	2019/20 £	2020/21 £
Taxable trade profits	10,500	Nil	350
Less: Loss relief b/f	–	–	(350)[3]
	10,500	Nil	Nil
Employment income	12,000	12,000	12,000
Interest	220	8,715	8,700
Total income	22,720	20,715	20,700
Less: Loss relief			
– preceding year	(22,720)[1]		
– current year		(20,715)[2]	
Net income after reliefs	Nil	Nil	20,700

Notes:

1   Relief against total income can be in any order.

2 The question says offset the loss as early as possible, therefore the claim is made against 2018/19 first, then 2019/20.

3 The remaining loss is then carried forward to 2020/21 and set against the first available trading profits.

Loss memorandum

		£
Loss in 2019/20 – year ended 31 December 2019		45,000
Less: Claim 2018/19 (preceding year)	(1)	(22,720)
		22,280
Less: Claim 2019/20 (year of loss)	(2)	(20,715)
		1,565
Less: Carry forward claim 2020/21	(3)	(350)
Loss carried forward		1,215

Test your understanding 3

1 False Loss relief claims cannot be restricted to preserve the personal allowance.

2 True

3 False Each partner can choose independently what loss relief to claim.

Test your understanding 4

Belinda

The correct answer is C.

Explanation

The trading loss can be carried forward and set against future trading profits, but the loss is incurred in 2020/21 and will therefore be available to carry forward to 2021/22, not 2020/21.

The trading loss can be set against total income of 2020/21 and/or 2019/20. There is no need for the claim for 2020/21 to be made before that of 2019/20 or vice versa.

Test your understanding 5

Bourbon

(a) **Alternative means of loss relief**

   (i)   Carry forward for set off against the next available taxable trading income from the same trade until the loss is fully relieved.

   (ii) Claim against the total income of:

   –   the tax year of loss; and/or

   –   the preceding tax year.

(b) **Advice on relief**

From the following computations it can be seen that the best method of obtaining relief is for Bourbon to claim relief against total income for 2019/20 to obtain relief as early as possible.

A claim against total income should also be made in 2020/21 for the balance of the loss, as there will still be enough income remaining after the loss claim to use up the personal allowance of £12,500.

	2019/20 £	2020/21 £	2021/22 £
Trading profits	12,200	Nil	12,750
Less: Loss relief b/f	–	–	–
	12,200	Nil	12,750
Interest	7,250	17,100	5,250
	19,450	17,100	18,000
Less: Loss relief			
– Current year		(4,600)	
– Carry back	(19,450)		
Net income after reliefs	Nil	12,500	18,000

Payment and administration – individuals

13

Introduction

This chapter covers tax returns and amendments, the payment of tax and compliance checks for individuals.

At the end of each section you will find a summary showing which information from that section is provided in the AAT reference material, and which information is not provided and therefore needs to be learnt.

ASSESSMENT CRITERIA
Tax return filing deadlines (3.1)
Payment rules for sole traders and partnerships: amounts and dates (3.1)
Penalties for late filing of tax returns and failing to notify chargeability (3.2)
Late payment interest and surcharges (3.2)
The enquiry window and penalties for incorrect returns (3.2)
What records need to be maintained by a business, how long these records need to be maintained and the penalties for failing to keep these records (4.3)

CONTENTS

1 Introduction to the self-assessment return
2 Payment of income tax and capital gains tax
3 Interest and penalties on payments of tax
4 HM Revenue and Customs' compliance checks
5 Penalties for incorrect returns

1 Introduction to the self-assessment return

1.1 The self-assessment return

Certain individuals are required to complete a return for every tax year.

Amongst other things the return covers trading income and capital gains and, in some cases, a calculation of the tax payable.

The key details to grasp concerning the return are the filing dates.

The taxpayer has the choice of filing a paper return or filing electronically online. The date by which a return must be filed depends on the method used.

All completed and signed paper returns must be filed by:

- 31 October following the end of the tax year.

All online electronic returns must be filed by:

- 31 January following the end of the tax year.

The relevant dates for a 2020/21 return are therefore 31 October 2021 for a paper return and 31 January 2022 for an electronic return.

Where a taxpayer submits a paper return HMRC will calculate the tax due. If a taxpayer chooses to file online then the tax will be calculated automatically.

HMRC normally issue an individual with a notice to complete a tax return in April/May following the end of the tax year.

However, where HMRC issue a notice to complete a tax return late, the taxpayer has until the later of the filing dates mentioned above and 3 months after the notice is issued in which to file their return.

An individual who receives a notice to file a 2020/21 tax return from HMRC on 15 August 2021 therefore has until 15 November 2021 to file a paper return or until 31 January 2022 to file the return electronically.

31 January following the end of the tax year is known as the 'filing date', regardless of whether the return is filed on paper or electronically. This must be distinguished from the date on which the return is filed/submitted to HMRC (known as the 'actual' filing date).

The return consists of an eight page summary form with six supplementary pages for self-employed individuals.

In the assessment you will only be required to complete page 2 of the self-employment supplementary pages and/or page 6 of the partnership return.

Where a notice to file a tax return is not issued, an individual is required to notify HMRC by **5 October** following the tax year where there is chargeable income (i.e. new sources of income) or gains arising.

Notification is not required where there are no assessable gains or where the income is either covered by allowances or the full tax liability has been deducted at source.

Failure to notify may result in a penalty. The penalty is calculated in broadly the same way as penalties for incorrect returns (see below) and is a maximum of 100% of the tax outstanding.

The taxpayer is permitted to correct or 'repair' his/her self-assessment return within 12 months of the filing date (i.e. by 31 January 2023 for a 2020/21 return). HMRC can correct 'obvious errors' and anything else which they believe to be incorrect by reference to the information they hold in the period of nine months from actual filing.

Where an assessment is excessive due to an error or mistake in a return, the taxpayer can claim overpayment relief. The claim must be made within four years of the end of the tax year concerned.

Note that many of the details about dates, time limits and penalties are contained in the AAT reference material set out below in section 8. You should refer to this throughout this chapter.

1.2   Records

An individual must retain certain records to support the completed tax return, to assist with providing evidence to support information given to HMRC.

Self-employed people (i.e. sole traders and partners in a partnership) must keep records for five years after the filing date (i.e. until 31 January 2027 for 2020/21 information).

Examples of records to be kept include the following:

- accounts
- supporting documentation such as receipts and invoices
- dividend vouchers.

Failure to keep records can lead to a penalty of up to £3,000 per tax year.

1.3 Penalties for late filing

Failure to submit a return by 31 January following a tax year will result in a penalty.

The system operates as follows:

Immediate penalty	£100
Delay of more than three months	an additional £10 per day (maximum 90 days = £900)
Delay of more than six months	an additional 5% of tax due
Delay of more than 12 months	the penalties above, plus:
No deliberate withholding of information	5% of tax due
Deliberate withholding of information	70% of tax due
Deliberate withholding of information with concealment	100% of tax due

The penalties based on the tax due are each subject to a minimum of £300.

A penalty will not be charged if the taxpayer has a reasonable excuse for the late filing, for example a serious illness. A lack of knowledge of the tax system is not a reasonable excuse.

Test your understanding 1

Bob

Bob understands that he has responsibilities under the self-assessment system and is required to meet a number of deadlines. In particular, he needs confirmation of the deadlines for the following actions.

1   Notifying HMRC that he started receiving rent for the first time on 1 January 2021. *A*

2   Filing a paper return for 2020/21. *C*

3   Filing his 2020/21 return electronically. *B*

4   Amending his 2020/21 tax return. *D*

Match each of Bob's responsibilities with the correct deadline:

A   5 October 2021 *(1)*

B   31 January 2022 *(3)*

C   31 October 2021 *(2)*

D   31 January 2023 *(4)*

1.4 Summary of reference material

Item	Included in reference material	Not included in reference material
Paper and online filing deadlines	✓	
Extension to deadline where notice to file given late		✓
Deadline to notify chargeability	✓	
Penalties for failure to notify chargeability		✓
Deadline for taxpayer to amend return	✓	
Deadline for HMRC to amend return		✓
Deadline to claim overpayment relief	✓	
Deadline for keeping records	✓	
Examples of records to keep		✓
Penalty for failure to keep appropriate records for required period	✓	
Penalties for late filing	✓	

2 Payment of income tax and capital gains tax

2.1 The instalment system

As well as submitting a tax return certain individuals will also need to make payments of tax.

Self-employed individuals are required to pay their tax liability in instalments.

The instalment system operates as follows:

- 31 January in the tax year: first payment on account (POA).

- 31 July *following* the tax year: second payment on account (POA).

- 31 January *following* the tax year: final payment.

For example, for 2020/21 the following dates are relevant:

The payments on account are estimated, in that they are based on the previous year's income tax and class 4 national insurance contributions (NICs) payable. Note that the tax payable figure used in the payments on account calculation is net of any tax deducted under PAYE.

The taxpayer can claim to make reduced payments on account where this year's income tax payable is expected to be less than that of last year. The taxpayer will be charged a penalty if the claim to make reduced payments on account was made either fraudulently or negligently.

In the assessment a detailed understanding of the payments on account system is expected, including when payments are due and how to pay them.

Example

Roderic is self-employed. His only source of income is from his trade. The income tax payable for 2019/20 was £5,100.

His income tax payable for 2020/21 based on his taxable trade profits for the year ended 31 July 2020 is £7,032.

Ignoring NICs, state Roderic's payments in respect of his 2020/21 income tax liability.

Solution

Step 1: Determine the relevant dates

31 January 2021	–	first payment on account
31 July 2021	–	second payment on account
31 January 2022	–	final payment

Step 2: Determine the amounts due

- The amounts due for the 'payments on account' are based on an equal division of the previous year's tax payable, hence £2,550 (£5,100 ÷ 2).

- The final payment on account will be based on the final liability for 2020/21 less the payments on account already made.

	£
2020/21 IT liability	7,032
Payments on account (2 × £2,550)	(5,100)
	————
Final payment	1,932
	————

Step 3: Prepare a final summary

	£
31 January 2021	2,550
31 July 2021	2,550
31 January 2022	1,932

The amount due on 31 January following the end of the tax year consists of the final payment on account for the year just ended and the first payment on account for the new tax year.

In Roderic's case this means that on 31 January 2022 he will start the instalment option all over again, by making the first payment on account of his 2021/22 liability based on 2020/21 tax payable.

Hence his 31 January 2022 payment is £5,448 ((£7,032 × ½) + £1,932).

The class 4 national insurance contributions payable by a self-employed person are also paid by the instalment system (see Chapter 14).

 Test your understanding 2

Kazuo

Kazuo is required to pay tax in instalments.

For 2019/20, his income tax liability was £18,700, of which £2,000 was collected via PAYE. He estimates that his income tax payable for 2020/21 will be £22,000.

What is the amount of the first payment on account that Kazuo should make on 31 January 2021 in respect of his income tax liability for 2020/21?

Ignore national insurance.

A   £8,350

B   £9,350

C   £10,000

D   £11,000

2.2 No requirement for payments on account

Payments on account are not required in the following circumstances:

- The income tax and class 4 NICs payable for the previous tax year by self-assessment is less than £1,000, or

- More than 80% of the income tax liability for the previous tax year was met through tax deducted at source.

2.3 Class 2 NICs

Class 2 NICs (see Chapter 14) are payable on 31 January following the end of the tax year, together with the final payment of income tax. They are not subject to payments on account.

2.4 Capital gains tax

The capital gains tax due for a tax year (see Chapter 18) is payable on 31 January following the end of the tax year, together with the final payment of income tax.

CGT is therefore paid in one instalment on 31 January following the tax year regardless of whether there was a CGT liability for the previous year.

The CGT liability is not taken into account when determining the payments on account for income tax.

Payments on account of capital gains tax are never required.

 Test your understanding 3

(a) State the latest date by which the taxpayer should submit the 2020/21 tax return if:

    (i) he/she wishes to file his return online, or *31-Jan-2022*

    (ii) he/she wishes to file a paper return. *31-oct-2021*

(b) State:

    (i) the normal dates of payment of income tax and class 4 NICs for a sole trader in respect of the tax year 2020/21, and *31/Jan-2021 - Prev*

    (ii) how the amounts of these payments are calculated. *31 July - 2021 - Prev*
31 Jan- 2022 - Bud.

(c) State:

    (i) the penalties that can be charged where a tax return is submitted within six months after the due date, and *100+900 = 1000*

    (ii) the penalties that can be charged where a tax return is submitted more than six months late. *100+900 +5% tax due (mn. 300)*

2.5 Recovery of overpaid tax

Taxpayers who believe that they have paid too much income tax or capital gains tax can submit a claim in order to have the excess tax repaid. The claim must be submitted within four years of the end of the relevant tax year.

2.6 Summary of reference material

Item	Included in reference material	Not included in reference material
Due dates for payments on account and balancing payment	✓	
Instances where payments on account are not required	✓	
Class 2 NIC due date	✓	
Capital gains tax due date	✓	
Recovery of overpaid tax	✓	

3 Interest and penalties on payments of tax

3.1 Interest

Taxpayers that fail to make payments, whether payments on account (POA) or final payments, by the due date will be charged interest.

Interest is not perceived as being a penalty but merely as commercial compensation for late payment. It is not a deductible expense when computing taxable income.

Interest is charged from the day the tax is due until the day it is paid.

In addition to the interest charge there is also a penalty where tax is paid late.

An individual who receives a tax repayment may receive interest in respect of the amount repaid. This interest income is not taxable.

The tax treatment of interest on underpayments/overpayments of corporation tax paid by or to companies is different from that for individuals and is covered in Chapter 7.

 Example

Rodney was due to make the following payments of tax for 2020/21.

		Actual date of payment
31 January 2021	£2,100	28 February 2021
31 July 2021	£2,100	31 August 2021
31 January 2022	£1,000	31 March 2022

For what periods will interest be charged?

Solution

On first POA	31 January 2021 – 28 February 2021	1 month
On second POA	31 July 2021 – 31 August 2021	1 month
On final payment	31 January 2022 – 31 March 2022	2 months

3.2 Penalty for late payment of tax

A penalty will be charged where there is income tax or capital gains tax outstanding after the day on which the final payment of tax is due (31 January after the end of the tax year). This penalty is in addition to any interest that is charged.

- More than 30 days late   5% of tax overdue

- More than six months late   further 5% of tax overdue

- More than 12 months late   further 5% of tax overdue

A late payment penalty may be mitigated (i.e. reduced) where the taxpayer can provide a reasonable excuse, for example a serious illness.

Insufficiency of funds or lack of knowledge of self-assessment are not reasonable excuses.

No penalties are due in respect of late payments on account.

Example

Star made the final payment in respect of his 2019/20 self-assessment return on 31 August 2021.

What penalties will be charged in respect of the late payment of the tax?

Solution

The final payment in respect of the 2019/20 self-assessment return was due on 31 January 2021. The payment is more than six months but less than 12 months late.

Because the payment is more than six months late there will be a total penalty of 10% of the tax outstanding, i.e. 5% for being 30 days late and an additional 5% for being six months late.

(Note that Star will also be charged interest on the late paid tax from 31 January 2021 to 31 August 2021. However, the question only asked for the penalties.)

3.3 Summary of reference material

Item	Included in reference material	Not included in reference material
Interest on tax paid late/overpaid tax	✓	
Dates between which interest will be charged		✓
Penalties on late paid tax	✓	
Details of which payments penalties are charged on		✓
Mitigation of penalties where there is a reasonable excuse		✓

4   HM Revenue and Customs' compliance checks

4.1   Introduction

HMRC have the right to enquire into an individual's tax return (similar to the system on corporation tax returns) under their compliance check powers. This may be a random check or because they have reason to believe that income or expenses have been misstated in the tax return.

Where the return is filed on time they must make their compliance check (enquiry) within 12 months of the date the return was filed.

Where a return is submitted late HMRC can give notice of a compliance check (also referred to as an enquiry) within a year of the 31 January, 30 April, 31 July or 31 October following the actual date of delivery of the return.

4.2   Compliance check (enquiry) procedure

Once the compliance check notice is given, an Officer can request relevant documents and written particulars. If the individual fails to do so, a penalty of £300, plus up to £60 a day, may be imposed.

At the end of the compliance check a closure notice is issued stating the outcome of the enquiry, for example, no amendment made or business profits increased by a particular amount.

In more complex cases, if the compliance check covers several different aspects, then a partial closure notice (PCN) may be issued to bring one particular part of the compliance check to an end ahead of the final closure notice.

The taxpayer has 30 days from completion to ask for their case to be reviewed.

4.3   Discovery assessments

Although HMRC usually only have 12 months from the date a return is filed to open a compliance check (enquiry), they can replace a self-assessment at a later date by making a discovery assessment.

A discovery assessment can be made where tax has been lost perhaps because of insufficient information in the tax return.

The taxpayer can appeal to the Tax Tribunal against a discovery assessment.

4.4 Appeals procedure

The taxpayer can request an informal review of a disputed decision.

Alternatively, a formal appeal may be made to the Tax Tribunal.

Appeals from the Tax Tribunal on a point of law (but not on a point of fact) may be made to the Court of Appeal and from there to the Supreme Court.

The Tax Tribunal is independent of HMRC.

4.5 Summary of reference material

Item	Included in reference material	Not included in reference material
Reasons why HMRC may open an enquiry	✓	
Deadline for HMRC to open an enquiry where the return was filed on time	✓	
Deadline for HMRC to open an enquiry where the return was filed late		✓
Penalty for failure to produce enquiry documents	✓	
Details of closure notice/partial closure notice		✓
Discovery assessments		✓
Appeals		✓

5 Penalties for incorrect returns

5.1 Penalties for incorrect returns

The common penalty regime described in Chapter 7 applies to income tax returns as well as corporation tax returns.

The penalties are the same for individuals in that a penalty will be charged where an inaccurate return is submitted to HMRC or where the individual fails to notify HMRC where an under assessment of tax is made by them.

Example

State the maximum and minimum penalties that may be levied on each of the following individuals who have submitted incorrect tax returns.

Lars   Deliberately understated his tax liability and attempted to conceal the incorrect information that he had provided. HMRC have identified the understatement and Lars is helping them with their enquiries. *100% / 50%*

Sven   Accidentally provided an incorrect figure even though he checked his tax return carefully. He realised his mistake a few days later and notified HMRC. *Nil*

Jo   Completed his tax return too quickly and made a number of errors. The day after he had submitted the tax return he decided to check it thoroughly and immediately provided HMRC with the information necessary to identify the errors. *30% / 0%*

Solution

Penalties for incorrect tax returns are a percentage of the under declared tax.

Lars   The maximum percentage for a deliberate understatement with concealment is 100%. The minimum percentage for prompted disclosure of information (where the taxpayer provides information in response to HMRC identifying the error) in respect of deliberate understatement with concealment is 50%.

Sven   No penalty is charged where a taxpayer has been careful and has made a genuine mistake.

Jo   The maximum percentage for failing to take reasonable care is 30%. The minimum percentage for unprompted disclosure is nil.

Test your understanding 4

1   James commenced his own business in February 2021.

    If he does not receive a notice to complete a tax return for 2020/21, by what date should he notify HMRC that he is chargeable to tax for 2020/21? *31/May/2021*

2   Isabel made her second payment on account of tax for 2020/21 on 15 September 2021.

    What are the consequences? *No penalties on PoA*

3   Mike filed his 2020/21 tax return on 18 January 2022.

    What is the latest date for HMRC to open a compliance check (enquiry)? *18/Jan – 2023*

5.2   Summary of reference material

Item	Included in reference material	Not included in reference material
Penalties for incorrect returns	✓	

6 Test your understanding

Test your understanding 5

Payments on account

State the appropriate dates in respect of the following payments.

1   First instalment for tax year – 2020/21   *31/Jan/2021*

2   Second instalment for tax year – 2020/21   *31/July/2021*

3   Final instalment for tax year – 2020/21   *21/Jan/2022*

4   Payment date for capital gains tax for tax year – 2020/21   *31/Jan/2022*

Test your understanding 6

Income tax self-assessment

Read the following statements and state whether they are true or false.

1   An individual must retain tax records for 2020/21 until 5 April 2026.   *(F)*

2   If an individual is two months late in submitting his/her tax return for 2020/21, he/she will receive a penalty of £100.   *(T)*

3   Penalties for errors made by individuals in their tax returns vary from 30% to 100%.   *(F)*

4   Late payment penalties can be imposed on balancing payments made late.   *(T)*

> ### Test your understanding 7
>
> **Income tax self-assessment**
>
> Clark is a new client who has come to you for information about the self-assessment system.
>
> Explain to Clark:
>
> (a) The latest date by which income tax returns for the year 2020/21 should be submitted to HM Revenue and Customs (HMRC).
>
> (b) The date by which Clark should notify HMRC that he has received income in the year 2020/21 which is liable to income tax where no notice to complete an income tax return has been issued.
>
> (c) The potential penalties for the late submission of income tax returns and when they apply.
>
> (d) The penalty for the submission of an incorrect income tax return.
>
> (e) The penalty for failing to maintain or retain adequate records to back up an income tax return.

(a) The paper submissions to done by 31/oct/2021 and electronic submission to be done by 31/Jan/2022.

(b) You should notify HMRC by 5/oct/2021.

(c) Immediate Penalty of 100 applies and If its 3 months

7 Summary

This chapter covers a core topic – self-assessment.

Traders have to self-assess their tax liability and pay any tax due because they receive trading income gross, i.e. without deduction of tax at source.

Payment dates

31 January 2021

- Balance of income tax and class 4 NICs payable for 2019/20.
- CGT liability for 2019/20.
- First POA for 2020/21 (based on previous year's liability).

31 July 2021

- Second POA for 2020/21.

31 January 2022

- Balance of income tax and class 4 NICs payable for 2020/21.
- CGT liability for 2020/21.
- First POA for 2021/22 (based on liability for 2020/21).

Filing returns (2020/21 return)

Paper return   –   31 October 2021

Electronic return   –   31 January 2022 (the 'filing date')

Main penalties

Late filing – an immediate £100 penalty with further penalties if the return is more than three, six or 12 months late.

Incorrect returns – same as Corporation tax (see Chapter 7).

Tax unpaid 30 days after 31 January – 5% penalty with further 5% penalties if the tax remains outstanding after six and 12 months.

If no compliance check (enquiry) notice issued by the anniversary of the date the return is filed, the taxpayer can assume it is 'final'.

However, if HMRC are able to show they had insufficient information supplied in the tax return, they can make a 'discovery' assessment.

✳ Links to other syllabus areas

A professional adviser needs to know when, and how, the business must discharge its legal responsibilities and the penalties for failing to do things correctly or on time.

One of the fundamental ethical principles is that of professional competence and due care. This means having a thorough understanding of the underlying legal and regulatory rules such that we are in a position to provide advice which is technically correct.

Tax is a key part of a business's legal obligations and ethics is a recurring theme in all of your AAT units.

KAPLAN PUBLISHING

8 AAT reference material

Payment and administration – sole traders and partners

The return must be filed by:

- 31 October following the end of the tax year if filing a paper return.
- 31 January following the end of the tax year if filing online.

Penalties for late filing and payment

Late filing	Late payment	Penalty
Miss filing deadline		£100
	30 days late	5% of tax outstanding at that date
3 months late		Daily penalty £10 per day for up to 90 days (max £900)
6 months late		5% of tax due or £300, if greater
	6 months late	5% of tax outstanding at that date
12 months late		5% of tax due or £300, if greater
	12 months late	5% of tax outstanding at that date
12 months and information deliberately withheld		Based on behaviour: • deliberate and concealed withholding 100% of tax due, or £300 if greater. • deliberate but not concealed 70% of tax due, or £300 if greater. Reductions apply for prompted and unprompted disclosures and for cooperation with investigation.

Disclosure and errors

- Taxpayer must notify HMRC by 5 October following end of the tax year if a tax return is needed.

- Taxpayer can amend a tax return within 12 months of filing date or make a claim for overpayment relief within 4 years of the end of the tax year.

Payments on account (POA)

- Due 31 January (in tax year) and 31 July (after tax year end). Each instalment is 50% of the previous year's tax and Class 4 National Insurance contribution (NIC) liability after taking into account any tax deducted at source.

- Balancing payment made 31 January after tax year end.

- No POA due if:

  - last year's tax and Class 4 NIC liability less than £1,000 or

  - if greater than 80% of last year's liability was deducted at source.

- Can reduce this year's POA if this year's liability expected to be less than last year's. Penalties and interest will be charged if a deliberate incorrect claim is made.

- Capital gains tax (CGT) liability and Class 2 National Insurance is paid 31 January following the tax year end. No POA needed for CGT and Class 2 National Insurance.

Interest on tax paid late/overpaid tax

- Interest charged daily on late payment.

Enquiries and other penalties

- HMRC must notify individual of enquiry within 12 months of submission of return.

- Basis of enquiry – random or HMRC believe income/expenses misstated.

- Penalty for failure to produce enquiry documents = £300 + £60 per day.

- Penalty for failure to keep proper records is up to £3,000. Records must be kept for five years after the filing date for the relevant tax year.

- Penalties for incorrect returns are detailed in the table below:

Type of behaviour	Maximum	Unprompted (minimum)	Prompted (minimum)
Genuine mistake: despite taking reasonable care	0%	0%	0%
Careless error and inaccuracy is due to failure to take reasonable care	30%	0%	15%
Deliberate error but not concealed	70%	20%	35%
Deliberate error and concealed	100%	30%	50%

Test your understanding answers

Test your understanding 1

1   A
2   C
3   B
4   D

Test your understanding 2

Kazuo

The correct answer is A.

Explanation

The payment on account is calculated as follows:

	£
2019/20 income tax liability	18,700
Less: PAYE	(2,000)
Income tax payable under self-assessment	16,700
First payment on account for 2020/21 (£16,700 ÷ 2)	8,350

Test your understanding 3

Self-assessment

(a) (i) 31 January following the tax year to which the return relates (i.e. 31 January 2022 for 2020/21).

(ii) 31 October following the tax year to which the return relates (i.e. 31 October 2021 for 2020/21).

(b) (i) (1) 31 January in the tax year (i.e. 31 January 2021).

(2) 31 July following the tax year (i.e. 31 July 2021).

(3) 31 January following the tax year (i.e. 31 January 2022).

(ii) Payments (1) and (2) are equal amounts each amounting to half the income tax and class 4 NIC payable in respect of the preceding tax year.

Payment (3) is the balancing figure (i.e. it is the amount of the final income tax and class 4 NIC liability for the year, less any tax deducted at source, less payments (1) and (2)).

(c) (i) There will be an immediate penalty of £100.

A further penalty of £10 per day for a maximum of 90 days can be charged once the return is more than three months late.

(ii) As well as the penalties listed above, there will be a further penalty of 5% of the tax due (minimum £300) once the return is more than six months late.

Once the return is more than 12 months late there will be a further penalty equal to a percentage of the tax due (minimum £300). The percentage is determined by the reason for the delay.

No deliberate withholding of information	5%
Deliberate withholding	70%
Deliberate withholding with concealment	100%

Test your understanding 4

1   James must notify HMRC by 5 October 2021.

2   Isabel will be charged interest from the due date of 31 July 2021 until 15 September 2021, the day of payment.

3   The latest date for opening a compliance check (enquiry) is 18 January 2023; one year after Mike filed the return.

Test your understanding 5

Payments on account

1   31 January 2021

2   31 July 2021

3   31 January 2022

4   31 January 2022

Test your understanding 6

Period of assessment

1   False   The records must be retained until 31 January 2027.

2   True

3   False   The penalties start at 0% for a genuine mistake.

4   True

Test your understanding 7

Income tax self-assessment

(a) The date by which a return must be filed depends on the filing method used.

A paper return must be filed by 31 October 2021 for the tax year 2020/21 (i.e. 31 October following the end of the tax year).

An electronic return must be filed by 31 January 2022 for the tax year 2020/21 (i.e. 31 January following the end of the tax year).

(b) Notification is due by 5 October 2021 if a new source arises in 2020/21 and a tax notice to complete a tax return has not been issued.

(c) If a tax return is submitted late, a £100 fixed penalty is charged.

If it is still outstanding after 3 months, a further £10 per day can be charged for a maximum of 90 days.

If it is still outstanding after 6 months, a further penalty equal to 5% of the tax due is charged.

If the return is still outstanding after 12 months, a penalty of up to 100% of the tax outstanding is charged.

(d) The penalty for submitting an incorrect tax return is a percentage of the revenue lost.

The percentage ranges from 0% (where the taxpayer has simply made a mistake) to 100% (where the taxpayer has deliberately understated the return and concealed the error).

(e) The penalty for failing to maintain adequate records is up to £3,000.

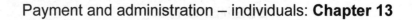

National insurance contributions payable by self-employed individuals

Introduction

A self-employed individual has his/her own national insurance contributions to pay, but may also have to pay contributions as an employer.

ASSESSMENT CRITERIA	CONTENTS
Determine who is liable to pay NI contributions (1.5) Calculate NI contributions (1.5)	1 Contributions as an employer 2 Contributions as a sole trader 3 Effect of partnerships

1   Contributions as an employer

1.1   Class 1 secondary and class 1A contributions

A sole trader or partnership may employ staff.

As an employer, they may be liable to class 1 secondary and class 1A contributions in relation to the remuneration paid to their employees.

However, calculations of these contributions are outside the syllabus for business tax.

2   Contributions as a sole trader

2.1   Class 4 NICs

A self-employed person, whether operating as a sole trader or as a partner, pays two types of national insurance contributions:

- class 2 and
- class 4.

Class 4 NICs are calculated by applying a fixed percentage (currently 9%) to the amount by which the taxpayer's 'profits' (or share of 'profits', where the taxpayer is a member of a partnership) exceed a lower limit (£9,500 for 2020/21).

Example

If Nicholas has 'profits' of £12,775 for 2020/21, he will be liable to pay class 4 NICs calculated as follows:

	£
'Profits'	12,775
Less: Lower limit	(9,500)
Excess	3,275
Class 4 NICs (9% × £3,275)	294.75

The 9% rate only applies up to an upper limit of profits (£50,000 for 2020/21).

Where a taxpayer's 'profits' exceed the upper limit, the excess profit is liable to class 4 NICs at 2%.

For example, if a taxpayer has taxable trading profits of £54,500 for 2020/21 he/she is liable to class 4 NICs of £3,735.00 calculated as follows:

	£
(£50,000 – £9,500) × 9%	3,645.00
(£54,500 – £50,000) × 2%	90.00
	3,735.00

Note that where a taxpayer's 'profits' do not exceed the lower limit (i.e. £9,500 for 2020/21); there is no liability to class 4 NICs.

2.2 Profits

The 'profits' to be used in the calculation of the taxpayer's liability to class 4 NICs are:

	£
Taxable trade profits	X
Less: Trading losses brought forward	(X)
Profits for class 4 NICs	X

2.3 Payments of class 4 NICs

Class 4 NICs are payable under self-assessment at the same time as the related income tax liability (i.e. two payments on account and a balancing payment).

Interest will be charged on late payments.

A taxpayer does not have to pay class 4 NICs if he/she is:

- of state pension age or over at the beginning of the tax year
- aged under 16 at the beginning of the tax year.

In 2018 the state pension age was 65 for both men and women, and this is gradually increasing. It would be clear in the assessment that someone had reached state pension age.

2.4 Class 2 NICs

In addition to class 4 NICs, a trader is also liable for class 2 NICs which are payable at a fixed rate of £3.05 per week. The liability relates to the individual trader, such that it does not increase where an individual has more than one trade.

There is no liability if the 'profits' are below the small profits threshold of £6,475.

'Profits' for class 2 NIC purposes are the same as for class 4 purposes (i.e. tax adjusted trading profits less losses brought forward).

Class 2 NICs are payable under the self-assessment system. They are reported on the tax return and payable on 31 January following the end of the tax year (i.e. 31 January 2022 for 2020/21). There are no payments on account for class 2 NICs.

A taxpayer does not have to pay class 2 NICs in respect of any week in which they are:

- aged under 16, or

- of state pension age or over.

Note that the AAT reference material set out in section 6 below includes some details on class 2 and 4 NIC.

3 Effect of partnerships

3.1 Each partner is treated as a separate sole trader

Each partner must pay:

- his/her own class 2 contributions, and

- his/her own class 4 contributions.

Both class 2 and class 4 contributions are based on his/her share of profits, as assessed to income tax for the tax year.

Test your understanding 1

1 A taxpayer has self-employed income of £81,750 for the tax year 2020/21. The amount of income which will be chargeable to class 4 NICs at 2% is £ 31750

2 A taxpayer has self-employed income of £30,000. The amount of class 4 NICs payable would be £ 1845

3 Anne has tax adjusted trading profits for 2020/21 of £6,600.

   Her accounts show a net profit of £6,000 for the year to 31 March 2021.

   • What class 4 NICs are due? £ Nil

   • What class 2 NICs are due? £ Nil ✗ 158·6

4 Which one of the following statements is correct?

   A Self-employed taxpayers pay either class 2 or class 4 NICs, but not both (F)

   B Every self-employed taxpayer must pay class 2 NICs, regardless of the level of their profits (F)

   C Class 4 NICs are based on the amount of income a taxpayer withdraws from the business (F)

   D In a partnership, each partner is responsible for his/her own NICs (T)

4 Test your understanding

 Test your understanding 2

Naomi

Naomi, aged 45, has been self-employed for many years.

Required:

State the national insurance contributions payable by Naomi for 2020/21, assuming her taxable trade profits are:

(a) £6,500   *Class 2 = 158·6*   *Total*

(b) £24,500   *class 2 = 158·6 / class 4 = 1350 (1508·6)*   *Total*

(c) £51,200   *class 2 = 158·6 / class 4 = 3645 + 24 = 3669 (3827·6)*

 Test your understanding 3

Wei

Wei's tax liability for 2019/20 was as follows:

	£
Income tax liability	9,400
Less: PAYE	(2,100)
Income tax payable	7,300
Class 2 NICs	156
Class 4 NICs	700
CGT	5,000
	13,156

What will each of the payments on account be for 2020/21?

A   £6,578

B   £4,078

C   £4,000

D   £3,650

5 Summary

Sole traders and partners may have to pay the following contributions:

- class 2, and
- class 4.

Links to other syllabus areas

National insurance contributions are another form of tax – there is a direct link here with the Professional level Personal Tax Unit where NICs payable by employers and employees are considered.

6 AAT reference material

National Insurance contributions

- Self-employed individuals pay Class 2 and Class 4 contributions.

  Class 4 contributions are at 9% on profits between the lower and upper limits, then 2% on profits above the upper limit.

- Percentages and limits are provided in the Taxation Tables.

Test your understanding answers

Test your understanding 1

1 £31,750 (£81,750 − £50,000)

2 £1,845 (£30,000 − £9,500) × 9%

3 Anne's NICs for 2020/21 are:

- class 4 – £Nil, taxable profits less than £9,500

- class 2 – £158.60 (£3.05 per week for 52 weeks), as taxable profits exceed £6,475.

4 The correct answer is D.

Explanation

Taxpayers are required to pay class 2 NICs if their taxable profits for the tax year exceed £6,475 and class 4 NICs if their taxable profits exceed £9,500, so they can be liable to both classes 2 and 4.

Class 4 NICs are based on the taxable trading profits, **not** the amount of income a taxpayer withdraws from the business.

Test your understanding 2

Naomi

Naomi must pay class 2 NICs of £3.05 per week. In all cases her taxable profits exceed the small profits threshold of £6,475.

She is liable to pay class 4 NICs as follows:

		£
(a)	Profits do not exceed lower limit, no class 4 NIC	Nil
(b)	Class 4 NICs (£24,500 − £9,500) × 9%	1,350.00
(c)	Class 4 NICs (£50,000 − £9,500) × 9% + (£51,200 − £50,000) × 2%	3,669.00

Test your understanding 3

Wei

The correct answer is C.

Explanation

The relevant amount for income tax is   £7,300
The relevant amount for class 4 NIC is   £700

Payments on account will be due for 2020/21 as follows:

	£
31 January 2021 ((£7,300 + £700) = £8,000 × 1/2)	4,000
31 July 2021	4,000

No payments on account of class 2 NICs or capital gains tax are required.

Introduction to chargeable gains

Introduction

Both individuals and companies pay tax on chargeable gains.

Individuals pay capital gains tax on their chargeable gains.

Companies include chargeable gains in their taxable total profits and therefore pay corporation tax on them.

This chapter helps identify when chargeable gains arise.

ASSESSMENT CRITERIA	CONTENTS
Apply the rules relating to chargeable persons, disposals and assets (5.1)	1 Principle of a chargeable gain 2 Chargeable disposal 3 Chargeable person 4 Chargeable asset

1 Principle of a chargeable gain

1.1 The three essential elements

In order for a chargeable gain to be calculated there are three essential requirements.

2 Chargeable disposal

2.1 Main types of disposal

A chargeable disposal includes:

- a sale of an asset (whole or part of an asset)
- a gift of an asset
- an exchange of an asset
- the loss or destruction of an asset.

Where a gift is made the sale proceeds are deemed to be the asset's market value.

Where an asset is lost or destroyed the sale proceeds are likely to be nil or insurance proceeds.

2.2 Exempt disposals

The following occasions are exempt disposals and so no CGT computation is required:

- the sale is a trading disposal (badges of trade – Chapter 9)
- on the death of an individual
- on a gift to a charity.

In the assessment it will be obvious whether the disposal is of:

- stock/inventory, therefore dealt with as trading income, or
- a capital item (for example land), therefore calculate a gain.

3 Chargeable person

3.1 Types of person

Chargeable gains will be calculated on disposals by:

- Individuals ⎫
- Partners in partnership ⎭ – pay capital gains tax

- Companies – pay corporation tax on chargeable gains (see Chapter 5 pro forma)

4 Chargeable asset

4.1 Exempt assets

All assets are chargeable unless they are on the specific list of exempt assets. The main types of exempt asset are listed below.

Exempt assets in the list below need to be learned so that you can identify them in a question.

- Motor vehicles, including vintage and veteran cars.

- Cash (i.e. legal tender in the UK).

- Gilt edged securities.

- Wasting chattels:

    - a chattel is property that is tangible and moveable

    - 'wasting' means that it has a life of less than or equal to 50 years.

    The most common examples of wasting chattels that you will encounter in an assessment are:

    - all animals (racehorses, greyhounds etc.), boats and caravans.

- Non-wasting chattels, which have both sale proceeds and cost of £6,000 or less.

    The most common examples of non-wasting chattels are works of art, jewellery and antique furniture.

The following are exempt assets for individuals only:

- Any form of loan stock, loan notes, debentures which are qualifying corporate bonds (QCBs).

- Shares held in an ISA.

 Test your understanding 1

Chargeable disposals

For each of the following transactions, state whether it is a chargeable or an exempt disposal for the purpose of capital gains.

1   Bill gave his trading premises to his daughter Beatrice. *(Yes)*

2   ABC Ltd is a building company. It built a small development of five houses and sold them. *No*

3   DEF Ltd, a manufacturing company, sold a racehorse for £10,000. *No*

4   DEF Ltd also sold a portrait for £10,000 which had been hanging in the boardroom. *(Yes)*

---

5 Test your understanding

Test your understanding 2

Chargeable disposals

For each of the following transactions, state whether it is a chargeable or an exempt disposal for the purpose of capital gains.

1 Sale of a motor car that was purchased for £12,000 and sold for £13,000 and used for business purposes throughout the period of ownership. *(N)*

2 Sale of a half share in a racehorse that was purchased for £12,000 and sold for £17,000. *(N)*

3 Gift of a painting which was purchased for £5,000 and sold for £8,500. ✓

4 Sale of land that was purchased for £2,900 and sold for £5,800. ✓

6 Summary

The requirements for a chargeable gain to be calculated are:

- a chargeable disposal, by
- a chargeable person, of
- a chargeable asset.

Links to other syllabus areas

Profits and losses made on the disposal of capital assets have already been considered from a financial accounting perspective in AVBK (Advanced level). An appreciation of the tax consequences of such transactions is also important. The understanding and insight gained in your earlier studies will assist in this regard, as you consider many of the underlying principles which apply for tax purposes.

Test your understanding answers

Test your understanding 1

1	Chargeable	Even though Bill receives no actual payment for the property, a gift of a capital item is still a chargeable disposal.
2	Exempt	As ABC Ltd is a building company, the proceeds will be dealt with as trading income.
3	Exempt	A racehorse is a wasting chattel (i.e. life of 50 years or less).
4	Chargeable	The painting is a non-wasting chattel which was sold for more than £6,000. It is not a wasting chattel as it will have a life of more than 50 years.

Test your understanding 2

1	Exempt	Motor cars are exempt regardless of the use of the asset, cost or sale proceeds.
2	Exempt	A racehorse is a wasting chattel.
3	Chargeable	The painting is a non-wasting chattel that was bought for less than £6,000 but sold for more than £6,000. It would only be exempt if it had also been sold for less than £6,000.
4	Chargeable	The land, although bought and sold for less than £6,000, is not moveable property and therefore not a chattel.

Gains and losses for companies

16

Introduction

A company pays corporation tax on its chargeable gains.

A calculation of gains may be required in your assessment.

This chapter sets out the pro forma for calculating a chargeable gain, and explains the separate entries required in the computation.

ASSESSMENT CRITERIA	CONTENTS
Apply the rules relating to disposals and assets (5.2)	1 Pro forma computation
	2 The chargeable gain computation
Calculate the computation of chargeable gains and allowable losses (5.2)	3 Special rules

1   Pro forma computation

1.1   The pro forma computation (for corporation tax)

Gains and losses are calculated for accounting periods.

Once you have calculated all the individual chargeable gains and allowable capital losses for an accounting period, summarise them as follows:

	£
Chargeable gain (1)	X
Chargeable gain (2)	X
Allowable loss (3)	(X)
	____
Net chargeable gains/(losses) for the current year	X
Less: Capital losses brought forward	(X)
	____
Net chargeable gains	X
	____

The net chargeable gains are then put into the computation of taxable total profits and the corporation tax liability is calculated in the normal way.

If there is an overall capital loss, it is carried forward and set against future chargeable gains. It cannot be relieved against other income.

 Example

Alpha Ltd made three disposals in its year ended 31 March 2021, giving the following results:

Asset	Gain/(loss)
	£
1	20,000
2	5,000
3	(8,000)

Calculate the net chargeable gains shown on the corporation tax computation.

Solution

Included within taxable total profits will be net chargeable gains of £17,000 (£20,000 + £5,000 – £8,000).

If the loss on asset 3 had been £28,000, the corporation tax computation would show net chargeable gains of nil.

A net loss of £3,000 (£20,000 + £5,000 – £28,000) would then be carried forward to offset against the next available net chargeable gains.

 Test your understanding 1

Bubbles Ltd

Bubbles Ltd disposed of two assets during its accounting period to 31 March 2021, realising a chargeable gain of £13,000 and an allowable loss of £4,000.

It had allowable capital losses brought forward of £2,000.

How much will be included in taxable total profits for the year to 31 March 2021?

The remainder of this chapter considers how to calculate the gains and losses on each chargeable disposal made by a company.

2 The chargeable gain computation

2.1 The standard pro forma

The following pro forma should be used:

	Notes	£
Gross sale proceeds	1	X
Less: Selling costs	2	(X)
Net sale proceeds (NSP)		X
Less: Allowable cost	3	(X)
Unindexed gain	4	X
Less: Indexation allowance (IA) = Cost × 0.XXX	5	(X)
Chargeable gain		X

Notes to the pro forma

1   The sale proceeds are usually given in the question.

   However, where a disposal is not a sale at arm's length (e.g. a gift) then *market value* will be substituted for sale proceeds in the computation.

2   The selling costs incurred on the disposal of an asset are an allowable deduction.

   Examples of such allowable costs include valuation fees, advertising costs, legal fees, auctioneer's fees.

3   The purchase price of an asset is the main allowable cost, but this will also include any incidental purchase expenses, including legal fees, stamp duty, etc.

4   The gain after deducting the costs above is known as an unindexed gain.

5   An indexation allowance (IA) may then be available to reduce that gain.

   The indexation allowance is intended to give relief for inflation and is based upon the movement in the retail prices index (RPI).

2.2 The indexation allowance (IA)

The IA is relief for inflation covering the period since the asset was purchased up to the date of disposal.

The indexation allowance generally runs:

- from the month of the purchase (i.e. when the cost was incurred)

- to the month of disposal.

It is computed by multiplying the acquisition cost by an indexation factor.

The formula for calculating the indexation factor is:

$$\frac{\text{RPI for month of disposal} - \text{RPI for month of acquisition}}{\text{RPI for month of acquisition}}$$

This produces a decimal figure which must be rounded to three decimal places.

In the assessment you will be given the indexation factor or the amount of the indexation allowance.

Companies do not get the benefit of indexation allowance beyond 31 December 2017.

Therefore, if an asset acquired before 1 January 2018 is sold on/after 1 January 2018 then the December 2017 RPI should be used as the RPI at disposal.

If an asset is both acquired and disposed of on/after 1 January 2018 then no indexation allowance will be available.

 Example

Eli Ltd sells a chargeable asset on 31 March 2021 for £24,600 after deducting auctioneer's fees of £400. The asset was acquired on 1 May 2005 for £10,000.

Calculate the chargeable gain. Assume that the indexation factor for May 2005 to December 2017 is 0.448 and from May 2005 to March 2021 is 0.572.

Solution

	£
Gross sales proceeds (March 2021)	25,000
Less: Selling costs	(400)
Net sale proceeds	24,600
Less: Allowable cost (May 2005)	(10,000)
Unindexed gain	14,600
Less: Indexation allowance (£10,000 × 0.448)	(4,480)
Chargeable gain	10,120

Be careful to ensure that you index the allowable cost and not the unindexed gain – a very easy mistake to make!

Note also that the indexation allowance:

- cannot be used to turn a gain into a loss
- is not available where there is an unindexed loss.

Example

JNN Ltd is considering selling a field at auction in August 2020. It acquired the field in August 1995 for £10,000 and the sale proceeds are likely to be one of three results.

(a) £25,000

(b) £12,000

(c) £8,000

Calculate the chargeable gain or loss under each of these alternatives.

Assume the indexation factor from August 1995 to December 2017 is 0.855.

Solution

	(a) £	(b) £	(c) £
Sale proceeds	25,000	12,000	8,000
Less: Cost	(10,000)	(10,000)	(10,000)
Unindexed gain or (loss)	15,000	2,000	(2,000)
Less: Indexation allowance			
(0.855 × £10,000) = £8,550	(8,550)	(2,000)*	Nil**
Chargeable gain/(allowable loss)	6,450	Nil	(2,000)

Notes:

* Restricted, because indexation cannot create a loss.

** No indexation because indexation cannot increase a loss.

 Test your understanding 2

JHN Ltd

JHN Ltd made the following disposals in the year ended 31 March 2021.

1   On 9 June 2020 it sold a machine for £15,000. The machine was bought in October 1999 for £8,000.

2   On 5 September 2020 it sold a building which had been purchased for £27,500 in November 2000. Sale proceeds were £26,500.

3   On 1 March 2021 it sold a car, which was bought in February 1994 for £3,000. By the time of the sale, it had become a collector's item and JHN Ltd managed to obtain proceeds of £9,000, out of which it paid £450 in auctioneer's fees.

4   On 3 March 2021 it sold a collection of military memorabilia for £19,000. The collection had cost £7,000 in March 1994.

5   Also on 3 March 2021, it sold some land which was purchased in April 1993 for £15,000. The land was sold for £25,000.

Calculate the chargeable gain on each of the above transactions and the net chargeable gains for the year ended 31 March 2021.

You should use the following indexation factors.

April 1993 – December 2017	0.978
Feb 1994 – December 2017	0.957
March 1994 – December 2017	0.952
Oct 1999 – December 2017	0.670
Nov 2000 – December 2017	0.616

Approach to the question

It is important that the chargeable gain or allowable loss on each transaction is *separately* computed.

Finally, prepare a summary adding gains and losses together to arrive at one overall net chargeable gains figure.

Note that details of the pro forma computation and treatment of indexation allowance is included in the AAT reference material set out in section 6 below.

3 Special rules

3.1 Changes to the calculation of the gain

There are a number of special situations that will give rise to slight changes in the calculation of the gains. They are:

- Enhancement expenditure (see section 3.2 below)
- Part disposals (see section 3.3 below)
- Non-wasting chattels (see section 3.4 below).

3.2 Enhancement expenditure

The main allowable cost in computing an unindexed gain is the purchase cost (including incidental acquisition costs).

Any additional capital expenditure incurred at a later date on the asset is also an allowable cost. This normally takes the form of improvement (i.e. enhancement) expenditure.

As the additional expenditure is incurred later than the original expenditure, there will be an impact on the calculation of the indexation allowance.

Indexation allowance can only be calculated from the actual date of expenditure; therefore, where there is cost plus enhancement expenditure, *two* indexation allowance calculations will be required. Remember not to index past 31 December 2017.

 Example

RMY Ltd bought a shop in November 1997 for £13,200. The company spent £3,800 on improvements in May 2000. The shop was sold for £49,000 in October 2020.

The indexed rise from November 1997 to December 2017 is 0.742 and from May 2000 to December 2017 is 0.629.

Calculate the chargeable gain on the sale of the shop.

Solution

	£
Sale proceeds (October 2020)	49,000
Less: Cost (November 1997)	(13,200)
Enhancement (May 2000)	(3,800)
	———
Unindexed gain	32,000
Less: Indexation allowance	
Cost £13,200 × 0.742	(9,794)
Enhancement £3,800 × 0.629	(2,390)
	———
Chargeable gain	19,816
	———

 Test your understanding 3

Lindham Ltd

On 15 February 2021, Lindham Ltd sold a factory building for £420,000.

The factory had been purchased on 14 October 2004 for £194,000, and was extended at a cost of £58,000 during March 2006.

During May 2008, the roof of the factory was repaired at a cost of £12,000 following damage in a fire.

Lindham Ltd had incurred legal fees of £3,600 in connection with the original purchase of the factory, and £6,200 in connection with the disposal.

What is the chargeable gain on the disposal?

A   £24,116

B   £39,632

C   £8,878

D   £158,200

You should use the following indexation factors, where relevant.

October 2004 – December 2017	0.475
October 2004 – February 2021	0.596
March 2006 – December 2017	0.426
March 2006 – February 2021	0.544
May 2008 – December 2017	0.293
May 2008 – February 2021	0.399

3.3   Part disposal

A disposal can be of all or part of an asset. It could for example apply to a disposal of part of a plot of land.

When only part of an asset is sold, we know how much the proceeds are, but we cannot immediately determine what the cost was of that part of the asset.

The allowable cost of the part disposed of is calculated using the following formula:

Allowable cost of the part disposed of = Cost of whole asset $\times \dfrac{A}{A+B}$

Where   A =   gross sale proceeds of part disposed of
(i.e. before deducting selling costs).

B =   market value of the remaining part
(will be given in assessment).

Example

Jetsburg Ltd bought a piece of land in January 2001 for £5,000.

In March 2021 the company sold part of the land for £4,500. At the same time the remaining part was valued at £20,500.

The indexation factor from January 2001 to December 2017 is 0.625.

Calculate the chargeable gain arising on the part disposal of land.

Solution

	£
Sale proceeds	4,500
Less: Allowable cost (£5,000 × $\frac{£4,500}{£4,500+£20,500}$)	(900)
Unindexed gain	3,600
Less: Indexation allowance (0.625 × £900)	(563)
Chargeable gain	3,037

 Test your understanding 4

Smith Ltd

Smith Ltd sold three hectares out of a 12 hectare plot of land on 14 December 2020 for £15,000. The whole plot had been purchased for £4,500 on 15 June 2013. On 14 December 2020 the unsold hectares had an agreed market value of £25,000.

What is the chargeable gain?

13120 ✓

You should use an indexation factor of 0.114.

3.4 Non-wasting chattels

In the previous chapter we noted that wasting chattels (i.e. expected life of no more than 50 years) are exempt (e.g. animals, boats, caravans).

Special rules apply to non-wasting chattels (e.g. furniture, works of art, jewellery, antique furniture).

> ### Example
>
> Harwood Ltd sold an antique table for £5,000 in January 2021. It had originally purchased the table in August 2006 for £8,000.
>
> Calculate the chargeable gain or allowable loss on disposal.
>
> **Solution**
>
> | | £ |
> |---|---|
> | Sale proceeds (deemed) | 6,000 |
> | Less: Allowable cost | (8,000) |
> | | |
> | Unindexed loss | (2,000) |
> | Less: Indexation allowance | Nil |
> | (restricted as it cannot increase a loss) | |
> | | |
> | Allowable loss | (2,000) |

Example

Kelsall Ltd sold a painting for £6,600 incurring selling expenses of £500. It was originally purchased for £2,000. The indexation factor is 0.800.

Calculate the chargeable gain on disposal.

Solution

	£
Sale proceeds	6,600
Less: Selling costs	(500)
	———
Net sale proceeds	6,100
Less: Allowable cost	(2,000)
	———
Unindexed gain	4,100
Less: Indexation allowance (0.800 × £2,000)	(1,600)
	———
Chargeable gain	2,500
	———
Chargeable gain cannot exceed:	
5/3 × (£6,600 – £6,000)	1,000
	———

 Test your understanding 5

Chattel disposals

1   ABC Ltd sold a non-wasting chattel for £6,500 realising a gain of £2,000.

 What is the chargeable gain?

2   DEF Ltd sold a non-wasting chattel for £4,000. It had originally cost £7,500.

 How much of the loss is allowable?

3   GHI Ltd sold a painting for £14,000 in March 2021. The painting had been acquired for £5,000 in November 2009. The indexation factor from November 2009 to December 2017 was 0.284.

Complete the following computation.

	£
Proceeds	14000
Less: Cost	5000
	9000
Less: Indexation allowance	1420
Gain	7580
Chargeable gain cannot exceed: $\left(5/3 \times (14000 - 6000)\right) =$	13333
Chargeable gain	7580

KAPLAN PUBLISHING

4 Test your understanding

 Test your understanding 6

RBQ Ltd

RBQ Ltd made the following disposals in the year ended 31 March 2021.

(1) On 11 August 2020, it sold a shop for £15,000. The shop was bought in May 2003 for £8,000.

(2) On 16 October 2020, it sold a painting which had been purchased for £30,000 in November 2000. Sale proceeds were £25,000.

(3) On 1 February 2021, it sold a car, a VW Beetle, which was bought in February 1997 for £2,000.

   By the time of the sale, it had become a collector's item and RBQ Ltd managed to obtain proceeds of £10,000.

(4) On 3 January 2021, it sold a piece of land for £29,000. It had cost £6,000 in May 2001.

Calculate the total net chargeable gains on the above transactions in the year ended 31 March 2021.

You should use the following indexation factors, where relevant:

February 1997 – December 2017	0.794
November 2000 – December 2017	0.616
May 2001 – December 2017	0.596
May 2003 – December 2017	0.532

Test your understanding 7

Jackson Ltd

During the year to 30 September 2020, Jackson Ltd had the following capital transactions:

(a) In October 2019 it sold land for £27,000. It bought the land in February 1998 for £14,000.

(b) It also sold a factory unit in December 2019 for £100,000. Out of that the company had to pay legal fees of £1,200. It had originally bought the factory unit in March 1997 for £10,500, extended it in April 2001 for £3,000 and extended it again in June 2004 for £4,600.

(c) In March 2020, Jackson Ltd sold a racehorse for £22,000. It had purchased the horse for £4,000 on 1 December 2009.

Calculate the chargeable gain on each of the above transactions in the year ended 30 September 2020.

Use the following indexation factors, where relevant:

March 1997 – December 2017	0.790
February 1998 – December 2017	0.735
April 2001 – December 2017	0.607
June 2004 – December 2017	0.489
December 2009 – December 2017	0.276

Test your understanding 8

Alphabet Ltd

1   Alphabet Ltd sold an antique table for £7,500 realising an indexed gain of £3,000. What will be the chargeable gain?

2   Delta Ltd sold a painting for £3,000. It had originally cost £8,500.

     How much of the loss is allowable?

3   Golf Ltd sold an antique desk for £17,000 in January 2021. The desk had been acquired for £4,000 in September 2009. The indexation factor from September 2009 to December 2017 was 0.292.

     Complete the following computation.

	£
Proceeds	17000
Less: Cost	(4000)
	13000
Less: Indexation allowance	(1168)
Gain	11832
Chargeable gain cannot exceed	18333

⁵/₃ × (17000 − 600)

$$\tfrac{5}{3} \times (17000 - 600)$$

Chargeable gain	11832

5 Summary

There is a pro forma computation for the calculation of gains and losses on individual asset disposals.

The gains and losses of the accounting period are netted off to give the net chargeable gains to include in the company's corporation tax computation.

Companies receive an indexation allowance. Original and improvement costs are indexed from the month the cost is incurred to the month of disposal (or to December 2017 if disposal is after 31 December 2017).

Special rules exist for the treatment of improvement costs, part disposals (using the formula A/A+B), and for chattels.

 Links to other syllabus areas

The way in which companies record their chargeable gains feeds directly into their tax computation and their corporation tax liability. This in turn has a direct impact both in terms of the way in which their results are reported (FSLC) and future budgeting and forecasting exercises (MABU and MDCL).

An external auditor has a duty to ensure that the tax liability for a period is fairly stated and thus that it has been accurately calculated (ETAU) – the tax on the chargeable gains made by the company can comprise a very significant part of a company's overall tax liability for any given period.

6   AAT reference material

Calculation of gains and losses for companies

Pro forma computation

	£	£
Consideration received		X
Less Incidental costs of sale		(X)
Net sale proceeds		NSP
Less Allowable expenditure		
Acquisition cost + incidental costs of acquisition	X	
Indexation allowance [indexation factor × expenditure]	X	
Enhancement expenditure	X	
Indexation allowance	X	
		(Cost)
Chargeable gain		Gain

- Companies are entitled to an indexation allowance, based on the changes in the retail price index (RPI) from the date when expenditure was incurred to the date of disposal (or deemed disposal).

- Indexation allowance is frozen at 31 December 2017.

- Disposals taking place from 1 January 2018 will use the RPI at December 2017 for indexation allowance purposes.

- Indexation allowance is not available where there is an unindexed loss; nor can it turn an unindexed gain into an indexed loss.

- Note that companies do not get an annual exempt amount.

- Losses relieved in order – current year first followed by losses brought forward.

Only relief available to companies is rollover relief:

- Rollover relief is a deferral relief – see Chargeable gains – reliefs available to individuals for main rollover relief rules.

- Key differences applying for companies:

  - indexation is given on disposal of the original asset.

  - goodwill is not a qualifying asset for companies.

  - gain deferred is the indexed gain.

  - on disposal of the replacement asset, indexation is calculated on the 'base cost' not actual cost.

(Note that rollover relief is covered in Chapter 20 of this study text).

Test your understanding answers

Test your understanding 1

Bubbles Ltd

The amount to include in taxable total profits will be £7,000 (£13,000 – £4,000 – £2,000 b/f).

Test your understanding 2

JHN Ltd

Chargeable gains

	£
Machine (W1)	1,640
Building (W2)	(1,000)
Car – exempt	Nil
Memorabilia (W3)	5,336
Land (W4)	Nil
	———
Net chargeable gains	5,976
	———

Workings

(W1) Machine

	£
Proceeds	15,000
Less: Cost	(8,000)
	———
Unindexed gain	7,000
Less: Indexation allowance (£8,000 × 0.670)	(5,360)
	———
Chargeable gain	1,640
	———

(W2) Building

	£
Proceeds	26,500
Less: Cost	(27,500)
Allowable loss	(1,000)

No indexation is available to increase the loss.

(W3) Memorabilia

	£
Proceeds	19,000
Less: Cost	(7,000)
Unindexed gain	12,000
Less: Indexation allowance (£7,000 × 0.952)	(6,664)
Chargeable gain	5,336

(W4) Land

	£
Proceeds	25,000
Less: Cost	(15,000)
Unindexed gain	10,000
Less: Indexation allowance	
(£15,000 × 0.978) (restricted)	(10,000)
	Nil

The IA is restricted because indexation cannot create an allowable loss.

Test your understanding 3

Lindham Ltd

The correct answer is B.

Explanation

The gain is calculated as shown below.

	£	£
Disposal proceeds		420,000
Less: Incidental costs of disposal		(6,200)
Net proceeds		413,800
Less: Acquisition cost	194,000	
Incidental costs of acquisition	3,600	
		(197,600)
Enhancement expenditure		(58,000)
		158,200
Less: Indexation allowance		
Cost (£197,600 × 0.475)		(93,860)
Extension (£58,000 × 0.426)		(24,708)
Chargeable gain		39,632

The expenditure incurred in May 2008 for repairing the roof does not enhance the value of the factory and is therefore not an allowable deduction in the gain computation.

The repair is a revenue expense which is allowable against the company's trading profits.

Test your understanding 4

Smith Ltd

The correct answer is £13,120.

Explanation

The gain is calculated as shown below.

	£
Sale proceeds for 3 hectares	15,000
Less: Cost of 3 hectares £4,500 × (£15,000/(£15,000 + £25,000))	(1,688)
Unindexed gain	13,312
Less: Indexation allowance (£1,688 × 0.114)	(192)
Chargeable gain	13,120

Test your understanding 5

Chattel disposals

ABC Ltd

The chargeable gain cannot exceed:

5/3 × (£6,500 – £6,000) = £833.

Therefore, the chargeable gain will be restricted to £833.

DEF Ltd

The allowable loss will be restricted to (£6,000 – £7,500) = £1,500.

GHI Ltd

	£
Proceeds	14,000
Less: Cost	(5,000)
	9,000
Less: Indexation allowance (£5,000 × 0.284)	(1,420)
Gain	7,580
Chargeable gain cannot exceed: 5/3 × (£14,000 – £6,000)	13,333
Chargeable gain	7,580

Test your understanding 6

RBQ Ltd

	£
Shop (W1)	2,744
Painting (W2)	(5,000)
Car – exempt	Nil
Land (W3)	19,424
Total net chargeable gains	17,168

Workings

(W1) Shop

	£
Proceeds	15,000
Less: Cost	(8,000)
Unindexed gain	7,000
Less: Indexation allowance (£8,000 × 0.532)	(4,256)
Chargeable gain	2,744

(W2) Painting

	£
Proceeds	25,000
Less: Cost	(30,000)
Allowable loss	(5,000)

No indexation is available to increase the cost

(W3) Land

	£
Proceeds	29,000
Less: Cost	(6,000)
Unindexed gain	23,000
Less: Indexation allowance (£6,000 × 0.596)	(3,576)
Chargeable gain	19,424

Test your understanding 7

Jackson Ltd

		£	£
(a)	**Land**		
	Sales proceeds	27,000	
	Less: Cost	(14,000)	
	Unindexed gain	13,000	
	Less: Indexation allowance		
	(£14,000 × 0.735)	(10,290)	
	Chargeable gain		2,710

		£	£
(b)	**Factory**		
	Sale proceeds	100,000	
	Less: Legal fees	(1,200)	
		98,800	
	Less: Cost (March 1997)	(10,500)	
	Extension (April 2001)	(3,000)	
	Extension (June 2004)	(4,600)	
	Unindexed gain	80,700	
	Less: Indexation allowance		
	Cost (£10,500 × 0.790)	(8,295)	
	Extension (£3,000 × 0.607)	(1,821)	
	Extension (£4,600 × 0.489)	(2,249)	
	Chargeable gain		68,335
(c)	**Racehorse** – exempt asset (wasting chattel)		Nil

Test your understanding 8

Chattel disposals

Alphabet Ltd

The gain will be restricted to 5/3 × (£7,500 – £6,000) = £2,500.

Delta Ltd

The allowable loss will be restricted to (£6,000 – £8,500) = £2,500.

Golf Ltd

	£
Proceeds	17,000
Less: Cost	(4,000)
	13,000
Less: Indexation allowance (£4,000 × 0.292)	(1,168)
Gain	11,832
Chargeable gain cannot exceed: 5/3 × (£17,000 – £6,000)	18,333
Chargeable gain	11,832

Shares and securities – disposals by companies

Introduction

A company may hold another company's shares as an investment. Special rules apply to the calculation of chargeable gains on the disposal of shares.

ASSESSMENT CRITERIA	CONTENTS
Apply the rules relating to the disposal of shares (5.2)	1 The matching rules 2 Bonus issues and rights issues 3 Approach to assessment questions

1 The matching rules

1.1 Disposal of shares and securities

What distinguishes a share disposal from other asset disposals is the need for matching rules.

Before considering what these matching rules are, it helps to understand why we need them.

1.2 Principle of matching rules

Suppose that a company makes the following purchases of shares in another company, A plc:

1 September 1995	800 shares for	£2,000
3 February 1998	300 shares for	£1,000
1 July 2004	500 shares for	£1,000

On 1 November 2020, 400 of these shares are sold – but which 400?

- It could be the 300 acquired in 1998 and 100 acquired in 1995.

- It could be 400 out of the 500 acquired in 2004.

- It could be based on 400 out of the total 1,600 with costs being averaged.

We need matching rules so that we can establish *which* shares have been sold, and consequently what allowable costs and indexation allowances can be deducted from the sale proceeds.

The matching rules dictate the order in which the shares disposed of are matched with purchases.

1.3 The matching rules for companies

Shares of the same type in the same company (for example Lionel Ltd ordinary shares) are matched as follows:

(1) first, with shares bought on the same day, then

(2) second, with shares bought in the previous nine days (on a first in first out basis), then

(3) third, with shares in the 'share pool' (sometimes referred to as the s104 pool or the FA1985 pool).

The matching rules are given in the AAT reference material set out in section 6 below.

The 'share pool' is considered in detail below. For companies, shares are pooled together from 10 days after purchase.

Note that the matching rules for individuals are different and are covered in Chapter 19.

 Example

Minnie Ltd has sold 3,000 shares in Mickey plc for £15,000 on 2 February 2021. The shares in Mickey plc were purchased as follows:

Date	Number	Cost £
1 July 1997	1,000	2,000
1 September 2007	1,000	2,500
27 January 2021	500	1,200
2 February 2021	1,500	6,000

Explain which shares Minnie Ltd is deemed to have sold.

Solution

Using the matching rules, the 3,000 shares sold are as follows:

	Number
2 February 2021 (same day purchase)	1,500
27 January 2021 (in previous 9 days)	500
	2,000

Share pool:
All other shares were purchased more than 9 days ago, therefore must be in the pool.

1 July 1997	1,000	
1 September 2007	1,000	
Total number of shares in pool	2,000	
Out of the pool (1,000 out of 2,000)		1,000
Shares disposed of		3,000

Note: When dealing with the pool we do not identify which 1,000 shares are sold.

1.4 Calculation of gains on same day and previous 9 day purchases

If a disposal is matched with the first two rules (i.e. matching against a same day purchase or purchases in the previous 9 days), there will be no indexation allowance available (even in the unlikely event of the relevant dates occurring before 1 January 2018).

Hence, the gain is calculated as:

	£
Sale proceeds	X
Less: Allowable cost	(X)
Chargeable gain	X

Example

For Minnie Ltd in the previous example, calculate the gains on the shares purchased:

(1) on the same day, and

(2) in the previous 9 days.

Solution

Step 1: Calculate the gain on the same day purchase (1,500 shares)

3,000 shares are sold for £15,000.

	£
Sale proceeds (1,500/3,000 × £15,000)	7,500
Less: Allowable cost	(6,000)
Chargeable gain	1,500

Step 2: Calculate the gain on the previous 9 days purchase (500 shares)

	£
Sale proceeds (500/3,000 × £15,000)	2,500
Less: Allowable cost	(1,200)
Chargeable gain	1,300

1.5 The operation of a share pool

Any purchases from 1 April 1982 are 'pooled' in the 'share pool'.

Purchases before 1 April 1982 are not in the syllabus.

Indexation will apply to the pool from the date of acquisition to the date of disposal or December 2017, whichever is earlier

To enable the correct indexation to be calculated, a separate working is needed to identify the amount available. The working is also used to find the average cost of a partial disposal.

The pool is initially set up with three columns as follows:

	Number	Cost £	Indexed cost £
Purchases (say) June 1991	1,000	2,000	2,000

Then every time there is an 'operative event' (an event involving cash – i.e. a sale or a purchase), two steps must be performed.

Step 1: An indexation update.

In the indexed cost column, add in indexation from the last operative event until this one.

This is calculated by multiplying the balance in the indexed cost column by the increase in the RPI since the last operative event.

Step 2: Deal with the operative event.

- for a purchase add in the new shares. The cost must be added in to both the cost and indexed cost columns.

- for a sale eliminate some shares. The amounts to be deducted from the cost and indexed cost columns are calculated in proportion to the number of shares being removed from the pool.

The following working should be produced:

Pro forma for the share pool

	Number	Cost	Indexed cost
		£	£
Purchase	X	X	X
Index to next event			X
Record next event (e.g. purchase)	X	X	X
	X	X	X
Index to next event			X
	X	X	X
Record next event (e.g. sale)	(X)	(X) (W1)	(X) (W2)
Pool carried forward	X	X	X

Note: For the 'indexed rises' the indexation factor is **not** rounded in practice. This is the only situation where a non-rounded factor is ever used.

However, in the assessment you will always to be given a rounded indexation factor, therefore use the factor given.

Workings:

(W1) Total cost × (number of shares sold/number of shares in pool)

(W2) Total indexed cost × (number of shares sold/number of shares in pool)

The purpose of the share pool working is to find:

• the average pool cost of shares disposed of = working 1 (W1)

• the *indexation* of shares disposed of = (working 2 – working 1).

The gain on the shares is then calculated as normal:

	£
Sale proceeds	X
Less: Cost (W1)	(X)
Unindexed gain	X
Less: Indexation allowance (W2 – W1)	(X)
Chargeable gain	X

The indexation factor is **always** applied to the total on the indexed cost column **(not** cost).

A partial disposal from a share pool uses straight line apportionment of cost and indexation.

In your assessment you will be provided with a grid to enter your calculations (section 3).

Note that a basic pro forma is given in the AAT reference material set out in section 6 below.

 Example

For Minnie Ltd in the previous example, calculate the gain on the disposal from the share pool.

The indexation factors to use are as follows:

July 1997 – September 2007	0.321
September 2007 – December 2017	0.337

Solution

Step 1: Calculate cost and indexed cost from the share pool.

	Number	Cost £	Indexed cost £
July 1997 purchase	1,000	2,000	2,000
Index to next event			
(July 1997 to September 2007)			
Indexed cost × 0.321			
(£2,000 × 0.321)			642
September 2007 purchase	1,000	2,500	2,500
	2,000	4,500	5,142
Index to next event			
(September 2007 to December 2017)			
(£5,142 × 0.337)			1,733
	2,000	4,500	6,875
February 2021 sale (half)	(1,000)	(2,250)	(3,438)
Pool carried forward	1,000	2,250	3,437

Step 2: **Calculate the gain on share pool shares.**

	£
Sale proceeds (1,000/3,000 × £15,000)	5,000
Less: Allowable cost	(2,250)
Unindexed gain	2,750
Less: Indexation allowance	
(£3,438 – £2,250)	(1,188)
Chargeable gain	1,562

Step 3: **Calculate total chargeable gains on the disposal of all 3,000 shares in Minnie Ltd**

The total chargeable gains
= (£1,500 + £1,300 + £1,562) = £4,362

 Test your understanding 1

FDC Ltd

FDC Ltd has purchased shares in DCC Ltd. The share pool information of the shares in DCC Ltd is given below.

		Cost £
1 June 1993	4,000 shares for	8,000
30 July 2002	1,800 shares for	9,750

FDC Ltd disposed of 2,000 of its shares in DCC Ltd for £20,571 in March 2021.

The indexation factors to use are as follows:

June 1993 – July 2002	0.248
July 2002 – December 2017	0.581
July 2002 – March 2021	0.716

Calculate the chargeable gain on the share pool shares.

2 Bonus issues and rights issues

2.1 Principle of bonus issues and rights issues

A bonus issue is the distribution of free shares to shareholders based on existing shareholdings.

A rights issue involves shareholders paying for new shares, usually at a rate below market price and in proportions based on existing shareholdings.

Matching

In both cases, therefore, the shareholder is making a new acquisition of shares. However, for *matching* purposes, such acquisitions arise out of the original holdings.

Bonus and rights issues therefore attach to the original shareholdings for the purposes of the identification rules.

 Example

Alma Ltd acquired shares in S plc, a quoted company, as follows.

- 2,000 shares acquired in June 1994 for £11,500.
- In October 1995 there was a 1 for 2 bonus issue.
- In December 2001 there was a 1 for 4 rights issue at £3 per share.

Alma Ltd sold 2,600 shares in December 2020 for £30,000.

Calculate the number of shares in the share pool.

Solution

	Number
June 1994 purchase	2,000
October 1995 bonus issue (1 for 2)	
1/2 × 2,000	1,000
	3,000
December 2001 rights issue (1 for 4)	
1/4 × 3,000	750
	3,750
December 2020 sale	(2,600)
Balance in pool c/f	1,150

2.2 Bonus issue

A bonus issue is the issue of free shares (i.e. no cost is involved). As there is no expenditure involved it is not an operative event and therefore no indexation is calculated before recording the event.

Simply add the number of bonus issue shares received to the pool.

When the next event occurs (a sale, purchase or rights issue), index from the operative event prior to the bonus issue.

 Example

For Alma Ltd in the previous example, set up the share pool and deal with events up to and including the bonus issue.

Solution

Share pool	Number	Cost	Indexed cost
		£	£
Purchase June 1994	2,000	11,500	11,500
Bonus issue October 1995			
(1 for 2) 1/2 × 2,000	1,000	Nil	Nil
	3,000	11,500	11,500

Note: We have NOT indexed the pool before recording the bonus issue (as no cost is involved).

Therefore, next time there is an operative event we will index from June 1994 (the last operative event involving cost).

2.3 Rights issue

A rights issue involves a payment for new shares. Accordingly, it is treated simply as a purchase of shares (usually at a price below the market rate).

Hence, it should be treated in the same way as a purchase in the share pool:

- index up to the rights issue, then
- add in the number and cost of new shares.

Example

For Alma Ltd in the previous example, you are required to calculate the gain on disposal.

Assume that the indexed rise from June 1994 to December 2001 is 0.198 and from December 2001 to December 2017 is 0.604.

Solution

Share pool	Number	Cost	Indexed cost
		£	£
Purchase June 1994	2,000	11,500	11,500
Bonus issue October 1995 (1 for 2)	1,000	Nil	Nil
	3,000	11,500	11,500
Indexed rise to December 2001 (£11,500 × 0.198)			2,277
	3,000	11,500	13,777
Rights issue (1 for 4) at £3	750	2,250	2,250
	3,750	13,750	16,027
Indexed rise to December 2017 (£16,027 × 0.604)			9,680
	3,750	13,750	25,707
Disposal December 2020	(2,600)		
Allocate costs (2,600/3,750) × £13,750/£25,707		(9,533)	(17,824)
Balance c/f	1,150	4,217	7,883

Computation of gain – share pool

	£
Proceeds	30,000
Less: Cost	(9,533)
Unindexed gain	20,467
Less: Indexation (£17,824 – £9,533)	(8,291)
Chargeable gain	12,176

Note that the indexed cost is updated prior to the rights issue, because there is a purchase which involves additional cost.

Following the disposal there are 1,150 shares in the pool with a cost of £4,217 and an indexed cost of £7,883. This will be used as the starting point when dealing with the next operative event.

In the assessment you may be given details of brought forward amounts, rather than the complete history of the share pool.

 Test your understanding 2

Scarlet Ltd

On 20 September 2020, Scarlet Ltd sold 1,500 ordinary shares in Red plc for £4,725. The company's previous transactions were as follows.

Balance on the share pool at 5 May 2004 is 2,500 shares with a qualifying cost of £3,900 and an indexed cost of £4,385.

Transactions from 5 May 2004 were as follows:

| 4 April 2005 | Took up 1 for 2 bonus issue |
| 19 January 2006 | Took up 1 for 3 rights issue at 140p per share |

The indexed rise from May 2004 to January 2006 is 0.037, from January 2006 to September 2020 is 0.536 and from January 2006 to December 2017 is 0.438.

Calculate Scarlet Ltd's chargeable gain on the disposal on 20 September 2020.

3 Approach to assessment questions

In the assessment you will normally be asked to calculate a gain on shares. If so, this question will be manually marked. Hence it is important that you enter your answer into the table supplied correctly and show your workings.

In the specimen assessment a table is supplied with up to 5 columns. The first one or two columns are for description and narrative whilst the other columns are for numerical entry.

This should allow you to enter your answer in the same layout as used throughout this chapter although with a little less detail. For example, you do not need to include lines marking totals and subtotals.

Example

JTD Ltd bought 1,000 shares in VPZ plc for £4.40 each in December 2006.

In July 2014 it received a 1 for 5 rights issue at £4.80 each.

In May 2020 it sold 400 shares for £35,000.

The indexed rise from December 2006 to July 2014 is 0.263 and from July 2014 to December 2017 is 0.086.

What is the chargeable gain? Your answer should clearly show the balance of shares carried forward. Show all workings.

Solution

Pool	Number	Cost (£)	Indexed cost (£)
December 2006 Purchase	1,000	4,400	4,400
Index to July 2014			
(£4,400 × 0.263)			1,157
			5,557
July 2014 Rights issue			
1,000/5 × £4.80	200	960	960
			6,517
Index to December 2017			
(£6,517 × 0.086)			560
	1,200	5,360	7,077
May 2020 Sale			
(400/1,200) ×	(400)		
£5,360 / £7,077		(1,787)	(2,359)
Balance c/f	800	3,573	4,718
		£	
Proceeds		35,000	
Less cost (pool)		(1,787)	
		33,213	
Indexation			
(£2,359 – £1,787)		(572)	
Gain		32,641	

4 Test your understanding

Test your understanding 3

Share disposals for companies

Read the following statements and state whether they are true or false.

1   The matching rules for a company are as follows:

  –   first with same day acquisitions, then

  –   acquisitions within the previous nine days, then

  –   finally with the share pool.

  (handwritten: T)

2   You must apply an indexed rise when there is a bonus issue which happens before 1 January 2018. *(handwritten: F)*

3   For identification purposes rights issues are treated as separate acquisitions. *(handwritten: F)*

4   You must apply an indexed rise when there is a rights issue which happens before 1 January 2018. *(handwritten: T)*

Test your understanding 4

Jester Ltd

Jester Ltd sold ordinary 25p shares in Blue plc as follows:

	Number of shares	Proceeds
September 1999	2,000	£9,000
March 2021	2,000	£14,500

At 1 July 1995, Jester Ltd had 4,100 shares in the share pool, with an indexed cost of £10,744 and a cost of £8,200.

Purchases were made as follows:

	Number of shares	Cost
January 2001	200	£450

Compute the gains arising on all of the above transactions in quoted securities.

Use the following indexation factors as appropriate:

July 1995 – September 1999	0.115
September 1999 – January 2001	0.029
January 2001 – December 2017	0.625
January 2001 – March 2021	0.764

 Test your understanding 5

Purple Ltd

On 8 August 2020, Purple Ltd sold 5,000 ordinary shares in Indigo plc for £15,000. The company's previous transactions were as follows.

Balance on share pool at 9 June 1998, 3,000 shares with a qualifying cost of £4,000 and an indexed cost of £5,010.

Transactions from 9 June 1998 were as follows:

12 August 2003	Took up 1 for 3 bonus issue
7 May 2008	Took up 1 for 2 rights issue at 150p per share
4 August 2020	500 shares purchased for £1,410

The indexed rise from June 1998 to May 2008 is 0.316 and from May 2008 to December 2017 is 0.293.

Calculate Purple Ltd's chargeable gain on the disposal on 8 August 2020.

Test your understanding 6

Chrome Ltd

Chrome Ltd sold all of its ordinary shares in Copper plc for £17,760 on 1 October 2020.

Chrome Ltd acquired its shares in Copper plc as follows:

10 May 2007	Purchased 3,200 shares for £9,600
9 June 2011	Took up 1 for 4 rights issue at 260p per share
20 January 2013	Purchased 2,100 shares for £4,400

Indexation factors were:

May 2007 to June 2011	0.141
June 2011 to January 2013	0.045
January 2013 to December 2017	0.131
January 2013 to October 2020	0.212

Calculate Chrome Ltd's chargeable gain on the disposal on 1 October 2020.

5 Summary

When disposing of shares we apply matching rules to identify which shares have been disposed of.

These rules are needed so that we can deduct the appropriate acquisition costs from the disposal proceeds.

The matching rules for companies generally match disposals with shares held in the share pool.

Bonus and rights issues attach themselves to the original shareholdings.

 Links to other syllabus areas

Shares form the capital structure of a company and elsewhere in your syllabus (FSLC and earlier papers) you have considered how to account for share capital and changes thereto. This links in with gaining an understanding of the tax consequences of certain share transactions which may occur.

---

6 AAT reference material

Shares and securities – disposals by companies

The identification rules – a disposal of shares is matched:

- firstly, with same-day transactions

- secondly, with transactions in the previous 9 days (FIFO). No indexation allowance is available

- thirdly, with shares from the 1985 pool (shares bought from 1 April 1982 onwards).

1985 pool – pro forma working	No.	Cost £	Indexed cost £
Purchase	X	X	X
Index to next operative event			X
			X
Operative event (purchase)	X	X	X
	X	X	X
Index to next operative event			X
			X
Operative event (sale)	(X)	(X)	(X) A
Pool carried forward	X	X	X

Operative event = purchase, sale, rights issue. Bonus issue is not an operative event.

Computation

	£
Proceeds	X
Less indexed cost (A from pool)	(X)
Indexed gain	X

Test your understanding answers

Test your understanding 1

FDC Ltd

Share pool working	Note	Number	Cost	Indexed cost
			£	£
Purchase 1 June 1993	1	4,000	8,000	8,000
Indexed rise to July 2002	2			
£8,000 × 0.248				1,984
Purchase – July 2002		1,800	9,750	9,750
		5,800	17,750	19,734
Indexed rise to December 2017	3			
£19,734 × 0.581				11,465
		5,800	17,750	31,199
Sale of 2,000 shares	4	(2,000)		
$\dfrac{2,000}{5,800}$ × £17,750/£31,199			(6,121)	(10,758)
Carried forward		3,800	11,629	20,441

Notes:

(1) Any entry in the cost column must also be made in the indexed cost column.

(2) Indexation must be added before the purchase in July 2002 is added to the pool.

(3) No indexation is given after 31 December 2017.

(4) Use apportionment to allocate cost and indexed cost.

Gain on share pool shares

	£
Sale proceeds	20,571
Less: Cost	(6,121)
Unindexed gain	14,450
Less: Indexation allowance (£10,758 – £6,121)	(4,637)
Chargeable gain	9,813

Note: If the proceeds exceed the indexed cost then it is an acceptable short cut to just deduct the indexed cost from the proceeds in calculating the gain on the pool shares.

Test your understanding 2

Scarlet Ltd

Share pool	Number	Cost	Indexed cost
		£	£
Balance at 5 May 2004	2,500	3,900	4,385
4 April 2005 Bonus issue (1 for 2)	1,250	–	–
	3,750	3,900	4,385
Indexed rise to January 2006 £4,385 × 0.037			162
19 January 2006			4,547
Rights issue (1 for 3) × 140p	1,250	1,750	1,750
	5,000	5,650	6,297
Indexed rise to December 2017 £6,297 × 0.438			2,758
	5,000	5,650	9,055
Cost of sale $\frac{1,500}{5,000}$ × £5,650/£9,055	(1,500)	(1,695)	(2,717)
Pool balance c/f	3,500	3,955	6,338

Gain on the disposal of shares

	£
Proceeds	4,725
Less: Cost	(1,695)
Unindexed gain	3,030
Less: Indexation allowance (£2,717 – £1,695)	(1,022)
Chargeable gain	2,008

Test your understanding 3

Share disposals for companies

1 True

2 False   You do not apply an indexed rise as you do not need to add or deduct anything to or from the cost column.

3 False   The rights shares relate to the underlying shares.

4 True

📝 **Test your understanding 4**

Jester Ltd

	£
Disposal – September 1999	
Proceeds	9,000
Less: Cost (W)	(4,000)
Unindexed gain	5,000
Less: Indexation (£5,844 – £4,000)	(1,844)
Chargeable gain	3,156
Disposal – March 2021	
Proceeds	14,500
Less: Cost (W)	(4,043)
Unindexed gain	10,457
Less: Indexation (£9,558 – £4,043)	(5,515)
Chargeable gain	4,942

KAPLAN PUBLISHING

Share pool working

	Number of shares	Unindexed cost £	Indexed cost £
Balance at 1 July 1995	4,100	8,200	10,744
Indexed rise to September 1999 (0.115 × £10,744)			1,236
			11,980
September 1999 Sale (2,000/4,100) × £8,200 and £11,980	(2,000)	(4,000)	(5,844)
	2,100	4,200	6,136
Indexed rise to January 2001 (0.029 × £6,136)			178
January 2001 Acquisition	200	450	450
	2,300	4,650	6,764
Indexed rise to December 2017 (0.625 × £6,764)			4,228
			10,992
March 2021 Sale (2,000/2,300) × £4,650 and £10,992	(2,000)	(4,043)	(9,558)
	300	607	1,434

📝 Test your understanding 5

Purple Ltd

Disposal – 8 August 2020

(Sale of 500 shares purchased in previous 9 days)

	£
Sale proceeds (500/5,000 × £15,000)	1,500
Less: Cost	(1,410)
Unindexed gain	90
Less: Indexation allowance	Nil
Chargeable gain	90

Disposal – 8 August 2020 (Sale of 4,500 shares from the pool)

	£
Sale proceeds (£15,000 – £1,500)	13,500
Less: Cost	(5,250)
Unindexed gain	8,250
Less: Indexation allowance (£9,303 – £5,250)	(4,053)
Chargeable gain	4,197

Total gains (£90 + £4,197) = £4,287

Share pool working

	Number	Cost	Indexed cost
		£	£
Balance at 9 June 1998	3,000	4,000	5,010
12 August 2003			
Bonus issue (1 for 3)	1,000	Nil	Nil
	4,000	4,000	5,010
Indexed rise to May 2008			
(£5,010 × 0.316)			1,583
7 May 2008 Rights issue			
(1 for 2 × 150p)	2,000	3,000	3,000
	6,000	7,000	9,593
Indexed rise to December 2017			
(£9,593 × 0.293)			2,811
			12,404
8 August 2020 Sale			
$\frac{4,500}{6,000}$ × £7,000/£12,404	(4,500)	(5,250)	(9,303)
Pool c/f	1,500	1,750	3,101

Test your understanding 6

Chrome Ltd

	£
Disposal – October 2020	
Proceeds	17,760
Less: Cost (W)	(16,080)
	———
Unindexed gain	1,680
Less: Indexation (£20,382 – £16,080)	
Restricted, indexation allowance cannot create a loss	(1,680)
	———
Chargeable gain	Nil
	———

Share pool working

	Number of shares	Unindexed cost £	Indexed cost £
Purchase May 2007	3,200	9,600	9,600
Indexed rise to June 2011			
(0.141 × £9,600)			1,354
9 June 2011 Rights issue (1 for 4)			
(3,200/4 × £2.60)	800	2,080	2,080
	———	———	———
	4,000	11,680	13,034
Indexed rise to January 2013			
(0.045 × £13,034)			587
20 January 2013 Purchase	2,100	4,400	4,400
	———	———	———
	6,100	16,080	18,021
Indexed rise to December 2017			
(0.131 × £18,021)			2,361
			———
			20,382
1 October 2020 Sale	(6,100)	(16,080)	(20,382)
	———	———	———
	Nil	Nil	Nil
	———	———	———

Gains and losses for individuals

Introduction

An individual (including a sole trader or a partner) pays capital gains tax on his/her chargeable gains.

This chapter compares and contrasts the rules for capital gains for individuals with those for companies.

ASSESSMENT CRITERIA	CONTENTS
Calculate chargeable gains and allowable losses (5.1)	1 Individual v company – similarities
Apply the rules relating to the disposal of chattels and wasting assets (5.1)	2 Individual v company – differences
Apply current reliefs and allowances (5.1)	
Apply capital gains tax rates (5.1)	

1 Individual v company – similarities

1.1 Calculation of individual gains and losses

The standard pro forma used to calculate a gain or loss on disposal of an asset is essentially the same as for companies except that individuals are not entitled to an indexation allowance.

	£
Gross sale proceeds	X
Less: Selling costs	(X)
	——
Net sale proceeds (NSP)	X
Less: Allowable cost	(X)
	——
Capital gain	X
	——

1.2 Special rules

The special rules discussed in Chapter 16 also apply for individuals:

- enhancement expenditure
- part disposals
- non-wasting chattels.

Note that the AAT reference material set out in section 5 below has details of these special computational rules.

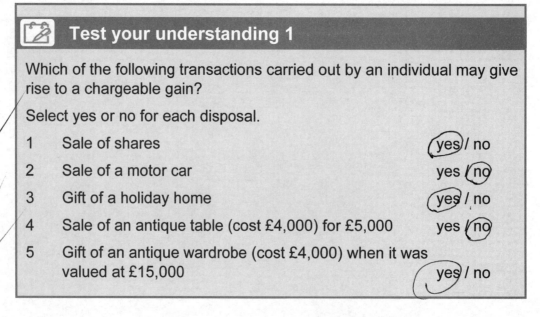

Test your understanding 1

Which of the following transactions carried out by an individual may give rise to a chargeable gain?

Select yes or no for each disposal.

1	Sale of shares	yes / no
2	Sale of a motor car	yes / no
3	Gift of a holiday home	yes / no
4	Sale of an antique table (cost £4,000) for £5,000	yes / no
5	Gift of an antique wardrobe (cost £4,000) when it was valued at £15,000	yes / no

2 Individual v company – differences

2.1 Capital gains tax

Individuals pay capital gains tax on their taxable gains for the tax year (e.g. 2020/21).

Individuals are entitled to an annual exempt amount (AEA) for each tax year (£12,300 in 2020/21).

The AEA is deducted from the total net chargeable gains of the year to give the taxable gains.

	£
Capital gains	X
Less: Capital losses	(X)
	―――
Net chargeable gains	X
Less: AEA	(12,300)
	―――
Taxable gains	X
	―――

If an individual has trading losses for the tax year he/she can claim to set them against his/her income, but if any loss remains then a claim can be made to treat the trade loss like a capital loss of the same tax year.

Note that this does not work the other way round. Capital losses cannot be offset against income.

Capital gains tax is then calculated on the taxable gains.

2.2 The AEA and brought forward losses

Brought forward capital losses are set off against gains after deducting the AEA, so the AEA is not wasted.

This rule does not apply to current tax year capital losses, which must be set off against current year gains and cannot be restricted to preserve the AEA.

The offset of current year losses may therefore result in wastage of the AEA.

Note that the AAT reference material set out in section 5 below covers the treatment of current year and brought forward capital losses.

Example

Mica has the following capital gains and losses for the two years ended 5 April 2021.

	2019/20 £	2020/21 £
Gains	12,500	14,900
Losses	(14,000)	(2,000)

What gains (if any) are chargeable after considering all reliefs and exemptions?

Solution

	2019/20 £	2020/21 £
Current gains	12,500	14,900
Current losses	(12,500)	(2,000)
	Nil	12,900
Less: AEA	Wasted	(12,300)
	Nil	600
Less: Brought forward losses		(600)
Taxable gain	Nil	Nil
Loss carried forward		
(£14,000 – £12,500)	1,500	
(£1,500 – £600)		900

 Test your understanding 2

Read the following statements and state whether they are true or false.

1   Brought forward capital losses are deducted after the AEA. (T)

2   Excess capital losses can be offset against taxable income. (F)

3   Excess trading losses can be offset against capital gains. (T)

4   Current tax year capital losses must always be relieved in full. (F)

Test your understanding 3

Manuel made chargeable gains and allowable losses for 2020/21 as set out below:

Gain of £60,100

Gain of £12,500

Capital loss of £4,000

Calculate Manuel's taxable gains for 2020/21.

A £56,300

B £60,300

C £68,600

D £72,600

2.3 Calculating the tax payable

Taxable gains are treated as an additional amount of income in order to determine the rates of CGT. However, the gains must not be included in the income tax computation.

Where the taxable gains fall within any remaining basic rate band (after income has been taxed) they are taxed at 10%. For 2020/21 the basic rate band is £37,500.

The balance of the taxable gains is taxed at 20%.

 Example

Carl sold some assets in 2020/21 and made chargeable gains of £31,700 and a capital loss of £2,500.

Carl has capital losses brought forward as at 6 April 2020 of £3,300.

Carl's taxable income for the year, after deducting the personal allowance, is £35,715.

What is Carl's CGT liability for 2020/21?

Solution

	Total £
Chargeable gains for the year	31,700
Less: Current year capital losses	(2,500)
Net chargeable gains for the year	29,200
Less: AEA	(12,300)
	16,900
Less: Capital losses brought forward	(3,300)
Taxable gains	13,600
CGT	
£1,785 (£37,500 – £35,715) × 10%	179
£11,815 (£13,600 – £1,785) × 20%	2,363
Capital gains tax liability	2,542

Test your understanding 4

Bert made chargeable gains of £13,600 and capital losses of £5,000 in 2020/21. He had losses brought forward of £3,000.

How much capital loss will be carried forward to 2021/22?

3,000

2.4 Connected persons

Where a disposal is between connected persons:

(i) sale proceeds are deemed to be market value (any actual sale proceeds are ignored), and

(ii) if a loss arises on a disposal to a connected person it can only be offset against a gain made on a disposal to the **same** connected person.

Connected persons are mainly relatives and their spouses/civil partners or relatives of your spouse/civil partner.

Note that connected persons are covered in the AAT reference material set out in section 5 below.

An individual is also connected with a company he/she controls and a partner is connected with his/her other business partners.

Whilst an individual is connected to his/her spouse, transactions between spouses are not made at market value but on the basis that no gain or loss arises.

Transfers between civil partners also take place on a no gain/no loss basis.

This gives an opportunity for tax saving as assets can be transferred to the spouse or civil partner with unused AEA, available capital losses or unused basic rate band to pay capital gains tax at a lower rate.

 Test your understanding 5

Fred sold a painting to his wife on 1 March 2021 for £10,000. The market value of the painting at that date was £20,000.

Fred had purchased the painting in June 2007 for £22,000.

A loss arises on the disposal which can only be offset against gains arising on future disposals to his wife.

True or False?

3 Test your understanding

Test your understanding 6

1   Mary made a capital loss of £4,000 in 2019/20. In 2020/21 she made a chargeable gain of £12,700 and a capital loss of £3,000.

How much capital loss is carried forward at the end of 2020/21?

A   £Nil

B   £4,000

C   £6,600

D   £7,000

2   What would your answer be if Mary had only made the chargeable gain of £12,700 in 2020/21 and not the capital loss?

A   £Nil

B   £400

C   £3,600

D   £4,000

Test your understanding 7

Misha sold two assets in 2020/21 and made two chargeable gains of £17,300 and £11,700. Her taxable income for the year, after deducting the personal allowance, is £24,900.

What is Misha's capital gains tax liability for 2020/21?

Handwritten working:

(2680)

$C.G = 17300 + 11700 = 29000$

Basic Rate Threshold

37500

A.E

(12300) Taxable   24900

Earned 37,400

16700   Left Suppt 12600

P.A. (12500) to CGT

Taxable   24,900

$CGT = 10\% (Basic\ Rate) + 20\%$ High Rate

1260   +   820 (4100)

Test your understanding 8

John

John made the following disposals in the tax year 2020/21. John's taxable income for the year, after deducting the personal allowance, is £33,715.

(1) On 20 June 2020 he sold an antique vase for £74,200. The vase was bought in October 2004 for £29,000.

(2) On 12 August 2020 he sold a collection of military memorabilia. It had been purchased for £30,000 in November 2000. Sale proceeds were £26,000.

(3) On 31 March 2021 he sold 2 hectares out of a 10 hectare plot of land that he had acquired in June 2010 for £50,000. He sold the 2 hectares for £60,000.

In March 2021 the remaining 8 hectares were worth £250,000.

Calculate John's capital gains tax liability for the tax year 2020/21.

Capital Gain (1) = 45200

Capital Loss (2) = (4000) ✓

Capital Gain (3) = 50323 ✓
(60000 - 9677)

Total Gain 91523

Less AEA (12,300)

79223

Basic Band Rate

(37,500 - 33715) = 3785 × 10% = 379 ✓

(79223 - 3785) = 75438 × 20% = 15088

15467 ✓

Working(3)

$50000 \times \dfrac{60000}{60000 + 250,000}$

= 9677

---

4 Summary

The main differences between calculating gains for individuals and those for companies are:

- individuals are not entitled to the indexation allowance
- individuals are entitled to an AEA which is deducted from chargeable gains in arriving at taxable gains
- individuals pay capital gains tax on the taxable gains arising in a tax year at 10% and 20% depending on the level of their taxable income and gains.

 Links to other syllabus areas

There is a direct link here to the other Professional level tax paper (PLTX) and a high degree of overlap between the two papers when it comes to calculating the capital gains made by individuals for a particular tax year. If you have already sat that unit, you will encounter a high degree of familiarity; alternatively, if you are intending to study it, the knowledge gained here will stand you in good stead going forwards.

5 AAT reference material

Introduction to chargeable gains

- Individual pays Capital Gains Tax (CGT) on net chargeable gains in a tax year.

- For companies, chargeable gains are included as income in calculating total profits.

- Individuals receive an annual exempt amount from CGT – for 2020/21 this is £12,300.

- Gains/losses arise when a chargeable person makes a chargeable disposal of a chargeable asset.

- Chargeable person – individual or company.

- Chargeable disposal – sale, gift or loss/destruction of the whole or part of an asset. Exempt disposals – on death and gifts to approved charities.

- Chargeable asset – all assets unless exempt. Exempt assets include motor cars and some chattels.

Calculation of capital gains tax

Net chargeable gains – total gains in the tax year after netting off any current year or brought forward losses and the annual exempt amount.

Annual exempt amount (AEA)

- For individuals only.

- AEA cannot be carried forward or carried back.

- Current year losses must be netted off against current year gains before AEA. This means AEA can be wasted.

- Brought forward capital losses are set off against current year gains after AEA so AEA is not wasted.

Calculation of gains and losses for individuals

Pro forma computation

	£	£
Consideration received		X
Less Incidental costs of sale		(X)
Net sale proceeds		NSP
Less Allowable expenditure		
– Acquisition cost	X	
– Incidental costs of acquisition	X	
– Enhancement expenditure	X	
		(Cost)
Gain/(Loss)		X/(X)

- Consideration received is usually sales proceeds, but market value will be used instead of actual consideration where the transaction is a gift or between connected persons.

- An individual is connected with their spouse, relatives (and their spouses) and spouse's relatives (and their spouses). Relative means brother, sister, lineal ancestor or lineal descendent.

- Husband and wife/civil partner transfers – nil gain nil loss.

Part disposals – the cost allocated to the disposal = Cost × (A/(A+B))

A = consideration received on part disposal

B = market value of the remainder of the asset

Chattels – tangible moveable object. Two types:

- Wasting – expected life of 50 years or less (e.g. racehorse or boat). CGT exempt.

  Non-wasting – expected life greater than 50 years (e.g. antiques or jewellery).

CGT, £6,000 rule

Buy Sell	£6,000 or less	More than £6,000
Less than £6,000	Exempt	Allowable loss but proceeds are deemed = £6,000
More than £6,000	Normal calculation of the gain, then compare with 5/3(gross proceeds – £6,000) – Take the lower gain	Chargeable in full

Test your understanding answers

Test your understanding 1

1	Yes	A chargeable disposal of a chargeable asset by a chargeable person.
2	No	A motor car is not a chargeable asset.
3	Yes	Gifts are chargeable disposals.
4	No	A chattel sold at a gain where the proceeds are less than £6,000 is exempt.
5	Yes	The proceeds (i.e. the value) exceed £6,000.

Test your understanding 2

1	True	
2	False	Capital losses cannot be set against anything except gains.
3	True	Once trade losses have been set against total income for the tax year, they can be treated like a capital loss of the year and deducted from capital gains.
4	True	Current year losses must be relieved in full, which means that the AEA may be wasted.

Test your understanding 3

The correct answer is A.

Explanation

Taxable gains are defined as net chargeable gains after the deduction of the AEA, as follows:

	£
Total chargeable gains (£60,100 + £12,500)	72,600
Less: Capital loss	(4,000)
Net chargeable gains	68,600
Less: AEA	(12,300)
Taxable gain	56,300

 Test your understanding 4

Bert

The correct answer is £3,000.

Explanation

Bert's net gains for 2020/21 are £8,600.

The capital losses brought forward of £3,000 will be carried forward to 2021/22 as the net gains for 2020/21 are less than the AEA of £12,300.

 Test your understanding 5

False – The transaction is between husband and wife and therefore takes place on a no gain/no loss basis.

Test your understanding 6

Mary

1   The correct answer is B.

2   The correct answer is C.

Explanation

1   Net chargeable gains for 2020/21 are £9,700 (£12,700 – £3,000). As this is less than the AEA, the loss brought forward of £4,000 is carried forward to 2020/21.

2   If Mary had only made the chargeable gain of £12,700 in 2020/21, her AEA would be used first leaving a figure of £400. Brought forward losses of £400 would be utilised here.
The balance of the capital losses of £3,600 (£4,000 – £400) would have been carried forward.

Test your understanding 7

Misha

The correct answer is £2,080.

	£
Chargeable gains (£17,300 + £11,700)	29,000
Less: AEA	(12,300)
Taxable gains	16,700
£12,600 (£37,500 – £24,900) × 10%	1,260
£4,100 (£16,700 – £12,600) × 20%	820
Capital gains tax liability	2,080

Test your understanding 8

John

	£	£
Vase		
Proceeds	74,200	
Less: Cost	(29,000)	
	————	45,200
Military memorabilia		
Proceeds	26,000	
Less: Cost	(30,000)	
	————	(4,000)
Land		
Proceeds	60,000	
Less: Cost		
$£50,000 \times \dfrac{60,000}{60,000 + 250,000}$	(9,677)	
	————	50,323
		————
Net chargeable gains		91,523
Less: AEA		(12,300)
		————
Taxable gains		79,223
		————
CGT		
£3,785 (£37,500 – £33,715) × 10%		379
£75,438 (£79,223 – £3,785) × 20%		15,088
		————
Capital gains tax liability		15,467
		————

Shares and securities – disposals by individuals

Introduction

As part of the assessment you may be required to calculate the gain on a disposal of shares by an individual.

As for companies, there are special rules applying to share disposals as it is necessary to determine which particular shares have been sold.

ASSESSMENT CRITERIA	CONTENTS
Apply the rules relating to the disposal of shares (5.1)	1 The matching rules 2 Same day and next 30 days 3 Share pool 4 Bonus issues and rights issues 5 Approach to assessment questions

1 The matching rules

As for companies, matching rules are required so that, if only some of the shares are sold we know which they are in order to identify their cost.

However, the matching rules for individuals are different to those for companies.

In relation to *individuals,* we match shares disposed of in the following order:

- first, with shares acquired on the same day as the disposal

- second, with shares acquired within the *following* 30 days (using the earliest acquisition first, i.e. on a FIFO basis)

- third, with the share pool (sometimes referred to as the s104 pool or the FA1985 pool).

  This pool of shares brings together the shares bought by the individual since 6 April 1982 to the date before the day of disposal.

Note that the matching rules for individuals are covered in the AAT reference material set out in section 8 below.

 Example

Frederic had the following transactions in the shares of DEF plc, a quoted company.

1 June 1995	Bought	4,000 shares for	£8,000
30 July 2002	Bought	1,800 shares for	£9,750
20 May 2010	Bought	1,000 shares for	£8,500
15 March 2021	Sold	3,500 shares for	£36,000
20 March 2021	Bought	400 shares for	£3,900

You are required to match the shares sold with the relevant acquisitions.

Solution

	Number	Number
Shares sold		3,500
(1) Shares acquired on same day		Nil
(2) Shares acquired in following 30 days		(400)
		3,100
(3) Share pool		
1 June 1995	4,000	
30 July 2002	1,800	
20 May 2010	1,000	
	6,800	
The disposal from the pool is therefore 3,100 out of 6,800		(3,100)
		Nil

 Test your understanding 1

Petra sold 200 shares in Red plc on 13 December 2020. She had acquired her shares in the company as follows:

	Number of shares
1 January 2008	650
14 February 2009	250
5 January 2021	50

In accordance with the share matching/identification rules the 200 shares sold by Petra are correctly identified as follows:

A The 50 shares acquired on 5 January 2021 and then 150 of the remaining 900 shares in the pool

B The 50 shares acquired on 5 January 2021 and then 150 of the shares acquired on 14 February 2009

C 200 of the shares acquired on 1 January 2008

D 200 shares in the share pool which includes all 950 shares acquired

Once the correct acquisition is identified, then the computation of the gains can be carried out. This is looked at in detail over the next few sections.

2 Same day and next 30 days

2.1 Calculation of the gain

The calculation of the gain on disposal is straightforward.

	£
Sale proceeds or market value	X
Less: Allowable cost	(X)
Chargeable gain	X

Example

Using the example details above (Frederic) calculate the gain on the sale of the shares acquired in the 30 days following the sale.

Solution

This consists of the sale of 400 shares.

Sale proceeds of £36,000 relates to 3,500 shares so must be apportioned. The proceeds relating to 400 shares will be:

$$\frac{400}{3,500} \times £36,000 = £4,114$$

	£
Sale proceeds	4,114
Less: Cost	(3,900)
Chargeable gain	214

The balance of the proceeds (£36,000 − £4,114) = £31,886 will be applied to shares sold from the share pool.

3 Share pool

3.1 Calculation of the pooled cost

The share pool consists of all shares of the same type in the same company purchased since 6 April 1982 (we do not need to consider those purchased before 6 April 1982).

The pool is used to calculate the cost of shares sold by reference to the average cost of all shares purchased.

The pool is set up with two columns; number (of shares) and cost.

Shares purchased are added to the pool and shares sold are deducted.

- For a purchase, add the number of shares acquired to the number column and the cost to the cost column.

- For a sale, deduct the number of shares sold from the number column and an appropriate proportion of the cost from the cost column.

Note that there is no indexed cost column for individuals, as individuals are not entitled to indexation.

> ### Example
>
> Using the example details above (Frederic), calculate the cost to be eliminated from the pool.
>
> **Solution**
>
> **Share pool**
>
> | | | Number | Cost £ |
> |---|---|---|---|
> | 1 June 1995 | purchase | 4,000 | 8,000 |
> | 30 July 2002 | purchase | 1,800 | 9,750 |
> | 20 May 2010 | purchase | 1,000 | 8,500 |
> | | | 6,800 | 26,250 |
> | 15 March 2021 | disposal | | |
> | £26,250 × (3,100 / 6,800) | | (3,100) | (11,967) |
> | Pool balance c/f | | 3,700 | 14,283 |

3.2 Calculation of the gain on the share pool

The gain is calculated as normal:

	£
Sale proceeds	X
Less: Allowable cost	(X)
Chargeable gain	X

Example

Using the details from the example Frederic, what is the gain on the share pool disposals?

Solution

Sale proceeds are £31,886 (from Frederic example above).

	£
Sale proceeds	31,886
Less: Allowable cost (above)	(11,967)
Chargeable gain on share pool shares	19,919

Hence, the total chargeable gain on disposal of the 3,500 shares = (£214 + £19,919) = £20,133

Test your understanding 2

Patrizia has carried out the following transactions in shares in CYZ plc.

	Number	Cost £
Purchase (8 February 2001)	1,800	3,100
Purchase (12 September 2010)	1,200	4,400
Purchase (10 October 2020)	400	6,000
	Number	Proceeds
Sale (10 October 2020)	2,000	£33,000

What is the chargeable gain? $\left(2240 + 600\right) = 23000$

4 Bonus issues and rights issues

4.1 Principles of bonus issues and rights issues

A bonus issue is the distribution of free shares to existing shareholders based on existing shareholdings.

The number of shares acquired is added to the number column but there is no cost to add to the cost column.

A rights issue involves shareholders acquiring new shares in proportion to their existing shareholdings. The shares are not free but are usually priced at a rate below the market price.

The number of shares acquired is added to the number column and the cost to the cost column. Accordingly, a rights issue is no different from any other purchase of shares.

Note that the rules for share pools, including the treatment of bonus and rights issues, is included in the AAT reference material set out in section 8 below.

Example

Alma acquired shares in S plc, a quoted company, as follows.

2,000 shares acquired in June 1996 for £11,500.

In October 2006 there was a 1 for 2 bonus issue.

In December 2008 there was a 1 for 4 rights issue at £3 per share.

Alma sold 1,350 shares in November 2020 for £30,000.

What is the chargeable gain?

Solution

	£
Sale proceeds	30,000
Less: Cost (W)	(4,950)
Chargeable gain	25,050

Working: Share pool

	Number	Cost £
June 1996 purchase	2,000	11,500
October 2006 bonus issue (1 for 2) No cost so simply add in new shares	1,000	–
	3,000	11,500
December 2008 rights issue (1 for 4) (£3 × 750)	750	2,250
	3,750	13,750
November 2020 disposal $\frac{1,350}{3,750} \times £13,750$	(1,350)	(4,950)
Pool carried forward	2,400	8,800

Test your understanding 3

Omar

In October 2020 Omar sold 3,000 shares in Smith plc for £36,000.

He had purchased 4,200 shares in June 1994 for £11,600. In August 2008 there was a 1 for 3 rights issue at £5.60 per share.

Calculate the chargeable gain on disposal.

5 Approach to assessment questions

In the assessment you will normally be asked to calculate a gain on shares. If so, this question will be manually marked. Hence it is important that you enter your answer correctly into the table supplied and show your workings.

In the specimen assessment a table is supplied. The first one or two columns can be used for description and narrative whilst the other columns are for numerical entry.

This should allow you to enter your answer in the same layout as used throughout this chapter although with a little less detail. You will not be able to type in lines to indicate totals and subtotals.

 Example

Jason bought 1,000 shares in VZ plc for £4.20 each in December 2007.

In July 2016 he received a 1 for 5 rights issue at £6.52 each.

On 4 May 2020 he sold 400 shares for £45,000.

On 12 May 2020 he bought 100 shares for £10,000.

What is the chargeable gain? Your answer should clearly show the balance of shares carried forward. Show all workings.

Solution

100 shares		£	
(following 30 days)			
Proceeds	100/400 × £45,000	11,250	
Cost		(10,000)	
Gain		1,250	
300 shares – pool			
Proceeds	£45,000 – £11,250	33,750	
Less cost (pool)		(1,376)	
Gain		32,374	
Total gain		33,624	
Pool		Number	Cost (£)
December 2007 Purchase		1,000	4,200
July 2016 Rights issue	1,000/5 × £6.52	200	1,304
		1,200	5,504
May 2020 Sale	300/1,200 ×	(300)	
	£5,504		(1,376)
Balance c/f		900	4,128

6 Test your understanding

Test your understanding 4

Viktoriya bought 1,000 shares in XYZ plc on 1 May 2008 and a further 500 shares on 5 September 2020. She sold 750 shares on 25 August 2020.

Which shares are the shares sold identified with?

A   750 of the shares acquired on 1 May 2008

B   500 of the shares acquired on 1 May 2008 and 250 of the shares acquired on 5 September 2020

C   The 500 shares acquired on 5 September 2020 and 250 of the remaining 1,000 shares in the pool

D   750 of the shares in the share pool which includes 1,500 shares acquired

Test your understanding 5

Tony bought 15,000 shares in Last Chance Ltd for £6 per share in August 2006. He received a bonus issue of 1 for 15 shares in January 2009.

In November 2020 Tony sold 9,000 shares for £14 per share.

Calculate the gain made on the sale of the shares and show the balance of shares and their value to carry forward.

All workings must be shown in your calculations.

Test your understanding 6

Leonardo sold all of his 2,145 ordinary shares in Turnip plc on 19 November 2020 for net sale proceeds of £8,580.

His previous dealings in these shares were as follows:

July 2013 purchased 1,750 shares for £2,625

May 2014 purchased 200 shares for £640

June 2015 took up 1 for 10 rights issue at £3.40 per share

Calculate the gain made on the sale of the shares.

All workings must be shown in your calculations.

 Test your understanding 7

Zineb bought 2,000 shares in PQR plc for £4,000 on 6 October 2004 and a further 1,000 shares for £3,000 in March 2010.

PQR plc made a rights issue of 1 new share for every 5 held at £4 per share in February 2012. Zineb sold 400 shares in September 2020 for £4,150.

What is the cost of the shares sold?

A   £3,106

B   £1,600

C   £933

D   £1,044

	Number	Cost
Purchase 1	2000	4000
Purchase 2	1000	3000
	3000	7000
Rights @4	600	2400
	3600	9400
Sold 400/3600 ×9400	(400)	(1044)
	3200	8356

Test your understanding 8

Irving sold 1,500 ordinary shares in Corniche plc on 9 September 2020 for net sale proceeds of £5,550.

His previous dealings in these shares were as follows:

3 June 2012	purchased 4,800 shares for £15,360
11 April 2016	received a 1 for 4 bonus issue
4 October 2020	purchased 700 shares for £2,450

Calculate the gain on the sale of the shares on 9 September 2020.

All workings must be shown in your calculations.

7 Summary

Share disposals require special matching rules.

Shares sold by individuals are matched with:

- purchases on the same day
- purchases within the following 30 days
- share pool.

Bonus issues increase the number of shares held in the pool.

Rights issues affect both the number of shares held in the pool and the pool cost.

 Links to other syllabus areas

There is a direct link here to the other Professional level tax paper (PLTX) and a high degree of overlap between the two papers when it comes to calculating the capital gains made by individuals when disposing of shares. If you have already sat that unit, you will encounter a high degree of familiarity; alternatively, if you are intending to study it, the knowledge gained here will stand you in good stead going forwards.

8 AAT reference material

Shares and securities – disposals by individuals

CGT on shares and securities

Disposal of shares and securities are subject to CGT except for listed government securities (gilt-edged securities or 'gilts'), qualifying corporate bonds (e.g. company loan notes/debentures) and shares held in an Individual Savings Account (ISA).

The identification rules

Used to determine which shares have been sold and so what acquisition cost can be deducted from the sale proceeds (e.g. match the disposal and acquisition).

Disposals are matched:

- firstly, with acquisitions on the same day as the day of disposal
- secondly, with acquisitions made in the 30 days following the date of disposal (FIFO basis)
- thirdly, with shares from the share pool.

The Share Pool

- The share pool contains all shares acquired prior to the disposal date.
- Each acquisition is not kept separately, but is 'pooled' together with other acquisitions and a running total kept of the number of shares and the cost of those shares.
- When a disposal from the pool is made, the appropriate number of shares are taken from the pool along with the average cost of those shares.
- The gain on disposal is then calculated.

Bonus issues and rights issues

- Bonus issue – no adjustment to cost needed.
- Rights issue – adjustment to cost needed.

Test your understanding answers

 Test your understanding 1

Petra

The correct answer is A.

Explanation

A is the correct answer because the share identification rules match shares in the following priority.

1   Shares acquired on the same day as the disposal – not applicable here.

2   Shares acquired in the following 30 days – 50 shares acquired on 5 January 2021.

3   Shares in the share pool (all acquisitions up to date of disposal).

Test your understanding 2

Patrizia

10 October 2020 disposal of 2,000 shares identified with:

		£
(a)	Shares acquired on the same day	400
(b)	Shares from share pool	1,600
		2,000

Sale proceeds are £33,000 for 2,000 shares = £16.50 each

(a) 10 October 2020 acquisition

	£	£
Sale proceeds (400 × £16.50)	6,600	
Less: Cost	(6,000)	
Chargeable gain		600

(b) Share pool

	£	£
Sale proceeds (1,600 × £16.50)	26,400	
Less: Cost (W)	(4,000)	
Chargeable gain		22,400
Total chargeable gains		23,000

Working: Share pool

	Number	Cost £
February 2001 purchase	1,800	3,100
September 2010 purchase	1,200	4,400
	3,000	7,500
October 2020 disposal	(1,600)	(4,000)
Pool balance c/f	1,400	3,500

Test your understanding 3

Omar

	£
Sale proceeds	36,000
Less: Cost (W)	(10,414)
Chargeable gain	25,586

Working: Share pool

	Number	Cost £
June 1994 purchase	4,200	11,600
August 2008 rights issue (1/3 × 4,200) = 1,400 × £5.60	1,400	7,840
	5,600	19,440
October 2020 disposal $\frac{3,000}{5,600} \times £19,440$	(3,000)	(10,414)
Pool balance c/f	2,600	9,026

Test your understanding 4

Viktoriya

The correct answer is C.

Explanation

C is the correct answer because the share identification rules match shares in the following priority.

1   Shares acquired on the same day as the disposal – not applicable here.

2   Shares acquired in the following 30 days – 500 shares acquired on 5 September 2020.

3   Shares in the share pool.

Test your understanding 5

Tony

	£
Sale proceeds (9,000 × £14)	126,000
Less: Cost (W)	(50,625)
Chargeable gain	75,375

Working: Share pool

	Number	Cost £
August 2006 purchase (15,000 × £6)	15,000	90,000
January 2009 bonus issue	1,000	
	16,000	90,000
November 2020 disposal $\frac{9,000}{16,000} \times £90,000$	(9,000)	(50,625)
Pool balance c/f	7,000	39,375

Test your understanding 6

Leonardo

		£
Proceeds		8,580
Less: Cost (W)		(3,928)
Chargeable gain		4,652

Working: Share pool

		Shares number	Cost £
July 2013	purchase	1,750	2,625
May 2014	purchase	200	640
		1,950	3,265
June 2015 (1 for 10)	rights issue @ £3.40	195	663
		2,145	3,928
Nov 2020	sale	(2,145)	(3,928)
		Nil	Nil

KAPLAN PUBLISHING

Test your understanding 7

Zineb

The correct answer is D.

Explanation

Working: Share pool		*Shares number*	*Cost £*
October 2004	purchase	2,000	4,000
March 2010	purchase	1,000	3,000
		3,000	7,000
February 2012 (1 for 5)	rights issue @ £4.00	600	2,400
		3,600	9,400
September 2020	sale	(400)	(1,044)
		3,200	8,356

Test your understanding 8

Irving

September 2020 disposal of 1,500 shares identified with:

		£
(a)	Shares acquired in the next 30 days	700
(b)	Shares from share pool	800
		1,500

Net sale proceeds = £5,550 for 1,500 shares = £3.70 each

(a) 4 October 2020 acquisition

	£	£
Sale proceeds (700 × £3.70)	2,590	
Less: Cost	(2,450)	
Chargeable gain		140

(b) Share pool

	£	£
Sale proceeds (800 × £3.70)	2,960	
Less: Cost (W)	(2,048)	
Chargeable gain		912
Total chargeable gains		1,052

Working: Share pool

	Number	Cost £
June 2012 purchase	4,800	15,360
April 2016 bonus issue (4,800/4)	1,200	
	6,000	15,360
September 2020 disposal	(800)	(2,048)
Pool balance c/f	5,200	13,312

Chargeable gains – reliefs

Introduction

The sale of a substantial asset within a business, or the sale of a whole business, could give rise to a large gain. If all of the gain was subject to tax it would make it difficult for business assets to be sold if the owner could not afford the tax due.

Reliefs exist to reduce the tax payable or the gain in specific circumstances, including when a replacement asset is acquired or when an asset is given away.

ASSESSMENT CRITERIA
Apply current reliefs and allowances (5.1, 5.2)
Apply capital gains tax rates (5.1)

CONTENTS	
1	Business asset disposal relief
2	Investors' relief
3	Rollover relief
4	Gift relief

1 Business asset disposal relief

Business asset disposal relief (BADR) reduces the capital gains tax payable by an individual on qualifying business disposals; for example, where an individual sells all or part of his/her unincorporated business.

1.1 The relief

The relief operates as follows:

- Gains on 'qualifying business disposals' of up to £1 million are taxed at a lower rate of 10%.

- Any gains above the £1 million limit are taxed at the normal rates of 10% and 20%.

- The limit is a lifetime limit that is diminished each time a claim for the relief is made.

- In order to maximise tax savings, allowable losses and the annual exempt amount (AEA) should be deducted from gains on disposals of assets that do not qualify for BADR wherever possible.

- The amount of qualifying gains that is taxed at 10% must be deducted from the remaining basic rate band when determining the rate of tax to be paid on non-qualifying gains (which will therefore usually be 20%).

The relief must be claimed within 12 months of the 31 January following the end of the tax year in which the disposal is made.

For 2020/21 disposals, the relief must be claimed by 31 January 2023.

The relief is not available to companies.

1.2 Qualifying business disposals

The relief applies to the disposal of:

- the whole or part of a business carried on by the individual either alone or in partnership

- assets of the individual's or partnership's trading business that has **now ceased**

- shares, provided:
  - the shares are in the individual's 'personal trading company', and
  - the individual is an employee of the company (part time or full time).

An individual's 'personal trading company' is one in which the individual:

- owns at least 5% of the ordinary shares
- which carry at least 5% of the voting rights, entitlement to distributable profits and entitlement to net assets.

Note in particular that:

- the disposal of an individual business asset used for the purposes of a continuing trade does not qualify. There must be a disposal of the whole or part of the trading business; the sale of an asset in isolation does not qualify.

1.3　Qualifying ownership period

In the case of the disposal of a business it must have been owned by the individual making the disposal in the 24 months prior to the disposal.

Where the disposal is of an asset of the individual's or partnership's trading business that has now ceased the individual must have owned the business for 24 months prior to the date of cessation and the disposal of the asset must also take place within three years of the cessation of trade.

In the case of shares individual must have been an employee of the company and the company must have been his/her personal trading company for at least 24 months prior to the disposal.

Note that the AAT reference material set out in section 7 below includes details of the qualifying assets and ownership period.

1.4　Applying the relief

When a qualifying disposal is made:

- Calculate the qualifying gains arising on the disposal of the individual assets as normal.
- Add the individual gains arising on the qualifying disposals together.
- Deduct any capital losses and the AEA from gains that do **not** qualify for the relief.
- Deduct any remaining capital losses and/or AEA from the gains qualifying for the relief.

- The taxable qualifying gains are taxed at 10%.
- The non-qualifying gains are taxed at 10%/20% depending on the amount of basic rate band (currently £37,500) available.

⚪ Example

In July 2020, Katie sold her unincorporated trading business which she set up in 1996. The following gains arose on the disposal of the business:

	£
Factory	275,000
Goodwill	330,000
Warehouse	100,000

In August 2020 Katie also realised a gain of £20,300 on the sale of a painting.

Calculate the capital gains tax payable by Katie in respect of 2020/21.

Solution

	Qualifying gains £	Non-qualifying gains £
Business:		
Factory	275,000	
Goodwill	330,000	
Warehouse	100,000	
Painting		20,300
Less: AEA		(12,300)
Taxable gains	705,000	8,000

CGT payable:	
£705,000 × 10%	70,500
£8,000 × 20%	1,600
Capital gains tax payable	72,100

Note: The gain on the painting is taxed at 20% because the gains qualifying for BADR are deemed to use up any basic rate band available.

Test your understanding 1

Oliver

In 2020/21 Oliver sold his unincorporated business and made a total gain on the assets used in the business of £600,000. He also made a gain of £9,700 on the sale of an antique table. Oliver has capital losses brought forward as at 6 April 2020 of £22,000.

How much of the gain on the sale of the business is taxed at 10%?

A   £575,400

B   £600,000

C   £565,700

D   £578,000

2 Investors' relief

As we have seen, BADR is only available on the disposal of shares if the shares are in the individual's personal trading company (i.e. he/she holds at least 5% of the shares) and the individual is also working for the company. Investor's relief extends the benefit of BADR to certain disposals of shares which would not satisfy the conditions for BADR.

2.1   The relief

The relief operates as follows:

- Gains on 'qualifying share disposals' of up to £10 million are taxed at a lower rate of 10% (this is in addition to the £1 million lifetime limit that applies for BADR).

- Any gains above the £10 million limit are taxed at the normal rates of 10% and 20%.

- The limit is a lifetime limit that is diminished each time a claim for the relief is made.

2.2 Qualifying share disposals

The relief applies to the disposal of:

*   unlisted ordinary shares in a trading company (i.e. shares in a Ltd company rather than a plc)

*   subscribed for on, or after, 17 March 2016 (i.e. newly issued shares)

*   which have been held for a minimum period of three years

*   by an individual who is **not** an employee of the company.

2.3 Applying the relief

The relief operates in a similar way to BADR. Allowable losses and the AEA should be deducted from gains on disposals of assets that do not qualify for investors' relief wherever possible, and the amount of qualifying gains that is taxed at 10% must be deducted from the remaining basic rate band when determining the rate of tax to be paid on non-qualifying gains.

The relief must be claimed within 12 months of the 31 January following the end of the tax year in which the disposal is made.

For 2020/21 disposals, the relief must therefore be claimed by 31 January 2023.

The relief is not available to companies.

Note that the AAT reference material set out in section 7 below includes details of the key conditions.

 Example

In January 2021, Ahmed sold his shares in Stellar Ltd (a trading company). Ahmed had subscribed for the shares in August 2016 and made a gain of £78,100 on their disposal. Ahmed has never been an employee of Stellar Ltd.

Ahmed made no other disposals during the tax year 2020/21.

Calculate the capital gains tax payable by Ahmed in respect of 2020/21.

Solution

	Gains qualifying for investors' relief £
Shares in Stellar Ltd	78,100
Less: AEA	(12,300)
Taxable gains	65,800
CGT payable: £65,800 × 10%	£6,580

 Test your understanding 2

Irene

In September 2020 Irene disposed of shares in East Ltd and shares in West Ltd. Irene acquired the shares in East Ltd in May 2017 when she purchased them from her cousin who had subscribed for them several years ago. The shares in West Ltd were subscribed for by Irene in June 2017. Both companies are unquoted trading companies and Irene does not work for either of them.

Which of the disposals will qualify for investors' relief?

A   Neither of them

B   Both of them

C   The shares in East Ltd only

D   The shares in West Ltd only

3 Rollover relief

3.1 Principle of rollover relief

Rollover relief allows a company to defer a chargeable gain, provided certain conditions are met.

This relief is also available for unincorporated businesses (sole traders and partnerships).

This is the only relief in this chapter which is available to both companies and unincorporated businesses.

In order to qualify for relief, the company, sole trader or partnership must reinvest the proceeds from the sale of a qualifying business asset into another qualifying business asset.

Any gain on the disposal of the first asset is then 'rolled over' (i.e. deferred) against the capital gains cost of the new asset.

Unlike BADR or investors' relief, which *reduce* the tax paid, rollover relief simply *defers* the gain on the sale of the asset until the later disposal of the replacement asset. A typical situation can be depicted as follows.

A company sells a building and then buys a new bigger building.

		£
Building (1)	Sale proceeds	100,000
	Less: Cost and indexation allowance	(40,000)
	Indexed gain	60,000
	Less: Rollover relief	(60,000)
	Chargeable gain	Nil
Building (2)	Purchase price	150,000
	Less: 'Rolled over gain'	(60,000)
	Base cost	90,000

The gain on building (1) has been deferred against the base cost of building (2).

Provided that *at least* an amount equal to the proceeds received is reinvested, then *full* deferral applies.

On the sale of the second building, a higher gain will result as the building's allowable cost has been reduced by the rolled over gain from the first building. This higher gain represents both the gain on the second asset and the deferred gain from the first.

	If no rollover relief claimed on building (1) £		If rollover relief is claimed on building (1) £
Sale of building (2) Sale proceeds, say		Sale proceeds	200,000
	200,000		
Less: Original cost	(150,000)	Less: Base cost	(90,000)
Unindexed gain	50,000	Unindexed gain	110,000

The benefit of rollover relief is that tax which would otherwise be payable now is deferred, possibly for many years.

There is a drawback however in that, for companies, if the replacement asset was acquired before December 2017 the indexation allowance on the second gain is calculated on a lower base cost (rather than the full cost) if rollover relief is claimed.

3.2 Conditions for relief

Now that we have considered the mechanics, it is necessary to look at the other conditions which apply.

There must be a disposal of and reinvestment in:

- a qualifying business asset
- within a qualifying time period.

Qualifying business assets

The assets must be used in a *trade.* Where they are only partly used in a trade then only the gain on the trade portion is eligible.

The main qualifying assets are:

- land and buildings (freehold and leasehold)
- fixed plant and machinery
- goodwill (for unincorporated business only, see below).

The following assets are **not** qualifying assets:

- shares in a company

- buildings rented out to tenants.

Note that the replacement asset does not have to be the same type as the asset sold. A company could sell a factory and reinvest in fixed plant and still claim the relief.

Qualifying time period

The qualifying period for reinvestment in the replacement asset is up to 12 months before the sale to within 36 months after the sale.

Goodwill

For a company, goodwill is not a chargeable asset so cannot be used as a qualifying replacement asset for rollover relief purposes.

However, goodwill is a qualifying asset for unincorporated businesses (sole traders and partnerships).

Claims

A claim for rollover relief must be made within four years from the later of the end of the tax year (individuals) or accounting period (companies) in which:

- the disposal takes place or

- the replacement asset is purchased.

Therefore, for a sole trader disposal and replacement in 2020/21, the election must be made by 5 April 2025.

For a company disposal and replacement in the year ended 31 December 2020, the election must be made by 31 December 2024.

Note that it is not possible to make a partial claim for rollover relief. If a claim is made then the whole of the eligible gain must be rolled over.

3.3 Partial reinvestment

Rollover relief may still be available even where only part of the proceeds is reinvested. However, it will be restricted, as there is some cash retained which is available to settle tax liabilities. This is logical as the main purpose of the relief is not to charge tax where cash has been reinvested in the business.

The amount which is chargeable now is the lower of:

- the proceeds not reinvested
- the chargeable gain.

This amount cannot be rolled over (i.e. cannot be deferred).

The following example will demonstrate where full relief is available, partial relief is available and no relief is available.

Note that the AAT reference material set out below in section 7 includes details of the rollover relief rules.

 Example

AB Ltd sold an office block for £500,000 in December 2020. The office block had been acquired for £200,000 and was used throughout AB Ltd's ownership for trade purposes. The indexation allowance on the disposal was £213,100. A replacement office block was acquired in February 2020.

Assuming rollover relief is claimed where possible, calculate the gain assessable on AB Ltd and the base cost of the replacement office block if it cost:

(a) £610,000

(b) £448,000

(c) £345,000

Solution

Gain on sale of old office block.

	£
Proceeds	500,000
Less: Cost	(200,000)
Unindexed gain	300,000
Less: Indexation allowance	(213,100)
Chargeable gain before reliefs	86,900

(a) New asset cost £610,000

As all the proceeds have been reinvested, the full gain is rolled over and no gain is immediately chargeable.

	£
Chargeable gain before reliefs	86,900
Less: Rollover relief	(86,900)
Chargeable gain	Nil
Base cost of new asset	
Cost	610,000
Less: Gain rolled over	(86,900)
Base cost	523,100

Note that it is not possible to elect to rollover less than £86,900 i.e. a partial claim cannot be made.

(b) New asset cost £448,000

As not all of the proceeds have been reinvested, a gain arises when the old office block is sold as follows:

Gain chargeable now = lower of

(i)	Proceeds not reinvested (£500,000 – £448,000)	£52,000
(ii)	The whole of the chargeable gain	£86,900

	£
Chargeable gain before reliefs	86,900
Less: Rollover relief (£86,900 – £52,000)	(34,900)
Chargeable gain now	52,000
Base cost of new asset	
Cost	448,000
Less: Gain rolled over	(34,900)
Base cost	413,100

(c) New asset cost £345,000

As not all of the proceeds have been reinvested, a gain arises immediately.

Gain chargeable now = lower of

(i)	Proceeds not reinvested (£500,000 – £345,000)	£155,000
(ii)	The whole of the chargeable gain	£86,900

	£
Chargeable gain before reliefs	86,900
Less: Rollover relief (balance)	(Nil)
	———
Chargeable gain now	86,900
	———

As the proceeds not reinvested exceed the gain, the full gain of £86,900 is chargeable and no rollover relief is available.

Base cost of new asset	£345,000
	———

 Test your understanding 3

Karim

Karim purchased a freehold building in September 1995 and sold it for £450,000 in May 2020, generating a chargeable gain before reliefs of £190,000. The asset qualifies as a business asset.

Karim purchased a new building in February 2020 for £415,000. This building is also a qualifying business asset.

Assuming a claim for rollover relief is made, what is the chargeable gain on the sale of the original building?

A   £190,000

B   £155,000

C   £35,000

D   £14,778

Test your understanding 4

Spares Ltd

An office building was sold by Spares Ltd on 30 April 2020. Spares Ltd has a year end of 31 December.

The dates during which the proceeds must be reinvested are:

From:

A   30 April 2019

B   30 April 2020

C   31 December 2019

D   31 December 2020

To:

A   30 April 2023

B   30 April 2024

C   31 December 2023

D   31 December 2024

4 Gift relief

4.1 Principle of gift relief

When a gift is made by an individual, the capital gains tax rules require any gain to be calculated as if the disposal had been a sale at full market value.

The legislation allows a claim to defer the gain where the asset is a qualifying 'business asset' as defined for 'gift relief' purposes.

The broad purpose of gift relief is to enable sole traders and shareholders of family companies to pass on their business or shares to the next generation. Note that this relief is not available for gifts by companies.

Gift relief works by 'deducting' the gain (often described as 'holding over' the gain) from the base cost to the donee (i.e. the person receiving the asset).

	Donor		**Donee**
	£		**£**
Market value	50,000	Deemed cost	50,000
Less: Cost	(10,000)		
	———		
	40,000		
Less: Gift relief	(40,000)	Less: Held over gain	(40,000)
	———		———
Chargeable gain	Nil	CGT base cost	10,000
	———		———

In effect, the donee 'takes over' the responsibility for the donor's gain until such time as he makes a disposal of the asset.

4.2 Conditions for relief

There are various conditions which must be considered before applying gift relief. We discuss them under the following headings:

- assets which qualify for the relief
- administration of the election.

Assets which qualify for the relief include the following:

- assets used in a trade by the donor or by his/her personal trading company
- shares and securities in an unquoted trading company (regardless of how many shares are owned)
- shares and securities in the donor's personal trading company (quoted or unquoted).

A 'personal company' is one in which the donor holds at least 5% of the voting rights.

There is no requirement for the taxpayer to be an employee of the company.

Note that relief is therefore only available for quoted company shares if the donor holds at least a 5% interest in the company.

Administration of the election

Gift relief requires a joint election by the donor and the donee.

This must be made within four years of the end of the tax year in which the gift takes place. Therefore, for a gift in 2020/21, the election must be made by 5 April 2025.

It is not possible to specify the amount of the gain to holdover in a claim. All the gain qualifying is held over if a claim is made.

Note that the AAT reference material set out below in section 7 has some details about gift relief.

 Example

Jonas, aged 48, gave the factory that he used in his business to his son on 16 June 2020 when it was valued at £600,000. The factory cost him £150,000 on 16 October 2003.

Calculate the chargeable gain arising and show the base cost of the factory for Jonas' son, assuming gift relief is claimed.

Solution

Step 1: Calculate the gain on the gift using market value

	£
Proceeds (use market value)	600,000
Less: Cost	(150,000)
Chargeable gain before reliefs	450,000

Step 2: Consider whether the gift relief conditions are satisfied

- Asset used in Jonas' trade.

- Factory is a qualifying asset.

Step 3: Hold over the gain against the base cost of the factory

	£
Chargeable gain before reliefs	450,000
Less: Gift relief	(450,000)
Chargeable now	Nil

Base cost of factory for Jonas' son.

	£
Market value of factory	600,000
Less: Gain held over	(450,000)
Base cost	150,000

Test your understanding 5

Matt and Ella

Matt gave a business asset to Ella on 1 February 2021. The asset originally cost Matt £21,000. On 1 February 2021 the asset had a market value of £60,000. A joint election for gift relief is made.

Which one of the following statements is correct?

A Ella's deemed cost is £21,000

B Ella's deemed cost is £60,000

C Ella's deemed cost is £39,000

D Matt has a chargeable gain of £39,000

 Test your understanding 6

Gift relief

Which one of the following statements is false?

A Gift relief is available on the gift of quoted shares or securities in a trading company provided the individual holds at least 5% of the voting rights in the company

B Gift relief is available on the gift of unquoted shares or securities in a trading company regardless of the number of shares held by the individual

C Gift relief is only available on the assets of a trade when the trade is disposed of as a whole or after it has ceased

D Gift relief is available on any assets used in a trade by the donor or by his/her personal trading company

5 Test your understanding

Test your understanding 7

Business asset disposal relief

Which of the following statements is correct?

A   The maximum business asset disposal relief available is £1,000,000 per business disposal

 B   Business asset disposal relief is not available in respect of a gain on a sale of shares

C   Where a gain qualifies for business asset disposal relief the relief is given automatically

D   Gains qualifying for business asset disposal relief are taxed at 10% even if the vendor is a higher rate taxpayer

Test your understanding 8

Leon

Leon is a sole trader. He sold a factory in December 2020 which he had used in his business since 2006.

Leon can claim to rollover the gain on the factory against which of the following?

A   The purchase of a commercial property in January 2021 which will be let to tenants

B   The purchase of a shop in December 2020 which will be rented by his sister

 C   The purchase of a new factory in May 2020 which will be used in Leon's trade

D   The purchase of a new forklift truck in December 2020 for use in Leon's trade

Test your understanding 9

Brian

Brian bought a factory for £600,000 in March 2008. In November 2020, it was sold for £900,000. In the same month another factory was bought for £825,000.

The amount of the gain that can be rolled over is:

A   £Nil

B   £75,000

C   £225,000

D   £300,000

Handwritten notes:
Sold 900,000
Cost 600,000
300,000

75,000
225,000

 Test your understanding 10

Taylor

Taylor disposed of his freehold factory on 18 July 1995 for £120,000, realising a gain of £30,000.

On 1 December 1995, he invested £115,000 of the proceeds in a warehouse for use in his business.

On 22 December 2020, he sold the warehouse for £320,000.

Compute the amount of Taylor's taxable gains which would be subject to capital gains tax as a result of the above transactions, showing the years in which they would be assessed.

Assume the AEA is £12,300 in all years.

Handwritten notes:
Roll over
17,700
(20,000) 2,700
5000
325,000
(12,700)
307,700

320,
1995/96 = 5000
2020/21 = 307,700
313,700

Test your understanding 11

Jonald

On 5 June 2020 Jonald, aged 49, gifted his 80% shareholding in Jonald Limited (with a market value of £5 million) to his son Reg.

The resulting gain for the purposes of capital gains tax was £900,000.

Assuming gift relief is claimed, compute:

(a)   the amount chargeable on Jonald in 2020/21 *(nil)*

(b)   Reg's base cost in respect of the shares gifted. *£100,000*

Test your understanding 12

DRV Ltd (1)

DRV Ltd prepares accounts to 31 March annually.

The company sold the freehold of a factory on 3 March 2021 for £325,000, having previously purchased it as a replacement freehold factory for £200,000 in October 1995.

The factory which it replaced was acquired in May 1991 for £65,000 and sold in December 1995 for £140,000.

Calculate the chargeable gains, assuming all available reliefs are claimed. The indexation factors are:

May 1991 – December 1995	0.129
October 1995 – December 2017	0.856
October 1995 – March 2021	1.015

Test your understanding 13

DRV Ltd (2)

DRV Ltd prepares accounts to 31 March annually.

The company sold the freehold of a factory on 3 March 2021 for £325,000, having previously purchased it as a replacement freehold factory for £115,000 in October 1995.

The factory which it replaced was acquired in May 1991 for £65,000 and sold in December 1995 for £140,000.

Calculate the chargeable gains, assuming all available reliefs are claimed.

The indexation factors are:

May 1991 – December 1995	0.129
October 1995 – December 2017	0.856
October 1995 – March 2021	1.015

 Test your understanding 14

Columbus

Columbus sold one of his factories on 30 April 2020 for £900,000. The factory had been purchased in September 1991 for £300,000.

In March 2020, Columbus purchased another factory for £700,000 and claimed rollover relief on the gain on the factory sold in April 2020.

Calculate the chargeable gain on the sale of the first factory, the amount of any rollover relief available and the base cost of the second factory.

Test your understanding 15

Astute Ltd

Astute Ltd sold a factory on 15 February 2021 for £320,000. The factory was purchased on 24 October 2006 for £164,000, and was extended at a cost of £37,000 during March 2008.

Astute Ltd incurred legal fees of £3,600 in connection with the purchase of the factory, and legal fees of £6,200 in connection with the disposal.

Astute Ltd is considering the following alternative ways of reinvesting the proceeds from the sale of its factory.

(1)   A freehold warehouse can be purchased for £340,000.

(2)   A freehold factory building can be purchased for £300,000.

The reinvestment will take place during May 2021. All of the above buildings have been, or will be, used for business purposes.

(a)   State the conditions that must be met in order that rollover relief can be claimed.

    You are not expected to list the categories of asset that qualify for rollover relief.

(b)   Before taking account of any available rollover relief, calculate Astute Ltd's chargeable gain in respect of the disposal of the factory.

(c)   Advise Astute Ltd of the rollover relief that will be available in respect of EACH of the two alternative reinvestments.

    Your answer should include details of the base cost of the replacement asset for each alternative.

Indexation factors are as follows:

October 2006 to December 2017	0.388
October 2006 to February 2021	0.502
March 2008 to December 2017	0.311
March 2008 to February 2021	0.419

Test your understanding 16

Roy and Colin

In September 2020 Roy gave his business premises to his son Colin.

At that time the premises had a market value of £500,000 and had been purchased by Roy in September 1990 for £100,000.

Roy and Colin made a joint claim for any capital gain to be held over.

Calculate the gain assessable on Roy for 2020/21, before deduction of the annual exempt amount, and the cost which will be available to Colin when computing the gain on a future disposal of the premises.

 Test your understanding 17

Aya

On 1 August 2020 Aya sold the trade and assets of her business for £13,000,000.

The only assets of the business chargeable to capital gains tax were goodwill and a factory. The goodwill and the factory were acquired in June 2009 for £10,000 and £1,300,000 respectively.

The proceeds received on the sale of the business included £5,500,000 for goodwill and £6,000,000 for the factory.

Aya is a higher rate taxpayer and made no other disposals in 2020/21.

Calculate the capital gains tax payable by Aya for 2020/21 on the assumption that all beneficial claims are made.

Test your understanding 18

Hamza

In 2020/21 Hamza, a higher rate taxpayer, made the following disposals:

(1)   On 1 July 2020 he sold his 25% shareholding in Osprey Ltd, a trading company for which he had worked for the last five years. Hamza acquired his shares in the company in May 2013 for £20,000. He sold the shares for £500,000.

(2)   On 1 August 2020 he sold an antique table for £8,000, incurring selling costs of £900. He had acquired the table for £2,000 in May 2009.

(3)   On 1 September 2020 he sold a painting for £20,000. He had acquired the painting for £22,000 in June 2008.

Calculate the capital gains tax payable by Hamza for 2020/21.

 Test your understanding 19

Which of the following statements is incorrect with regard to investors' relief?

A   The shares must have been subscribed for on or after 17 March 2016.

B   The shares concerned must be shares in an unlisted trading company.

C   The shares must have been held for a minimum of three years.

D   The shareholder must be an employee of the company.

6 Summary

The reliefs available are as follows:

	For companies	For individuals
Business asset disposal relief – first £1 million of gains taxed at 10%	✗	✓
Investors' relief – first £10 million of gains taxed at 10%	✗	✓
Rollover relief – defer the gain against cost of the new asset	✓	✓
Gift relief – defer the gain by reducing the donee's cost	✗	✓

※ Links to other syllabus areas

Reliefs are ways in which capital gains liabilities can be mitigated or deferred – often these are the result of taxpayer discretion and therefore there are time limits within which any available options need to be exercised.

Understanding which reliefs apply and the conditions attaching to each ensure that liabilities will be accurately recorded in the financial statements (FSLC) or that known commitments are properly forecast and budgeted for (MABU and MDCL).

If liabilities are reduced as the result of any claims, the external auditor would need to be confident that such claims are validly made and their overall net impact is properly understood for financial reporting purposes (ETAU).

7 AAT reference material

Chargeable gains – reliefs available to individuals

Replacement of business assets (Rollover) relief – when a qualifying business asset is sold at a gain, taxpayer can defer gain by reinvesting proceeds in a qualifying replacement asset.

- Deferred gain is deducted from the cost of the replacement asset so gain crystallises when the replacement asset is sold.

- Qualifying assets (original and replacement) – must be used in a trade by the vendor and be land and buildings, fixed plant and machinery or goodwill.

- Qualifying time period – replacement asset must be purchased between 1 year before and 3 years after the sale of the original asset.

- Partial reinvestment – only some of the sales proceeds reinvested then the gain taxable is the lower of the full gain and the proceeds not reinvested.

Gift relief (holdover relief) – donee takes over asset at donor's base cost i.e. the gain is given away along with the asset.

- Qualifying assets – trade assets of donor or shares in any unquoted trading company or personal trading company (individual owns at least 5% of company).

Business asset disposal relief – gain taxable at 10% capital gains tax rate.

- The £1 million limit is a lifetime limit which is reduced each time a claim for the relief is made.

- For 2020/21 claim must be made by 31 January 2023.

- Qualifying business disposals (assets must be owned for at least 24 months prior to sale).

  – The whole or part of a business carried on by the individual (alone or in partnership).

  – Assets of the individual's or partnership's trading business that has now ceased.

  – Shares in the individual's 'personal trading company' where they have at least 5% of shares, voting rights, entitlement to distributable profits and entitlement to net assets. Individual must have owned the shares and been an employee of the company for 24 months prior to sale.

Investors' relief – gain taxable at 10% capital gains tax rate

- The £10 million limit is a lifetime limit which is reduced each time a claim for the relief is made.

- For 2020/21 a claim must be made by 31 January 2023

- the individual subscribes for shares which are issued on or after 17 March 2016

- the shares are ordinary shares

- the issuing company is a trading company or holding company of a trading group

- the shares are not listed on a recognised stock exchange

- the individual has not been an officer or employee of the issuing company at any point during the ownership period

- the shares are held continuously for three years.

Test your understanding answers

 Test your understanding 1

Oliver

The correct answer is A.

Explanation

The gain is calculated as follows:

	£
Gain on disposal of business assets	600,000
Less: AEA (£12,300 – £9,700)	(2,600)
Capital losses b/f	(22,000)
Chargeable gain	575,400

The AEA is offset against the gain on the sale of the antique table in preference to the gain on the sale of the business as this is more tax efficient.

 Test your understanding 2

Irene

The correct answer is D.

Explanation

All of the conditions for investors' relief are satisfied with respect to the shares in West Ltd but Irene did not subscribe for the shares in East Ltd and therefore investors' relief is not available on the disposal of those shares.

Test your understanding 3

Karim

The correct answer is C.

Explanation

The gain on the sale of the original building can be rolled over against the cost of the new building as follows:

	£
Gain on sale of building	190,000
Less: Rollover relief	(155,000)
	————
Chargeable gain = proceeds not reinvested (£450,000 − £415,000)	35,000
	————

 Test your understanding 4

Spares Ltd

The correct answers are both A.

Explanation

A business or company has from 12 months before the disposal to 3 years after the disposal to reinvest the proceeds.

Test your understanding 5

Matt and Ella

The correct answer is A.

Explanation

Matt's gain is deducted from Ella's deemed cost, which is market value, to arrive at the base cost.

	£
Market value	60,000
Less: Cost	(21,000)
Chargeable gain before reliefs	39,000
Less: Gift relief	(39,000)
Chargeable gain	Nil
Base cost to Ella:	
Deemed cost (MV)	60,000
Less: Gift relief	(39,000)
Base cost	21,000

Test your understanding 6

Gift relief

The correct answer is C.

Explanation

C is the correct answer because gift relief is available on:

- quoted shares or securities in a trading company provided the individual holds at least 5% of the voting rights in the company

- unquoted shares regardless of the number of shares held, and

- any assets used in a trade by the donor or by his/her personal trading company.

It is business asset disposal relief that is only available on the assets of a trade when the trade is disposed of as a whole or after it has ceased.

 Test your understanding 7

Business asset disposal relief

The correct answer is D.

Explanation

The maximum business asset disposal relief is £1,000,000 per lifetime not per disposal.

Business asset disposal relief is available on the disposal of shares in the individual's personal trading company in which he/she is employed.

The relief must be claimed within 12 months of the 31 January following the end of the tax year in which the disposal occurs.

Test your understanding 8

Leon

The correct answer is C.

Explanation

C is the correct answer because rollover relief is available against qualifying assets purchased within 12 months before and 3 years after the sale of the original factory.

However, property let out to tenants does not qualify for rollover relief, nor does moveable (rather than fixed) plant and machinery (i.e. the forklift truck).

 Test your understanding 9

Brian

The correct answer is C.

Explanation

The rollover relief is restricted because the proceeds have not been fully reinvested.

The chargeable gain now will be calculated as follows:

	£
Proceeds	900,000
Less: Cost	(600,000)
	300,000
Less: Rollover relief (balancing figure)	(225,000)
Chargeable gain (£900,000 − £825,000)	75,000

Test your understanding 10

Taylor

Disposal of freehold factory (18 July 1995)

£115,000 has been reinvested in a business asset (warehouse) within three years and therefore part of the gain may be rolled over.

The £5,000 (£120,000 – £115,000) proceeds not reinvested is taxed in 1995/96, but will be covered by the AEA.

The gain rolled over is £25,000 (£30,000 – £5,000).

Disposal of warehouse (22 December 2020)

	£	£
Proceeds		320,000
Less: Cost	115,000	
Gain rolled over	(25,000)	
	————	
Base cost of warehouse		(90,000)
		————
Capital gain		230,000
Less: AEA		(12,300)
		————
Taxable gain in 2020/21		217,700

 Test your understanding 11

Jonald

(a) **Amount chargeable on Jonald in 2020/21**

Gain eligible to be held over = £900,000

The gain assessable in 2020/21 is therefore £Nil.

(b) **Reg's base cost for shares gifted**

Market value at date of gift less gain held over
= (£5,000,000 – £900,000) = £4,100,000

Test your understanding 12

DRV Ltd (1)

Sale of original freehold factory (purchased May 1991)

	£
Sale proceeds (December 1995)	140,000
Less: Cost	(65,000)
Unindexed gain	75,000
Less: Indexation allowance	
(May 1991 – December 1995) (0.129 × £65,000)	(8,385)
Chargeable gain before relief	66,615
Less: Rollover relief upon purchase of replacement factory in October 1995	(66,615)
Chargeable gain – year ended 31 March 1996	Nil

Sale of replacement factory

	£	£
Sale proceeds (March 2021)		325,000
Cost (October 1995)	200,000	
Less: Rolled over gain	(66,615)	
		(133,385)
Unindexed gain		191,615
Less: Indexation allowance		
(October 1995 – December 2017) (0.856 × £133,385)		(114,178)
Chargeable gain (Note)		77,437

Note: DRV Ltd may be able to roll this gain over if it makes a further qualifying purchase in the qualifying time period.

No indexation allowance is permitted after 31 December 2017.

Test your understanding 13

DRV Ltd (2)

Sale of original freehold factory (purchased May 1991)

	£
Sale proceeds (December 1995)	140,000
Less: Cost	(65,000)
	———
Unindexed gain	75,000
Less: Indexation allowance	
(May 1991 – December 1995) (0.129 × £65,000)	(8,385)
	———
Indexed gain (as above)	66,615
Less: Rollover relief (balancing figure)	(41,615)
	———
Chargeable gain – year ended 31 March 1996 (Note)	25,000
	———

Note: Not all of the sale proceeds are reinvested.

Therefore, the chargeable gain arising now is the sale proceeds not reinvested = £25,000 (£140,000 – £115,000).

Sale of replacement factory

	£	£
Sale proceeds (March 2021)		325,000
Cost	115,000	
Less: Rolled over gain	(41,615)	
	———	
		(73,385)
		———
Unindexed gain		251,615
Less: Indexation allowance		
(October 1995 – December 2017) (0.856 × £73,385)		(62,818)
		———
Chargeable gain		188,797
		———

Test your understanding 14

Columbus

Disposal of first factory

	£
Proceeds	900,000
Less: Cost	(300,000)
Chargeable gain before reliefs	**600,000**

Gain taxable in 2020/21:
Lower of
(1) Sale proceeds not reinvested
    (£900,000 – £700,000)   200,000
(2) Chargeable gain before reliefs   600,000

Therefore a gain of £200,000 is taxable in 2020/21

Rollover relief is therefore:
(£600,000 – £200,000)   400,000

Base cost of second factory

	£
Cost of second factory	700,000
Less: Gain rolled over	(400,000)
Base cost	**300,000**

Test your understanding 15

Astute Ltd

(a) **Conditions for rollover relief**

    (i)   The reinvestment must be within the period starting 12 months before the disposal and ending 36 months after the date of disposal of the original asset.

    (ii)   The original asset and the replacement asset must be qualifying business assets used for a trading purpose by the taxpayer.

    (iii)   The replacement asset must be brought into use by the taxpayer for a trading purpose on acquisition.

(b) Disposal of the factory – 15 February 2021

	£
Proceeds (£320,000 – £6,200)	313,800
Less Cost (October 2006)	(164,000)
Legal fees of purchase	(3,600)
Extension (March 2008)	(37,000)
	_____
Unindexed gain	109,200
Less Indexation allowance	
On cost: (£164,000 + £3,600) × 0.388	(65,029)
On extension: (£37,000 × 0.311)	(11,507)
	_____
Chargeable gain	32,664
	_____

(c) Alternative reinvestments

(1) Freehold warehouse costing £340,000

As the full sale proceeds will have been reinvested, the company can claim to rollover the gain in full.

The base cost of the warehouse will be £307,336 (£340,000 – £32,664).

(2) Freehold factory building costing £300,000

As less than the full proceeds will have been reinvested, only part of the gain can be rolled over.

The proceeds not reinvested of £20,000 (£320,000 – £300,000) results in a gain of £20,000 remaining chargeable (see notes).

The balance of £12,664 (£32,664 – £20,000) is rolled over.

The base cost of the factory building becomes £287,336 (£300,000 – £12,664).

Note: HMRC allow the 'proceeds not reinvested' to be calculated as the difference between the **net** sale proceeds (i.e. after selling costs) and the purchase cost (including purchase expenses) of the replacement asset.

In (c) (2) this would mean only £13,800 (£313,800 – £300,000) of the gain remaining chargeable. However, you are not expected to know this and would not be penalised either way.

Test your understanding 16

Roy and Colin
Roy

	£
Deemed disposal proceeds	500,000
Less: Cost	(100,000)
Chargeable gain before reliefs	400,000

If a joint claim for gift relief is made, there will be no chargeable gain arising on Roy in 2020/21.

Colin

The cost available to Colin when computing the gain on a future disposal of the building is (£500,000 – £400,000) = £100,000.

Test your understanding 17

Aya

	£	£
Goodwill		
Proceeds	5,500,000	
Less: Cost	(10,000)	
		5,490,000
Factory		
Proceeds	6,000,000	
Less: Cost	(1,300,000)	
		4,700,000
Total chargeable gains		10,190,000
Less: AEA		(12,300)
		10,177,700
Qualifying gains (£1,000,000 × 10%)		100,000
Remaining gains (£9,177,700 × 20%)		1,835,540
Capital gains tax payable		1,935,540

Test your understanding 18

Hamza

	Qualifying for BADR £	Not qualifying for BADR £
Shares		
Proceeds	500,000	
Less: Cost	(20,000)	
Chargeable gain	480,000	
Table		
Proceeds		8,000
Less: Selling costs		(900)
Net proceeds		7,100
Less: Cost		(2,000)
Chargeable gain		5,100
Chargeable gain restricted to 5/3 × (£8,000 − £6,000)		3,333
Painting		
Proceeds		20,000
Less: Cost		(22,000)
Allowable loss		(2,000)
Total net chargeable gains on non-qualifying assets (£3,333 − £2,000)		1,333
Less: AEA	(10,967)	(1,333)
Taxable gains	469,033	Nil
Capital gains tax payable (£469,033 × 10%)		46,903

Test your understanding 19

The incorrect statement is D.

Explanation

Investors' relief is not available when the individual concerned was an employee of the company.

Duties and responsibilities of a tax adviser

Introduction

Tax advisers must ensure that they have the best interests of their clients in mind at all times, whilst ensuring that they comply with their legal duties.

ASSESSMENT CRITERIA	CONTENTS
The distinction between tax planning, tax avoidance and tax evasion (4.3) AAT's ethical standards relating to tax advice and professional conduct in relation to taxation (4.3)	1 Duties and responsibilities 2 Confidentiality 3 Ethical issues 4 Money laundering 5 Tax advice

1 Duties and responsibilities

1.1 AAT expectations

The AAT expects its members to:

- master skills and techniques through learning and maintain them through continuing professional development

- adopt an ethical approach to work as well as to their employers and clients

- acknowledge their professional duty to society as a whole

- maintain an objective outlook

- provide professional, high standards of service, conduct and performance at all times.

These expectations are discussed in greater depth in the 'Code of Professional Ethics' that can be found on the website (www.aat.org.uk).

A person advising either a company or an individual on taxation issues has duties and responsibilities towards both:

- his/her client, and

- HM Revenue and Customs.

An adviser owes the greatest duty to his/her client.

2 Confidentiality

2.1 Dealings with third parties

A tax adviser has an overriding duty of confidentiality towards his/her client. Under normal circumstances a client's tax affairs should not be discussed with third parties. This duty remains even after the adviser no longer works for the client.

The exceptions to this rule mentioned in the Guidelines are where:

- authority has been given by the client, or

- there is a legal, regulatory or professional duty to disclose (e.g. in the case of suspected money laundering).

2.2 Dealings with HM Revenue and Customs

The duty of confidentiality also relates to dealings with HMRC.

However, the tax adviser must ensure that, whilst acting in the client's best interests, he/she consults with HMRC staff in an open and constructive manner (see below).

3 Ethical issues

3.1 Dealing with problems

In spite of guidelines being available, there can be situations where the method of resolving an ethical issue is not straightforward.

In those situations additional advice should be sought from:

- a supervisor
- a professional body, or
- a legal adviser.

3.2 Tax planning, tax avoidance and tax evasion

Tax planning is arranging your tax affairs, using legal methods, to result in paying less tax. Examples of this could be utilising reliefs and allowances. It is acceptable to advise a client on ways in which their tax liabilities may be reduced.

Tax avoidance is legal but does not follow the intent of the law. Examples of tax avoidance include exploiting loopholes in the legislation or artificially using foreign jurisdictions with low tax rates. Businesses should exercise caution where using tax avoidance schemes as they can often result in reputational damage.

Tax evasion is unlawful. A taxpayer who dishonestly withholds or falsifies information in order to evade tax may be subject to criminal proceedings or suffer civil penalties.

3.3 Dealing with errors in clients' tax returns

Where a tax adviser realises that an error has been made in a client's or employer's tax return he/she must recommend that the client/employer informs HMRC.

If the client/employer refuses to do so, the member must not act for them in connection with that return or related matters.

Test your understanding 1

Which of the following statements is not correct?

A   Accountants need to follow the rules of confidentiality even in a social environment.

B   If money laundering is suspected; accountants are allowed to break the rules of confidentiality.

C   Rules of confidentiality towards a client must be followed even after the business relationship has ended.

D   Accountants must follow the rules of confidentiality irrespective of the situation.

 Test your understanding 2

When an accountant is advising a client, to whom does the accountant owe the greatest duty of care?

A   HMRC

B   The professional body to which the accountant belongs

C   The client

D   The public

 4   Money laundering

4.1   What is money laundering?

Money laundering is the exchange of funds acquired through crime for funds that do not appear to be linked to crime.

The AAT and its members are required to comply with the money laundering laws and regulations.

4.2   Requirements under the laws and regulations

A tax adviser should check the identity of prospective clients via a review of appropriate documentation, for example, a passport.

A firm of accountants must appoint a money laundering officer.

Suspicion that a person is involved in money laundering should be reported to the money laundering officer who will determine whether it needs to be reported to the appropriate authorities.

5 Tax advice

5.1 Providing tax advice

When providing tax advice and preparing tax returns, a person should act in the best interests of his/her client.

However, he/she must ensure that his/her services are consistent with the law and are carried out competently.

At all times an adviser 'must not in any way impair integrity or objectivity'.

5.2 Providing information to HM Revenue and Customs/ other authorities

The 'Code of Professional Ethics' states that:

'A member should not be associated with any return or communication where there is reason to believe that it:

- contains a false or misleading statement
- contains statements or information furnished recklessly, or
- omits or obscures information required to be included and such omission or obscurity would be misleading.'

Test your understanding 3

1   All individuals must submit a tax return – TRUE or FALSE?

2   A member of the AAT working for a firm of accountants should report any suspicion that a person is involved in money laundering to the AAT.

6 Summary

A tax adviser has an overriding duty of confidentiality towards his/her client.

However, his/her responsibilities include openness in dealing with HMRC and reporting suspicion of money laundering.

✳ Links to other syllabus areas

Ethics runs through all of your AAT units (and indeed all other professional papers which you may subsequently go on to sit). As advisers we need to comply with the principle of professional competence and due care. Also, we need a strong understading of the difference between tax planning, tax avoidance and evasion so that we have clarity in terms of executing the responsibilities imposed upon us by the relevant money laundering regulations.

HMRC is a significant third party in any tax engagement and in this respect the professional responsibilities and obligations which we owe extend to others beyond just the interests of our immediate client. This emphasises and reinforces the need and importance for a rigid set of fundamental ethical principles which have been noted at every stage in your studies, past, future and present.

7 AAT reference material

Duties and responsibilities of a tax adviser

- Maintain client confidentiality at all times.
- AAT members must adopt an ethical approach and maintain an objective outlook.
- Give timely and constructive advice to clients.
- Honest and professional conduct with HMRC.
- A tax advisor is liable to a penalty if they assist in making an incorrect return.

Test your understanding answers

Test your understanding 1

The answer is **D**.

The duty of confidentiality can be overridden if the client gives authority or if there is a legal, regulatory or professional duty to disclose.

Test your understanding 2

The correct answer is **C**.

Test your understanding 3

1   **False** – Individuals only have to submit a tax return if the tax legislation requires them to do so. Some individuals are not required to submit a return because they are non-taxpayers or all of their tax liability is settled by deduction at source (e.g. PAYE).

2   **False** – a suspicion that a person is involved in money laundering should be reported to the firm's money laundering officer.

MOCK ASSESSMENT
AQ 2016

1 Mock Assessment Questions

This assessment contains 11 TASKS and you should attempt to complete every task.

Each task is independent. You will not need to refer to your answers to previous tasks.

Read every task carefully to make sure you understand what is required.

Where the date is relevant, it is given in the task data.

You may use minus signs or brackets to indicate negative numbers UNLESS task instructions say otherwise.

You must use a full stop to indicate a decimal point.

For example, write 100.57 NOT 100,57 or 100 57

You may use a comma to indicate a number in the thousands, but you don't have to.

For example, 10000 and 10,000 are both acceptable.

If rounding is required, normal mathematical rounding rules should be applied UNLESS task instructions say otherwise.

Task 1 (12 marks)

(a) For each item, tick whether the following items are capital or revenue expenditure for tax purposes for a trading company.

(4 marks)

	Capital	Revenue
Stationery		✓
Legal costs on purchase of a second-hand building	✓	
Repairs to the building to make it useable	✓	
Computer software which will be replaced in two years		✓

(b) **Tick the appropriate box to show how the following items should be dealt with when calculating adjusted profit for a sole trader. All items have been charged or credited (as appropriate) in arriving at net profit of £190,000.** **(8 marks)**

	Increase net profit	Decrease net profit	No adjustment needed
Staff salaries			✓
Profit on the sale of a capital asset		✓	
Decrease in general bad debt provision		✓	
Legal fees for an unsuccessful appeal against a business rating assessment	✓		
Costs of installing new machinery	✓		
Food hampers given to staff as Christmas gifts			✓
Boxes of chocolates given to customers who spent over £250	✓		
Leasing costs for car for sales person. The car has CO_2 emissions of 100g/km			✓

Task 2 (14 marks)

Armin is a sole trader who has prepared annual accounts to 31 March in the past. He decides to change his year end and prepares accounts for the period to 31 May 2021. His capital allowance information is as follows:

	£
Tax written down value at 1 April 2020	
General pool	74,000
Armin's car	8,200

Armin's car originally cost £14,000, has CO_2 emissions of 100g/km and 60% business use.

During the period ended 31 May 2021, Armin makes the following additions and disposals.

Additions:

1 April 2020	Car for employee – CO_2 emissions 45g/km (private use 40%)	12,000
1 June 2020	Plant and machinery	37,000
15 June 2020	New car for Armin – CO_2 emissions 170g/km and 60% business use	22,000

Disposals:

13 June 2020	Armin's old car	10,000

Using the following grid, calculate the total capital allowances and show the balances to carry forward to the next accounting period.

(14 marks)

Description		General	Armin Car Special 60%	Spend	C.A
B/F 1/4/20		74000	8200		
1/4/20 Car FYA (100%)	12000×60				12000
1/6/20 ATA Plant & Machine 12-Month	37000				37000
15/6/20 New Car 170 g/km (60%)				22000	
13/6/20 Disposal old car			(10000)		
Sub-Total		74000	(1800)	22000	
WDA 14/12 (18%)	13320×14/12	(15540)			15540
Balancy charge	1800 60%		(1800)		(1080)
WDA 14/12 (6%) (60%)	1540×14/12 (60%)			(1540)	924
Bal c/f		58460	—	20460	
Total C.A.					64384

Task 3 (12 marks)

(a) Wasim ceased to trade on 31 January 2021. His previous tax adjusted trading profits were as follows:

	£
Year ended 30 September 2018	70,000
Year ended 30 September 2019	81,000
Year ended 30 September 2020	56,000
Period ended 31 January 2021	13,000

His overlap profits from the commencement of his business were £8,000. Wasim has calculated that if this amount was inflated to today's value it would be £11,200.

Calculate the taxable profits and state the tax year and basis period for the last three tax years of trading. (6 marks)

Tax year	Basis period	Profit £
2018/19	Year ended 30/9/208	70,000
2019/20	Year ended 30/9/2019	81,000
2020/21	01 – 10 – 19 – 31 – 1 – 21	61000

(b) David, George and Nick are in partnership sharing profits equally. On 1 August 2020 they changed their profit sharing arrangements so that David received a salary of £24,000. The balance of profits was to be shared 2:3:1 for David, George and Nick.

For the year ended 31 March 2021, their tax adjusted trading profit was £180,000.

Show the division of profit between the partners. (6 marks)

	Total £	David £	George £	Nick £
Period to 31/7/2020	60000	2000		
Salary				
Balance 180,000 × 4/12	60000	20000	20000	20000
Period to 31/3/21	120000			
Salary David (8m)	16000	16000		
Balance 2:3:1	104000	34667	52000	17333
Total	180,000	70667	72000	37333

Task 4 **(12 marks)**

(a) Sirtis Ltd has prepared accounts for the 15 months to 30 June 2021.

(i) **How will this period be split for tax purposes?** **(1 mark)**

A 3 months to 30 June 2020: Year ended 30 June 2021

B 9 months to 31 December 2020: 6 months to 30 June 2021

C 10 months to 31 January 2021: 5 months to 30 June 2021

D 12 months to 31 March 2021: 3 months to 30 June 2021

(ii) The tax adjusted trading profit before capital allowances is £450,000.

How will this be split between the two periods? **(2 marks)**

| 360,000 (480000×12/15) | 90,000 (3/15) |

(iii) Sirtis Ltd has a tax written down value of £70,000 on its capital allowances pool at the beginning of the 15 month period. There are no additions or disposals during the 15 month period.

What are the capital allowances for each period? **(3 marks)**

| 70000 × 18% 12600 | (70000 − 12600) × 18%/12 = 2583 |

(iv) Sirtis Ltd does not pay tax by instalments.

State the due dates for payment of the corporation tax for the period ended 30 June 2021. **(2 marks)**

First period	31 Jan 22
Second period	31 Jan 22

(v) Riker Ltd's tax liability for the year ended 31 December 2020 is £112,000. The company filed its corporation tax return and paid its tax liability on 1 August 2022.

It has always filed its returns on time in previous years.

What is the maximum late filing penalty that Riker Ltd can be charged? **(2 marks)**

| 10%. 11200 |

(b) XYZ plc owns the 80% of the ordinary share capital of PQR Ltd, 20% of the ordinary share capital of DEF Ltd and 10% of the ordinary share capital of STU Ltd.

XYZ plc has taxable total profits of £420,000 for the eight months ended 30 September 2020. It received dividends of £35,000 from PQR Ltd and £12,000 from DEF Ltd.

Complete the following for XYZ plc for the eight months ended 30 September 2020: **(2 marks)**

£

Augmented profits

Limit for determining the date on which the corporation tax liability is due

Task 5 (4 marks)

Your answers for parts (a) and (b) should be to the nearest penny. If your answer is zero enter 0.

(a) A 40 year old taxpayer has taxable business profits of £61,500 for 2020/21.

How much class 4 NIC is due on these profits? **(2 marks)**

£

(b) A 67 year old taxpayer receives the state pension and also has taxable business profits of £8,000 for 2020/21.

How much class 2 NIC is due for 2020/21? **(1 mark)**

£

(c) **Which one of the following statements is correct?** **(1 mark)**

A Class 2 NIC is paid monthly.

B Joseph is a sole trader who will reach state pension age on 7 April 2020. He has taxable business profits of £35,000 for 2020/21 but he pays no NIC for 2020/21.

C Class 4 NIC is paid on a trader's taxable trading profits less any trading losses brought forward.

D Class 2 NIC is a tax allowable expense for a self-employed trader.

Task 6 (6 marks)

Mark the following statements as true or false. (6 marks)

	True	False
When a partnership makes a trading loss, all the partners must claim the same method of loss relief.		
When a company makes a trading loss, it can choose not to offset the loss in the current year but instead offset it first in the previous 12 months.		
When a sole trader makes a trading loss, he/she can choose not to offset the loss in the current year but instead offset it first in the previous tax year.		
A company wishing to offset a trading loss in the current year must submit an election within nine months and one day after the end of the year.		
When a company carries back a trading loss, it can only deduct it from previous periods' trade profits.		
When a company carries forward a trading loss it can never deduct it from total profits.		
When a sole trader claims to offset a loss against income of the current year, they cannot restrict the claim to preserve their personal allowance.		

Task 7 (10 marks)

Zahera is a client of your firm. You have agreed the following tax liabilities in recent years.

	2019/20 £	2020/21 £
Income tax liability	16,350	17,550
Tax deducted under PAYE	(9,280)	(7,420)
Income tax payable	7,070	10,130
Class 2 NIC	156	159
Class 4 NIC	2,500	2,370
Capital gains tax	1,670	1,965
	11,396	14,624

Zahera does not understand the tax payment system and wants you to explain:

(a) how her tax liabilities for 2020/21 are paid (7 marks)

(b) the effect of making a payment late. (3 marks)

Task 8 (6 marks)

James is a sole trader running a music shop. He has prepared his accounts for the year ended 31 March 2021 and they include the following expenses:

	£
Wages and salaries includes:	
James' drawings	15,000
Motor expenses include:	
Van expenses (van used by shop staff for business use only)	3,200
Car expenses (car used by James with 40% private use)	4,300
Repairs and renewals include:	
Repair to broken window	250
New till for the shop	820
Entertainment expenses include:	
Cost of staff Christmas party	315
Supplier entertaining	230
Miscellaneous expenses include:	
Donation to local cat rescue	60
Donation to political party	150
Gifts of bongo drums costing £25 each to shop staff	100

Complete page 2 of the self-employment supplementary pages for the relevant expenses for James in the year ended 31 March 2021.

Boxes 17 to 31 have already been completed. **(6 marks)**

Business expenses

Please read the 'Self-employment (full) notes' before filling in this section.

Total expenses	Disallowable expenses
If your annual turnover was below £85,000, you may just put your total expenses in box 31	Use this column if the figures in boxes 17 to 30 include disallowable amounts

17 Cost of goods bought for resale or goods used

£ 1 3 2 5 3 8 . 0 0

32

£ . 0 0

18 Construction industry – payments to subcontractors

£ . 0 0

33

£ . 0 0

19 Wages, salaries and other staff costs

£ 4 1 9 2 0 . 0 0

34

£ . 0 0

20 Car, van and travel expenses

£ 8 0 0 0 . 0 0

35

£ . 0 0

21 Rent, rates, power and insurance costs

£ 1 2 8 5 0 . 0 0

36

£ . 0 0

22 Repairs and maintenance of property and equipment

£ 1 5 3 0 . 0 0

37

£ . 0 0

23 Phone, fax, stationery and other office costs

£ 6 1 0 . 0 0

38

£ . 0 0

24 Advertising and business entertainment costs

£ 7 4 5 . 0 0

39

£ . 0 0

25 Interest on bank and other loans

£ . 0 0

40

£ . 0 0

26 Bank, credit card and other financial charges

£ . 0 0

41

£ . 0 0

27 Irrecoverable debts written off

£ . 0 0

42

£ . 0 0

28 Accountancy, legal and other professional fees

£ 8 3 0 . 0 0

43

£ . 0 0

29 Depreciation and loss/profit on sale of assets

£ 1 1 2 0 . 0 0

44

£ . 0 0

30 Other business expenses

£ 2 3 1 9 . 0 0

45

£ . 0 0

31 Total expenses (total of boxes 17 to 30)

£ 2 0 2 4 6 2 . 0 0

46 Total disallowable expenses (total of boxes 32 to 45)

£ . 0 0

Task 9 (8 marks)

(a) **For each of the following assets, tick the appropriate box to show whether the item is chargeable or exempt for capital gains tax.** **(3 marks)**

	Chargeable	Exempt
Half of a racehorse owned jointly with a friend		
£10,000 of 5% Treasury Stock		
Car used by Joe in his business		

(b) Obscure Ltd purchased ten hectares of land in December 2010 for £120,000. On 15 March 2021 it sold two hectares out of the ten hectares for £80,000 incurring £3,420 of legal costs. On 15 March 2021 the remaining eight hectares were worth £240,000.

The indexation factors are:

December 2010 – December 2017	0.218
December 2010 – March 2021	0.321

Complete the following computation. Use brackets to indicate numbers to be deducted. **(5 marks)**

	£
Proceeds	
Selling costs	
Cost	
Unindexed gain	
Indexation allowance	
Indexed gain/loss	

Task 10 (10 marks)

Immense plc bought 40,000 shares in Smith plc for £2.20 each in August 2010. There was a bonus issue of 1 for 1 in February 2013 and a rights issue of 1 for 4 at £2.11 each in September 2015. Immense plc took up all its rights. Immense plc sold 75,000 shares in February 2021 for £350,000.

Indexation factors were:

August 2010 – February 2013	0.103
August 2010 – September 2015	0.156
February 2013 – September 2015	0.048
September 2015 – December 2017	0.071
September 2015 – February 2021	0.159

Using the grid below calculate the gain made on this disposal and show the balance of shares carried forward. **(10 marks)**

Task 11   **(6 marks)**

(a) **Tick the correct box to show whether the following statements about capital gains are true or false.**   **(3 marks)**

	True	False
A company can offset a capital loss against its total income of the same accounting period.	✓	
Opera Ltd sells a painting for £12,000. This painting had hung on the wall of the boardroom. This is an exempt disposal.		✓
An individual taxpayer cannot carry his/her unused capital gains tax annual exempt amount forward for one year.		

(b) Overs Ltd made a capital gain on the sale of a factory building of £124,300. The building was sold for £500,000 in March 2021.
In January 2020, Overs Ltd had bought a new factory building for £481,500.

   How much of the gain of £124,300 can be rolled over into the purchase of the new factory?   **(1 mark)**

   [   ]

(c) **Which of the following statements about business asset disposal relief is correct? Select one answer only.**   **(2 marks)**

   A   The first £1 million of gains on each qualifying disposal is charged at 10%.

   B   Manuel has owned 10% of the shares in ABC Ltd, a trading company, for 20 years. He does not work for the company. If he sells his shares in ABC Ltd he will be able to claim business asset disposal relief.

   C   Jonah bought a sole trader business, ran it for nine months and then sold it making a gain of £500,000. Jonah will be able to claim business asset disposal relief on this disposal.

   D   Abigail bought a sole trader business which she ran successfully for 10 years. Due to illness she ceased to trade in June 2020. She was unable to sell her business until July 2021. Abigail will be able to claim business asset disposal relief on this disposal.

2 Mock Assessment Answers

Task 1

(a) Capital or revenue

	Capital	Revenue
Stationery		✓
Legal costs on purchase of a second-hand building	✓	
Repairs to the building to make it useable	✓	
Computer software which will be replaced in two years	✓	

(b) Treatment in adjustment of profits computation

	Increase net profit	Decrease net profit	No adjustment needed
Staff salaries			✓
Profit on the sale of a capital asset		✓	
Decrease in general bad debt provision		✓	
Legal fees for an unsuccessful appeal against a business rating assessment			✓
Costs of installing new machinery	✓		
Food hampers given to staff as Christmas gifts			✓
Boxes of chocolates given to customers who spent over £250	✓		
Leasing costs for car for sales person. The car has CO_2 emissions of 100 g/km			✓

Task 2

Capital allowances computation – period ended 31 May 2021

	AIA/FYA	Pool	Armin's car (1)	(2)	Total
	£	£	£	£	£
Tax WDV b/f		74,000	8,200		
Additions – no AIA or FYA				22,000	
Additions with AIA	37,000				
Less: AIA	(37,000)				37,000
	———	Nil			
Disposals			(10,000)		
			———		
			(1,800)		
BC			1,800	× 60%	(1,080)
			———		
		74,000		22,000	
WDA at 18% × 14/12		(15,540)			15,540
WDA at 6% × 14/12				(1,540)	
				× 60%	924
Addition with FYA	12,000				
FYA 100%	(12,000)				12,000
	———	Nil			
Tax WDV c/f		58,460		20,460	
					64,384

Note: In the assessment you do not need to enter lines marking totals and subtotals.

Task 3

(a) Taxable profits

Wasim ceases to trade in 2020/21

Tax year	Basis period	Profit £
2018/19	Year ended 30 Sept 2018	70,000
2019/20	Year ended 30 Sept 2019	81,000
2020/21	1 Oct 2019 – 31 Jan 2021	61,000

Working:

£56,000 + £13,000 – £8,000 overlap = £61,000

The figure to use for overlap profits brought forward is the original figure with no adjustment for inflation.

(b) Division of profits between partners

	Total £	David £	George £	Nick £
Period to 31 Jul 2020				
Salary	0	0	0	0
(4/12 of £180,000)	60,000	20,000	20,000	20,000
Period to 31 Mar 2021				
(8/12 of £180,000) = £120,000				
Salary (8m)	16,000	16,000		
Balance 2:3:1	104,000	34,667	52,000	17,333
	180,000	70,667	72,000	37,333

Task 4

(a) Long period of account

(i) The answer is D.

When a company prepares accounts for a period exceeding 12 months the profits must be split into a 12 month period and a balance period, in this case 3 months.

(ii) Profits before capital allowances are time apportioned.

12/15 £360,000	3/15 £90,000

(iii) Capital allowances are calculated for each period separately. For the second period the WDA must be time apportioned.

£70,000 × 18% = £12,600	(£70,000 – £12,600) × 18% × 3/12 = £2,583

(iv) Corporation tax is due 9 months and 1 day after the end of the accounting period.

First period	1 January 2022
Second period	1 April 2022

(v) The return is filed 7 months late as it was due on 31 December 2021. The penalty will be a fixed penalty of £200 plus 10% of the tax outstanding making a total of £11,400 (£200 + 10% of £112,000)

£11,400

(b) Short period of account – XYZ plc

	£
Augmented profits £420,000 + £12,000 (note 1)	432,000
Limit for determining the date on which the corporation tax liability is due £1,500,000 × 8/12 × 0.5 (note 2)	500,000

Notes:

(1) The dividend from PQR Ltd is not included because it is a 51% group company.

(2) The limit is divided by two because there is a 51% group company, PQR Ltd.

Task 5

(a) **Class 4 NICs**

£3,875.00

Working:	**£**
(£50,000 – £9,500) × 9%	3,645.00
(£61,500 – £50,000) × 2%	230.00
	3,875.00

(b) **Class 2 NICs**

No class 2 NIC is due as the taxpayer is over state pension age.

(c) **NICs**

The answer is C.

A is incorrect because class 2 is paid through the self-assessment system on 31 January following the end of the tax year.

B is incorrect because in order to be exempt from class 4 NIC, Joseph must be of state pension age at the start of the tax year on 6 April 2020.

D is incorrect because the trader's own NIC is never an allowable expense.

Task 6

Losses

	True	False
When a partnership makes a trading loss, all the partners must claim the same method of loss relief.		✓
When a company makes a trading loss, it can choose not to offset the loss in the current year but instead offset it first in the previous 12 months.		✓
When a sole trader makes a trading loss, he/she can choose not to offset the loss in the current year but instead offset it first in the previous tax year.	✓	
A company wishing to offset a trading loss in the current year must submit an election within nine months and one day after the end of the year.		✓
When a company carries back a trading loss, it can only deduct it from previous periods' trade profits.		✓
When a company carries forward a trading loss it can never deduct it from total profits.		✓
When a sole trader claims to offset a loss against income of the current year, they cannot restrict the claim to preserve their personal allowance.	✓	

Task 7

(a) Payment of 2020/21 tax liabilities

Payments on account must be made for income tax and class 4 NIC on 31 January 2021 and 31 July 2021. These payments are 50% of the income tax and class 4 NIC payable for 2019/20. Any balance of tax due, together with all the 2020/21 capital gains tax and class 2 NICs, is paid on 31 January 2022. This gives a payment schedule as follows:

Date		Amount £
31 January 2021	First payment on account 50% × (£7,070 + £2,500)	4,785
		────
31 July 2021	Second payment on account	4,785
		────
31 January 2022	Balancing payment (£10,130 + £2,370 − £9,570)	2,930
	2020/21 CGT	1,965
	2020/21 Class 2 NICs	159
		────
	Total	5,054
		────

The whole process starts again with the first payment on account of £6,250 (50% × (£10,130 + £2,370) for 2021/22, also due on 31 January 2022.

(b) Effect of late payments

Interest will be charged on any tax paid late from the due date until the date the tax is paid.

In addition, if the tax (excluding class 2 NIC) of £4,895 due on 31 January 2022 is paid more than 30 days late there will be a penalty equal to 5% of the tax due. Further 5% penalties will be due if the tax is still outstanding after 6 and 12 months after 31 January 2022.

Task 8

Self-employment Form

Business expenses

Please read the 'Self-employment (full) notes' before filling in this section.

Total expenses	Disallowable expenses
If your annual turnover was below £85,000, you may just put your total expenses in box 31	Use this column if the figures in boxes 17 to 30 include disallowable amounts
17 Cost of goods bought for resale or goods used £ 1 3 2 5 3 8 . 0 0	**32** £ . 0 0
18 Construction industry – payments to subcontractors £ . 0 0	**33** £ . 0 0
19 Wages, salaries and other staff costs £ 4 1 9 2 0 . 0 0	**34** £ 1 5 0 0 0 . 0 0
20 Car, van and travel expenses £ 8 0 0 0 . 0 0	**35** (£4,300 × 40%) £ 1 7 2 0 . 0 0
21 Rent, rates, power and insurance costs £ 1 2 8 5 0 . 0 0	**36** £ . 0 0
22 Repairs and maintenance of property and equipment £ 1 5 3 0 . 0 0	**37** £ 8 2 0 . 0 0
23 Phone, fax, stationery and other office costs £ 6 1 0 . 0 0	**38** £ . 0 0
24 Advertising and business entertainment costs £ 7 4 5 . 0 0	**39** £ 2 3 0 . 0 0
25 Interest on bank and other loans £ . 0 0	**40** £ . 0 0
26 Bank, credit card and other financial charges £ . 0 0	**41** £ . 0 0
27 Irrecoverable debts written off £ . 0 0	**42** £ . 0 0
28 Accountancy, legal and other professional fees £ 8 3 0 . 0 0	**43** £ . 0 0
29 Depreciation and loss/profit on sale of assets £ 1 1 2 0 . 0 0	**44** £ 1 1 2 0 . 0 0
30 Other business expenses £ 2 3 1 9 . 0 0	**45** £ 1 5 0 . 0 0
31 Total expenses (total of boxes 17 to 30) £ 2 0 2 4 6 2 . 0 0	**46** Total disallowable expenses (total of boxes 32 to 45) £ 1 9 0 4 0 . 0 0

Task 9

(a) Chargeable or exempt assets

	Chargeable	Exempt
Half of a racehorse owned jointly with a friend		✓
£10,000 of 5% Treasury Stock		✓
Car used by Joe in his business		✓

Note: A racehorse is exempt as a wasting chattel. It does not matter if two or more people own it.

(b) Chargeable gain – part disposal

	£
Proceeds	80,000
Selling costs	(3,420)
Cost (£120,000 × (£80,000/(£80,000 + £240,000)))	(30,000)
Unindexed gain	46,580
Indexation allowance Cost (£30,000 × 0.218)	(6,540)
Indexed gain/loss	40,040

Note: Indexation allowance has been frozen at December 2017 so the factor to March 2021 should be ignored.

Task 10

Chargeable gain – Share disposal

Gain calculation		£	
Proceeds		350,000	
Less: Cost (W)		(97,650)	
Less: Indexation (W)			
(£115,610 – £97,650)		(17,960)	
Chargeable gain		234,390	
Working: Share pool			
	Number	*Cost*	*Indexed cost*
August 2010 Purchase	40,000	88,000	88,000
Feb 2013 Bonus issue 1 for 1	40,000	Nil	Nil
Indexed rise to Sep 2015			
£88,000 × 0.156			13,728
Sep 2015 Rights issue 1 for 4	20,000	42,200	42,200
	100,000	130,200	143,928
Indexed rise to Dec 2017			
£143,928 × 0.071			10,219
			154,147
Feb 2021 Disposal	(75,000)	[1] (97,650)	[2] (115,610)
Balance c/f	25,000	32,550	38,537
[1] 75,000/100,000 × £130,200			
[2] 75,000/100,000 × £154,147			

In the assessment you do not need to enter lines marking totals and subtotals.

Task 11

(a) True or False

	True	False
A company can offset a capital loss against its total income of the same accounting period. (Capital losses can only be offset against capital gains)		✓
Opera Ltd sells a painting for £12,000. This painting had hung on the wall of the boardroom. This is an exempt disposal.		✓
An individual taxpayer cannot carry his/her unused capital gains tax annual exempt amount forward for one year.	✓	

(b) Rollover relief

The answer is Nil.

None of the gain can be rolled over because the purchase of the new factory building is more than 12 months before the disposal of the old factory.

(c) Business asset disposal relief

The answer is D.

Abigail's disposal qualifies as it is within 3 years of the cessation of her business and she operated the business for more than 24 months prior to the date of cessation.

A is incorrect because the £1 million is a cumulative lifetime limit covering all disposals, not each disposal.

B is incorrect because business asset disposal relief would only be available if Manuel worked for the company.

C is incorrect because qualifying assets must be owned for at least 24 months before disposal.

APPENDIX

Advice on answering extended writing tasks

Advice on extended writing tasks

The chief assessor has offered some tips to help you understand the best way to answer the written task, which will always be marked by an AAT assessor.

These tips were specifically written for the personal tax assessment; however, they are also extremely helpful when answering the written task in the business tax assessment.

Layout of answer

Before we look at the technical aspects of this task, we should begin by considering the practical issues.

Firstly, it's important you understand that the software in which you are answering the task is **not** Microsoft Word. So there's no:

- spell checker
- grammar checker
- automatic correcting of typos.

You won't see any different coloured lines highlighting any of these issues. It's quite clear from assessments we've marked so far that too many students are not proofreading their answers, and are failing to correct obvious mistakes.

So, when you type:

"i DON'T LIKE ANWSERING WRITEN QUETSIONS."

… this is exactly how it will look to the assessor. While the sentence can be read and understood, it's poor practice and would certainly not be allowed in the workplace.

You **must** proofread what you've written and correct any obvious spelling and grammatical errors.

There's often a mark for presentation of the answer, and the assessor is looking for whether the way you've presented your work would be acceptable in the workplace. This mark is independent of the technical answer, and what we look for is whether a client would find the answer acceptable from a visual perspective.

Length of answer

It may not be obvious when you first look at the answer box on the screen, but this is a never-ending answer box. When you get to the last visible line, you can scroll down for extra writing space. So don't start your answer assuming that it needs to be condensed or short.

You should also remember that in many cases, the model answer the assessor is working from is in much more depth than the answer you'd need to give to gain full marks. It's acknowledged that it can be very difficult to write every aspect of all the areas applicable in a written question, and usually it's not necessary to do so.

Before you start to type

You **must** read the question in detail. We've noticed that students often scan read a question, decide what it's about in an instant and then write the answer without giving any thought or consideration to the details. You should:

- read through once to get the general feel of the question

- read through again, slower this time, concentrating on key words or phrases

- plan your answer, ensuring all key areas are covered

- decide the structure of your answer, considering where you'll use things like an email, a memo or bullet points

- type up your answer

- proofread your answer, correcting any errors

Too many times it would seem that students only follow the fifth of these points. If you do this it **will** affect your marks.

Consider exactly who you're writing to. Most likely it will be a client, so this needs to influence your approach.

Remember, if the client is writing to you for advice, they don't know the answer. We often see students give half answers which the assessor will understand, but which a client would not. As a result, they lose marks.

Similarly, be sure to avoid:

- abbreviations

- technical jargon

- SMS/text message speak.

Technical content

What exactly are you going to write?

Let's take the written task from an AQ2010 sample assessment, updated.

Shania has written to you with the following query:

"I am writing to you for some clarification on my father's tax affairs. He is no longer capable of handling his own money, and I have a letter of authorisation allowing me to deal with his tax matters.

I have received notification from HMRC of how much tax he has to pay on 31 January 2021. It says he owes £1,400 from 2019/20, and needs to pay £3,500 for 2020/21. I thought he had paid all the tax due for 2019/20, so I don't understand what the £1,400 is for. Also, I know that he has hardly any income this tax year, so where does the £3,500 come from?

If you could explain this to me, it would be much appreciated."

You need to respond appropriately to her query.

Let's break this task down to see exactly what you need to do.

The first line is an introduction only, and gives you the name of the person you are addressing.

The first paragraph of her query is also background, but lets you know two things.

1   It's fine to discuss the father's affairs with Shania.

2   As this tax bill is not hers, Shania will have no understanding of how it has arisen or why, and so you need to explain this in simple but detailed terms.

The second paragraph is the crux of the query, and you must spend time working out the figures and dates from the information given. Let's take a look at the details.

There's a total tax bill of £4,900 to be paid on 31 January 2021. Shania can't understand this, as she knows her father has little income for 2020/21.

Now, ask yourself this question: before you started studying tax, did you know how payments on account worked?

For the majority of people, the answer is 'No'; so you need to put yourself in Shania's position and consider how you're going to clearly and simply explain the £4,900 her father needs to pay.

The question already tells you that £1,400 is from 2019/20, so that must be the balancing figure from that year. But why would there be a balancing figure?

You need to explain the payments on account system, but in very simple terms.

Before you read any further, write your answer to this question and then compare it to the examples below.

Your answer

Now consider the following three typical student answers.

Read them carefully and decide how well they answer the question, before reading the feedback from the chief assessor.

Answer 1

Half of the tax liability for any year is paid by 31 January in that tax year, and the other half is paid by 31 July following the tax year. This is based on an estimate, using the preceding tax year's liability. Therefore, when your father paid his tax liability on 31 January 2020 and 31 July 2020 for 2019/20, this was based on his liability for 2018/19. When the final figures were sent to HMRC, they have worked out that these two instalments are not enough to cover the full liability; hence the £1,400 is the balance of tax due.

Feedback from the chief assessor

Answer 1 is from the model answer and will obviously get full marks.

Answer 2

This is to do with the payments on account system. You need to pay half of your tax bill on 31 January in the year and the other half on 31 July in the year. Anything still to pay needs paying on 31 January after that. So the £1,400 is what is left from 2019/20.

Feedback from the chief assessor

Answer 2 has some good points. Firstly, it uses short sentences, which always makes it easier to read and understand. There are no jargon words. It would therefore get the mark for communication.

However, the crux of the answer, explaining the payments on account, is a problem. The assessor will know which year the answer is referring to, but there's no way a client would. When the answer says '31 January in the year', which year is the student referring to? The tax year, the financial year or the calendar year?

A client wouldn't understand this, so dates written in this manner will lose the student marks. This answer would attract a few marks, but certainly not full marks.

Answer 3

This is to do with POA. You need to pay half of your tax bill in January in the year, and other half in July following that. Then anything left over to pay gets paid in January after that. So the £1,400 is what is left from 2019/20.

Feedback from the chief assessor

Answer 3 will simply attract no marks at all.

How will a client know what POA means? A day in January in some year also means nothing, and the last sentence is lifted from the question.

How did you do?

Now be honest, and compare the three examples above to your answer and see which one you're the closest to. Ask yourself these questions.

- Have I used abbreviations?
- Have I given the day, month and year accurately?
- Have I proofread my answer?

To finish off, let's consider the rest of the model answer to the question and see if you can understand how to judge the quality of your answer. Again, be honest with yourself on this.

Do you, for instance, realise that as Shania knows her father has 'hardly any income' she needs to understand the implications of this? This leads to the last paragraph of the answer where you can explain to her that he may be entitled to a refund; but that if he makes an incorrect claim to reduce his payments, this may have negative implications.

And finally, when you start the written question, remember this sequence:

- read
- read again
- plan
- structure
- type
- read once again.

Note: below is the full answer to the question to help you.

Half of the tax liability for any year is paid by 31 January in that tax year, and the other half is paid by 31 July following the tax year. This is based on an estimate, using the preceding tax year's liability. Therefore, when your father paid his tax liability on 31 January 2020 and 31 July 2020 for 2019/20, this was based on his liability for 2018/19.

When the final figures were sent to HMRC, they have worked out that these two instalments are not enough to cover the full liability; hence the £1,400 is the balance of tax due.

As explained, the instalment on 31 January 2021 for this current tax year is based on the accurate liability for 2019/20. If he overpays for 2020/21, he will receive a refund from HMRC.

However, he can claim to reduce these instalments if he knows that his income will not be as high as it was last year. Whilst this is fine, your father needs to be careful. If he makes an incorrect claim to reduce these instalments, then HMRC will charge him interest on the difference between what should have been paid and what was actually paid.

AAT qualification
Business Tax BSTX (Level 4)
Reference material

inance Act 2020 – for assessments from January 2021

Reference material for AAT assessment of Business Tax

Introduction

This document comprises data that you may need to consult during your Business Tax computer-based assessment. The material can be consulted during the practice and live assessments through pop-up windows. It is made available here, so you can familiarise yourself with the content before the test.

Do not take a print of this document into the exam room with you. Unless you need a printed version as part of reasonable adjustments for particular needs, in which case you must discuss this with your tutor at least six weeks before the assessment date.

This document may be changed to reflect periodical updates in the computer-based assessment, so please check you have the most recent version while studying. This version is based on *Finance Act 2020* and is for use in AAT assessments from January 2021.

Contents

1. Taxation tables for business tax – 2020/21

1.1. Capital allowances

Annual investment allowance

Prior to 1 January 2019	£200,000
Between 1 January 2019 and 31 December 2020	£1,000,000
From 1 January 2021	£200,000

Plant and machinery writing down
   allowance

Assets other than motor cars	18%

Motor cars

CO_2 emissions up to 50 g/km	100%
CO_2 emissions between 51 and 110 g/km	18%
CO_2 emissions over 110 g/km -Prior to 1 April 2019/6 April 2019	8%
CO_2 emissions over 110 g/km -From 1 April 2019/6 April 2019	6%

1.2. Capital gains

Annual exempt amount	£12,300
Basic rate	10%
Higher rate	20%
Business asset disposal relief rate	10%
Investors' relief rate	10%
Business asset disposal relief lifetime allowance	£1,000,000
Investors' relief lifetime allowance	£10,000,000

1.3. National Insurance rates

Class 2 contributions:	£3.05 per week
Small profits threshold	£6,475p.a.
Class 4 contributions:	
Main rate	9%
Additional rate	2%
Lower profits limit	£9,500
Upper profits limit	£50,000

1.4. Trading allowance

This allowance is available to individuals only. £1,000

1.5. Corporation tax

Financial year	2020	2019
All profits and gains	19%	19%

2. Introduction to business tax

2.1. Administration

- Taxation administered by HM Revenue & Customs (HMRC).
- Rules covering tax are contained in statute (law) which is passed every year (*Finance Act*).
- Decisions reached by the courts interpreting the law are known as case law.
- HMRC also issue guidance – Extra Statutory Concessions and Statements of Practice.

2.2. Taxes

- Corporation Tax – paid by companies on both income and chargeable gains.
- Income Tax – paid by individuals on their income.
- Capital Gains Tax – paid by individuals on their capital gains.

2.3. Tax evasion, tax avoidance and tax planning

- Tax evasion: any action taken to evade tax by illegal means; this carries a risk of criminal prosecution. Examples of tax evasion include failing to declare income and claiming false expenses.
- Tax avoidance: bending the rules of the tax system to gain a tax advantage that Parliament never intended. It involves operating within the letter of the law but not the spirit of the law.
- Tax planning: use of legitimate means to minimise taxpayer's tax liability, for example by investing in a tax-free ISA (Individual Savings Account).

3. Adjustment of profits – sole traders, partnerships and companies

3.1. Pro forma for adjustment of profits

	£	£
Net profit as per accounts		X
Add: Expenses charged in the accounts that are not allowable as trading expenses	X	
		X
		X
Less: Income included in the accounts which is not assessable as trading income	X	
		(X)
Adjusted profit/(loss)		X

3.2. Disallowed expenses

- Expenses that fail the remoteness test so not "wholly and exclusively" for trading purposes.
- Fines on the business or fraud by directors/owners.
- Donations to charity are generally disallowed in calculating trading profits (however qualifying charitable donations are deductible in the corporation tax computation).
- Political donations are never allowable.
- Capital expenditure e.g. purchase of equipment included in profit and loss account.
- Depreciation. Capital allowances granted instead.
- Costs of bringing newly acquired second-hand assets to useable condition.
- Legal and professional expenses relating to capital items or breaking the law.
- Customer entertaining. Staff entertaining can be allowable.
- Customer gifts, unless gift incorporates business advertising, cost is less than £50 per annum per customer, and gift is not food, drink, tobacco or cash vouchers.

3.3. Non-assessable income

- Income taxed in any other way, e.g. interest or property income for individuals.
- Profits on sale of fixed assets.

4. Unincorporated businesses – trading income

4.1. Trading income calculated for each period of account:

	£
Adjusted accounting profit	X
Less: Capital allowances:	(X)
Less: Balancing allowances	(X)
Plus: Balancing charges	X
Trading income for the period of account	X

4.2. Expenses charged in the accounts which are not allowable as trading expenses

- See adjustment of profits – sole traders, partnerships and companies.
- Transactions with the owner of the business. For example:
- Add back salary paid to owner. Salaries paid to family members do not need to be added back.
- Private expenditure included in accounts.
- Class 2 and Class 4 National Insurance contributions.
- Goods taken for own use.

5.   Sole traders – basis periods

Tax year – 2020/21 tax year runs from 6 April 2020 to 5 April 2021.

5.1.   Basis period rules

- First year – runs from start date of trading to the next 5 April.
- Second year and third year:

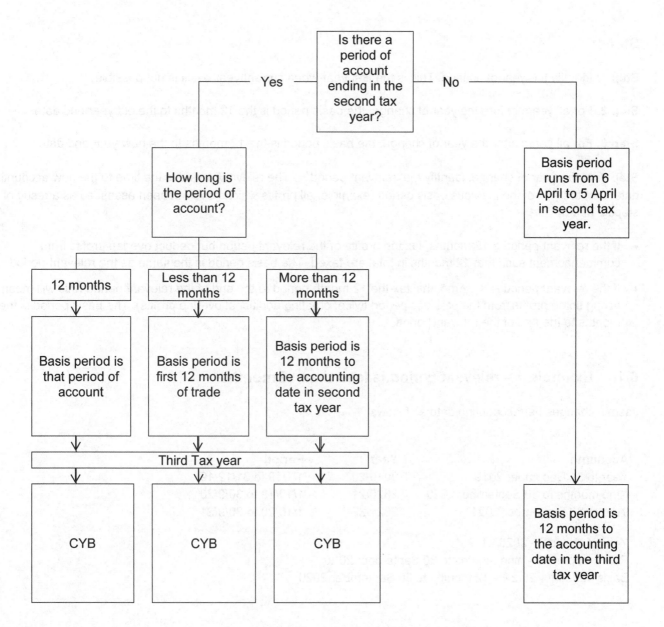

Later years – basis period is the period of account ending in the tax year = Current Year basis (CYB).

Final year – basis period is the period from the end of the basis period for the previous tax year to cessation date.

Overlap profits – opening year rules may lead to profits being taxed twice. Relief is given on cessation of the business.

6. Sole traders – change of accounting date

For an accounting date change to be recognised for tax purposes the following conditions must be satisfied:

- the first accounts ending on the new date must not exceed 18 months in length
- the sole trader or partnership must give notice of the change in the tax return by the filing date of the tax return
- the change will not be permitted if there has been a change of accounting date in the previous five years unless there are genuine commercial reasons for the change.

Steps:

Step 1: Identify the year of change. This is the first year when current year basis is not possible.

Step 2: For all years before the year of change, the basis period is the 12 months to the old year end date.

Step 3: For all years after the year of change, the basis period is the 12 months to the new year end date.

Step 4: In the year of change, identify the relevant period'. The relevant period is the time to the new accounting date from the end of the previous basis period (example: all profits which have not been assessed as a result of steps 2 and 3)

- If the relevant period > 12 months, tax the profits of the relevant period but deduct overlap profits from commencement such that 12 months in total are taxed. The basis period is the same as the relevant period.
- If the relevant period is < 12 months, tax the 12 month period to the end of the relevant period (this will mean taxing some profits from the previous period twice, creating additional overlap profits). The basis period is the 12 months to the end of the relevant period.

6.1.   Example 1 – relevant period is less than 12 months

Jasmin changes her accounting date as follows:

Accounts	Year	Period
Year to 31 December 2019	2019/20	1/1/19 to 31/12/19
Nine months to 30 September 2020	2020/21	1/10/19 to 30/9/20
Year to 30 September 2021	2021/22	1/10/20 to 30/9/21

Year of change – 2020/21
Relevant period – nine months to 30 September 2020
Basis period for 20/21 – 12 months to 30 September 2020

6.2. Example 2 – relevant period is greater than 12 months

Vaughan changes his accounting date as follows:

Accounts	Year	Period
Year to 31 December 2019	2019/20	1/1/19 to 31/12/19
15 months to 31 March 2021	2020/21	1/1/20 to 31/3/21
Year to 31 March 2022	2021/22	1/4/21 to 31/3/22

Year of change – 2020/21
Relevant period – 15 months to 31 March 2021
Basis period for 20/21 – 15 months to 31 March 2021

7. Capital allowances on plant and machinery

7.1. Layout of capital allowances on plant and machinery computation

(see taxation tables for rates)

	First Year Allowance (FYA)	Annual Investment Allowance (AIA)	General pool	Special rate pool	Short Life Asset	Total allowances
	£	£	£	£	£	£
WDV b/f			X	X	X	
Additions	X	X	X			
Disposals			(X)		(X)	
	X	X	X	X	X	
Balancing allowance/balancing charge (BA/BC)					X/(X)	X/(X)
					Nil	
AIA/FYA	(X)	(X)				X
Writing down allowance@ 18% pa			(X)			X
Writing down allowance@ X% pa				(X)		X
WDV c/f	Nil	Nil	X	X		
	===	===	===	===		
Total allowances						X
						===

- Plant – defined by 'function/setting' distinction and case law.

- AIA – 100% allowance for expenditure (other than cars) in 12-month period (pro rata). Expenditure in excess of AIA qualifies for writing down allowance (WDA). If the accounting period straddles 1 January 2019 or 1 January 2021, the AIA must be pro-rated.

- Full WDA for the period is given regardless of date of purchase of item. WDA is scaled for periods other than 12 months.

- The WDA % on the special rate pool is calculated as: ((8 x number of months before 1 April 2019) + x number of months after 1 April 2019))/number of months in the chargeable period. This % should rounded to two decimal places.

- FYA – 100% allowance given on purchase of low CO_2 emission cars. FYA is not scaled for short accounting periods.

- If the written down value (WDV) on the general pool (= WDV b/f + additions-disposals) is £1,000 or less then an election can be made to write off the pool balance, known as a 'small pools allowance'.

- Short life assets (SLA) – de-pool asset if life expected to be less than 8 years. Not available for cars

7.2. Unincorporated businesses – Private use assets

- Private use assets have separate column in Capital Allowance computation.
- Disallow private use % of WDA/AIA/FYA.

7.3. Capital allowances – business cessation

- In the cessation period of account, no WDA/AIA/FYA.
- Include additions and disposals as normal. Any asset taken over by owner, treat as a disposal at market value. Balancing adjustment made (balancing charge or balancing allowance).

8. Partnerships

- Each partner is taxed like a sole trader on their share of the partnership profits.
- First step is to share accounting profits between partners:
- allocate the correct salaries and interest on capital for the period to each partner
- divide the remaining profit for each set of accounts between the partners based upon the profit shari arrangement
- you may need to split the period if there is a change such as a partner joining or leaving.
- Opening year and cessation rules apply to partners individually when they join or leave the partnersh
- Allocate the profit for each partner to the correct tax year using usual basis period rules.
- Basis periods for continuing partners are unaffected by joiners or leavers.
- Each partner enters their share of profits for a tax year in the partnership pages of their own tax retur

9. Trading losses for sole traders and partners

9.1. Trading losses for sole traders and partners

- A loss is computed in the same way as a profit, making the same adjustments to the net profit as per the accounts and deducting capital allowances.

9.2. Set off of trading loss against total income

- Set off loss against total income of the preceding tax year and/or the tax year of loss, e.g. loss in 2020/21 set off against total income in 2019/20 and/or 2020/21.
- Cannot restrict loss to preserve use of personal allowance so personal allowance may be wasted.
- For 2020/21 loss claim needed by 31 January 2023.

9.3. Carry forward of trading losses

- If any loss remains unrelieved after current year and carry back claim has been made, or no such claims are made, then carry forward the loss against first available profits of the same trade.

9.4. Choice of loss relief – consider the following:

- utilise loss in the tax year in which income is taxed at a higher rate
- possible wastage of personal allowance
- review the projected future profits to ensure the loss can be utilised
- if cash flow is important, a loss carry back claim may result in a tax refund being paid to the business.

10. Payment and administration – sole traders and partners

10.1. The return must be filed by:

- 31 October following the end of the tax year if filing a paper return
- 31 January following the end of the tax year if filing online.

10.2. Penalties for late filing and payment

Late filing	Late payment	Penalty
Miss filing deadline		£100
	30 days late	5% of tax outstanding at that date
3 months late		Daily penalty £10 per day for up to 90 days (max £900)
6 months late		5% of tax due or £300, if greater
	6 months late	5% of tax outstanding at that date
12 months late		5% of tax due or £300, if greater
	12 months late	5% of tax outstanding at that date
12 months and information deliberately withheld		Based on behaviour: • deliberate and concealed withholding 100% of tax due, or • £300 if greater. • deliberate but not concealed 70% of tax due, or £300 if greater. Reductions apply for prompted and unprompted disclosures and for cooperation with investigation.

10.3. Disclosure and errors

- Taxpayer must notify HMRC by 5 October following end of the tax year if a tax return is needed.
- Taxpayer can amend a tax return within 12 months of filing date or make a claim for overpayment rel within four years of the end of the tax year.

10.4. Payments on account (POA)

- Due 31 January (in tax year) and 31 July (after tax year end). Each instalment is 50% of the previous year's tax and Class 4 National Insurance contribution (NIC) liability after taking into account any tax deducted at source.
- Balancing payment made 31 January after tax year end.
- No POA due if:
- last year's tax and Class 4 NIC liability is less than £1,000 or
- if greater than 80% of last year's liability was deducted at source.
- Can reduce this year's POA if this year's liability expected to be less than last year's. Penalties and interest will be charged if a deliberate incorrect claim is made.
- Capital gains tax (CGT) liability and Class 2 National Insurance is paid 31 January following the tax year end. No POA needed for CGT and Class 2 National Insurance.

10.5. Interest on tax paid late/overpaid tax

- Interest charged daily on late payment.

11. Enquiries and other penalties

- HMRC must notify individual of enquiry within 12 months of submission of return.

- Basis of enquiry – random or HMRC believe income/expenses misstated.

- Penalty for failure to produce enquiry documents = £300 + £60 per day.

- Penalty for failure to keep proper records is up to £3,000. Records must be kept for five years after the filing date for the relevant tax year.

- Penalties for incorrect returns are detailed in the table below:

Type of behaviour	Maximum	Unprompted (minimum)	Prompted (minimum)
Genuine mistake: despite taking reasonable care	0%	0%	0%
Careless error and inaccuracy are due to failure to take reasonable care	30%	0%	15%
Deliberate error but not concealed	70%	20%	35%
Deliberate error and concealed	100%	30%	50%

12. National Insurance contributions

- Self-employed individuals pay Class 2 and Class 4 contributions.

- Class 4 contributions are at 9% on profits between the lower and upper limits, then 2% on profits above the upper limit.

- Percentages and limits are provided in the Taxation Tables.

13. An outline of corporation tax

- Companies pay corporation tax on their profits for each accounting period.
- There is one rate of corporation tax set each financial year.
- Profits = Income + Gains - Qualifying charitable donations
- Accounting periods are usually 12 months long but can be shorter.
- If a company's accounts are longer than 12 months, the first 12 months will be one accounting period and the remainder a second accounting period.
- All UK property income is pooled as a single source of income and taxed on an accruals basis.
- Borrowing or lending money by a company is a loan relationship.
- Trading loan relationships are part of trading income.
- Non-trading loan relationships (NTL-R) are pooled to give NTL-R credits or deficits.
- Donations to charities are qualifying charitable donations.
- Company A is a related 51% group company of company B if:
  - A is a 51% subsidiary of B, or
  - B is a 51% subsidiary of A, or
  - A and B are both 51% subsidiaries of the same company.

'A' is a 51% subsidiary of 'B' if more than 50% of its ordinary share capital is beneficially owned (directly or indirectly) by 'B'.

14. The calculation of total profits and corporation tax payable

ABC Ltd

Corporation tax computation for the year/period ended DD/MM/20XX

	£
Trading income – accruals basis	X
Interest income (NTL-R) – accrual basis	X
Property income – accruals basis	X
Chargeable gains	X
	X
Less Qualifying charitable donations	(X)
Total taxable profits	X
Corporation tax payable – Total taxable profits × Corporation tax rate	X

14.1. Key points

- Trading income is adjusted from net profit per company accounts less capital allowances.

- Companies receive interest gross.

- Virtually all interest receivable is taxed as interest income (NTL-R).

- Dividends payable by a company are not an allowable expense.

- UK dividends receivable by a company are not taxable.

- Net-off current year capital losses against current year capital gains. If there is a net capital loss carry it forward.

- See taxation tables for corporation tax rates.

14.2. Long periods of account

- Will consist of two accounting periods = first 12 months and remainder of period.

- Split profits as follows:

- Adjusted trading profit – time apportion.

- Capital allowances – separate computations for each accounting period.

- Interest income (NTL-R) and property income – accruals basis.

- Chargeable gains – according to date of disposal.

- Qualifying charitable donations– according to date paid.

15. Corporation tax – trade losses

- Can elect to set trading losses against current accounting period 'total profits'. Qualifying charitable donations will remain unrelieved.

- If the above election is made, can also carry back trading loss to set against 'total profits' within the previous 12 months.

- Losses not relieved in the current accounting period or previous 12 months are carried forward and an election can be made to set against total profits in future periods.

- If there is a choice of loss relief, firstly consider when the loss was incurred, the rate of loss relief and then the timing of relief.

- Set out the use of the losses in a loss memorandum.

16. Corporation tax – payment and administration

16.1. Payment dates

- Small companies (annual profits less than £1.5 million): nine months + 1 day after end of the accounting period (AP).

- Large companies (annual profits greater than £1.5 million) must estimate year's tax liability and pay 25% of the year's liability:

- six months and 14 days after start of AP

- nine months and 14 days after start of AP

- 14 days after end of AP

- three months and 14 days after end of AP.

- Estimate must be revised for each quarter. Penalties may be charged if company deliberately fails to pay sufficient instalments.

- No instalments due for first year company is large unless profits are greater than £10 million.

- 51% group companies share the annual profit limit of £1.5 million equally.

16.2. Interest on late payments

- Interest charged daily on late payment. Overpayment of tax receives interest from HMRC. Interest is taxable/tax allowable as interest income.

16.3. Filing the return

- Filed on the later of 12 months after end of AP or three months after the notice to deliver a tax return has been issued.

- Late filing penalties are: less than three months late: £100; greater than three months late: £200; greater than six months late: 10% of tax due per return; greater than 12 months late: 20% of tax due per return.

- Company must notify HMRC it is within scope of corporation tax within 3 months of starting to trade.

- Company can amend return within 12 months of the filing date.

16.4. Enquiries and other penalties

- HMRC must notify company of enquiry within 12 months of submission of return.

- Basis of enquiry – random or HMRC believe income/expenses misstated.

- Penalty for failure to produce enquiry documents: £300 + £60 per day.

- Penalty for failure to keep proper records is up to £3,000. Records must be retained for six years after the end of the relevant accounting period.

- Penalties for incorrect returns are the same as for sole traders and partners – see sole traders and partners link.

17. Current tax reliefs and other tax issues

17.1. Research and development (R&D) tax credits for small and medium sized companies

A small or medium sized enterprise (SME) is a company with less than 500 employees with either:

- an annual turnover under €100 million, or
- a balance sheet under €86 million.

17.2. The SME tax relief scheme

The tax relief on allowable R&D costs is 230%.

17.3. R&D tax credits

If a company makes a loss, it can choose to receive R&D tax credits instead of carrying forward a loss.

17.4. Costs that qualify for R&D tax relief

To qualify as R&D, any activity must contribute directly to seeking an advance in science or technology or must be a qualifying indirect activity. The costs must relate to the company's trade – either an existing one, or one that they intend to start up based on the results of the R&D.

17.5. Intermediaries (IR35) legislation

IR35 legislation prevents personal service companies ("PSC") being used to disguise permanent employment.

The rules apply where the relationship between the worker and the client, would be considered to be an employment relationship if the existence of the PSC was ignored.

If the rules apply, a **deemed employment income tax charge** is charged on the PSC.

The **deemed employment income tax charge** is calculated based upon the actual payments made to the PSC by the client.

18. Introduction to capital/chargeable gains

- Individual pays Capital Gains Tax (CGT) on net chargeable gains in a tax year.
- For companies, chargeable gains are included as income in calculating total profits.
- Individuals receive an annual exempt amount from CGT – for 2020/21 this is £12,300.
- Gains/losses arise when a chargeable person makes a chargeable disposal of a chargeable asset.
- Chargeable person – individual or company.
- Chargeable disposal – sale, gift or loss/destruction of the whole or part of an asset. Exempt disposals – on death and gifts to approved charities.
- Chargeable asset – all assets unless exempt. Exempt assets include motor cars and some chattels.

18.1. Calculation of capital gains tax

Net chargeable gains – total gains in the tax year after netting off any current year or brought forward losses and the annual exempt amount.

18.2. Annual exempt amount (AEA)

- For individuals only.
- AEA cannot be carried forward or carried back.
- Current year losses must be netted off against current year gains before AEA. This means AEA can be wasted.
- Brought forward capital losses are set off against current year gains after AEA so AEA is not wasted.

19. Calculation of gains and losses for individuals

19.1. Pro forma computation

	£	£
Consideration received		X
Less Incidental costs of sale		(X)
Net sale proceeds		NSP
Less Allowable expenditure		
- Acquisition cost	X	
- Incidental costs of acquisition	X	
- Enhancement expenditure	X	
		(Cost)
Gain/(Loss)		X/(X)

- Consideration received is usually sales proceeds, but market value will be used instead of actual consideration where the transaction is a gift or between connected persons.

- An individual is connected with their spouse, relatives (and their spouses) and spouse's relatives (and their spouses). Relative means brother, sister, lineal ancestor or lineal descendent.

- Husband and wife/civil partner transfers – nil gain nil loss.

Part disposals – the cost allocated to the disposal = Cost × (A/(A+B))

A = consideration received on part disposal   B = market value of the remainder of the asset

- Chattels – tangible moveable object. Two types:

  - Wasting – expected life of 50 years or less (e.g. racehorse or boat). CGT exempt.

  - Non-wasting – expected life greater than 50 years (e.g. antiques or jewellery).

19.2. CGT, £6,000 rule

Sell	Buy £6,000 or less	More than £6,000
Less than £6,000	Exempt	Allowable loss but proceeds are deemed = £6,000
More than £6,000	Normal calculation of the gain, then compare with 5/3(gross proceeds – £6,000) – Take the lower gain	Chargeable in full

20. Shares and securities – disposals by individuals

20.1. CGT on shares and securities

Disposal of shares and securities are subject to CGT except for listed government securities (gilt-edged securities or 'gilts'), qualifying corporate bonds (e.g. company loan notes/debentures) and shares held in an Individual Savings Account (ISA).

20.2. The identification rules

Used to determine which shares have been sold and so what acquisition cost can be deducted from the sale proceeds (e.g. match the disposal and acquisition).

Disposals are matched:

- firstly, with acquisitions on the same day as the day of disposal

- secondly, with acquisitions made in the 30 days following the date of disposal (FIFO basis)

- thirdly, with shares from the share pool.

20.3. The share pool

- The share pool contains all shares acquired prior to the disposal date.

- Each acquisition is not kept separately, but is 'pooled' together with other acquisitions and a running total kept of the number of shares and the cost of those shares.

- When a disposal from the pool is made, the appropriate number of shares are taken from the pool along with the average cost of those shares.

- The gain on disposal is then calculated.

20.4. Bonus issues and rights issues

- Bonus issue – no adjustment to cost needed.

- Rights issue – adjustment to cost needed.

21. Chargeable gains – reliefs available to individuals

Replacement of business assets (Rollover) relief – when a qualifying business asset is sold at a gain, taxpayer can defer gain by reinvesting proceeds in a qualifying replacement asset.

- Deferred gain is deducted from the cost of the replacement asset so gain crystallises when the replacement asset is sold.

- Qualifying assets (original and replacement) – must be used in a trade by the vendor and be land and buildings, fixed plant and machinery or goodwill.

- Qualifying time period – replacement asset must be purchased between 1 year before and 3 years after the sale of the original asset.

- Partial reinvestment – only some of the sales proceeds reinvested then the gain taxable is the lower of the full gain and the proceeds not reinvested.

Gift relief (holdover relief) – donee takes over asset at donor's base cost i.e. the gain is given away along with the asset.

- Qualifying assets – trade assets of donor or shares in any unquoted trading company or personal trading company (donor owns at least 5% of company).

Business asset disposal relief – gain taxable at 10% capital gains tax rate.

- The £1 million limit is a lifetime limit which is reduced each time a claim for the relief is made.

- For 2020/21 a claim must be made by 31 January 2023.

- Qualifying business disposals (assets must be owned for at least 24 months prior to sale).

  - The whole or part of a business carried on by the individual (alone or in partnership).

  - Assets of the individual's or partnership's trading business that has now ceased.

- Shares in the individual's 'personal trading company' where they have at least 5% of shares, voting rights, entitlement to distributable profits and entitlement to net assets. Individual must have owned the shares and been an employee of the company for 24 months prior to sale.

Investors relief – gain taxable at 10% capital gains tax rate

- The £10 million limit is a lifetime limit which is reduced each time a claim for the relief is made.

- For 2020/21 a claim must be made by 31 January 2023:

  - the individual subscribes for shares which are issued on or after 17 March 2016

  - the shares are ordinary shares

  - the issuing company is a trading company or holding company of a trading group

  - the shares are not listed on a recognised stock exchange

  - the individual has not been an officer or employee of the issuing company at any point during the ownership period

  - the shares are held continuously for three years.

22. Calculation of gains and losses for companies

22.1. Pro forma computation

	£	£
Consideration received		X
Less Incidental costs of sale		(X)
Net sale proceeds		NSP
Less Allowable expenditure		
Acquisition cost + incidental costs of acquisition	X	
Indexation allowance [indexation factor × expenditure]	X	
Enhancement expenditure	X	
Indexation allowance	X	
		(Cost)
Chargeable gain		Gain

- Companies are entitled to an indexation allowance, based on the changes in the retail price index (RPI) from the date when expenditure was incurred to the date of disposal (or deemed disposal).

- Indexation allowance is frozen at 31 December 2017.

- Disposals taking place from 1 January 2018 will use the RPI at 31 December 2017 for indexation allowance purposes.

- Indexation allowance is not available where there is an unindexed loss; nor can it turn an unindexed gain into an indexed loss.

- Note that companies do not get an annual exempt amount.

- Losses relieved in order – current year first followed by losses brought forward.

22.2. Only relief available to companies is rollover relief:

- Rollover relief is a deferral relief – see Chargeable gains – reliefs available to individuals for main rollover relief rules.

- Key differences applying for companies:

- indexation is given on disposal of the original asset.

- goodwill is not a qualifying asset for companies.

- gain deferred is the indexed gain.

- on disposal of the replacement asset, indexation is calculated on the 'base cost' not actual cost.

23. Shares and securities – disposals by companies

The identification rules – a disposal of shares is matched:

- firstly, with same-day transactions

- secondly, with transactions in the previous nine days (FIFO). No indexation allowance is available.

- thirdly, with shares from the 1985 pool (shares bought from 1 April 1982 onwards).

1985 pool – pro forma working	No.	Cost £	Indexed cost £
Purchase	X	X	X
Index to next operative event			X
			X
Operative event (purchase)	X	X	X
	X	X	X
Index to next operative event			X
			X
Operative event (sale)	(X)	(X)	(X)A
Pool carried forward	X	X	X
	===	===	===

Operative event = purchase, sale, rights issue. Bonus issue is not an operative event.

Computation

	£
Proceeds	X
Less indexed cost (A from pool)	(X)
Indexed gain	X

24. The badges of trade

- Profit seeking motive
- Number of transactions
- Nature of asset
- Existence of similar trading transactions or interests
- Changes to the asset
- The way the sale was carried out
- The source of finance
- Interval of time between purchase and sale
- Method of acquisition

25. Duties and responsibilities of a tax advisor

- Maintain client confidentiality at all times.
- AAT members must adopt an ethical approach and maintain an objective outlook.
- Give timely and constructive advice to clients.
- Honest and professional conduct with HMRC.
- A tax advisor is liable to a penalty if they assist in making an incorrect return.

The Association of Accounting Technicians
140 Aldersgate Street
London
EC1A 4HY
t: +44 (0)20 7397 3000
f: +44 (0)20 7397 3009
e: aat@aat.org.uk
aat.org.uk

INDEX